A NARRATIVE OF THE ESTABLISHMENT AND PROGRESS OF THE MISSION TO CEYLON AND INDIA

BY
W. M. HARVARD

First Fruits Press
Wilmore, Kentucky
c2016

A narrative of the establishment and progress of the mission to Ceylon and India.
By W.M. Harvard.

First Fruits Press, ©2016
Previously published by the author, 1823.

ISBN: 9781621715351 (print), 9781621715368 (digital) 9781621715375 (kindle)

Digital version at http://place.asburyseminary.edu/firstfruitsbooks/12/

First Fruits Press is a digital imprint of the Asbury Theological Seminary, B.L. Fisher Library. Asbury Theological Seminary is the legal owner of the material previously published by the Pentecostal Publishing Co. and reserves the right to release new editions of this material as well as new material produced by Asbury Theological Seminary. Its publications are available for noncommercial and educational uses, such as research, teaching and private study. First Fruits Press has licensed the digital version of this work under the Creative Commons Attribution Noncommercial 3.0 United States License. To view a copy of this license, visit http://creativecommons.org/licenses/by-nc/3.0/us/.

For all other uses, contact:

First Fruits Press
B.L. Fisher Library
Asbury Theological Seminary
204 N. Lexington Ave.
Wilmore, KY 40390
http://place.asburyseminary.edu/firstfruits

Harvard, W. M. (William Martin), 1790-1857.

A narrative of the establishment and progress of the mission to Ceylon and India / by W.M. Harvard. Wilmore, Kentucky : First Fruits Press, ©2016.

lxxii, 404 pages, 2 leaves of plates : illustrations, map ; 23 cm.

Reprint. Previously published: A narrative of the establishment and progress of the mission to Ceylon and India : founded by the late Rev. Thomas Coke, L.L.D., under the direction of the Wesleyan-Methodist Conference, including notices of Bombay and the superstitions of various religious sects at that presidency, and on the continent of India : with an introductory sketch of the natural, civil, and religious history of the Island of Ceylon. London : printed for the author, 1823.

ISBN: 9781621715351 (paperback)

1. Methodist Church--Missions--Sri Lanka. 2. Wesleyan Methodist Church—Mission--Sri Lanka. 3. Methodist Church--Missions--India. 4. Wesleyan Methodist Church--Mission--India. 5. Mission--Sri Lanka. 6. Mission--India. 7. Sri Lanka--Church history. 8. India--Church history. 9. Christianity--Sri Lanka--19th century. 10. Christianity--India--19th century. I. Title.

BV3275.H3 2016

Cover design by Jonathan Ramsay

asburyseminary.edu
800.2ASBURY
204 North Lexington Avenue
Wilmore, Kentucky 40390

This publication has been digitized and made freely available as the result of a generous gift from the Association of Professors of Mission

First Fruits Press
The Academic Open Press of Asbury Theological Seminary
204 N. Lexington Ave., Wilmore, KY 40390
859-858-2236
first.fruits@asburyseminary.edu
asbury.to/firstfruits

A Front View of the Wesleyan Mission House & Premises, Colombo. With a representation of Ceylonese Costume & Modes of Conveyance.

A

NARRATIVE

OF

THE ESTABLISHMENT AND PROGRESS

OF

The Mission

TO

CEYLON AND INDIA,

FOUNDED BY

THE LATE REV. THOMAS COKE, L.L.D. UNDER THE DIRECTION OF THE
WESLEYAN-METHODIST CONFERENCE:

INCLUDING

Notices of Bombay,

*And the Superstitions of various Religious Sects at that Presidency,
and on the Continent of India.*

WITH

AN INTRODUCTORY SKETCH

OF THE

NATURAL, CIVIL, AND RELIGIOUS HISTORY

OF THE

ISLAND OF CEYLON.

BY W. M. HARVARD,
ONE OF THE MISSIONARIES WHO ACCOMPANIED DOCTOR COKE.

LONDON:
PRINTED FOR THE AUTHOR,
AND SOLD BY T. BLANSHARD, 14, CITY ROAD; F. WESTLEY, STATIONERS'
COURT; BAYNES AND SON, PATERNOSTER ROW; ALSO, BY SWINBOURN
AND WALTER, AND CHAPLIN, COLCHESTER.

1823.

TO THE

PREACHERS OF THE CONNEXION FORMED BY THE

LATE REV. JOHN WESLEY, A.M.

AND TO THE

SUBSCRIBERS AND FRIENDS

TO

The Wesleyan Missions

THROUGHOUT THE WORLD,

THE FOLLOWING NARRATIVE OF THE MISSION TO
CEYLON AND INDIA,

*Commenced under their Auspices, conducted under their Direction,
and supported by their enlightened Liberality,*

Is Inscribed,

WITH SINCERE RESPECT AND AFFECTION,

By their Servant in the Gospel of Christ,

THE AUTHOR.

ADVERTISEMENT.

The following pages have been prepared at the suggestion of some esteemed friends; who were desirous that a comprehensive record should be preserved of the principal events connected with the formation and progress of the Wesleyan Mission to Ceylon and India.

The Author has enlarged upon his original design, by introducing an account of Bombay, (where he resided several months,) and of the Superstitions of various religious sects at that Presidency, and on the Continent of India; also a sketch of the Natural, Civil, and Religious History of Ceylon, derived from authentic, and in many instances original sources.

These, though they have encreased the size and price of the volume, will, it is hoped, impart an additional value to the work.

The Author is happy to have the present opportunity of bearing his testimony to the importance of this Asiatic Mission. After his intimate acquaintance with all its concerns, an absence of four years has only tended to increase his attachment to its interests—to confirm his satisfaction in its progress—and to animate his expectation of results (under the Divine blessing,) still more important and extensive.

CONTENTS.

INTRODUCTION: Historical sketch of the Island of Ceylon---*Sect. I.* Situation, Climate, and Productions, page i.---*Sect. II.* Political and Civil History, page xxiii.---*Sect. III.* Ceylonese Superstitions and idolatrous Ceremonies --- Present state of Christianity in Ceylon, page xlix.

CHAP. I.

Mr. Wesley's universal charity—The Formation of the Wesleyan Connexion—Its progress—Established Church of England—Dissenting Denominations—Doctor Coke—His Missionary character—America—First Wesleyan Foreign Mission in 1769—To the enslaved Africans in 1778—Mr. Baxter—Western Africa, 1792, and 1811—Europe—Asia—Mr. Wesley's lively interest in an Asiatic Mission—Doctor Coke's correspondence on the subject in 1784—Bengal—Application from Madras—Communication from Lieut. Col. Sandys in 1805—Letter from Surat in 1808—Plummer—Successful exertions of other Denominations in Asia—Visit to England of the Chief-Justice of Ceylon in 1809—State of the Island—Mr. Wilberforce's recommendation of the Wesleyan Missions—Ceylon Mission proposed by the Chief-Justice—Former policy of the Hon. East India Company—Doctor Moreton—Sanctified affliction—Doctor Coke's application to the Rev. W. Ault—and the Author in 1812—Rev. I. Bradnack—Letter from Doctor Coke to Mr. Ault in 1813—The Doctor determines himself to embark in the Mission—His plan—the General Wesleyan Methodist Missionary Society—Doctor Buchanan—Mission proposed in the London District—Rev. Benjamin Clough—Irish Conference—Rev. Messrs. Lynch, Erskine, and M'Kenny—Liverpool Conference—Devotion to the Mission Cause—Final adoption and limitation of the plan—The original appointment for Asia—Doctor Coke's letter to the Author—His pious submission. . . . . Page 1.

CHAP. II.

Doctor Coke's application to preparatory duties—Portuguese Studies—Decline of the Portuguese power in India—Subscriptions for Ceylon—Recommendatory Letters—The subject considered—Doctor Coke's successful applications—Earl Bathurst—Right Hon. Lord Teignmouth— Mr. Grant—Mr. Stevens—Mr. Wilberforce—Doctor Buchanan, &c. &c.—Piety and simplicity—Interesting scene—Interview in London—Doctor Coke's last Circular letter—Replies—Missionary motto of the Rev. Doctor Carey—The Ceylon Missionaries encouraged and animated—The Rev. Walter Griffith—Thomas Thompson, Esq. M. P.—Joseph Butterworth, Esq. M. P.—The late Reverend John Barber—Portuguese teacher—Search for a vessel—Cabalva, Captain Birch—Lady Melville, Captain Lochner—Outfit—Printing-press and types—Missionary Ordinations—Marriages of Missionaries—Dismissal from the Committee, preparatory to the Voyage—Meeting at Portsmouth—Mr. Clough's Account of Doctor Coke—Kindness of Friends at Portsmouth and Portsea, &c.—The Rev. Jon. Edmondson—The Rev. Messrs. Aikenhead, Fish, and Beal—The only meeting of the entire Missionary family—Missionary emotions—Rev. Henry Moore—Xavier—Dr. Coke's last Sermon at Portsea—Mrs. Ault's distressing illness—Division of the party—Embarkation at Portsmouth Point. p. 29.

CONTENTS.

CHAP. III.

Commencement of the Voyage—Sea-sickness—Scrutiny of motives and object—Doctor Coke—Extract from Madame Guion—Portuguese Vulgate—The Doctor's Journal—Mr. Clough's Account—The situation of a Missionary during a Voyage—Public worship on the Lord's-day—Services in the Lady Melville—Mr Squance—Cautious reserve with respect to the Doctor—Journal—Mr. Clough's elucidation—Sabbath-evening reading--Social meetings for prayer, &c. in the author's cabin—Behaviour of the Passengers—Encouraging effects of Christian conversation with them—Note on Grace before Meat—Ship Newspaper—Signals—Mrs. Ault's illness—Visit from Messrs. Ault and Squance—Mrs. Ault's death—Her amiable and devout character—Her death greatly lamented—Its effect on the Doctor's mind—The health of Mr. Squance seriously affected—Visits the Cabalva—We pass the Equator—The Visit of Neptune, &c.—Isles of Bourbon and France—Another Mission contemplated for Mr. Squance—He recovers, and returns on board the Melville—Doctor Coke's attentions to the spiritual interests of the Soldiers on board—Pleasing results—Melancholy cases—Asiatic Journal for June, 1820—Effects of intoxication—A singular interview—The Doctor's hopes in reference to the Soldiers—Separated from the fleet, and rejoin—" *O cabo dos tormentados*"—Volcano—Second approach to the Line—Illness of Mrs. Harvard, and of the Author—Dr. Coke's anxiety and prayers—They recover—the Doctor discovers symptoms of illness—Solemn and affecting parting—His Death and Funeral. . . . . p. 55.

CHAP. IV.

Difficulty of reconciling the Death of Doctor Coke, with his actual Call to embark in the Asiatic Mission—Destitute situation of the Missionaries, and their painful exercises—Spend several days in searching for, and examining the deceased Doctor's papers—Disappointments—Anecdote on " Trust in Providence "— Captain Birch's generous and humane attentions—Extracts from the Author's Journal—Recommendatory letters to the Governor, and to W. T. Money, Esq.—Conversation with J. Anderson, Esq.—Divine service on board.—Exchange signals with the party on board the Melville. The statement furnished by the Author to Captain Birch, at his request, of the doctrines, discipline, &c. of the Wesleyan Methodists; the character and extent of their Missions, and the circumstances connected with the formation of the present Mission to Ceylon—Captain Birch's reply to the Author. . . . . p. 86.

CHAP. V.

Termination of our voyage—Indian Scenery—Meeting with the Brethren on board the Lady Melville—Difference of opinions—First Sabbath in India—Press-gang—Visited by the Rev. S. Newell—Disembarkment—Palanquin-stands—Breakfast at the Bombay Tavern—Causes of disquietude—Interview with Mr. Money—Reception—Gratifying information respecting Ceylon—Ride with Captain Birch to the Governor's country seat—Native washermen—Persee women—Toddy—Native village—Persee burial place—A Fakeer—An idol—Audience with the GOVERNOR—His Excellency's condescension, and remarks on the Rev. J. Wesley—Return to Bombay.—Rev. Messrs. Hall and Nott—The Governor's house at Parell prepared for our reception—Sensations produced by the arrival of the Missionaries. . . . . p. 109.

CONTENTS.

CHAP. VI.

Description of Parell House and Grounds—Gentoo Temple—Disgusting objects of Worship—Aversion of the Natives to the entrance of Europeans—Impositions practised by Native servants—Certificates of character—Present from Capt. Beaty—Sabbath—Attend the Fort Church—Native carriage—Visit from the Governor—Mr. Hart—Lieut. Wade—Visit to the Island of Elephanta—Its dimensions—Description of the wonderful Cave—Extracts from Maurice's Indian Antiquities—Amazing specimens of ancient sculpture—Description of the principal figure—The design of these astonishing works involved in obscurity—Tempest—The visitors to the Island exposed to considerable peril—Safe arrival—Service at the Fort Church—Lord's Supper—Letters to the Committee and our Families, franked by the Governor—The party, with the exception of the Author and his wife, proceed to CEYLON, in the Earl Spencer. . . . . p. 128.

CHAP. VII.

Voyage of Messrs. Ault, &c. to Ceylon—Kind reception from the Government authorities—The Government house at Galle prepared for their reception—Condescension of Lord and Lady Molesworth—His Lordship's estimate of their character—The Rev. G. Bisset—Liberal proposal of His Excellency, the Governor, to endow schools—First Ceylon Conference—Deliberations—Wesleyan plan of stationing the preachers—Their resignation of themselves to God, and satisfaction with their respective stations—Celebration of the Lord's Supper previous to their separation—Arrival of Messrs. Lynch and Squance at Colombo—Hospitable reception by the Honourable and Reverend Archdeacon Twisleton, &c.—Introduced to His Excellency, the Governor—Invited to dine—Important assistance rendered by the Right Honourable Sir A. Johnston, Chief Justice of Ceylon—Mr. Armour; his history and character Preach in the Baptist Mission Chapel—A Native Convert—Proceed to Jaffnapatam—J. N. Mooyart, Esq.—Christian David, a pupil of Swartz—School opened—Preach in the Dutch Church—Mr. Erskine proceeds to Matura—Encouraging reception—The Rev. T. G. Erhardt—Matura school opened—Service in the Dutch church—Importance of Matura, as a Missionary station—Mr. Ault sails from Galle to Batticaloa—Dangerous voyage—Reception—Acts as Chaplain—His labours among the Europeans and Natives—Mr. Clough commences his Mission at Galle—Lord Molesworth's important patronage and advice—Mr. C's labours among the Europeans, and efforts to benefit the Natives—Visited by Don Abraham Dias Abeysinha Ameresekera, who generously offers a residence and school-house—The Galle school opened—Native enquirers—Mr. Clough's unwearied and successful application to the study of the Singhalese language. . . . . p. 146.

CHAP. VIII.

The Author's residence at Bombay—Derivation of name—Teak wood—Birds, reptiles, and insects—Climate—Population—Various classes of inhabitants—The GENTOO superstition—Mode of worship—Distinction of caste—Pagodas—Festivals, fasts, processions, &c. The Gentoo female character—The swinging ceremony—The MAHOMEDANS, their mosques and worship—Marriage and funeral processions—Juvenile merchants—Language—PERSEES—Worship, &c.—Refuse to extinguish fire—Processions at marriages, funerals &c.—Superstitious notions founded on the decay of the body—Conversion from their idolatry difficult—JEWS—PORTUGUESE ROMAN CATHOLICS—Opulence—Chapels—Superstition and

CONTENTS.

idolatry—Mendicants—ARMENIAN CHRISTIANS—Wealth and respectability—Their various establishments—Their history—BRITISH and AMERICAN CHRISTIANS--Miscellaneous information. 172.

CHAP. IX.

Peculiar situation of the Author at Bombay—Native Curiosity—Conversation with a Gentoo youth—Meetings for prayer, religious conversation, &c.—Extract from Journal—Pleasing indications of usefulness—Visit from a Portuguese lady—Interesting and affecting conversation with some invalid soldiers—Portuguese studies—Sentiments of a military officer respecting Christian Missions—Conversation with a Gentoo physician—Chinese merchant at the prayer-meeting—Lieutenant Wade, his shipwreck, and death—The Author engages a passage to Ceylon—Various incidents during the voyage—Its unexpected termination. . . . . 201.

CHAP. X.

Arrival at CEYLON—Interview with Messrs. Clough and Squance—Point-de-Galle—Bay, Scenery, &c.—Description of Mr. Clough's residence—Prayer-meeting—Visit from the Guard Moodeliar—Lord Molesworth—His Lordship's character and affecting death—Loss of the Bengal Indiaman by fire—Service in the Dutch church—Illness of Mr. Squance—Receives kind attention from the Hon. Chief Justice—Preaches by an interpreter—Necessity of adopting such a medium of instruction—Narrative of the Conversion and Baptism of PANDITTA SEKARA, a learned Budhuist Priest—His subsequent appointment to a situation under the local government—Meeting of the Mission party at Galle---The Author's appointment to Colombo---Letter from New South Wales---Mr. Ault's illness---Journey of the Author and his family to Colombo Rest Houses---Caltura---Slow travelling---Met by Mr. Armour---Cinnamon gardens---Relative of the late Queen Charlotte . . . 225

CHAP. XI.

Interview with Archdeacon Twisleton---Visit from the Chief Justice---Submission of the Kandyan territory to the British Crown---Audience with His Excellency the Governor---Death of Mr. Ault at Batticaloa---His epitaph---Mr. Lynch preaches his funeral sermon before the Governor---Baptist Mission church---Arrival of Mr. Clough---Village preaching---Singhalese interpreter---Weekly meeting of preachers---Dutch church---Malabar Christians---Purchase of estate---Public subscription---Captain Schneider---Sunday school---Levee---Lady Johnston---Colombo theatre and Orphan House---Mission printing press---Government press---Day school Ava priest---Head printer---Illness of the Author---Kindness of the Catholic Missionaries---Journey to Galle---Preaches in an idol temple---Visits the Government schools---The Ava priest embraces Christianity, and is baptized 251

CHAP. XII.

Attendance of native females on Christian Worship---Opening of the Malabar church---Missionary estate at Colombo---Printing of the Singhalese Scriptures---Arrival of Wesleyan and Church Missionaries---Village labours---Milagria and Galkeece---Favourable circumstances---The late Bishop of Calcutta---Pagan enquirers---An aged Naiaka---Kandyan headman---Adikar---Kandyan priest baptized---Affecting case of a converted priest---Preaching in the Garrison---Arrival of Baptist and American Missionaries---Mr. Warren--Missionary union--Conference--Singular visitor--Shrewd

CONTENTS.

remark of an idiot---Assistant Missionary---Madras Mission---Missionary estate at Galle---Preaching to Budhuist priests---Baptism of one---Matura station---Missionary estate at Colpetty---Native school---Opening of Colombo Mission-House---Services---Mr. Clough's translation of the Liturgy---Contributions---Death of Mr. Tolfrey---Type Foundry---Unsuccessful attempt to commence a Kandyan Mission---Providential interposition 274

CHAP. XIII.

Apathy of the Malabar natives---Points of difference in the Singhalese and Malabar characters---Discouraging circumstances in the south---Establishment of a native school at Negombo---Opening of the Colpetty school-house---Compelled to recognize the distinction of caste---Attachment of the children to the school---Purchase of Mission premises at Negombo---Native marriages---Plan for establishing Mission schools throughout the island---Encouraging proofs of success---Meeting of the Mission Conference---New Stations---Schools---Execution of a soldier---Conversion of two Budhuist priests---Sir Hardinge Giffard---J. Sutherland Esq.---His son, Mr. J. Sutherland, placed with the Missionaries---Received on trial as a Missionary---Illness of several of the Missionaries---Singular application---Establishment of regular worship---Review ---Church Missionaries. . . . . 297.

CHAP. XIV.

Pleasing results of the native schools---Colpetty school---Juvenile piety ---Mrs. Harvard's visits to the female schools---Happy deaths---Remarks on immediate effects of Missionary effort---Success from the Lord alone---Kallibowilla school---the author's illness and removal from Ceylon---Missionaries meet at Galle---Commencement of the Voyage---Landing at Falmouth---Retrospect and Conclusion. . . . . 317.

ERRATA.

Page iii. line 25, for *Kullu-ganga*, read *Kallu-ganga*.
—— iv. —— 35, for *feet*, read *inches*.
—— xv. —— 9, insert *poisonous* before *tree*.
—— xvii. note, insert *of the same size* after *specimen*.
—— xxxiii. —— 20, for *eighteen* read *eighty*.
—— xxxvii. —— 13, for *uncultivated* read *maritime*.
—— 185, —— 9, insert *no* after *ascendancy*.
—— 234, ——25, for Sehara, read Sekara.
—— 137, —— 5, for *Hallibowitta*, read *Kallibowilla*.

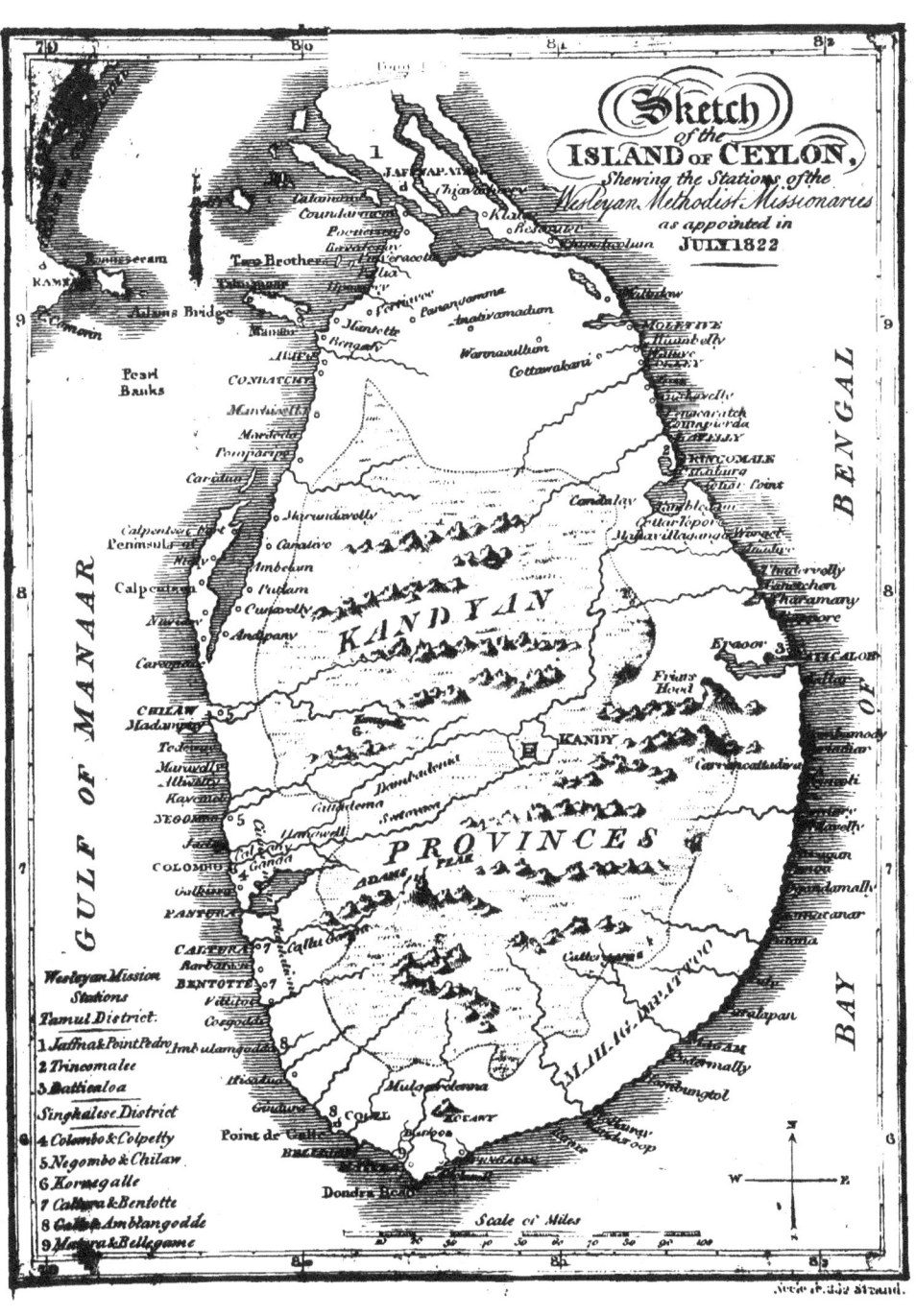

INTRODUCTION.

HISTORICAL SKETCH

OF

THE ISLAND OF CEYLON.

SECT. I.

SITUATION, CLIMATE, AND PRODUCTIONS.

CEYLON is situated at the entrance of the Bay of Bengal, by which it is bounded on the north; and on the south and east by the great Indian Ocean. On the west, it is separated from the Coast of Coromandel by the Gulf of Manaar, which issues in a narrow strait, full of shoals, and impassable by large ships. Across the Gulf, the island is estimated to be about sixty leagues from Cape Cormorin, the southernmost point of Peninsular India. It lies between 5° 49′ and 9° 50′ north of the Equator; and its longitude is from 7° 34′ to 81° 50′ east of Greenwich. Travellers differ respecting its dimensions. Mr. Cordiner, whose opportunities for forming a correct estimate were most favourable, states, that its greatest length from Dondera Head, near Matura, to the northern extremity of Point Pedro, is about 280 miles; and that its broadest part is the tract of country lying between Colombo and Komaree, which he supposes to be nearly 150 miles. Its circumference is generally admitted to be about 900 miles. The form of the island, as exhibited on correct maps, bears some resemblance in its shape to a ham; and the Dutch named the narrow peninsula of Jaffnapatam, *Ham's-heel*, and the projecting corner of Point Pedro, *Ham' heel Point*.

INTRODUCTION.

That Ceylon was once connected with the main land of India, is highly probable. A range of rocks, extending about thirty miles, usually called Ramas, or Adam's Bridge, and connected with the small islands of Manaar and Ramisseram, is supposed to have formed the basis of an isthmus, by which it was united to the continent; but by the force of the waters the connecting soil is entirely washed away, and small vessels, when the tide is favourable, pass between the separated masses of rocks.

Though situated so near the equator, the air is generally of a very moderate and salubrious temperature; and the frequent showers of rain to which it is subject in the south-east and south-west districts, cause those parts to be clothed with an almost constant verdure.

The northern division of the island, comprehending Jaffna and Trincomalee, with the adjacent stations, possesses much of the same climate and temperature as Continental India. The lofty ranges of Kandyan mountains are supposed to cause this difference between the districts they separate. Both sides are, however, subject to periodical rains, though at different seasons of the year; and they equally share in those violent storms of thunder and lightning which are so terrible to Europeans, but which do not occasion more injury to life and property than the less violent conflicts of the elements in Europe. In the south and western districts, the range of the thermometer in the shade, is from $73°$ to $88°$, throughout the whole year; this comprehends all the variations to which the temperature in those parts are subject; but Fahrenheit's thermometer usually fluctuates in the shade about the point of $80°$. The north and eastern coasts are much warmer, and the variations greater. In the shade, the range is from $69°$ to $95°$; the usual temperature $83°$. It is on this account, principally, that the former is the more healthy and pleasant, and the latter most subject to agues and fevers.*

* "From the situation of this island, so near the equator, the days and nights are necessarily always of equal length; the variation during the two seasons not exceeding fifteen minutes. The seasons are more regulated by the monsoons than by the course of the sun; for, although the island lies to the north of the line, the coolest season is during the

INTRODUCTION.

The interior of Ceylon, long under the power of a despotic and barbarous race of native princes, but now forming a part of the British Empire, is very mountainous and woody.* Some of the towns are situated in cool and airy spots; while others, and by far the greater number, are extremely unfavourable to the health of Europeans. During the rainy season in March and April, it is said to be inundated by torrents of rain, accompanied by storms of thunder and lightning. Captain Percival states, that " owing to the thick and close woods, and the hills which crowd upon each other, the heat is many degrees greater than on the sea-coast, and the climate often extremely sultry and unhealthy." The judicious improvements which were introduced into these districts, under General Brownrigg's government, and which proceeded with great spirit under his immediate successor, Lieutenant General Sir Edward Barnes, will greatly conduce to the health and comfort both of the native and European inhabitants of the Kandyan Provinces.

" Ceylon is well supplied with LAKES and RIVERS, which facilitate inland navigation, and might be rendered highly serviceable to the purposes of agriculture. The four principal rivers take their rise from Adam's Peak, and the adjacent hills. These are, the Maha-villa-ganga, the Walluwy, or Neel-ganga, the Kullu-ganga, and the Kalaany-ganga, or Mootwall. They are in general rapid, but smooth streams; and some of them are navigable with

summer solstice, while the western monsoon prevails. Their spring commences in October; and the hottest season is from January to the beginning of April. The heat during the day is nearly the same throughout the year; the rainy season, however, renders the nights much cooler, from the dampness of the earth, and the prevalence of winds during the monsoons." The climate, upon the whole, is much more temperate than on the continent of India. " This is owing to the constant sea-breezes by which it is fanned, without being subject to the hot and suffocating land-winds, which so frequently annoy the continent. This temperate climate, however, is chiefly confined to the coast, where the sea breezes have room to circulate." *Captain Percival's Ceylon*, p. 35.

* *Adam's Peak*, and all the principal mountains of Ceylon, are situated in that part of the island formerly under the Kandyan monarchy; and which is now officially denominated, *The Kandyan Provinces.*

INTRODUCTION.

small boats to a considerable distance up the country."* The smaller rivers and streams, by which the country is watered, are without number. Some of the lakes are of great extent. Of the numerous HARBOURS which present their inviting shelter to the mariner on the Ceylon coast, none are of sufficient importance to require a particular mention, except Trincomallee and Point-de-Galle. The former is generally admitted to be the noblest and most commodious harbour in the known world. Cordiner says of it—" The communication with the sea being concealed in almost every direction, it resembles a beautiful and extensive lake. Hills diversified by a variety of forms, and covered with luxuriant verdure, rise steeply all around, completely enclosing the capacious basin. Five hundred ships of the line may enter it with ease, and ride at anchor without the smallest inconvenience."†

Few countries have been more liberally supplied with interesting varieties of the animal, vegetable, and mineral kingdoms, than the Island of Ceylon. Within its limits, an extensive field of research offers itself to the naturalist, which has hitherto been imperfectly explored. But many obstacles to the natural researches and literary pursuits of our countrymen in Ceylon are removed. The interior now maintains a peaceful intercourse with the coast; and a Literary and Agricultural Society has been formed at Colombo;‡ which, with the intellectual and moral improvement of the native population, by a general system of education, will tend to advance the progress of science.

The ANIMALS of Ceylon are numerous, and many of them remarkable; among which the elephant must be noticed. They live in herds, and are of immense size. Gomera, a well-known elephant which is full fourteen feet high, but completely tame, is often seen in the streets of Colombo. A tusk of one found at Galle measured six feet three inches long, and three feet in diameter. The elephant is granivorous, and does much injury to the plantations; but seldom directs his attack against the human species, except previously irritated. Much ingenuity is displayed by the natives

---

* Cordiner, vol. 1. p. 8.   † Ibid. p. 270.
‡ Asiatic Journal, vol. xii. p. 515, 583.

in hunting, for the purpose of taking them alive, in which
the tame elephants are very serviceable, and produce a
considerable revenue to the government.* Bears are seen
in a few districts; also leopards, the cheeta, (a species of

* " The proceeding is briefly this: When the government has fixed
on the time of hunting elephants, the snare, (which consists of an extensive piece of ground) is marked out with large stakes of wood, in a
triangular shape, having an open base towards the forest; and at the
apex, a narrow funnel like the cod of a fish-net. The people of the
district are then ordered to drive the herds towards the snare; employing for this purpose guns, and drums, and trumpets, torches and
fire-works; or, in the words of a Dutch author, which are in themselves enough to frighten the stoutest elephant—'*schietgeweer, flam-
bawen, en vuurstuckeryen, pypers, en hoorenbluazers, trommels, en
tambolin-heros.*' On the present occasion, (August 1800) this tremendous assemblage commenced its operation at the distance of thirty
miles from the trap, advancing slowly in a chain of three thousand men,
who were employed in this service two months. As the circle nar-
rows, the fires and the noises approach each other: and when the
elephants get within the gaping jaws of the trap. ' the grand business
of the campaign is considered as brought to a termination.' The governor and other spectators then resort to the scene of action, and the
' *guns, drums, trumpets, blunderbusses and thunder,*' once more rend the
air; as their incessant din is judged necessary to terrify the animals,
and prevent them from making a retrograde movement. The first com-
partment of the inclosure is about 1800 feet in circumference; the
fold, with which it communicates by a single gate, is not more than
100 feet long and 40 broad; and the space is narrowed by a rivulet or
canal five feet deep: beyond this, the funnel gradually contracts into
a straight passage, five feet broad, and 100 feet long.

" The next process was, to drive the entrapped elephants into the
water-fold. From the water-snare, they are next driven into the long
and narrow tube of the funnel, just wide enough to admit one elephant at a time; and as they singly arrive at the farthest extremity, a
huge beam is let down behind each; when thus hemmed in, the
hunters contrive to secure him, by binding his legs with ropes. Two
tame elephants are then brought to the gate, and the captive is passed
between them. They feel his tusks, if he has any, and his proboscis;
sometimes, seemingly, to soothe his anger, and to reconcile him to his
new condition; and sometimes, if refractory, they batter him with their
heads, till they have reduced him to perfect submission. Thus is he
marched to ' the garden of stalls,' where he is very soon completely
trained. ' The marching off of this venerable trio,' says Cordiner, ' is
a sight truly magnificent; and exhibits a noble specimen of the skill of
man, united with the sagacity of the elephant.'"—*Quarterly Review,*
October, 1815.

tiger) and the tiger-cat. The hyæna is also found in the jungles, or woods, with the porcupine and ichneumon; and thousands of monkeys and squirrels, who sport and live among the trees. The wild hog, the rabbit, the hare, and a species of deer, are frequently hunted. Jackalls abound in great numbers; as do also the dog and the cat, in a state of nature.

The *domestic animals* are found in great varieties; some natural to the island, and many introduced from other countries. Among these, the buffalo, the sheep, the pig and the goat are recognized; but the flesh of these animals is inferior to those of Europe. Every description of English poultry, turkies excepted, is produced in the island. Ducks, geese, and pheasants, both wild and tame, abound. Snipes, storks, cranes, herons, and water-fowls of several kinds; woodpeckers, wild and tame pigeons, partridges, honey-birds, Indian rollers, thrushes, taylor-birds,* fly-catchers, and swallows, are seen in great numbers. The beautiful peacock is often seen among the trees. The jungle fowl is about the size of our common fowl, but in appearance resembles the pheasant. Kites and vultures, of which there are many, make great havoc among the smaller birds.

Rats of various kinds infest the houses and the fields. The musk-rat is remarkable for the strong scent it communicates to whatever it touches. Wine is sometimes rendered unfit for use, from these unpleasant animals running among the bottles. The bandacoot is almost as large as a young puppy, and will often have the courage to attack a man. " The flor-mouse, or flying-fox, like the bat, partakes of the appearance both of the bird and quadruped; and its name is derived from the great resemblance of its head and body to the fox. Its body is about the size of an ordinary cat. The wings, when extended, measure six feet; and the length of the animal from the nose to the tail, is about two feet. These animals live in the woods, and perch on the tallest trees; when asleep, or inactive, they

---

* A singular little-bird, that forms its nest of a large leaf, which it sews into a suitable shape. Its bill is very long; with this it pierces the leaf, and introduces the thread.

hang, suspended by their feet, from the branches. They fly in flocks, like the rooks in England." Not having seen this singular animal myself, the above account is given on the authority of Captain Percival; but, both in Bombay and Ceylon, I have frequently seen various species of the bat hanging by the trees in the day-time, perfectly indifferent to the noisy crowds beneath them.

The SERPENTS of Ceylon are much of the same kind as those found in other parts of India.* The cobra-capella is from six to fifteen feet long, and its bite is very poisonous: it is therefore much dreaded by the natives; but some are found hardy enough to take it alive. One was killed in my presence at Caltura, by Doctor De Hoet, to whom it had been brought in a rush bag. When dying, its skin exhibited by turns all the lively colours of the rainbow. Other poisonous snakes are found in the island. Some, however, are perfectly harmless. Of the latter description is the rock-snake; which grows to the length of many feet, and proportionably thick. The rat-snake is of a smaller size; and so inoffensive, that the inhabitants allow it to reside in the roofs of their houses, which it keeps clear of rats, and from which its name is derived. When a contest between a rat and this snake is obstinate, they sometimes both fall together from the roof, to the no small annoyance of the company below.

Very large crocodiles, or, more properly speaking, alligators, are numerous in the rivers of Ceylon, and often prove fatal to bathers. During the progress of an embassy to the interior country, in the year 1800, an English soldier of the 19th regiment, being employed in washing some clothes on the bank of a river, was suddenly seized by an alligator, which sprung at him, and dragged him into the deeper parts of the river; the unfortunate man was seen no more! One of these terrific creatures was killed about thirty miles from Colombo, and being sent for the inspection of the Lieutenant Governor, it was measured, and found to be full twenty feet in length, and as thick round the body as a horse; two carts, drawn by eight bullocks, were required to convey its

* A brief enumeration of these will be found in the notices of the Island of Bombay.

body; which, on being opened, was found to contain the head and arm of a black man not completely digested. The skin was of a hard, knotty texture, impenetrable to a musket-ball. A few days previous to my arrival at Galle, an alligator was caught near that place; and the remains of an unfortunate native were taken out of his stomach. This creature had destroyed several people, and the inhabitants at length united to accomplish his destruction.

The gwana in form resembles a young alligator, but is perfectly harmless. The natives esteem its flesh for food, which it is said tastes like that of rabbit. Toads, bloodsuckers, camelions, and lizards, and a vast variety of other reptiles of the same class, swarm in the fields and gardens throughout the island. A small and inoffensive species of lizard is permitted to live in the houses of the inhabitants. It possesses the faculty of running horizontally on the walls and cielings, in a manner similar to flies, on which they feed, and in which they manifest great dexterity. They, however, occasionally miss their hold, and sometimes fall on the plate or face of a person sitting beneath them.*

A species of leech which infests the woods of the interior occasions great inconvenience to travellers. They are so diminutive, as to intrude themselves imperceptibly into the shoes, and have not been suspected, until they have covered the feet with blood. I have seen persons who have been so desperately wounded by these assailants, as to render amputation necessary. A description of *flying* lizard is sometimes met with; but never came within my observation. Captain Percival describes it as having membranes extended along its sides, in the form of wings, with which it is enabled to take its flight from tree to tree: "it is not above nine inches long, and is perfectly harmless; although it is the only animal known which resembles the fabled dragon."

---

* A recent discovery, (I believe by Doctor Woolaston) ascertains that spiders, flies (and probably lizards) possess the extraordinary power of walking on ceilings, by exuding a viscous matter, which resides in their feet; and which, from its glutinous properties, enables them successfully to counteract the force of gravitation.

The INSECTS of Ceylon are extremely numerous, and many of them very troublesome; in which class we may reckon the musquito, a kind of gnat, and various kinds of ants: the white ant, which possesses the power of devouring almost every substance but metal and stone: large spiders, whose bite is poisonous: the tarantula, having legs four inches long, and the body covered with hair: the scorpion, which inflicts a wound which sometimes proves fatal: and the centipede, the bite of which causes the wounded part to inflame. Many other insects might be named, curious in shape, and brilliant in colours.

The island is well supplied with both fresh and salt-water FISH, many of them delicate. The shark is frequently caught of a prodigious size. This tyrant of the Indian seas not only strikes terror into the finny tribes, but preys also on the human species. Some English gentlemen, one day amusing themselves with bathing in the surf a short distance from Colpetty, were alarmed by the appearance of a shark. In the midst of their uneasiness, one of the company, a young gentleman named May, exclaimed that he was wounded. The water was instantly discoloured with blood; and, as he was hastening to the shore, the monster inflicted a second wound. On being taken out of the sea, he was unable to stand. It was found that the femoral artery was so completely divided, as to cause almost instantaneous death!

The fishermen, when angling among the rocks, sometimes stand for hours, with incredible patience, in expectation of their uncertain prey; but are compelled to use the utmost caution, lest they should be surprised by the shark. He is, however, sometimes caught with their large hooks; and when cut up into small pieces, is sold to inexperienced purchasers as *king-fish;* by which the imagination of the eater is preserved from the disgusting association occasioned by partaking of a fish which devours men. The *real* king-fish is a favourite at a Ceylon table, its flavour very much resembling the salmon, but of a different colour. Several kinds of flat-fish are brought to the Ceylon markets; among which the pomfret is highly esteemed: soals are not uncommon, and are very fine. The coast also supplies a species of mackerel, and also of herring, in great abundance. Lobsters, crabs, and prawns abound; and, in some few places, muscles and oysters are obtained.

The Ceylon fisheries produce a considerable income to the government. They are let to the highest bidders; and the fishermen contract with the public renters. Whether this be the most excellent arrangement is questionable. Some are of opinion, that to throw open the fisheries, unrestrained by impost, to the industry of the fisherman, would in the end benefit the revenue, and encourage habits of industry in the natives.

Ceylon has long been celebrated for its excellent PEARLS. They are found in a small oyster, which is caught in the neighbourhood of Arrippo and the Bay of Condatchy, on the north-western coast of the island. At the proper season of the year, generally in the month of February, these two places are thronged with natives of various tribes with their respective priests and conjurers, on whose powers they calculate for preservation from danger. The officers of government are present to superintend the fishery; and a small detachment of soldiers is generally found necessary for the preservation of order. The government sometimes conducts the fishery on its own account; but it is more frequently let after the manner of the other fisheries.

The banks on which the pearl oysters are found extend several miles along the coast, and some of them equally as far out to sea. They are procured by the process of diving, a practice in which the natives are peculiarly expert. It is very common for the divers to remain under water two or three minutes, and some for nearly double that time, without taking breath. In the year 1797, it is said, a native of Anjango remained immersed full six minutes!

It is seldom that any of the divers are drowned; but the shark occasionally makes sad havoc among these intruders upon his dominions, and fills them with dismay and consternation. To preserve them from these voracious and destructive creatures, they are accompanied by the conjurers; who, standing on the shores, impose on their deluded followers, by muttering during the whole day a kind of incantation, in which they have great confidence. When it happens, as it sometimes does, that a diver loses his leg, or his life, the conjurers are allowed so unlimited a range of excuses, that a cause for the mischief is soon assigned; and a promise to keep the mouths of the sharks closer shut for the future, induces the infatuated divers to resume their hazardous employ with their wonted confidence.* The oysters when caught are buried, and taken up again when they have reached a state of putrefaction; by which the pearl is taken out without injury.

The government receipt from this fishery is precarious: some years it is very unproductive, in others very considerable. Of those who have speculated in it, a few have gained amazing sums; while a much greater number have been disappointed, impoverished, and ruined.

In the neighbourhood of Manaar, a chanque fishery is carried on, and proves a valuable source of revenue to government. The shells are obtained by divers, at about two fathoms; but not after the same manner as the pearl oysters. When the weather is calm, the chanques are seen from a boat, moving in the bottom of the sea; and the diver often follows a single one with his eye for a considerable space; when he is always sure of being conducted to a richly covered bank, where he can fish with advantage. These shells, which are of a spiral form, are chiefly exported to Bengal; where they are sawed into rings of various sizes, and worn on the arms, legs, fingers and toes, of the Hindoos, both male and female. They are likewise used whole, to sound as a horn at funerals, and are employed for other purposes in religious ceremonies. A chanque opening towards the right hand is highly valued by the natives of India; and, being rarely found, always sells for its weight in gold.†

Even in the immediate vicinity of the sea, when it is

---

* An intelligent friend engaged in the Colne oyster-trade has suggested, that the oyster-drag, in use in this country, might be introduced with success into this fishery. It can be used even in thirty fathom water: and, could it be adopted, humanity would rejoice over the preservation of human life, and the prevention of human suffering.

† Cordiner, vol. ii. p. 7.

very sandy, the Ceylonese soil is in the general friendly to vegetation; and were it subjected to those modes of cultivation which are employed in England, its produce would be still more abundant.

The island is supplied with wheat from the upper provinces of India. As rice is the chief article of food to the Ceylonese natives, their principal agricultural labour consists in the cultivation of that grain. This, however, is not raised in a sufficient quantity to obviate the necessity of very large importations from other countries. It is hoped that foreign supplies will become less and less necessary, by the improvement and extension of cultivation, and as the noxious jungles of the interior give place to the healthful and productive corn-field. The rice is generally sown in level lands; as the hills are less favourable for retaining sufficient water to keep the soil continually moist, which is indispensably requisite in the cultivation of this grain. But even the sloping sides of the hills are occasionally brought to render their tribute to the Ceylon harvest; in accomplishing which, the natives manifest great ingenuity.

The mode of cultivating the rice is curious. Around the fields intended for the reception of the seed small embankments are raised, to the height of three feet, to retain the water; which is then let in upon the grounds, which are levelled for the purpose, and soon completely inundates them. When the fields begin to get dry, buffalos are introduced to tread them over,* or they are turned over with a sort of light plough. The ground thus prepared looks like one large tract of mud; and in this state it receives the rice, which is previously steeped in water, mixed with the lime of burnt shells. The soil is afterwards levelled, and prevented from caking into lumps, by a description of harrow, or rake, which consists of a piece of board fixed to a pole, drawn along edgewise. As the rice will not thrive except the ground be completely drenched, the fields are carefully embanked against the commencement of the rainy season. They usually sow in July and August, and reap

* Isa. xxxii. 20.

in February. If proper advantage be taken of the monsoons, they sometimes have two crops a year.

From the tenure under which their lands are held, they are required to clear the whole of their fields at the same time. This obliges them to arrange for the whole crop of rice to be ripe together. In this their agricultural skill principally consists. The several kinds of rice which ripen at different periods are, by the manner of sowing, and the quantity of water introduced, made to advance equally. When ripe, instead of reaping it according to the European custom, they pull it up by the roots, and then lay it out to dry. The straw is trodden by oxen, to separate the grain from the ear; and is afterwards beaten in a kind of wooden mortar, tor emove the husk. Their inundated fields attract a terrible enemy in the alligator, who frequently enters unperceived, and conceals himself among the embankments. The natives are obliged to examine them with great care, before they venture among the mud and water.*

In addition to different kinds of rice, Ceylon produces Indian corn—*gram*, a grain which is used principally for domesticated animals; also coriander seed, cardamoms, with a few other kinds of seed, which are brought to the bazaars. The bringal, the sweet potatoe, the yam, and considerable varieties of the bean, the portuguese green, and the Indian spinach, are plentiful; also, small onions, garlic, and ginger. The pumpkin is sometimes made, by cooking, to resemble turnips and carrots; various species of gourds are rendered by the same means palateable. French beans and green peas, and some other European vegetables, are raised in private gardens. The soil of the Kandyan hills, has been considered favourable for the cultivation of the potatoe; attempts are also making to raise the English cabbage. Some suppose that wheat will ultimately be grown successfully in the interior provinces. The sugar-cane is but very partially cultivated: it is sold at the bazaars to children, as a kind of luxury, in pieces a few inches long. The most delicious pine-apples are produced in the open fields, after the manner of turnips in England.

* Percival's Ceylon, p. 333.

Tobacco, when growing, resembles the leaf of the horse-radish. The betel, like the ivy, twines itself around the plants which are near it. The pepper plant*, which is of the same order, runs along the ground, or clings to the trees. Beautiful and fragrant flowers in an almost infinite variety, with innumerable plants, are left to the pen of the naturalist for description.

Among the TREES of Ceylon, may be ranked the chocolate and coffee trees. When mature in growth, they are about the size of the English filbert-tree. The coffee is produced in a small red berry; considerable quantities of which is raised throughout the island. A species of the cotton-tree, which resembles the English ash, grows to a considerable height; but there is also a smaller description, more generally cultivated. Several respectable Dutch gentlemen have assured me, that the tea-plant grows in some parts of the island. Captain Percival, in his "History of Ceylon," corroborates this statement. He says,—" I have in my possession a letter from an officer in the 80th regiment, wherein he states, that he had found the real tea-plant in the woods of Ceylon, of a quality equal to any that ever grew in China; and that it was in his power to point out to government the means of cultivating it in a proper manner." The vast advantages to be derived from the cultivation of the tea plant in our own dominions, might, at least, prompt a speedy and vigorous experiment on the subject.

The plantain-tree is of so peculiar a form, that it is not easy to convey an idea of it to an English reader. The wood is soft, and the leaves very broad, long, and green. When it has once produced fruit, the trunk dies, and a new one springs from the root. The fruit grows from the top of the tree, which bends towards the ground by the weight; and resembles in shape a bunch of large sausages, each from six to nine inches long, and from ten to twenty in a bunch. There are several varieties of this fruit, some of much the same flavour as a ripe pear. It is one of the most whole-

---

* The capsicum, or red pepper, is a shrub; the fruit grows in small oblong pods, which are at first green; but, when pulled and dried become red; and from them the Cayenne pepper is made.

some fruits in the world; and the leaf is a cooling and agreeable application to a blister, or wound of any kind.

A particular description of all the Ceylon fruit trees would include the grape-vine, mango, mangusteen, fig, custard-apple, pomegranate, guava, pumplemose, the pau-pau, the orange in several varieties, the lemon, tamarind, country gooseberry, cashoo, almond, jamboo, moringa, bread-fruit, areca-nut, rose-apple, castor-tree, and many others. There is in the island a tree called Eve's-apple; the fruit resembles an apple from which a piece has been cut, or bitten. By this fruit, it is gravely asserted, our first parents were tempted to disobedience; and hence the singular appearance, which has been perpetuated. The believers in this tradition state, that Ceylon was the primitive Eden: the Mahomedans, or Roman Catholics, were most probably the inventors of this fable. I have seen and examined the fruit: the blossom is remarkably and powerfully fragrant, and the form of the apple is singularly coincident with the tradition. A few other vegetable productions also inherit poisonous qualities; among which is the wild-pine: this plant generally grows in the sand near the sea-shore.

The cocoa-nut tree has long attracted the curiosity of Europeans, though it is not produced exclusively in Ceylon. It sometimes grows to the height of seventy feet, and continues productive for a great number of years. Its fruit supplies the natives with food, and with oil, which is expressed from the dried kernel;* they manufacture the shell into curious and ornamental vessels for domestic use; the integuments which surround the shell is formed into a kind of brush, and used to clean their houses; a useful cordage is also made from this coating. The trunk of the tree supplies timber, with which they build their cots and houses; the leaves serve as an excellent thatch for the roofs of their dwellings, and are made into a common school book, called *olla* books. By a simple process they extract the sap, or toddy, from the tree, which is a delicious drink, esteemed by some equal to champagne; from this is distilled a strong intoxicating liquor,

* Considerable quantities of this oil are exported to Europe. It has been recently discovered that some qualities reside in it which render it highly useful in the manufacture of cloth.

resembling whiskey, called arrack; and jaggery, a kind of sugar, is prepared from the toddy; it is also used by bakers instead of yeast; and very good vinegar is made from it. It is said, that this profitable tree is applied to nearly an hundred different uses.*

The palmyra tree is to the north of the island, what the cocoa-nut tree is to the inhabitants of the south; it is much slenderer than the cocoa-nut tree, and grows to a greater height.

The jaggery tree belongs to the same order as the two preceding, and derives its name from its peculiar fertility in the production of sugar. In its general appearance it resembles the cocoa-nut tree, with the addition of blossoms, and clusters of fruit hanging down in perpendicular strings three or four feet long, from the bottom of the leaves all around the top of the stem. The pith of this tree, when dried and granulated, is well known by the name of sago.†

The talipot tree, the largest of the palms, is perhaps one of the most remarkable trees in the world. Its trunk is nearly seven feet in circumference, and usually more than a hundred feet high. The fruit, or berries, which it bears, are only produced in the last year of its life, and are of no other value than as seeds; the size and peculiar construction of its leaf renders it an object worthy of particular notice. The following is a minute and accurate description of it by Capt. Robert Knox—"This tree is as big and as tall as a ship's mast, and very straight, bearing only leaves, which are of great use and benefit to the inhabibitants; one single leaf being so broad and large, that it will cover fifteen or twenty men [standing close together], and keep them dry when it rains. The leaf when dried is very strong and limber, and most wonderfully made for men's convenience to carry with them; for, though the leaf be thus broad when it is open, yet it folds close, like a lady's fan; and then it is no bigger than a man's arm, and extremely light. The people cut them

---

* Mr. Percival relates, that some ambassadors coming to Ceylon from the king of the Maldive Islands, were conveyed in a small ship, which was entirely built and rigged from the cocoa-nut tree, while those employed in fitting it out were fed upon the nuts.

† Cordiner, vol. i. p. 357.

into pieces, and carry them in their hands; the whole leaf spread out is round, almost like a circle, but the pieces cut for use are nearly like unto a triangle. When the sun is vehement, they use them to shade themselves from the heat. All soldiers carry them; for, besides the benefit of keeping them dry, in case it rain upon the march, those leaves make their tents to lie under in the night."* Strange as this account must appear to Europeans, its correctness may be relied on. A small one was presented to me by the Guard Moodeliar of Galle.† It is from this leaf that the most expensive native books, called *pooscoola*, are made. A curious preparatory process of boiling is necessary in order to make it receive and retain the impression of the *stylus*, or iron-pen, of the natives. When thus prepared they will resist the ravages of time for a great number of years.

A species of bread-fruit, known by the name of the jack-tree, also grows in Ceylon, and is invaluable to the natives. Its manner of growth resembles a chesnut tree, shooting forth branches in all directions. It often exceeds the bulk and height of the largest oak; the leaves are much used in feeding sheep, and other animals. The fruit grows from the trunk of the tree, or from the principal branches, is of an oval form, and sometimes a foot in length, and often more in circumference; and so heavy, that two native men will bend under the weight of a single apple. It is covered with a thick green coat of a scaly appearance, and contains a number of seeds, each enclosed in a fleshy substance, of the size and form of the green fig; this substance is of a yellow colour, and of a rich and delicious taste. The seeds resemble a chesnut, and are roasted and eaten in the same manner. The fruit has a strong unpleasant smell and taste when first cut open; but when well washed, and steeped in salted water,

---

* " Historical Relation."

† I also brought home with me a still larger piece of the talipot leaf, which we had some difficulty in preserving from perishing during the voyage, from the dampness of the air, and the heat of the ship. It is lodged with a few other curiosities in the Museum of the Wesleyan Mission House, Hatton Garden, London. This singular tree is found in perfection only in the interior of Ceylon. I am not aware of there being another specimen in this country.

these entirely disappear. The wood of this tree is employed in all substantial buildings. It is rather weighty, of a yellowish cast,* and receives a polish nearly as well as mahogany. It is used in the manufacture of household furniture, and looks very handsome. The interior of the Wesleyan Mission Chapel in Colombo is formed of this wood; which being constantly rubbed, and cleaned with a preparation of linseed oil, &c. has a very interesting and respectable appearance.

The cocoa-nut, palmyra, and jack trees, are highly esteemed by the natives; and furnish a certain resource against the failure of more precarious sustenance. "The man who plants any one of these useful trees confers a lasting benefit on himself, and hands down to posterity more certain riches, than can be procured in less genial climates by a life of the most toilsome labour. When the seeds, or slips, are once put into the ground they require no cultivation, no pruning, no kind of attention; but spontaneously advance to maturity, and yield a regular and never-failing produce."†

The banyan tree is sufficiently remarkable to be noticed. Branches from those which grow horizontally from the trunk strike into the earth, where they take root, and return their obligations to the parent tree, by giving it support from the newly formed root. This tree affords a shady and pleasant retreat to the traveller. The bogaha, or tree of the god Budhu, grows to a large size, and is held in high veneration by the Singhalese. Its leaves resemble the outline of a heart. The Singhalese pay divine honours to this tree, and make a pavement round it, which they keep constantly swept. They place lighted lamps, images, and sacred flowers under it, and bow before it with great veneration. Capt. Knox states, "that it is held meritorious to plant them; which, they say, he that does, shall die within a short time after, and go to heaven. But," he adds, "the oldest men only, who are nearest death, in the course of nature, do plant them, and none else; the younger sort

* The shavings of this wood make an excellent yellow dye.

† Cordiner, vol. i. p. 362.

desiring to live a little longer in this world, before they go to the other."

In a description of the natural productions of Ceylon, the cinnamon tree merits especial notice. In its wild state this tree grows to the height of from twenty to thirty feet, and is about three feet in circumference; but, when cultivated, is not suffered to attain so large a size. There are several species of the cinnamon tree; the finest and most valued is found in the government gardens, and is from four to ten feet in height: the trunk is slender, with numbers of branches shooting out from it on every side. The wood is soft, light and porous, in appearance somewhat resembling our osier; a vast number of fibres issue forth from the root, and, shooting out into slender twigs, form a bush around it. The leaf has the appearance of the laurel in shape, but is not of so deep a green; when bruised it has the scent and taste of cloves. The blossom is white, but not very fragrant. The fruit resembles an acorn, but is somewhat smaller; from this the Singhalese extract an oil, which is much esteemed by them. The Dutch Governor, M. Falck, who was a native of the island, and whose memory is still held in high esteem, was the first who devoted any particular attention to the culture of the cinnamon-tree. His plans were followed up by our government; and considerable tracts of many miles are at present occupied by this valuable tree, which are under the constant superintendance of the Chalias, or Mahabadde Singhalese. An English civilian is placed at the head of this department; and intelligent and assiduous headmen attend to the prosecution of the work.

The mode of obtaining the cinnamon, which is the inner bark of this tree, is curious and worthy of description. When about three years old, the branches are taken from the stock; the outer bark, or coating, is then scraped off with a knife of a peculiar form, concave on the one side, and curved on the other. With the point of this knife the bark is ripped up longwise, and the curved side is then employed in gradually loosening it from the branch, till it can be taken off entire. In this state it appears in the form of tubes open at one side, the smaller of which being inserted within the larger, they are thus spread out to dry, and by the heat of the sun they contract, until they attain the form in which they are seen in the European markets. The cinnamon thus prepared is safely lodged in the government storehouses, where it undergoes a careful examination, and is sorted according to its quality. It is brought to Europe in bundles of about eighty pounds weight, which are packed as closely as possible in the hold of the vessels, and all the interstices filled up with black pepper; which prevents the flavour from evaporating, or the article from being otherwise injured. The best cinnamon is rather pliable, and not much thicker than strong writing-paper. From the stout kind, and the refuse, the oil of cinnamon is prepared; and the water used in the process has also lately become an article of commercial speculation.

The tulip-tree is a conspicuous object, and especially attracts the eye by its beautiful flower. It is often planted by the road side, and emits a delightful fragrance. The bamboo has also a fine aspect on the borders of a stream; over which it hangs like a weeping willow.

Ceylon produces many kinds of ornamental wood, and useful timber. Thirty-nine species of these have been collected and sent to England.* The teak wood resembles our English oak.† The nadan wood is used in the manufacture of household furniture. The nandoo wood is finely streaked, and bears a high polish. Fine ebony grows in the jungles. Satin-wood makes very elegant furniture, and cabinet articles. But the choicest and most beautiful of all the Ceylon woods is the kallamandoo; which is extremly hard, of a dark chocolate colour, clouded like marble, and streaked with veins of black and pale yellow. The root of the kallamando tree is wrought up into ladies' work-boxes of the most handsome description. The variegated and singular viening of this wood sometimes presents a lively imagination with the appearance of a picturesque landscape.

In Ceylon the foundation of the SOIL is generally a deep

---

* Cordiner.

† A description of this wood is inserted among the natural productions of Bombay; Chap. VIII. of this work.

stratum of reddish clay, mixed with sandy ferruginous particles. In the country it is called by the name of *cabooc-stone*. When first broken up it is as soft as a stiff clay, and as easily cut into pieces; but upon being exposed to the sun it becomes indurated and brittle, and is used as a substitute for stone in building. This foundation of the soil is covered with strata of black mould and white sand, the latter of which forms the surface. Its fertility is remarkable; almost every where producing grass, shrubs and trees of a lively and perpetual verdure. Hard rock is found on some parts of the coast, particularly at Point-de-Galle and Trincomalee. All the shores are lined under water with ledges of white coral of various species. The earth abounds in useful minerals and beautiful fossils; iron ore is extremely plentiful. Mica, or glimmer, is found in large laminated masses, shivers of it are used in ornamenting talipot leaves. Plumbago is found with mica a the foot of mountains, in clay, or red earth, most frequently at a considerable depth, but sometimes by itself in a dry soil; crystallized pyrites, which contain a little copper, is manufactured into buttons. Quicksilver has been discovered in small quantities. The Kandyan territories are said to contain gold; but the working of the mines, or gathering of the dust, was prohibited by the jealous policy of the king.*

Upwards of twenty sorts of precious stones adorn and enrich the cabinet of the Singhalese collector. They are found among the hills and rocks, and along the banks and beds of rivers, whence they are frequently fetched up by the natives, some of whom derive considerable profit by their sale to Europeans. The diamond of Ceylon is seldom perfectly transparent, but generally appears of a milky colour. The ruby is esteemed according to its clearness, the deepness of its colour, and its freedom from flaws. The amethyst is a mountain crystal, tinged with a violet colour. Stones known by the name of tourmalins are found here of various colours; the red, the blue, the green, or cryso-prase, the yellow, or topaz-tourmalin. The topaz is generally

* This policy being no longer in operation, should the supposition be founded in fact, our own Government will, without doubt, avail itself of such an advantage.

found in yellowish splinters. The blue and the green sapphire are made into buttons and rings. Crystals—white, black, yellow and brown—are so plentiful, that much value is not attached to them. The cat's-eye is a deserved favourite with the virtuoso, and in its perfect state is often sold at an enormous price; imperfect stones may be procured on more reasonable terms. The moon-stone partakes of the appearance of the pearl and cat's-eye. Cornelians of different colours are also plentiful; and new varieties will, without doubt, continue to be discovered in the Kandyan territories.

SECT. II.

POLITICAL AND CIVIL HISTORY.

The early history of Ceylon is involved in comparative obscurity. Tradition has made it the scene of the creation of man, and of those important transactions which took place in the infancy of our world. In conformity with this idea, the isthmus by which the island and the continent are supposed to have been once united, is called *Adam's Bridge;* the highest mountain received the name of *Adam's Peak;* and early writers have amused the world by an account of a fountain of water on its summit, produced by the tears shed by our first parents on beholding the mangled body of Abel, the victim of a brother's rage, and the first human being who tasted death! The Mahomedans were, most probably, the authors of these tales; as a respectable author has asserted, on the authority of Marco Paulo, that " the Moors believe Adam to have been buried there."

Rejecting these accounts, as the reveries of a distempered imagination, the sober historian cannot but regret that his search for satisfactory information, respecting the early history of this interesting island, has been attended with success so little commensurate with the labour bestowed on the investigation.

From whence was Ceylon first peopled? This important enquiry can only be met by conjecture strengthened by analogy, in the absence of direct evidence. In a few points, the Singhalese exhibit marks of a Chinese origin. Some writers have supposed that the neighbouring coast of India supplied the first settlers; while others imagine them to have proceeded from the Maldive Islands. The latter opinion is opposed by the dissimilarity which prevails between the Singhalese and the natives of these islands, both in language, habits, and national character; a dissimilarity so entire, as to render it highly improbable that they had their origin from that source. Valentyn, a respectable and laborious historian of the Dutch nation, whose writings are not sufficiently known, states, that in the ancient Singhalese books, the first king of the island is said to have been a Chinese, who was accidentally driven in a junk upon the shore;* and that giving himself out to be a descendant from the sun, (which at that time was the object of national worship) the conceit being also favoured by his own companions, the islanders agreed to confer on him the sovereignty.†

The convulsion of nature which originally separated the island from the continent must have been terrible to those who witnessed it. This might occasion the first race of settlers to abandon the island, and seek a shelter on the continent. If, as the Singhalese ancient writings affirm, the Chinese vessel found the island inhabited by a people who worshipped the sun; might not a second colony, the progenitors of the present inhabitants, have been formed by *Persians,* (who worship the sun) driven by accident, or impelled by a spirit of adventure, here to take up their abode?

* " According to tradition, this island, or rather country, formerly comprehended a greater extent of territory than it does at present; having been separated from the Continent at its northern extremity; and having lost in the southern and eastern, a considerable extent of that part of the country in which the Basses *(Baxos)* are situated. These events, occasioned probably by some violent convulsion of nature, must have taken place in ages very remote; since the Veda makes mention of Ceylon *(Sirendip)* distinctly as an island."—*See a Memoir by the late Monsieur Burnard,* inserted in the ASIATIC JOURNAL for *May,* 1821, p. 440.

† " The naval skill of the Chinese seems not to have been superior to that of the Greeks, the Romans, or Arabians. The course which they held from Canton to Sitaf, near the mouth of the Persian Gulf, is described by their own authors. They kept as near as possible to the shore *until they reached the island of Ceylon;* and then, doubling Cape Comorin, they sailed along the west side of the Peninsula, as far as the mouth of the Indus; and thence steered along the coast to the place of their destination. *Mem. de Literat.* tom. xxvii. p. 367."— *Doctor Robertson's Notes and Illustrations.*

The following fanciful account is given of the derivation of the term *Singhalese;* which literally signifies *Lion-people.* The astrologers of an Asiatic king announcing that some peculiar fate awaited his infant daughter, she was educated in solitude, in a house of singular construction, in order to defeat the dreaded prediction. On coming of age, however, her curiosity to see the world, impelled her to escape from her seclusion; when she was met by a powerful lion, who, killing her attendants, carried her to his den; where she became the mother of two lion-children, a male and a female. The lion-son, having learned from the princess the story of his birth, forsook his native den, and repaired to the court of his grandfather, in company with his mother and sister. On his return from hunting, the lion-parent, enraged at the removal of his family, flew to the inhabited parts of the country, and committed great ravages among the people in revenge of his loss. That his kingdom might be delivered from so sanguinary a foe, the king offered an immense reward to any one who would accomplish his destruction; and the lion-prince, availing himself of the freedom with which his shaggy sire permitted his approach, shot him with an arrow, and presented his head to the king. The consequence of his exploit was, the highest honours at court; and, at length, the sovereignty of another nation; who, from him, and his extraordinary history, received the appellation of *Sing-ha-lese.* Most traditionary fables have their origin in some fact. Subsequent researches may trace out the connection of this marvellous tale with the real history of this people.

" The Sanscrit name of Ceylon is *Tapobon* (Taprobane) a word implying the wilderness of prayer—the hallowed groves consecrated to devotion, whether pious pilgrims repaired from the farthest corners of India, to offer gifts and adorations to the unknown God."* This name is by Mr. Dunstan, in the " Asiatic Researches," derived from *Tapoo-Rawan,* the island of *Rawan* the giant; who, according to Indian mythology, fought with *Raama* on this very spot. The island is called by the natives, *Lanka-Dwīpa,*

* The Rev. J. Cordiner's Description of Ceylon.

or the " Holy Land ;" which is the name it still bears in the Singhalese and Malabar languages, on the Government paper-currency.

" Prior to the age of Alexander the Great, the name of Taprobane was unknown in Europe. In consequence of the active curiosity with which he explored every country that he subdued or visited, some information concerning it seems to have been obtained. From his time, almost every writer on geography has mentioned it ; but their accounts of it are so various, and often so contradictory, that we can scarcely believe them to be describing the same island. STRABO, the earliest writer now extant, from whom we have any particular account of it, affirms that it was as large as Britain, and situated at the distance of seven days' sailing from the southern extremity of the Indian peninsula. POMPONIUS MELA, the author next in order of time, is uncertain whether he should consider Taprobane as an island, or as the beginning of another world. PLINY gives a more ample description of it. After enumerating the various and discordant opinions of the Greek writers, he informs us, that ambassadors were sent by a king of that island to the Emperor Claudius, from whom the Romans learned several things concerning it, which were formerly unknown. PTOLEMY, though so near to the time of Pliny, seems to have been altogether unacquainted with his description of Taprobane, or with the embassy to the emperor Claudius. He places that island opposite to Cape Comorin, at no great distance from the continent. AGATHEMERUS, who wrote after Ptolemy, and was well acquainted with his geography, considers it as the largest of all the islands, and assigns to Britain only the second place. The generally received opinion among the moderns is, that the Taprobane of the ancients is the island of Ceylon; and not only its vicinity to the continent of India, but the general form of the island as delineated by Ptolemy, as well as the position of several places in it, mentioned by him, established this opinion with a great degree of certainty.

" Under the Roman emperor Justinian, COSMAS, an Egyptian merchant, in the course of his traffic, made some voyages to India, whence he acquired the surname of

Indicopleustes; but afterwards, by a transition not uncommon in that age, he renounced all the concerns of this life, and assumed the monastic character. In the solitude and leisure of a cell, he composed several works; one of which, dignified by him with the name of *Christian Topography*, has reached us. Cosmas seems to relate what he himself had observed in his travels, or what he had learned from others, with great simplicity and regard for truth. From him we learn that the island of Taprobane, had become, in consequence of its commodious situation, a great staple of trade; that into it were imported the silk of the Sinæ, and the precious spices of the eastern countries, which were conveyed thence to all parts of India, to Persia, and to the Arabian Gulf. To this island he gives the name of *Sielediba*, nearly the same with that of *Selendib*, or *Serendib*, by which it is still known all over the East."*

The Portuguese was the first European state which established a regular intercourse with Ceylon. In 1505, Don Lorenzo, the son of the Vice-roy of Goa, was obliged to take refuge in a storm in the harbour of Galle; and, meeting with a hospital reception from the chief of that province, a regular intercourse was established, and the new visitors soon found means to erect a fort at Colombo, which they formed of clay and stone; and shortly after constructed fortifications of a class calculated to defend the possession they had acquired.

The Portuguese appear to have conducted themselves towards the natives more as conquerors than as friends; until the natives, roused to resentment by their insolence and oppression, attempted their forcible extirpation. They assembled an army of 20,000 men, with which they besieged the Portuguese in their fortifications; who, but for prompt supplies from Goa, would have been compelled to yield to the overwhelming numbers of their assailants. After a series of wars, attended with varied success; and negociations, in which the superior knowledge of the Portuguese gave them decided advantages; they so firmly established their power in the island, as to have the whole of the coasts, with the

* Doctor Robertson

maritime towns, ceded to them as their regular territory; and the interior of the island was so completely under their influence, that a regular tribute was levied, under some plausible pretext, for the service of the king of Portugal.

In 1603, the Dutch made a successful attempt to obtain a footing in Ceylon. The native princes, who had long groaned under the tyranny of the Portuguese, lent their strength and influence to aid the new-comers; and so effectually, that the Portuguese were at length driven from the island, and the whole of their territory taken possession of by the Dutch; who, sensible of the commercial advantages to be derived from a peaceful possession of the coasts, left the interior of the island to the native princes, with whom they kept up a friendly intercourse. This policy tended to the stability of their possessions, and the increase of their wealth; and to *policy* they were always more indebted than to the force of arms. Occasionally disputes arose, in course of time, between the colonists and the natives; but the wars which were the consequence of these quarrels, were oftentimes severely felt by the Dutch.

In 1782, the French fitted out an expedition against Ceylon, and succeeded in capturing Trincomalee. From thence the commander of the expedition sent an embassage to the king of Kandy, with offers to co-operate with the Kandyans in expelling the Dutch from the island. The embassy was favourably received; and the offers would have been accepted, but the French were unable to make any impression on the Dutch power. The embassy never returned from the interior, being detained under various pretences by the Kandyan court; and the island continued in the possession of the Dutch until 1795; when it was taken possession of by the British and East India Company's troops.

For some time after their conquest by the British, the European provinces of Ceylon remained under the administration of the Presidency of Madras; but being transferred to the English crown in 1798, the Hon. Frederic North was appointed Governor; whose administration is still remembered by the settlers with respectful affection. On his retirement, General Sir Thomas Maitland was appointed his successor; and the various interests of the colonists were watched over and promoted by his vigilance. But it was reserved for the government of General Sir Robert Brownrigg (the successor of Sir T. Maitland) to extend the blessings of civilization, and the invaluable privileges of British subjects, to the natives of the interior. Other European powers had sometimes obtained a temporary possession of the city of Kandy, and had compelled the king to seek shelter among the woods and fastnesses with which the country abounded; but these advantages were invariably abandoned, as their troops either fell sacrifices to the climate, or were worn-out by hunger and fatigue. A course of favourable events placed *the whole* of the Kandyan territories in the hands of Governor Brownrigg; by whose orders their sanguinary monarch was transported to a distance from the country he had polluted by his cruelties.*

The native population of Ceylon; which is estimated at about a million and a half; owes its origin to almost every nation in India; but the Ceylonese themselves may be divided into the following classes:—VEDDAS, KANDYANS, SINGHALESE, and MALABARS.†

---

* A particular account of these events will be found at page 252 of this work.—See also Appendix.

† The *Malabars*, who inhabit the northern and north-eastern parts of the island; and whose principal towns are Manaar, Jaffna, Trincomalee and Batticalao; are so similar in their habits and superstitions to the Continental Asiatics, an account of whom is included in my notices of Bombay; that the reader is referred to that part of the work for information respecting them. The Malabars in Ceylon were originally from the west coast of the Indian peninsula, which is still denominated *the Malabar Coast*. In ancient maps, we observe on that coast a town, of the name of *Male*, or *Ma-lee*, situated near Cannanore or Tillicherry; which in the seventh century was one of the most frequented of the Indian ports; and which, from its commercial importance, is very likely to have given its name to that part of India. This supposition is confirmed by Dr. Robertson; who observes, "From *Male* it is probable that this side of the continent has derived its modern name of *Malabar;* and the cluster of islands contiguous to it, that of the *Maldives*."

The Veddas;

long denominated *Wild Men,* from their living in the woods, and avoiding intercourse with any but their own tribe; are a singular people, and but very imperfectly known. Some suppose them to be the remains of the aboriginal inhabitants; while others imagine them to have sprung from a people who were cast away on the Ceylon coast; and who, refusing to submit to the Singhalese sovereign, betook themselves to the jungles, and by their wandering and isolated habits have continued to retain their original independence. What progress civilization has made among them, has not been accurately ascertained. They have a knowledge of the Singhalese language, and some of them even possess the ability of writing it. They have a few simple ideas of subordination to superiors of their own tribe; and have occasionally paid a tributary contribution to the king of Kandy; but they never acknowledged his sovereignty over them, nor were entirely subjected to his control. The Kandyan king, when they have been charged with any offence against his subjects, has sometimes endeavoured to chastise them by parties of soldiers, who harassed and destroyed numbers of them; but having satisfied his revenge, they left them to their former habits.

The Veddas have seldom called forth the attention of the British Government. Sometimes it has been found necessary to apprehend a few, and to bring them to our towns to answer for offences committed by their tribe; but I never heard of any punishment being inflicted upon them. By these captures alone have the Veddas been brought into contact with European society. Capt. Percival mentions his having seen, in 1798, a few who were brought into Colombo; and describes them as " a race entirely different from the other Singhalese : their complexions were fairer, and inclining to a copper-colour: they were remarkably well made; wore long beards, and their hair tucked up close to the crown of the head; their bodies had scarcely any other covering than they had received from nature." The same author speaks of another party of them, which had been apprehended by Colonel Champagne at a subsequent period: " they were wild and savage in their appearance, and armed with bows and arrows. After enjoining them to live in quiet, the Colonel made them a few presents, and then ordered them to be released; upon which they instantly fled away into the woods like deer."

The Veddas are found in various parts of the jungle-woods; the province of Bintenne, near Trincomalee and Batticalao, is their principal district, where numbers live in a state of barbarism, and are seldom seen by the other natives. In the year 1817, they afforded protection to some native miscreants who had taken up arms against the British crown, and very considerably annoyed and harassed our troops. The Veddas, in some of the other parts of the island are less untractable, and more disposed to trade and barter with their neighbours, than those of Bintenne.

Captain Knox, who had better opportunities of observing this people than any other author who has written on the subject, states:—" They speak the Singhalese language; they kill deer, and dry the flesh over the fire, which the country people buy of them; they never till the ground for corn, their only food being flesh; their arms are a bow and arrow and a small axe with which they cut honey out of hollow trees. They have no towns nor houses, living by the waters under a tree, with boughs cut and laid round-about them, that they may hear by the noise of the trampling on the boughs, should any wild beast come near them. The wilder sort of them, when they want arrows, will carry their load of flesh in the night, and hang it up in a smith's shop, also a leaf cut in the form they will have their arrows made, and hang by it; which if the smith do make according to their pattern, they will requite and bring him more flesh; but if he makes them not, they will do him a mischief one time or other by shooting him in the night; the smith leaves the arrows in the same place where the Veddas hang the flesh. They have boundaries, and some ideas of private property among themselves.* The wilder and tamer sort

---

* An infringement on these boundaries, is sometimes the cause of serious quarrels and skirmishes among them; which seems to indicate that

of them do both observe a religion : they have a god peculiar to themselves. The tamer do build temples ; the wilder only bring their sacrifice under trees; and while it is offering dance round it, both men and women."*

The total number of the Veddas cannot be ascertained. It is probable, however, from the importance which was attached to their connection with the rebellion of 1817, that their number is considerable.†

The Kandyans

and the Singhalese, most probably, owe their origin to the same stock; though, at present a very striking dissimilarity in many points is observable. The term *Kandy*‡ is derived from a Singhalese word, which denotes a *hill*, or *mountain*, or a *hilly country;* and has been employed by the inhabitants of the low countries to designate their highland

---

they have nothing among them resembling a regular administration of justice. " One company of them is not to shoot, nor gather honey or fruit, beyond those bounds. Near the borders stood a jack-tree; one Vedda being gathering some fruit from this tree, another Vedda of the next division saw him, and told him he had nothing to do to gather jacks from that tree, for that belonged to them: they fell to words, and from words to blows, and one of them shot the other; at which more of them met, and fell to skirmishing so briskly with their bows and arrows, that twenty or thirty were left dead on the spot."—*Knox's Historical Relation.*

* Ibid. See also the Appendix.

† A race of similar habits formerly existed in the neighbourhood of *the Wanny*, bordering on the province of Jaffnapatam. They are now considerably civilized ; and, except in seasons of revolt, live in subjection to the British government. They speak the Malabar language, and profess the faith of Brahma. Their country is less mountainous [than that of the Veddas,] but extremely woody, and barren of useful produce."—*Cordiner's Ceylon,* v. i. p. 91.

‡ The orthography of this word has been recently changed from *Candy* to *Kandy*. The former was the mode adopted, until the interior country became united to the British territories ; when the question being agitated, it was decided in favour of the latter mode, as more congenial with the derivation of the word. The Singhalese alphabet contains no letter corresponding with our *C*. The original is written with the Singhalese *Kāianoo,* answering to our *K*.

neighbourhood. Respecting the local situation of the Kandyan territory, Mr. Percival states, that the Kandyan provinces " are completely cut off on all sides from those long under the dominion of Europeans, by almost impenetrable woods and mountains. The passes which lead through these to the coasts are extremely steep and difficult, and scarcely known even by the natives themselves. As soon as we advance from ten to twenty miles from the coast, a country presents itself greatly differing therefrom both in soil, climate, and appearance. After ascending the mountains and passing the woods, we find ourselves in the midst of a country, not advanced many stages beyond the first stage of improvement; and which we are astonished to find in the neighbourhood of the highly-cultivated fields which surround Colombo. As we advance towards the centre of the island, the country gradually rises, and the woods and mountains which separate the several parts of the country become more steep and impervious."

The city of Kandy, which was formerly the royal residence of the native monarchs, is situated within eighteen miles of Colombo, the European seat of government; and about twice that distance from Trincomalee, where the British dock-yard and arsenal are established. It is built in a valley, and is a poor, miserable-looking place, surrounded by a mud-wall, of no strength whatever.— It has been several times in the possession of Europeans; but the amazing difficulties attending the furnishing supplies of men and stores, through a country so hilly and overgrown with jungle, have proved a better defence to the Kandyan metropolis than the largest army or the strongest fortifications could have afforded. From this cause, Kandy was never, till its recent conquest by the British, long in the possession of an invading power. When compelled by these causes to abandon the country, they have sometimes lost as many men in their retreat, from the harassing of the natives, and the influence of hunger and disease, as would have been more than sufficient for the reduction of an European fortress of considerable strength.

The embassy of General Macdowal to the Kandyan court in 1800, published some information respecting the city and its inhabitants; but as the ambassador entered it by torch-light, little opportunity was afforded for inspection. "From what could then be observed, the city consists of long straggling streets, built on the declivity of a hill; the houses mean and low, but with the foundations so raised above the level of the streets, that they appear quite lofty to passengers. The reason for this extraordinary taste is to enable the king to hold the assemblies of the people, and to have his elephant and buffalo fights in the streets, without interfering with the houses. When the king passes along the streets, none of the inhabitants are allowed to appear before their houses; or on the paths on a level with them; as that would be attended with the heinous indecorum of placing a subject higher than the prince descended from the sun!*"

The kings of Kandy were possessed of a power the most absolute over both the lives and property of their enslaved subjects. Among the titles by which they were addressed, were "Emperor: descendant of the Golden Sun; whose kingdom was higher than all others:" and he was supposed by his subjects to be the only monarch in the world who possessed the high dignity of wearing a crown! In approaching him, they paid him expressions of homage surpassing those exacted even by the Emperor of China; for, in addition to three profound prostrations, it was required of the persons approaching the throne, to repeat slowly all the titles of the monarch *with the greatest reverence*. In the royal presence the most profound silence reigned; the highest courtier was not allowed to address even a whisper to another; and an involuntary cough was punished as a crime. The king reserved to himself the privilege of having the walls of his residence whitened, and the roof covered with tiles; and no subject was allowed even to fold a letter in the form used by the king. By these, and many such particulars; the fruitful sources of vexation to his subjects, and made constant pretexts for the imposition of fines and the infliction of cruelties; did the vain and haughty tyrants of the Kandyan throne, labour to perpetuate a distinction between themselves and their subjects.

* Percival, p. 106.

The pomp with which the monarch appeared in public was equal to the state and etiquette observed within his court. He was supported in a palankeen, his attendants bearing flags and streamers; while another company made the most discordant noises with drums and uncouth instruments, by which his movements were announced. The *effect* produced by a Kandyan band of *music* may be imagined, when it is stated, that each performer is regulated by his own caprice, both with respect to *time* and *sound;* beating or blowing (as the nature of his instrument requires) with all his might, till he is completely tired, and then stopping to recruit his exhausted strength. But the most ludicrous attendants of Kandyan royalty consisted of a company of men called *crackers* or *smackers,* who preceded the procession, armed with whips several feet in length, which they incessantly cracked with great violence. Whether these were intended merely to clear the road; or were designed to express the contempt felt by the Kandyan kings for all inferior orders of beings; cannot be precisely determined. The *Adikars,* or native ministers of state, when they visit Colombo, are attended by several of these *crackers;* and the effect produced by their evolutions on the mind of an European spectator is ludicrous in the extreme. So expert are they in the use of their long whips, that though the streets be crowded with spectators, they are never known to touch even those who from their situation seem to be in the greatest danger of the lash.

Perfidy and barbarity were the prominent traits of the Kandyan character: and the monarchs appear to have been not more distinguished by their rank, than by their pre-eminence in these qualities. The crews of vessels wrecked on the Kandyan coasts were consigned to hopeless captivity. Traders, allured by commercial enterprize within the range of their authority, were ensnared and enslaved.*
Even ambassadors from other nations found no protection

---

* The reader is referred to Capt. Knox's pathetic and interesting Narrative, who was thus detained several years; the account of whose captivity and escape has been re-published, with an introductory preface and notes, by the author of this work. Sold by Blanshard, price 3s. 6d.

from their peculiar character, and were not unfrequently deprived of their liberty or lives. The tortures inflicted as punishments on criminals were expressive of the barbarity of those who possessed the supreme power; and the frequency of their recurrence habituated the people themselves to spectacles of horror, and went far to assimilate them to those for whose amusement they were sometimes inflicted. Among the modes of executing criminals, that by *elephants* was the most common. Men were frequently torn limb from limb by these animals, who were trained for the purpose. At other times, spikes were fastened to their tusks, with which they were instructed to wound and stab the victim. The docility and expertness of these animals in the work of torture was remarkable. In obedience to signs with which they were familiar, they prolonged or shortened the sufferings of the criminal: and, at command, most effectually inflicted the stroke of mercy, by placing one of their ponderous feet on the head of the wretched being. *Pounding to death in a large mortar*, was another mode of taking the life of offenders. The horrible punishment of death by *impalement* was frequently inflicted; often on innocent individuals, who had accidentally offended the sanguinary king. On the approach of the British troops to the city of Kandy in 1815, a native sentinel announced the unwelcome intelligence to the king; when the monster, in the ebullition of his rage, ordered him to be immediately impaled. The order was executed; and, a few hours after, the British soldiers found the unfortunate and unoffending victim transfixed to a stake! As they continued their march, similar spectacles of horror met their view. Even the *dogs* of the country had become so familiar with these scenes, that they recognized the instruments of torture; and instinctively followed the criminals to execution, in expectation of their accustomed meal on the mangled bodies.

Next in rank and authority to the king, were two *adikars*, or prime ministers, to whom the affairs of government were more immediately entrusted. Under these were several inferior officers; from the *dissauvas*, or governors of districts, to the *peon*, or native constable. These several gradations employed their power for the purposes of oppression; and the burdened people were impoverished by continual exactions, and harassed by the insolence of the exactors.

The Budhuist religion is generally professed in the interior of Ceylon; and the *Kappooa superstition* has obtained considerable influence over the inhabitants. The late king was a Malabar and a Hindoo; but he supported the Budhuist faith; and it is stated, that no inauguration to the priestly office was deemed valid, which had not the sanction of his concurrence. Some believers in the Mahomedan faith reside in that part of the country; and a settlement of native Christians of the Roman Catholic church was unexpectedly discovered during my residence on the island.*

The produce of the soil of Kandy is similar to the uncultivated parts of the island; and has been already described. Since the British have obtained the sovereignty, considerable improvements have been introduced; and civilization is gradually extending its influence to the soil, the buildings, and the manners of the natives. When the Gospel of the Son of God obtains access to this territory, it will afford the most effective aid to the efforts of the enlightened politician. By eradicating the principles of barbarism, it will raise the degraded native to the rank assigned him by his Creator in the scale of human existence; and will thus ameliorate his manners by purifying his heart.

This brief notice of the Kandyans will be concluded with a letter from an intelligent young Singhalese headman, which was addressed to me from the city of Kandy.

"*October* 23, 1815.

" REV. SIR,

" I would have written to you earlier, had I not been prevented both with business of moment, and the hope of very soon returning to Colombo. Since my arrival here, I continue, thank God, in good health. With regard to this city, it commands a beautiful prospect, and is surrounded by a range of mountains. The country is very cold, particularly in the morning. It produces abundance of marble

* Some account of this interesting Settlement will be preserved in the Appendix.

(stones) and good water, which issues out of springs and fountains; but what comes from the mountainous part is held to be of inferior excellency. The palace is crowded with houses; a turret of gold is affixed at the top of the palace, which is surrounded by a lake. In the midst of this, stands the king's house of pleasure, and has a gratifying appearance; all the pillars, door-frames, &c. are worked in relievo, the handles embossed with gold and silver. The adjoining edifice to the palace is the principal temple, called *Dalada Mauligauve*, its architecture is magnificent, and boasts of two golden turrets at both extremities of the roof. There are hundreds of *Wi-hā-rees*, (subordinate temples) and innumerable priests belonging to them. The streets are broad, but the construction of the side-houses is low, and the windows so small, that they could barely admit the head through.

" The people of the Kandyan provinces, particularly those of the lower classes, are wretchedly ignorant, and the latter very shy, and generally lead careless lives. Many inoffensive and good kind of people may be found among them; and should Christianity extend its benign influence to those remote parts, we might justly be elated with hope of their becoming in some years both wise and happy; while the country itself would flourish in proportion as they advance in knowledge. I hope you are in health, and beg you will accept my unfeigned respect and compliment, and that Mr. Clough will also be kind enough to accept of the same.

"I remain, Rev. Sir,
" Your devoted humble Servant,
" D. D. A. DASSENAIKE."*

* Mr. Dassenaike, (the writer) was a young man of a respectable Singhalese family. At the commencement of our Colombo Mission he attached himself to us, became one of our Sunday School teachers, and a regular attendant on our ministry. The respectability of his character obtained for him an appointment as Government Interpreter in the Kandyan Provinces; and he was in that situation when the bove was written. In 1817, some of the unprincipled of the Kandyan chiefs set up a Malabar pretender to the Kandyan throne, and called on all classes of their countrymen to destroy and exterminate from

The Singhalese

are chiefly found on the western coast of Ceylon; their district extending from several miles north of Colombo, to the eastern extremity of the province of Matura, in the south; and comprising a tract of country from ten to fifty miles in breadth, and about one hundred and fifty in length. It is by far the most *Europeanised* part of the island. Its principal towns are, Colombo, Negombo, Pantura, Caltura, Barbarene, Bentotte, Amblangodde, Hicgodde, Galle, Belligamme, Matura and Dickwella; all of which are situated close to the sea.

This class of Ceylonese are in general about the middle stature, and are slenderly made; though tall and robust men are occasionally found among them. The features of the Singhalese have a nearer resemblance to Europeans than is found in the continental natives. The families of the Singhalese native chiefs, and especially of the principal cast, contain many noble looking men. The native complexion varies very considerably, from that of the sable African to the English brunette; but the general hue is between a copper and a chocolate colour. The Singhalese females are generally smaller in stature, and fairer in complexion, than the men. Both sexes have black eyes, and long, smooth, black hair, which they wear turned up, and fastened on the crown of the head with a tortoise-shell comb, or other instrument. It is not common among the Singhalese for the men to wear their beards, as in some

---

their country the Europeans, and their native adherents. During this rebellion, which raged for nearly a year, the insurgents displayed the utmost hatred and cruelty to the natives in the service of the English; and this they strongly manifested in the case of our lamented native friend. Being one day with a British officer and a small detachment, proceeding from one station to another, the party were attacked by a body of the insurgents, whom they resisted till their ammunition was expended. Overpowered by numbers, and conducted to the Pretender, that wretched outlaw ordered the English officer, (a fine young man) to be immediately hanged on an adjacent tree; while a still more cruel fate was reserved for Mr. Dassenaike. After the most bitter reproaches and abuse, he was mutilated and tortured, till death released him from his tormentors.

tribes. But before a young man can become entitled to the privilege of shaving, he is compelled to give an entertainment to his relations and acquaintance. Without this festival, it is not considered that the first-fruits of the chin can be honourably removed.

The dress of the common people consists of nothing more than a piece of calico or muslin, wrapped round the waist, and a small jacket thrown over the shoulders. The Singhalese women, however, discover considerable taste in the shape and ornaments of their dress, and are often patterns of neatness, simplicity and cleanliness. The native chiefs and their families are distinguished by a greater quantity of clothing: the men often by a woollen coat of the fashion of the last century. Even the more respectable seldom wear breeches, except on horseback, and never cover their heads. They in general wear leather shoes, trodden down at the heels after the manner of slippers; but the poorer men have only a kind of sandal. The principal ladies wear stockings when full dressed; and then, of course, shoes also; but these are not commonly worn by the Singhalese females. Their *camboy*, or body-cloth, reaches to the instep; and hence stockings are the less needed.

There are some parts of dress which all ranks wear in common. But the different castes are restricted to the fashions adopted by their ancestors from the earliest ages. Some inferior castes are not allowed to assume jackets, but must have the upper part of their bodies uncovered; and this custom is rigidly enforced, without distinction of sex, or age, or circumstances. Female ingenuity is, however, equal to almost any exigency. Many of the women bring their *camboy* so high under their arms, as to obviate this inconvenience. The very low castes are even still more limited in respect to dress; but as they reside mostly in the jungle part of the country, they do not often come under the notice of Europeans.

Some of the fiercest contentions among the Singhalese arise from the encroachments of inferiors on the style of dress belonging to their superiors. The latter usually punish them, by forcibly depriving them of the assumed garment, as well as by the infliction of a severe chastisement. When a number of offenders are in company, this is not submitted to without considerable resistance, and a serious affray is frequently the consequence. The following instance fell under my own observation : a Singhalese barber was leading his bride to the hymeneal altar, both of them, of course, dressed as handsomely as their circumstances allowed; when a by-stander discovered that the comb in his head was of a quality too good for one of the barber-caste. The officious discoverer communicated this to others; and an immediate uproar took place, which disorganized the procession, and compelled the aspiring barber to fly to the church with his trembling bride; where he was under the necessity of removing the obnoxious comb, in order to the peaceful performance of the marriage service.

This prohibition does not extend beyond the original dress of the Singhalese. It does not prevent the poorer natives from assuming the European dress; which they are allowed to do with less interruption, though not without ridicule. In those parts of the island frequented by Europeans, the lower classes of the Singhalese frequently dress themselves in a jacket and trowsers, with hat and shoes, and then call themselves *Portuguese!* Their women also substitute the petticoat for the camboy, wear shoes, and occasionally stockings; and thus become as truly and really Portuguese, as their companions of the other sex. A female, whose complexion is sufficiently fair, will make yet higher pretensions, and denominate herself " *Hollanchi hum nonie,*" "*a Dutch lady!*" The actual descendants from the Dutch and Portuguese are, however, easily distinguished by their manners and appearance from those who merely assume the name.

On state occasions, the principal Singhalese chiefs are richly dressed. At such times they wear a curiously embossed gold or silver sword, suspended to a rich belt made of lace of the same materials. They have a number of attendants; and the talipot leaves, borne after them by their servants, are also richly ornamented.

Most Singhalese men contrive to borrow an European coat, in which to be married. For once in their lives, at least, they aspire to this ornament. But their appearance in the borrowed garb is often rendered highly amusing, from the difference between the size of the owner and the wearer of the garment. A tall man may occasionally be seen on such an occasion wearing a coat with sleeves which do not reach far below his elbows; and *vice versa*. Those who cannot provide the envied distinction of a European coat, consider themselves greatly dignified, if they can procure a boy to walk behind them, with a talipot leaf borne on his shoulder. The dress of the Singhalese females at marriages, and other festivals, is often very costly; they are, in general, at such times covered with a profusion of gold and jewels, according to the circumstances and rank of the wearer.

The distinction of *caste* which prevails among the natives of Continental India is found also among the Singhalese; though not in so rigid a degree as on the Continent. In Ceylon it is of a more political character than among the Hindoos. It is not a line of distinction between Christians and idolaters; but partakes of the nature of that general classification of society which prevails in most civilized countries. omething analagous to it exists even in England, in the division of the population into nobility, gentry, merchants, tradesmen, farmers and mechanics; and is a fair representation to a certain extent of the *caste* in Ceylon. This exception, among others, may be made, that in England, it is regulated by the influence of learning and religion; while in Ceylon it oftener becomes the parent of the baser passions of the human mind.

The *vellalahs,* or *cultivators of the ground,* are the principal caste. From this description most of the head native officers of government are selected; but the *velallahs* are engaged in almost every branch of trade; and those who are poor do not refuse domestic servitude, or even bearing burdens. The next caste is the *carawas,* or *fishers.* These are also found occupied in trade; as builders, carpenters, joiners; and many of them excel in their respective pursuits.

The *chandoos,* or *toddy-drawers,* are principally employed in the culture of the cocoa-nut tree, but are not restricted to that employment. There are several inferior castes; as the *tanners, potters, washers, barbers, lime-burners, tom-*

tom-beaters, charcoal-makers, mat-weavers, executioners, &c. All these different castes form so many different corporate bodies, headed by native chiefs of their respective classes, who are the usual channels of communication, through which the orders of government are conveyed to the people.

In addition to these castes, is a description of natives engaged in cultivating and preparing the cinnamon. The term *Maha-badde*, (formed of two Singhalese words, signifying *great*, or *principal*, and *revenue;* in allusion to the considerable revenues derived from the valuable tree they cultivate,) is applied to the government department to which they are attached; but the natives of the caste thus employed are termed *cha-lias*. These have also certain distinctions among themselves, according to the part assigned them in the work. The station which this class should occupy in the scale of caste is yet undecided; some assign to it an higher, and others a lower rank. It is supposed by some, that this class was originally formed of foreigners. They were considered of such importance by the Kandyan kings, that they had great privileges and immunities granted them. Many of their head-men are persons of superior minds, and manifest considerable generosity. The Maha-badde, or Chalia caste are placed under the superintendence of an English civilian, who is also their magisterial president; an office which was filled during my residence in Ceylon by James Maitland, Esq. to whose public worth honourable attestation has been recently borne by the Supreme Court of the island.*

The Singhalese are more remarkable for their patient endurance of suffering, than for an aptitude to face danger; and have been supposed better calculated for martyrs than for soldiers. In their intercourse with strangers they are harmless and timid; and to their superiors, and those in authority, subservient and polite, sometimes to sycophancy. Indolence, hypocrisy, and revenge may be considered as the national vices. But when brought under the influence of education and piety, they are capable of noble sentiments, and of strong, generous and honourable affections.

---

* See the Asiatic Journal, Vol. xiv. p. 620. (Dec. 1822.)

The domestic habits of the Singhalese are very simple. Their dwellings are usually formed by sticks fixed in the ground, tied together, and covered with the leaf of the cocoa-nut tree. Sometimes their huts are plastered with clay or mud; and some are built with *cabooc*, a species of brick-stone, common to Ceylon, and tiled: the latter are principally seen in the neighbourhood of towns. As they dress their food out of doors, the houses contain no chimnies, and the door answers the purpose of windows. The floors are made hard by the addition of lime, &c. to the earth, and plastered with the ordure of the cow, which renders them cleanly and healthful. Their articles of furniture are not numerous: a pillow rolled up in a mat serves them for a bed; with occasionally a rudely-constructed chair or two, and a bedstead of the same style; but for sitting and sleeping they generally prefer the ground. *Chatties*, or earthern pots, are their principal cooking utensils; setting up three bricks on one end, in the form of a triangle, they place their chatty on the top, and make a wood fire beneath it. Rice boiled, and curry, form their usual food; the latter is generally made of vegetables, as their religion prohibits the taking away of animal life. Flesh and fish, however, are eaten by the less strict of the different castes.

An extract from a work on the *language* of the Singhalese, by the Rev. John Callaway, one of our Missionaries; whose various and valuable literary labours have given such lasting efficiency to his ministerial efforts; will furnish an idea of its pronunciation and construction:

" Upwards of a century ago, it was observed by Capt. Knox, that the Singhalese language is '*copious; smooth, elegant,* and *courtly.*' The accuracy of the statement is confirmed by those who have had intercourse with the people, and made their language a subject of study. It contains no sound disagreeable to an English ear, or one whose utterance is very difficult to acquire. No language, perhaps, has a greater variety of vowels. Its aspirated consonants make a formidable figure in the alphabet, but are usually softened in discourse, and seldom appear in writing. The Singhalese characters are used by no other nation; but in sound and arrangement they have a near resemblance to those used in the greater part of Hindostan. Each sound has a distinct letter; and, which must be considered an excellence, the pronunciation and orthography always agree.

"The language of the Singhalese seems to have undergone no material alteration since their settlement in Ceylon. No tradition of any event, likely to have produced a considerable change in their speech, appears to exist among the people; and, it may be observed, that the names of their places have generally a reference to their local situation; and though given, it is probable, upwards of a thousand years ago, they are mostly compounded of words in use at this day. The Singhalese people seldom invent a name for any article newly introduced among them, but readily adopt the one used by those who introduce the thing. Many words have in this way been adopted since the settlement of Europeans in this country. Some are much changed, but others, being analogous in structure to Singhalese words, retain for the most part, their primary sound.

"Few words in this language are either abruptly short, or immoderately long. To contribute elegance to writing and discourse, they may be generally changed for others of the same import. They seldom depart from their primary meaning; nor can many terms of the same sound be produced which express opposite or different ideas. Little difference seems to prevail between the speech of different districts, or that of the higher and lower orders. The consequence, we may suppose, of the pitch of etiquette, which for ages has been maintained, rendering attention to *address* a matter of high consequence to all. The people, however, who are resident in the neighbourhood of Europeans, use more European words than the inhabitants of remote provinces. In other respects, the variation is by no means equal to the difference of dialect in different parts of Great Britain."

The following is the sound of the Lord's Prayer in Singhalese; with a literal English translation underneath.[*]

---

[*] In this specimen of Singhalese pronunciation, *a* sounds as in *hat;* *ā*, the same sound much lengthened; *e*, as in *men* ; *ē*, as *ay* in *hay;* *i*, as *ee* in *sweet;* *o*, as in *off*, &c. The other letters express the Singhalese words by their purely English sounds. The syllables are

xlvi   INTRODUCTION.

Swărr-ga-yē-hi wed-a-si-tin-a ap-pa-gē pi-yăn-an-wa-hăn-sē;
    In heaven   art   our   Father;
o-ba-wa-hăn-sē-gē nū-ma-ya sood-a-wē-wa : o-ba-wa-hăn-sē-gē
       your   name   holy be;   your
rā-jay-a ē-wa ; o-ba-wa-hăn-sē-gē kem-met-ta swārr-ga-gē-hi
kingdom come :   your   will   in heaven
men   *bhoo-mi-yē-hi-da   ka-roon-oo leb-e-wa :   appī*
as   in earth   be done   let :   our
da-was-pa-ta   bhō-jan-a-ya ap-pa-ta ad-da   di
   daily   bread[1]   to-day   to us give
wa-dā-la-men-a-wa :   ap-pī   na-ya-kā-ra-yan-ta   ap-pī
   grant :   our   debtors   we
ks-a-mā-wen-nāk-men ap-pī na-yat ap-pa-ta ks-a-m-āwi
   pardon us   our   debts   to us   forgive
wa-dā-la-men-a-wa : ap-pa pa-ri-ksā-wi-ma-ta no-pa-moon-
   grant :   as   to temptation   not
oo-wa : na-poo-ren ap-pa ga-la-wā wa-dā-la-men-a-wa :
 lead :   evil from   us   deliver   grant :
mak-ni-sā-da   rā-ja-yat,   pa-rā-kra-ma-yat,
   for   the kingdom also,   the power also,
ma-hi-ma-tā-wat, sad-hā-kā-li-ma o-ba-wa-hăn-sē-gē-ma-ya.
 the glory also,   for ever,   yours is.
āmen.
Amen.

 The Singhalese language was not much cultivated by Europeans, until some years after the island had been in the possession of the English. Under the auspices of the Dutch Government, an edition of the New Testament, and the five books of Moses were indeed printed in Singhalese. But the translation was made by some ministers who were natives of the island, and had been suitably educated in Holland. With all these advantages, however, their version is pronounced to be very faulty. The Hon. John D'Oyly, now Resident of the Kandyan provinces, was, I believe, the first Englishman who devoted himself to the study of Singhalese with success. He was followed by

divided for the sake of distinctness, and for the assistance of the English reader; but the several parts of the words should, in pronunciation, be united as quickly as may be consistent with the distinct expression of each.

the late W. Tolfrey, Esq. the indefatigable and lamented translator of the present authorised version of the Singhalese New Testament. The Rev. Andrew Armour has for many years preached to the natives in their own tongue. The Rev. John Chater, a Baptist Missionary, in the year 1816, published a Grammar of the language under the patronage of Governor Brownrigg; and it is now generally spoken by the superior civil and military servants of Government.

The Rev. B. Clough, has assiduously devoted himself to the critical study of the Singhalese language; and in concert with Messrs. Armour and Chater, and C. Layard, Esq. completed Mr. Tolfrey's translation of the Testament, upon the lamented death of that gentleman. The same worthy coadjutors; who have recently been joined by the Rev. Wm. B. Fox, another of our Missionaries; have made considerable progress in the translation of the Old Testament. Mr. Clough has also superintended the translation into Singhalese of several very useful works; and is at present employed in preparing for the press a large Singhalese and English Dictionary, which will be a work of great public utility. The Government has given considerable encouragement to Mr. Clough's design. A manuscript work of a similar description, which had been purchased by the Government of Mr. Tolfrey, has been generously given to aid him in his undertaking; and, in addition to the grant of paper for the work, one hundred copies of his Dictionary have been engaged for the servants of Government. Most of the Wesleyan Missionaries either read sermons, or preach *extempore*, in the Singhalese language, to the several native congregations under their care. Messrs. Fox and Callaway have also published useful works to facilitate the studies of others.*

Among the Singhalese, many (principally of the priesthood) have devoted their lives to literary pursuits, and have enriched their country with the result of their investigations. But their historical works are either entirely fabulous, or at

* The Rev. T. H. Squance, who has unhappily been under the necessity of returning to England from ill health, composed an excellent Tamul Grammar, and superintended the translation of various publications into that important language.

best exaggerated narratives, intermingled with fable. Their poetry is admired; and several of their old authors have written with great ability on the natural history of the island. Medical and mathematical books are numerous; as are also works on astrology, a science which is held in high repute by all eastern nations, and by none more highly prized than by the Singhalese. Their notions of geography, and of the heavenly bodies, are ludicrous; but on their own principles they have written very largely. Ceylon has also produced its *native* grammarians and lexicographers. The Pali and the Sanscrit are the learned languages, in which most of their standard works are written.*

Until the last few years, the ability of reading their own language was possessed but by a very inconsiderable part of the Singhalese; and those who had acquired the art, had received their education at the heathen temples, and in the use of superstitious books. By the extension of the blessings of education through the native schools, which are now in such pleasing operation, hundreds are annually added to the number of native readers. While by the Colombo Bible Society, the whole population of Ceylon are in the progress of being furnished with the means of reading in their own tongue the word of the living and true God.

* It gives me pleasure to add that Mr. Clough has completed the first European Grammar of the Pali Language. See the Asiatic Journal, Vol. xiv. p. 584.

SECT. III.

CEYLONESE SUPERSTITIONS AND IDOLATROUS CERE_ MONIES.—PRESENT STATE OF CHRISTIANITY IN CEYLON.

The superstitions of the Ceylonese might well employ a larger space in their description, than can be afforded them in this work. But I have the satisfaction of knowing that the subject has already fallen into abler hands, which will supercede the necessity of my proceeding in it, to any considerable length.* The Pagan inhabitants of the Tamul parts of the island are, as has been intimated, in general, disciples of Hindooism: a superstition with which the Christian world has, of late years, been made more acquainted than formerly; but of which, notwithstanding, a brief account will hereafter be given. The two principal religious systems which prevail among the Singhalese Natives, are, KAPPOOISM, or, the worship of Demons; and that which inculcates the superstition of BUDHU. The remarks on these two sections of heathenism will tend to bring into view another district of that empire of darkness, which in the wisdom and mercy of God is now beginning to yield, more rapidly than ever, to the cheering and vivifying beams of THE TRUE LIGHT.

In our review of the Singhalese system of

KAPPOOISM,

we cannot but be reminded of the solemn averment of the great apostle to the Gentiles:—*But I say that the things*

---

* Mr. Clough has been engaged for some time in collecting from the most authentic sources with a view to publication, information respecting the origin and character of the Singhalese superstitions.

INTRODUCTION.

*which the Gentiles sacrifice, they sacrifice to devils and not to God.** From all we can gather of the state of heathen countries in general, there appears very strong reason to conclude, that the superstitious fear and worship of evil spirits, is in fact the universal *religion of nature.* Travellers of the most undoubted veracity have informed us, that this superstition is found, more or less acknowledged, among all the uncivilized tribes of mankind; and undisputed vestiges of it still remain, even in countries where civilization and Christianity, its most powerful counteractions, have for ages been in active operation. In some benighted lands the sovereignty of that malignant spirit, known among us by the name of the devil, (because in the Scriptures so termed,) is openly and officially proclaimed. This is the case in the island of Ceylon.—The ascendency of Satan is THERE not merely *intimated* by the features of human conduct, as they are opposed to virtue and goodness. It is *avowed* in the most unequivocal manner. The visible kingdom of the Wicked One stands THERE erected, with unblushing front—in frightful images—in venerated temples—in an order of priesthood—in a round of ceremonies—in A DIRECT WORSHIP—in an endless series of terrifying fears and apprehensions—in amulets, and offerings—and in various abominable evils!†

From the ancient Singhalese records it appears, that the worship of evil spirits was the primitive religion of the Singhalese. This gloomy system is founded on the supposition, that all the pains and sufferings to which man is exposed, are occasioned by the baleful influence of dæmons on his person and concerns. Every misfortune and disease

---

* Appendix.

† " They may truly be said to be entangled in *the snare of the devil,* whose minds are laid prostrate by the degrading superstition of dæmon worship ; who, ignorant alike of the benignant love of the true God, and the merciful compassion of his blessed Son, fall down before the painted image of a ferocious monster, and beseech him to accept their sacrifice, and spare themselves and their children !—*Sermon on* 2 *Tim.* ii. 24—26, *by the Rev.* G. Bisset, *A. M. preached on the Fifth Anniversary of the Colombo Auxiliary Bible Society.*

has its presiding dæmon; and prayers are offered, and sacrifices made, to avert the evils which they are supposed to inflict. Their images represent Satanic beings, of the most horrible forms and propensities. Some of them have the semblance of men, of gigantic size, with several hands, each armed with an instrument of torture. Others are represented as monsters with tremendously large eyes, mouths, and teeth, in the act of devouring a human being; holding several more, suspended by the hair, in readiness for the same fate: and some are pictured as feeding on the reeking entrails of expiring men, whom they have massacred for the purpose. There are others of a character which forbids description!

The temples erected for this dæmon worship are of very humble construction, and are denominated *Dewallahs*.— Their priests are termed *Kappooas*;* who, though by no means respectable either for rank or learning, possess unbounded influence over the lower classes of Singhalese. As they do not wear sacerdotal garments, or any badge of distinction from the generality of natives, they frequently contrive to introduce themselves into situations which they would never be suffered to enter, were they always known. Some of this class actually gained admission into the religious establishment of the island, and procured appointments from the British government as schoolmasters of the districts in which they resided: they then employed the facilities furnished by their appointments, to instil privately into the minds of their pupils " the doctrines of devils." It is scarcely necessary to add, that no sooner were the deceivers detected, than they were discarded, and measures taken to prevent the recurrence of similar impostures.

The Kappooas are devoted to the study of astrology, and

---

* According to Doctor Davy, this word is derived from *kapu*, proper, and *ralle*, chief. If this be its real derivation, may it not be considered as indicative of the " proper," or legitimate claims to ascendency and influence which the Singhalese assign to this order of native priests; and thus afford a strong presumptive evidence of what the Author assumes to be the fact, that the *worship of dæmons* is the primitive offspring of the imagination of fallen man: and hence the " proper," or real and actual, *religion of nature?*

the people have recourse to them on all emergencies. A journey cannot be undertaken with safety, a marriage solemnized auspiciously, or a bargain made with success, except the Kappooa be first consulted. The presence of a Kappooa is deemed indispensable at the birth of a child; which, it often happens, that together with *its mother*, he has PREVIOUSLY *dedicated to Satan!* He announces the planet under which the infant is born, and the baleful or genial influence it possesses. The Singhalese who are attached to this system invariably step aside, when passing a *dewallah*, to make their profound obeisance to the image which represents the presiding dæmon of the place, and to deposit an offering according to their ability. Where they to omit either, they would be tormented with the apprehension, that some dreadful evil would be the consequence of the omission. Some of the *dewallahs* are esteemed highly sacred; and long and painful pilgrimages are periodically made, and expensive offerings presented, to propitiate the resident dæmon, and so to avert his dreaded wrath.

The sale of charms against particular evils is a source of considerable emolument to the Kappooas. A native with one of these charms suspended from his body esteems himself secure, and will boldly face the danger from which he would timidly fly, if destitute of the fancied protection. On examining some of these charms, they were found to consist of a piece of olla-leaf, covered with astrological signs and unintelligible jargon. These, rolled up in a peculiar form, may be seen hanging from the arms, legs, or necks of the natives; as they imagine that the evils which float about in the air, are prevented from alighting on the limbs of those who are thus protected. If an accident happen to a superstitious Singhalese, at a time when he has not one about his person, he has immediate recourse to a Kappooa; persuaded that his charm is as efficacious to cure, as it is powerful to preserve.*

† A curious illustration of this superstitious confidence was afforded me, when on a visit at Belligamme, in 1816. After preaching one day in the Government School House, I walked down to the seashore, followed by several of the natives, whose curiosity had induced them to attend me. Several fishing-boats had just entered the

The Superstition of Budhu*

may be considered as the established religion of the Singhalese, both of the coasts, and the interior of the island. Some writers are of opinion, that the worship of Budhu is a modification of the Hindoo superstition, from which they suppose it to have been originally derived. By others, it is regarded as the first step from the religion of nature; and once supposed to have been the prevailing religion of India. Respectable authorities may be quoted on either side.† It is still ascendant in the empires of China and Burmah.

harbour, and some young sharks which had been caught attracted my attention. I took up one of them to examine it, when it darted one of its armed fins into my thumb. The wound was very painful; and, as in that climate, comparatively trifling injuries are frequently productive of locked jaw, and end in death, an immediate remedy became necessary. A Singhalese, seeing the accident, affectionately addressed me in the language of tender sympathy, and entreated me to allow him to *fetch a Kappooa, to charm away the injury!*

The following occurrence may however be related as a pleasing counterpart. Once, while addressing a native congregation in the Government School House at Pantura, from John iii. 8; I endeavoured to show that the Kappooa system is one of *the works of the devil*, which the *son of God came to destroy;* and urged their immediate renunciation of all confidence in their vain *charms*, and to commit the keeping of their bodies and souls to God. Appealing to their understandings and consciences, I enquired, " Which of you will *now* cast away these *works of the devil*, and place himself under the protection of *the Son of God?*" I looked round upon the congregation for a reply. Presently a charm was handed up to the pulpit, which had been broken off for the purpose. I held it up, and gave thanks to God, that in that place he had began to destroy these works of the devil. I then repeated the enquiry, " *Who next?*" &c. and two or three more abandoned charms were handed up in a similar way. Before the close of the service a handful of these charms was in my possession.

* Worshipped in China, under the name of Fo. See the Appendix.

† From various authorities it sufficiently appears, that the worship of Boodh, or Boudha, has prevailed in several parts of India, at a period prior to that of the Brahmins; but that about the time of Christ, they gained a superiority over the worshippers of Buddha; and nine hundred years afterwards, they totally overthrew his doc-

When the Budhuist superstition was first introduced to the Island of Ceylon, has never been satisfactorily determined; but the circumstances attendant on its introduction are set forth by the Singhalese historians, in all the extravagant hyperbole of Eastern fable. According to their writings, Budhu visited Ceylon,* for the purpose of rescuing the natives from the tyranny of the dæmons, who covered the whole island, and exercised the most cruel tyranny over the inhabitants. So numerous were these malignant spirits, that on the arrival of Budhu, they covered the whole ground, and there was not sufficient space left for him to set his foot; and, had a pin fallen, it could not have found a passage to the ground. Budhu, confident of the efficacy of his doctrines, directed his discourse to a part of the vast mass before him; which immediately yielded to its force, and became panic-struck by the superior power which was opposed to them. Availing himself of the confusion into which the dæmons were thrown, and perceiving a vacant space, Budhu descended, and occupied the spot. As he continued to preach, directing his sermons to every part of the vast circle which was formed around him, the dæmons gradually retired farther from his presence; until they were all, at length, driven into the sea. Budhu then issued the following proclamation : " Behold, I have conquered the malignant spirits, who had so long, and with such irresistible sway, tyrannized over you. Fear dæmons no more !—worship them no more !"†

trine in its native country, and persecuted his followers. The Vedas, which are supposed to be the oldest books of the Brahmins, are of later date than the time of Bouddha, *as is evident from the mention which they make of that deity.*—See Encycl. Perthen. art. BOODH.

* Petrus Panditta Sekarra (a converted Budhuist priest) informed me, that the worshippers of Budhu believe that several incarnations of their deity have taken place; the last of which, they conceive to have happened about four hundred years before the Christian æra.

† The following legend of Budhu's personal success as a teacher of mankind may also be acceptable to the reader. " His days he devoted to men, in preaching to them and converting them; and his nights to the gods who assembled to listen to him. He was so success-

INTRODUCTION.

This tradition, divested of the absurdities in which it is clothed, represents Budhu as a religious reformer; who, finding the Singhalese devoted to the Kappooa system of dæmon worship, endeavoured, by preaching some portion of truth, though mixed up with much error, to raise their minds from the degraded and enslaved state in which they had been held for ages; success followed the persevering promulgation of the system; until it gained the ascendency, and became the established religion of the island. The principal doctrines he inculcated appear to have been these: He denied the existence of a Great First Cause of all things, and taught that matter is eternal; and that the affairs and destinies of men are invariably fixed by an uncontrolable fatality. As a rational effect of these principles, he rejected, as absurd, the practice of any form of religious worship.* With respect to a future state, he asserted, that

---

ful in convincing those whom he addressed of the truth of his doctrines, that he often *daily* converted *many asankeyas*, (a number too immense to be comprehended). The powers which he exercised in reforming mankind were more than human. He could assume any form he chose. He could multiply himself many hundred times; or, produce the appearance of many hundreds of Budhus, in every respect like himself, with rays of light issuing from every pore of their skin, differently occupied—some standing, some sitting, and some preaching. He could go any distance in an instant, even as fast as thought—through the air, water, or under the earth. When he preached, his face appeared to all his audience, though surrounding him in a circle; people of all languages understood him; and all, however distant, heard him distinctly; excepting those who were too deep in vice to be reformed, who were as the deaf, though close to him, and heard nothing. A learned man, who followed him every where during the space of six months, to ascertain if he were the true Budhu, never saw the impression of his foot, nor even a flower bent on which he trod, or a cushion pressed on which he sat. His good qualities equalled his extraordinary powers, and are said to have been boundless, and to baffle description."—DR. DAVY's *Travels in Ceylon*, p. 215.

* "It is not uncommon," observes DR. DAVY, "to see a *Dewallah* and a *Wihare* (a Budhuist temple) contiguous, or even under the same roof." This statement is correct, and has fallen within my own observation. But DR. DAVY adds, "This may be considered not merely tolerated, but *quite orthodox*." The general correctness of this respect-

human beings pass from one mode of existence into another, in an endless series of transmigrations; that these transmigrations are regulated according to their moral character; until, by repeated births and sufferings, they attain to that state of moral perfection which, as a necessary consequence, shall usher them into Nirri-wana.*

The Budhuist religion recognizes a moral law, in some points similar to the decalogue; requires reverence to the *ban-na*, the sermons, or sacred doctrines of Budhu;†— enjoins the support of priests, whose business it is to disseminate these doctrines; and the erection of temples to Budhu, in which images of him, in various postures, (sitting, standing, lying) are preserved, and before which they make profound salaams, and strew flowers of the most exquisite fragrance. Budhuism, in its original form, is probably the only system of undisguised Atheism ever promulgated; and presents the curious moral anomaly of the founder of a system (who himself denied a Creator) being at length constituted a god by his own disciples. He who rejected all religious worship, as vain and foolish, has now temples

---

able and learned author, to whose valuable work I beg to refer the reader, cannot be questioned; but I apprehend him inadvertently to have adopted a mistake in supposing that the worship of either the Brahminical gods, or the Kapooistic dæmons, is consistent with pure Budhuism; than which nothing can be more *heterodox*. It is true, the followers of Budhu, and even the priests themselves, will perform acts of worship to the Kapooistic deities, and have figures of dæmons painted on the walls of their own temples. But this, so far as I have been able to learn, is a corruption of the Budhuist system.

* *The Budhuist heaven.*—This word is formed of two Pali words, which signify the utter extinction of all desire; and, to the Singhalese in general, conveys no other idea than that of *annihilation*. The priests teach, that Budhu himself has long since ceased to exercise any power; he having reached *Nirri-wāna!*

† " So scrupulous are they with respect to books, that they will not touch them, until they have made obeisance, as to a superior; nor sit down, unless the books present are placed, as a mark of distinction, on a table or shelf above them."—DR. DAVY's *Ceylon.* p. 223.

reared to his name, in which he is worshipped: and his image is reverenced as a deity, wherever it is seen!*

The Budhuist *wihārees*, or temples, which have fallen under my observation, appear to have been constructed merely as receptacles of the sacred image; as they are not sufficiently capacious to have been designed for the accommodation of worshippers.† The natives generally perform their devotions standing at the door. The principal image of Budhu in these temples, represents the god in a recumbent posture, with the eyes open, and the head resting on one of the hands. The size of this image is sometimes fifteen or twenty feet long. The god is also represented by smaller images, sitting cross-legged, after the manner of the Asiatics; and by others standing, with the right arm extended, and the thumb and fore-finger compressed, as if in the act of communicating instruction. The temples also contain smaller images of the idol, molten and carved; with celestial attendants painted on the walls. A frightful dæmon, usually painted black or blue, armed with some instrument of destruction, is stationed at the door of the temple, as a guard of honour or defence. A priest is generally in attendance to receive the offerings of the worshippers: these consist of food, flowers, and money. The food is the portion of the priests; the flowers are placed on a table before the image; the money, of course, is at the disposal of the priests! A *dagobah*, or mausoleum, is erected within a few feet of most Budhuist temples: and the worshippers are made to believe that these contain some part of the real body of Budhu: they are therefore frequently the objects of adoration. An entire tooth of

* The reverence paid to an image of Budhu, may be conceived when it is stated, that a Kandyan Adikar discovering one on a sideboard in the Governor's drawing-room in Colombo, arose with great discomposure from the chair in which he had been sitting, and refused to resume his seat until the idol had been removed to another apartment.

† The interior of the island may contain Budhuist temples of larger dimensions; but those in the maritime parts are of the description here given.

Budhu is affirmed to be preserved in the principal temple at Kandy.*

The doctrines of Budhu, it is stated, were not committed to writing until several centuries after they were delivered; they were then collected together into one book, which they term *The Banna*. Besides this book, they have many others, to which they attach high importance, and from which passages are read in their religious assemblies. The common people apply the term *banna* to all their sacred books; and the *man-doos*, or temporary buildings of leaves, which are frequently erected in the country parts for Budhuist preaching, are termed *Banna Mandooas, or, Bible-houses*. These buildings are in the form of Chinese pagodas, and are tastefully ornamented. They contain two raised pulpits, from one of which the principal priest recites (sitting) from the Banna, in the Pali language; a subordinate priest occupies the other, who interprets the sentences to the people, as delivered, in the vernacular tongue.† While engaged in communicating instruction to the people, they skreen their faces from their auditors by a kind of fan; which they also carry about with them for the purpose of avoiding the sight of the other sex. As many priests are in attendance, the services are continued for several successive nights; the congregations assembling after sun-set. The people sit during the service on their heels; and, with admirable patience, will continue in that posture several hours; occasionally expressing by a kind of chorus (which may be heard at a considerable distance) their admiration of the doctrines. The priests are carried to and from the pulpits on the shoulders of their disciples. The expence of erecting the mando, and making the necessary preparations, is defrayed by the inhabitants of the neighbourhood. Great quantities of food are cooked, and sent to the priests at their lodging-rooms, which are built expressly for their reception. Instead

---

* Appendix.

† The natives being familiar with the practice of instruction by interpreters, were prepared for the reception of Christian preaching from the Missionaries by the same medium.

of stands for their lamps, at the public services, the natives will frequently undertake, as an act of merit, to bear them on their heads (each lamp weighing four or five pounds) during the whole night, and to supply it with oil, from a bottle in the right hand, as occasion requires.

The Budhuist priests are regularly educated for, and at the close of their prescribed studies appointed with great pomp to the duties of the priestly office. A description of hierarchy appears to exist in the Budhuist priesthood. The inferior orders are termed *Gan-nee-nāang-sees;* the next in dignity, *Tee-roo-nāang-sees;* and the yet higher orders, *Nāai-a-kas,* and *Ma-ha Naai-a-kas.* These degrees in most respects correspond with those of *deacon, priest, bishop,* and *archbishop,* in our own Establishment. The only distinction in dress which prevails among these various orders consists in the *quality* of their robes; the form and colour of all being alike. The priests are distinguished from the laity by a *yellow* robe of a peculiar form,* which is thrown over the left shoulder, and leaves the right arm and shoulder bare. The heads of the priests are closely shaven, and uncovered. The *Gan-nee-naang-sees* itinerate in the country parts; and may frequently be met, with an attendant boy carrying their bundle. They obtain food at the houses of their disciples; and recompense them by pronouncing a benediction at their

---

* *Yellow* is the sacred colour of the Budhuist; it being the colour of the flower which is consecrated to Budhu. Though some of the chief priests wear robes of silk, and even of satin and velvet, cotton is the usual material of which they are made. The dye is obtained from the shavings of the jack-wood, boiled in water. Each robe is formed of fifteen distinct pieces, sewed carefully together; and, (according to the explanation given us by one of the converted priests, a learned man,) are intended thus to perpetuate the rememberance of one of Budhu's charities. Fifteen paddy-fields were kept by him in a state of constant cultivation, and the produce given to supply the necessities of the poor. When a young man is about to enter on the priestly office, his friends meet together, on the evening previous to his inaugeration, to manufacture his first robe. The whole process must not occupy more than twelve hours. At sun-set they commence their operations; having previously collected together the materials; and before the next sun-rising the cotton is spun into yarn, woven into cloth, dyed, and made up of the prescribed number of patches.

departure; which is received by their host with clasped and uplifted hands. These itinerating priests find ample employment. Instructing the natives in the principles of Singhalese learning; reciting extracts from their sacred books; reading from the *Banna* to sick and dying persons; (it being deemed highly meritorious and efficacious to listen, in such circumstances, to the doctrines of Budhu;) and administering medicines prepared from herbs, in which they evince considerable skill; these varied duties may be considered as a fair outline of the labours in which the lowest class of the Budhuist priesthood is employed. The highest orders reside chiefly at the temples, where they are engaged in the cultivation of native literature, and occasionally visiting the houses of the wealthier natives, to perform the functions of their office.

The Budhuist priests are not allowed to marry; and individuals are, without doubt, found among them who keep their engagements with inviolable faith. Should, however, celibacy become irksome, the priest can lay aside his yellow robe, domesticate himself; and at any future time, without prejudice to his character, resume his vestments, and his functions. The influence of such permission on the interests of morality is obvious. " It must," as Dr. Davy observes, " tend greatly to exclude licentiousness and stop corruption, which (witness the old monasteries) are too apt to spring up, and grow to a monstrous height." It must, however, be admitted, that the internal history of the Budhuist seminaries is but very imperfectly known. " The rank of a priest, next to that of Budhu, is considered the most exalted—even superior to that of the gods. Priests may in consequence *sit* in a *wee-ha-ree*. They never worship the gods; but, when they preach, invite the gods to be of their audience; and, like Budhu himself, they are entitled to worship."[*]

With the exception of females, and those who support Budhuism from interested motives, the generality of the people manifest great indifference to every system of religion; and may at present be considered more inclined to infidelity than to superstition.

[*] Travels, p. 225.

Compared with the prevailing religion of the Hindoos, Budhuism wears an aspect amiable and humane. Unlike the worship of *Juggernaut*, (to instance one Hindoo deity only) whose rubric prescribes impurity and blood, as acceptable and even essential *acts of worship*, the worship of Budhu is simple and inoffensive. The sacred books of this system forbid cruelty, dishonesty, unchastity, and falsehood; and inculcate kindness, sympathy, and subordination in civil society. The system tends to correct the inveterate prejudices of *caste;* and has even produced institutions of benevolence and mercy in different parts of the island. On such a system the infidel looks with complacency; and the latitudinarian, in the exercise of a spurious candour, pronounces it to be *safe*. But the believer in Divine Revelation, while he admits its comparative excellence, when weighed in the balances with the impure and sanguinary systems of India, and other Pagan lands, beholds written on its portals in the indelible characters of inspired truth—
" WITHOUT GOD IN THE WORLD!"

CHRISTIANITY.

The *name* of *Christian* has been borne for many ages by multitudes of the natives of Ceylon; both of the Malabars in the north of the island, and of the Singhalese in the south. And charity dictates the pleasing hope that "the inward and spiritual grace" was possessed by some out of the thousands to whom the " outward and visible sign" was administered; yet it is to be feared they were but few. A benevolent and judicious clergyman, whose means of forming a correct estimate of the religious character of the natives professing Christianity, were as favourable as his exertions to improve that character were unremitting; and whose statement respecting them may be therefore received with implicit confidence; states:—" No race of people appear so easily convertible to Christianity as the Singhalese; for they have no fixed principles or prejudices. The greater part of the Singhalese whom I designate, *nominal Christians of the Reformed Religion,* are little more than Christians by baptism. They have *no objection* to the Christian religion;

but for their amusement are apt to attend the Budhuist festivals. Numbers of them make no difficulty in asserting that they are *both Budhuists and Christians;* and are willing to be sworn *either way,* or *both ways,* in a court of justice!"*

In addition to the above numerous class, usually designated *native,* Ceylon contains a considerable number of the descendants of the Dutch, who generally retain the language, religious creed, and forms of worship, of that nation. The fruit of marriages between Europeans and native females† also constitute a considerable class. The greater part of these profess the Roman Catholic faith; some few belong to the Dutch communion.

According to some writers, Christianity was first introduced to Ceylon in the fifth or sixth century, by Nestorian Missionaries from Persia. Whether any of the aborigines were converted by their labours, or whether they confined their attention to the factories established by their countrymen, cannot now be ascertained. The traders from Persia to Ceylon were very numerous; and one church, at least, was erected for their use. The Persia merchants were in high repute among the natives, on account of the valuable breed of horses which they imported for the use of the king.

The Singhalese annals record, that in the fourth century the throne of the island was usurped by *two Malabar Missionaries,* who administered the government with great prudence upwards of twenty years. If the Christian faith was first introduced from Persia, we shall be led to the conclusion, that these Malabar Missionaries were connected with the establishment formed by the natives of that country; and probably employed the influence of the priestly office to attain the temporal authority which they so long swayed. The Singhalese records, it is true, assign to these transactions a date considerably earlier than that to which the

* First Report of the Calcutta Bible Society, 1811.

† In some parts of India these are termed *half-caste;* in Ceylon they are denominated *filhos da terra;* children of the country, or country-born.

Nestorian Mission is referred; but, as the native annals are exceedingly loose and unsatisfactory with respect to *dates;* and as the two Missionaries are connected with the *trade in horses* throughout the whole history, the concurrence of these two circumstances furnish a *data* more satisfactory, than even the date assigned by a Singhalese historian, unsupported by collateral evidence.* The two usurpers were, at length deposed and slain by a member of the royal family; and, as the faith they professed would, as a matter of course, become odious to the restored government, the extinction of the Nestorian Mission may, possibly, be referred to that period.

The permanent introduction of the Christian faith to Ceylon, is generally attributed to the Portuguese;[†] who invariably elevated the *cross,* as the distinguishing characteristic of their religion, wherever they obtained temporal dominion, or succeeded in establishing commercial intercourse. The pliancy of the native character, probably exempted the Ceylonese from those coercive measures which were employed by the Jesuits in other places to proselyte the more unyielding. The whole of the inhabitants of the coast towns, not even excepting the Brahmins of the north, submitted to be called Christians; and to *hear, say,* and *do,* whatever they were enjoined by the ruling power.

When the spirit of political or commercial enterprize led the Portuguese to extend their views to the interior of the island, the zeal of the priests kept pace with the encroachments. The Kandyan territories were visited by the Missionaries of the Roman Catholic faith; and some illustrious examples of pious devotion to the Saviour's

---

* An attempt is here made to fill up a much-to-be-lamented chasm in the history of Christianity in Ceylon. The Author is aware that his hypothesis cannot be regarded as confirmed; and he will be highly gratified, if, from some hitherto undiscovered source, authentic documents should be furnished, which shall tend to shed a light on this department of Singhalese history.—See the Appendix.

† The celebrated XAVIER, styled, "the Apostle of the Indies," has been supposed by some writers to have had this honour; and is said by them to have preached Christianity at the Ceylon pearl fishery, so early as 1452.

cause, were furnished by these Missionaries. Memorials of the names and labours of a few have been preserved from oblivion. Among these, "Father Joseph Vaz" holds a distinguished place. The zeal which he evinced, and the spirit of piety and benevolence he manifested in the prosecution of his mission, to the inhabitants of the interior, entitle him to the appellation of "a second Xavier." There is ground for hope that his labours were not unproductive of fruit. Some members of the royal family embraced the Christian faith; and, according to the statements of the historian, exemplified its transforming influence.

When, about the year 1602, the Kandyans, assisted by the Dutch, emancipated themselves from the Portuguese yoke, Christianity was banished with those by whom it was introduced. The Kandyan dominions relapsed into the former idolatries; nor was it conjectured that any traces of Christianity remained within their limits. More than two centuries had been added to the annals of time, when two small colonies of Roman Catholic Christians, the fruit of the Portuguese Mission, were discovered embosomed in the Kandyan jungles. Though unsupplied with priests, they had continued a separate people, and preserved their attachment to the Christian name and ordinances. A copy of the New Testament, translated into the vernacular tongue by an European Catholic priest, was found in their possession: and, notwithstanding the errors of their system, the author cannot but avow his conviction, that such a translation, in connection with the singular preservation of the congregation referred to, furnishes a strong presumption of the purity and sincerity of those who laid the foundation of the work.

"*Names* and *sects* and *parties* fall—
"THOU, O CHRIST! art ALL IN ALL!"

The Kandyans had suffered too much from the oppressive treatment of the Portuguese, to permit the Dutch, to whom they owed their deliverance, to gain any authority within their territories. The attempts to promote the interests of Christianity were therefore necessarily confined to

INTRODUCTION. lxv

the coasts, which had been ceded to them, and were inhabited by their immediate subjects. These under the Portuguese government were all "*good Catholics*," beneath the care of regular priests, and subjected to papal authority: but, changing their creed, with a facility which proved their subserviency to their new rulers, nearly the whole population conformed to the worship of the Reformed Church.* Protestant ministers were provided at the government expense; and arrangements made to instruct the natives in the principles of Christianity, and to bless with its moralizing and cheering influence, the departments of domestic and social life. Copies of some of the Old Testament books, and a version of the entire New Testament, were issued from the Government Press for the use of the natives, and distributed gratuitously at the public expense.

That the people might be placed under regular ecclesiastical discipline, the Dutch territory was divided into districts, or schoolships; to each of these, two or three *schoolmasters* were appointed, who received a small monthly allowance from the government; and whose duties consisted in instructing all the children in what are still called "*the three prayers;*† and in an excellent historical and doctrinal catechism, which had been translated for the purpose. The first head master had the charge of the *Thombo*, or Registry of Baptisms and Marriages in the district; he also practised as a kind of notary. The masters were authorized by the government to *compel* the attendance of the children, and to punish such as absented themselves. Over a certain number of these districts a *catechist-master* was placed, with a higher salary. His duty was, to superintend the system of instruction by the schoolmasters, and to examine the scho-

* The Author once enquired of a Singhalese man, who had been educated in what they term *the Dutch time*, " Are you a Christian?" Confounding the term *Christian* with *Roman Catholic*, he replied in the negative, with a strong expression of disdain. " Of what religion are you?" His answer was, " *Reppremmado*," or, " of the Reformed Church!" Dr. Buchanan, in his " Christian Researches," relates, that while at Ceylon, he enquired of a boatman, what religion he professed? He replied, that " he was of the *Government religion!*"

† The Lord's Prayer, the Creed, and the Ten Commandments.

lars. By an order from the Dutch government, none could enter the marriage state who were not capable of repeating "*the three prayers;*" and it was part of his duty to ascertain their knowledge, and to certify the the same.

The next class of ecclesiastics employed by the Dutch Government were termed *proponents*, whose districts were more extensive, and sometimes comprehended two or three of those committed to the charge of catechists. The proponents were a description of unordained preachers, or exhorters, who performed divine service in their respective districts, and had authority from government to enforce the attendance of the people on public worship, at particular seasons. The president of their ecclesiastical system was a European minister, denominated the *Principal of Schools;* to whom a handsome salary was allowed, and under whose superintendence, all the schools in the island was placed. By his recommendation, the subordinate agents received their appointments from government, and to him all matters relating to the regulation of the schools were referred for sanction, previous to adoption. At regular intervals, the districts were visited by an ordained minister, who, after delivering a sermon in the Dutch language, baptized, married, and administered the Lord's Supper. The *Thombo holder*, or General Registrar of the island,* attended the minister on his visitation, to record the names of the parties baptized and married.

The Dutch government certainly exerted itself with considerable zeal to induce the natives to adopt the Protestant faith; and so far as *legislative enactments* could accomplish the object, succeeded with their Ceylonese subjects, without much difficulty. The attentions which were paid by that Government to the religious and moral improvement of the natives deserved to be recorded with respectful commendation. It is true the *form* of godliness is all that can be secured by the sanctions of human authority; the maintenance of its *power* and spirit must, in a great measure,

* This office was filled by a respectable Native Chief.

depend on the agency employed. But there is a blessing even in the form of Christianity, which it is only necessary to behold in a heathen country in order favourably to appreciate. Yet the Dutch had some active and zealous ministers at various periods of their Ceylonese sovereignty, whose earnest endeavours to promote the eternal interests of the natives, have procured for them the grateful recollection of all who love the " Holy Catholic Church."

During the possession of the island by the Dutch, the Pagan priests were placed under considerable restraint; and even those of the Roman Catholic communion, were restricted from exercising their functions within a certain distance of fortified towns. Notwithstanding these disadvantages, Romish Missionaries from the Portuguese settlement at Goa continued their exertions; they succeeded in erecting a considerable number of churches, and in attaching to their communion many thousands of devoted adherents. By a computation in 1813, founded on returns which were substantially correct, it appeared that at least 50,000 of the Ceylonese professed the Roman Catholic religion. It is but justice to this class of native Christians to state, that in general they are more detached from the customs of the pagan inhabitants; more regular in their attendance on the religious services of their communion; and their general conduct more consistent with the moral precepts of Christianity than any other religious body of any magnitude on the island. The number of Roman Catholic Missionaries in Ceylon is eighteen. When incapacitated by age, or removed by death, the vacancy is supplied from the seminary at Goa.

The island was taken possession of by the British in 1796, when the authority of the Dutch became extinct: and the operations of the system for the instruction of the natives ceased, for want of the impulse furnished by government patronage, and pecuniary rewards. The salaries of the various agents being withdrawn, the Dutch clergy either retired to colonies in the possession of their own countrymen, or returned to Europe. A pious schoolmaster was occasionally met with, who continued to perform the duties of his office, unrequited; but the majority (a hireling herd) abandoned their charge, and many actually became worshippers of dæmons! A people thus suddenly deprived of Christian teachers, and left defenceless to the artifices of idolatrous priests, presents a melancholy spectacle. The places erected for the worship of the true God fell by gradual decay into heaps of stone and timber;* and in a few years the croaking of the frog and the hisses of the serpent issued from within the walls erected for the reception of Christian worshippers!

No longer were the people summoned to learn and to pray. No public observances marked out to them the returns of sabbath-days, or checked the overweening tendencies of even lawful commerce with the things of this world. No spiritual monitor visited them with the remembrances of the lines of demarcation between the kingdom of error and vice, and the empire of truth and virtue. The ancient moral landmarks were taken away. Their children became domesticated without marriage, and their offspring were unsanctified by baptism. In this miserable period of Christian retrogression, the *enemy sowed his tares;* but he *went* not *his way. He remained,* unresisted, to superintend their growth; not *while men slept,* through unavoidable infirmity, but while they *neglected,* through infidel insensibility. *He remained:* he sowed many a crop, and reaped many a harvest! His *Budhuism* ensnared the people into forgetfulness of God—his *Kappooism* brought them to *fall down and worship* himself!

The new government was for a considerable time

* From the ruins of Christian churches materials were sometimes obtained for the erection of heathen temples. A correspondent, resident at Ceylon, writing under date of August 1815, says, " I was in company very lately with Sir Alexander Johnstone, the Chief Justice; and he mentioned the following circumstance. After I had finished my business at the criminal sessions at Jaffna, in my northern tour I went to Point Pedro; and while there visited a place where the celebrated Baldæus had formerly built an elegant church. But as there had been no minister to officiate in it for a length of time, it had gradually decayed, until at length it became a confused mass of ruins. Being in this condition, it was sold by government to a rich Gentoo; and, *at this time he is building,* or *converting the ruins into a Gentoo temple!!*"

too much engaged in political and civil arrangements, to attend to the moral and religious destitution of the natives. The effects were appalling.—" In the time of the Dutch government, the different places of worship dedicated to Budhu, and other deities of Singhalese superstition, were between *three and four hundred;* and during the *first ten years* of Ceylonese subjection to the British Crown, the number of such places of Pagan worship had increased to ONE THOUSAND TWO HUNDRED!"*

Nor was the growth of idolatry less rapid among the Malabars in the north. Under the Dutch government, there were, in the Province of Jaffna alone, *thirty four churches* appropriated to the use of the Malabar Christians; attended by nearly 63,000 auditors; exclusive of more than 2,000 baptized slaves; and the government-schools belonging to them included upwards of 16,000 native children, who were under regular tuition. It is not improbable, that this excellent system experienced some decay, even before the island fell into our hands; but when that event took place, it entirely ceased to exist. The Romish missionaries and the Brahmins divided the neglected population between themselves. But that the major part relapsed into Paganism, may be concluded from the following authentic statement; for which I am indebted to the kind-of the Chief Justice. In the year 1814, the Province contained *seventy-four Romish churches*, while of HINDOO TEMPLES, there were in the same district THREE HUNDRED AND TWENTY-NINE! And yet, this marks the condition of only one of the Tamul provinces of the island! May the zeal of British Christians be extensively aroused to repair the mighty mischief; nor deem the obligation discharged, until idolatry and superstition are *utterly abolished!*

When the affairs of the island had assumed a regular form, and the British government was established on a more firm basis, an atttempt was made, under the administration of Governor North, to restore and model the Dutch school system; a public grammar-school, called The Seminary,

* First Report of Colombo Auxiliary Bible Society.—See also Appendix to this volume.

was established at Colombo, to afford to the sons of the native chiefs the elements of an European education. Under the auspices of Governor North much was done. It must, however, be regretted that his benevolent plans were but partially executed, in consequence of orders from the government at home, restricting the expenditure to a sum very inadequate to the extensiveness of the object.

In 1810, the Hon. and Rev. Dr. Twisleton, (the present Archdeacon of Colombo,) succeeded in putting into operation a school system, formed on the basis of that established in the island by the Dutch. The enlightened and Christian policy of Governor Brownrigg's administration obtained for him all the assistance of the local government; and ninety-five native schools, the Seminary, the Orphan School, and a Military School, were placed under his jurisdiction, as *Principal of Schools.*† The important duties of the office could not have been entrusted to one more able, or more inclined to perform them with efficiency. At a visitation of fifty-three of these schools in the commencement of 1814, by the Rev. A. Armour, 2,297 children and adults were baptised; 793 couples married; and the sacrament of the Lord's Supper administered to 73 of the more serious; the greater part of whom were schoolmasters. Beside these, 3,482 were reported to be learners; of whom 527 boys and 18 girls were able to read in their own language with tolerable facility. Some of the schools were, however, without a single copy of the New Testament:* the children must therefore have been taught from heathen books, or have remained wholly without instruction. This deficiency is yet but very partially supplied.

The Rev. Henry Martyn, (a name dear to India, and to every lover of human souls) having pathetically and forcibly represented to the Europeans at the Presidency of Calcutta the dearth of the Holy Scriptures which prevailed throughout

† First Report of the Calcutta Bible Society.

* "There is, indeed, a lamentable scarcity of Singhalese New Testaments on our island: I question whether there be *twenty* copies in existence among a population of more than *one million* of souls!"— *Letter from Ceylon; Calcutta Report,* 1811.

our Indian territories, the Calcutta Auxiliary Bible Society was formed in February 1811; and one of the first steps taken by the Society in its career of Christian benevolence was to ascertain and supply the wants of the native Singhalese. An edition of the New Testament was printed at the Serampore press at the expense of the newly-formed institution, and forwarded to Ceylon for gratuitous distribution. A similar Society was soon after formed at Colombo, under the immediate patronage of His Excellency Governor Brownrigg, and the principal, civil and military officers of the island. The late Alex. Cadell, Esq. Paymaster General, and the Rev. George Bisset, Colonial Chaplain, were its first Treasurer and Secretary; while Sir Alexander Johnstone, the Chief Justice of the island, lent his powerful assistance to extend the benefits it was designed to convey to the natives throughout the island. The Missionaries of different denominations have derived from the bounty of this Society much valuable aid, in donations of the Holy Scriptures for the use of their schools and congregations; and if the number of copies supplied has not been commensurate with the necessities of the population, it must be referred, not to unwillingness in the Committee, but to the inadequacy of their funds. The Annual Reports of the Society, from the pen of its excellent Secretary, the Rev. G. Bisset, will be read with deep interest; as they not only detail the immediate operations of the Society, but refer (with a spirit truly catholic) to the exertions of the Missionaries of the various denominations, and to the result of their efforts to spread the influence of Christianity in the island.

The London Missionary Society appointed four Missionaries (Messrs. Vos, Palm, Erhardt, and Read) to labour in Ceylon, so early as 1805; who were encouraged in their laudable undertaking by Governor North, and the authorities of the island. Circumstances, however, induced the society to withdraw from Ceylon, which has not since been occupied by a Missionary from that body of Christians. The Rev. J. D. Palm remained at Colombo; and has undertaken the pastoral charge of the Dutch Church in that place. *The Baptist Missionary Society* established a

Mission to Ceylon, in 1812; and their Missionary, the Rev. J. Chater (from the Burman country) had, (in 1814,) under the Divine blessing, succeeded in raising a congregation, and in forming a church, which meet in a neat chapel in the Inner Pettah. The establishment and progress of the Mission under the direction of *The Wesleyan Missionary Society*, it is the object of the following pages to record.

The brief outline furnished by this sketch of the moral and religious circumstances of the Ceylonese, will, it is hoped, excite the friends of the human race to increased liberality, and more earnest prayer to the *God of all grace*, that the *heathen* in Ceylon may be *given to his Son for his inheritance;* and that in the hands of his devoted servants of every Christian communion, *the word of the Lord may have free course, and be glorified.*

CHAP I.

Mr. Wesley's universal charity—The Formation of the Wesleyan Connexion—Its progress—Established Church of England— Dissenting Denominations—Doctor Coke—His Missionary character——America—First Wesleyan Foreign Mission in 1769—To the enslaved Africans in 1778—Mr. Baxter—Western Africa, 1792, and 1811—Europe—Asia —Mr. Wesley's lively interest in an Asiatic Mission—Doctor Coke's correspondence on the subject in 1784—Bengal—Application from Madras—Communication from Lieut.-Col. Sandys in 1805—Letter from Surat in 1808—Plummer—Successful exertions of other denominations in Asia—Visit to England of the Chief-Justice of Ceylon in 1809—State of the Island—Mr. Wilberforce's recommendation of the Wesleyan Missions—Ceylon Mission proposed by the Chief-Justice—Former policy of the Hon. East India Company—Doctor Moreton—Sanctified affliction—Doctor Coke's application to the Rev. W. Ault—and the Author in 1812—Rev. I. Bradnack—Letter from Doctor Coke to Mr. Ault in 1813—The Doctor determines himself to embark in the Mission—His plan—the General Wesleyan Methodist Missionary Society—Doctor Buchanan—Mission proposed in the London District—Rev. Benjamin Clough—Irish Conference—Rev. Messrs. Lynch, Erskine, and M'Kenny—Liverpool Conference—Devotion to the Mission Cause—Final adoption and limitation of the plan—The original appointment for Asia—Doctor Coke's letter to the Author—His pious submission.

THE venerable Founder of the Methodist Societies was a lover of mankind on the most extensive scale. Adopting the principle which actuated the good Samaritan, his heart was open to every member of the human family. Deeply affected with the moral state of all who share our common nature, it was impossible for him to restrain his emotions of Christian sympathy and benevolence within a smaller circle of operation than the whole and entire generation of man; and when he commenced his laborious career of ministerial usefulness, it was by a recognition of the whole world as his parish, and with a determination to omit no means in his power of advancing the cultivation and improvement of the vast district.

There is no reason to suppose, that Mr. Wesley entertained any idea of originating a separate denomination of Christians, which should take any conspicuous part in the evangelization of the world. From all that can be gathered on the subject, nothing appears to have been farther than this from his primitive intentions. Candour and impartiality induce this conclusion in the mind of every person who is sufficiently acquainted with the determining incidents of Mr. Wesley's eventful life. His avowed and undeniable object, in the onset of his itinerant exertions, was to arouse and stimulate to increased piety and zeal, the existing bodies of the Christian Church, and especially the National Church of England, and by no means to give rise to a new and distinct denomination.

With this view he seems to have adopted two invariable principles with respect to the *matter* and the *manner* of his ministerial labours. In reference to *the former*, to preach without any studied ornaments of speech the plain and wholesome truths of the gospel; adopting the Articles and Homilies of the English Church as the basis of his expositions. And, in respect to *the latter*, to preach those truths in *any* and *every* place to which he might have a providential opening of usefulness. From these two principles he never deviated: and the results which followed his method, so far as related to the general diffusion of the gospel, present a growing illustration of that appropriate comparison of our Lord—" *The kingdom of heaven is like unto leaven, which a woman took and hid in three measures of meal, until the whole was leavened.*" Mr. Wesley's doctrines are before the world, in his excellent Sermons and Tracts; and the effects of them may be seen in the lives of multitudes who have been benefited by their dissemination.

Through an unhappy misapprehension of Mr. Wesley's doctrines and designs, those who had been converted by his ministry were, in the general, repelled from the communion of most of the denominations of the Christian church. It is not intended to revive controversies and persecutions long since happily become antiquated and unpopular. The fact is simply stated, in the course of accounting to the reader for the existence of his followers as a separate denomination of Christians. Repeated were the offers which Mr. Wesley made to various clergymen of the English National Church, to receive under their pastoral care those whom he had been instrumental in reclaiming from sin and error. But the compliance involved some deviations from episcopal usage, as to *mode;* and was therefore declined. Unfortunately, in that day, *every* parish in England was not supplied with a religious clergyman; and those excellent men, whose piety and zeal proved an ornament to the Establishment, and might have led them to a compliance, were prohibited by the canons of the National Church from interfering with the spiritual concerns of persons not residing within the limits of their own respective parishes.

In those circumstances, Mr. Wesley was reduced to one or the other of these alternatives: either to allow those persons who had been awakened by his ministry to a deeper sense of divine things, to fall back again into the general mass of moral slumberers, from whence they had been aroused,—or to unite them together in small societies, under his own superintendence, for their mutual edification and stability. The latter he could not do without committing an act of *irregularity* as a clergyman of the English Church. It is well known, that his own prepossessions were diametrically opposed to such a measure. It is possible, there may be persons who would not hesitate, even in the present day, to pronounce it to have been the greatest evil of the two. Mr. Wesley adopted it as the smallest. If he erred in this respect, his zeal for God, and his constraining concern for the everlasting interests of his fellow-men, will be his best apology on earth; while, waving any controversy on the subject, we await the final decision of Him, whose love to human souls was such, that he "*humbled himself, and became obedient,*" not only to circumstances, but "*unto death, even the death of the cross,*" in order to rescue them from eternal perdition.

Mr. Wesley, in the formation of his societies, avoided every thing which might have a sectarian tendency. Out of respect to the National Church, his preachers were not ordained by imposition of hands, and were forbidden to call themselves *Ministers*, or to take the title of *Reverend*. Divine service, also, was never performed in what are called church-hours; excepting in cases where the regular clergyman was an infidel or led a notoriously wicked life; or where the parish-church was too small to accommodate the inhabitants. And so liberal were the terms of admission into those societies, that no peculiar test of doctrine was prescribed; the only condition required, was " *a desire to flee from the wrath to come,*" evidenced by "*fruits meet for repentance.*" In the denomination of his Societies, Mr. Wesley adopted nothing which might present the idea of an independent church. It is true, he submitted to the term *Methodist*, applied in derision to himself and followers; and wrote a tract descriptive of " *The Principles of a Methodist;*" but in all things he wished to consider himself and them as auxiliaries of the Establishment, and as members of her communion.

It is possible, he might indulge the expectation, that, in some future day, the Church of England would be disposed to receive his Connexion more fully within her pale; and perhaps, on that account, united with his own firm attachment to her institutions, he sanctioned no usages among his people which might tend to multiply difficulties in the way of so desirable a measure. Several years afterwards, a proposal to that effect was made to some of the principal dignitaries of the English Church, which did not succeed. The pious and liberal of that Church being more disposed to look with a favourable and friendly eye on the Society under a distinct denomination, than to sanction what would be considered an anomaly in their Establishment, by such an incorporation.

This question, however, it is apprehended, may now be considered as set at rest. The Wesleyan Methodists, however unwillingly, form a distinct department of the catholic Church. But although it appears necessarily, and perhaps providentially, distinct from the National Church which gave it birth, the Connexion, in its general features, retains a greater measure of resemblance to that Church than it does to any other denomination of Christians. And, if an obscure individual may presume to offer an opinion on such a subject, in its providential growth, it appears most probable, that the resemblance will be increased rather than diminished.

It was while a young man, and but a short time

time after Mr. Wesley had quitted the University of Oxford, and had received English episcopal ordination, that his benevolent and expanding heart induced him to enter upon an episcopal mission to Georgia, in North America. On his return from that arduous station, he became, in fact, a home missionary to the end of his days. Through every part of the United Kingdom he continued regularly to itinerate and preach, for upwards of half a century. And it became one highly gratifying effect of the beneficial tendency of a life thus consecrated to the glory of God, that he was instrumental also in sending missionary-ministers, men like-minded with himself, to the North-American continent and archipelago; whose pious and self-denying labours abroad were followed by happy consequences, similar to those which attended the efforts of their venerable Founder at home. From its commencement, this unassuming system of moral re-action, apparently so adventitious in its origin, continued to receive the manifest blessing of the Almighty. On the death of Mr. Wesley, in the year 1791, there were associated within the bonds of Christian fellowship, in his various societies, at home and abroad, no less than 53,000 persons; independently of a far greater number, who, though attached to their modes of worship, and forming a part of their regular congregations, were not considered as incorporated members of the Connexion.

It was naturally anticipated by many, that, on the decease of their Founder, those societies would either become separated from the common bond, or, at best, that they would cease to increase their numbers, and extend their influence. But the event has been, happily, the reverse of either of these boding anticipations. While the National Church, as well as the Dissenting Denominations, have been enlarging their borders, the Wesleyan Connexion, as a distinct and separate body, has also enlarged. After the lapse of thirty years from the date just mentioned, their number of members has arisen from fifty-three thousand to half a million: exclusively of those individuals in their congregations, who are not viewed as members of their societies.

The Connexion continues to grow. To the Great Head of the Church Universal, the adorable Jesus, be the sole glory! To His gracious superintendence and spiritual influence alone, it is to be ascribed, that the piety and ardour which animated the breast of its original Founder, nearly a century ago, is found still to animate the rising Connexion which he was instrumental of originating. Its ministrations at home, and its missions abroad, bespeak the vigour of its moral pulsation. In the infancy of its existence, it was assailed both by churchmen and by dissenters; who would have rejoiced to see it expire; and who, by their treatment of it, seemed anxious to convince the world, that it possessed no right to the claims of consanguinity, on either side. It was thus cast on the bounty of Him "*in whom the fatherless find mercy;*" and on Him it professes its filial dependance. With this, it is intent upon visiting and relieving every benighted region under heaven. In its progress it breathes nothing but good-will and affection to all mankind. It retains its natural respect and deference for that National Church, who was the mother of its earthly existence, and but for whom it had never seen the day. To all its sister Denominations in every country, who acknowledge the same Father and Head, it extends the right hand of fellowship. And to the heathen world, it contributes its efforts and its savings to a pleasing amount, which increases every revolving year. It cherishes no principles of ambition, but to be instrumental in the conversion of the fallen children of Adam. Its plan includes the subversion of no other kingdom than that of Satan, which " *the Son of God was manifested that he might destroy.*"

In all these respects, its deportment for nearly a century has been the subject of public observation. Its principles and character are now generally known: and men well qualified to judge have favourably appreciated its influence upon human society. How many a reclaimed individual magnifies the Almighty for what it has taught him! How many a reformed family has improved in real enjoyment and respectability, under the Divine blessing, on the truth it spreads, and the discipline it maintains! The world has proved it to be safe and beneficial. The church exercises the offices of Christian affection towards it. And it has the satisfaction of being assured, that, neither its efforts nor its successes are viewed either with indifference or regret by the liberal and Christian Government under which we live.

Of the various co-adjutors of Mr. Wesley who survived him in the ministerial work, perhaps none more fully enjoyed his confidence, or more deeply imbibed his catholic and ardent spirit, than the late Rev. Doctor Coke, a gentleman commoner of Jesus' College, Oxford. To the lot of this venerable clergyman it fell more particularly to establish and superintend the Wesleyan Missions. It is truly affecting, to bring to recollection how unalienably and unabatingly he devoted himself to the interests of this department. It may seem harsh to the ears of a person unacquainted with his character, to pronounce, that, in that line of duty he has never been exceeded by any one, since the apostolical age. Yet, this is the opinion which the writer has formed. Doctor Coke's theatre of Missionary operations, included *the four quarters of the globe.* In *three* of them, he was the actual founder of Missions; for whose support, after spending two ample fortunes of his own, (by patrimony and marriage) he went about, begging from door to door, throughout the kingdom; and that not once or twice; but regularly, for several years, until the close of his life!

The first Wesleyan Missionaries visited North AMERICA in the year 1769. On that Continent the venerated names of the Reverend Richard Boardman, and the Reverend Joseph Pillmoor, are still cherished in grateful remembrance. And, perhaps, with every degree of propriety, the Missionary operations of the Wesleyan Methodists may be fixed, as having commenced at that date. The first subscriptions among us, for the support of a foreign Missionary ministry, were raised at that time. But it was not until the year 1778, that our Connexion had any agents among those who were purely Pagan. The attempt was made among the enslaved children of Africa, who were in West Indian bondage. The zealous and devoted Baxter, in correspondence with Mr. Wesley, proclaimed the unsearchable riches of Christ, to the Negroes of Antigua. And on the arrival of Doctor Coke in that place, on the Christmas day of 1786, nearly two thousand benighted Africans had, under the Divine blessing on his labours, been turned " *to God from idols, to serve the living and true God.*" In Western AFRICA, converted idolaters, in connexion with the Wesleyan Methodists, were settled in the year 1792; and their number continued to augment, until Missionaries from England were sent, to give their efforts greater efficiency, in the year 1811. OUR OWN QUARTER OF THE GLOBE has also furnished some very important stations, in which Wesleyan Missionaries, as well as the excellent agents of other denominations, have employed their energies, and expended their lives; and in which we may rejoice to add, they have not laboured in vain.

It remained, that the sleepless zeal of Doctor Coke should be permitted to exercise its influence, in behalf of the benighted idolaters of ASIA. A Mission to India had been the subject of serious conversation between himself and the venerable Founder of our Connexion; who anxiously desired to see the day, when the undertaking should be commenced. The plan of no Mission under the management of the Methodist Conference, more emphatically deserves the appellation of *Wesleyan*, than that of their Asiatic Mission. Mr. Wesley conceived no ordinary degree of interest in the success of such a measure. With a sanction, so likely to be influential with Doctor Coke, we are prepared to be informed, that so early as the year 1784, the Doctor had engaged in a correspondence on the subject, with an honourable gentleman, then residing in the Presidency of Bengal. The want of means, and not of zealous willingness, interfered to prevent the immediate establishment of the Mission. But Doctor Coke openly pledged himself as the Missionary friend of Asia, by publishing, in the Arminian Magazine for 1792, the intelligent and interesting letter of his Indian correspondent*.

Shortly after this, and perhaps in some degree owing to the publication of the letter referred to, the

---

* A respectable gentleman, one of our kind missionary subscribers in Colchester, who, about that time, filled an official situation at *Vellore*, informs me, that he also was addressed on the same subject by our late venerable friend. And I mention this circumstance, because it tends to confirm my opinion, that Doctor Coke had, for many years, most steadily and ardently aimed at the establishment of an Asiatic Mission.

Doctor was addressed by a merchant of the Madras Presidency on the same subject. It is with real concern, I find myself unable to present the reader with a copy of this gentleman's letter; which I have repeatedly perused, but which has been unhappily mislaid. The writer avows himself to have been formerly a minister in Mr. Wesley's Connexion in Ireland: refers to a conversation between Mr. Wesley and some of his preachers in that country, in company with Doctor Coke, at which he was present; and in the course of which, Mr. Wesley expressed his strong desire to have a providential opening for Missionary labour among the Asiatic Pagans: states, that, having subsequently engaged in commercial pursuits, he had, by the Divine blessing, realized a considerable property; and offers, in case the Doctor would send out an unmarried Missionary, to place him immediately in an encouraging sphere of usefulness; and himself to defray all expences connected with his voyage from England, and his settlement in India. This appeared, indeed, to be a very suitable opening; but there were some considerations which induced the Doctor to defer complying with the proposal at the time in which it was made. On my arrival in Bombay, in 1814, I immediately wrote to the address of the merchant; and was sorry to learn that he had been some time deceased.

The delays to which the Doctor's favourite design was subjected evidently had not the effect to weaken his purpose, or to lessen his ardour. With invariable interest he continued to prosecute his enquiries, and to collect information of every kind which tended to cast any light on the state of Christianity in India, or the means of its propagation among the Pagans of those extensive regions. In the year 1805, he entered largely into the subject, with a highly respectable and pious military gentleman, who had spent upwards of twenty years in various parts of India.* And he afterwards requested of his friend in writing, the substance of the valuable information and advice he had received from him, in reference to the submission of his plan to the Wesleyan Missionary Committee in London. Nor did he disregard communications from humbler sources. I have before me a letter, dated 1808, from Surat, in the Presidency of Bombay, written by a private soldier, in which he informs his parents, that being in the army on that station, he had obtained permission from the colonel of his regiment to hold a prayer-meeting in the barracks: that, in consequence, a number of his comrades had united with him, at the several seasons of worship, which were so fixed as not to interfere with their military duties: and that, from four to twelve, and ultimately forty-three of them, being under religious impressions, had begun to meet together, weekly, after the manner of the class-meetings among the Wesleyan Methodists in Europe.

This unassuming and gratifying document, indicative of the operation of Christianity in that part of India among our own countrymen, the Doctor had obtained from the parents of the young man in Ireland;† and after his death, I found it had been carefully preserved by him among a few papers of a similar description. We thus saw, beyond a doubt, that our venerable friend had steadily kept in view, for many successive years his original plan of an Asiatic Mission; and was carefully accumulating, as a pre-

---

* Lieut. Colonel William Sandys.

† See on this subject also an interesting and authentic little work, edited by the Rev. John Riles, and very recently published, under the title of " *A Journal of Samuel Plummer,* late a soldier in the Indian army."—*Blanshard,* London. 2s.

paratory measure, whatever information he could occasionally obtain on the subject.

The laborious, persevering, and successful efforts of our Christian brethren of other denominations, to plant the Gospel in the Indian Provinces, had long excited the most enthusiastic admiration of the Christian world in general. It was impossible to admire with sincerity, without a desire to imitate and co-operate with them in the laudable work. For many years the Wesleyan Methodists, as a body, had taken no other part in the evangelization of Asia, than merely giving a wider circulation, through the medium of their Magazine, to the animating accounts of the proceedings of other Christians. But at length the time arrived in which they also were admitted to the honour of contributing some small share of more active assistance towards the promotion of the glorious object. The following were the leading circumstances, by which their plan was matured and brought into operation.

In the year 1809, the Honourable Sir Alexander Johnston, the Chief Justice of the Island of Ceylon, paid a visit to England, for the purpose of securing to the various descriptions of Natives, within the jurisdiction of his Court, the British birth-right of Trial by Jury. This benevolent Judge, whose name will be handed down to posterity, as the giver of this privilege to the Ceylonese, was also desirous of bringing that interesting people more fully under the influence of the principles of our holy religion. Christianity had for ages, in some form or other, been the religion of a part of the Ceylonese: but by the political changes to which their island had been subject, owing to the European wars, most of their religious institutions had fallen into disuse and decay ; and at that time, little else but a Christianity extremely and inconceivably nominal could be found. Excepting among the Roman Catholics, who were furnished with subordinate objects of hope, and fear, and worship; there were very few even of those who called themselves Christians, but were open idolators—thousands of them worshippers of that evil and malignant spirit, termed in Scripture *"the Devil, and Satan"*—and many avowedly *Capoas*, or priests in attendance at his demon shrine and service.

The author speaks from personal knowledge: for no very considerable alteration had taken place, on the arrival of his colleagues and himself, five years after the memorable visit of the Chief Justice to England. And it may be satisfactory to the reader, and sufficient for the author, to observe, once for all, that he makes his statements under the influence of a conviction (ever present,) that it is more than probable what he writes in this country, will be read, and subjected to the test of examination, in the several countries and places to which the subject matter of his narrative may refer. The Protestant religion, (Dutch Church) was the established or Government-religion of the island. Dr. Buchanan estimates the number of Native Christians about that time to be 500,000: and at the same date, the Protestant ministry consisted of three clergymen of the Church of England, chiefly employed among the Europeans—one Church of Holland clergyman, engrossed by the Dutch descendants—one German clergyman, sent out by the London Missionary Society—one unordained European, licensed to preach in Singhalese—and a few native proponents; while the country abounded with pagan and demon priests, and presented every incitement to heathenism and wickedness.

During his stay in England, these unwelcome facts naturally became the theme of conversation between the Chief Justice and his friend, Mr. Wilberforce; the honour of whose name the author is peculiarly happy to be able to associate with the history of the commencement of this Mission. The same CAUSE which has added unperishable glories to that honourable name, brought Mr. Wilberforce into acquaintance with Doctor Coke, and our Missionary labours among the enslaved Africans. Doctor Coke had the gratification to enjoy the intimate friendship of Mr. Wilberforce to the end of his days; and it was in consequence of the honourable mention made by Mr. Wilberforce, of the Missionary system of the Wesleyan Methodists, that the Chief Justice desired to see a Mission undertaken by that Society to the important island, over whose best interests he had been accustomed to watch with so much lively concern.

The proposal of the Mission, and the promise of affording it every sanction and support in his power, as proceeding from the Chief Justice, was communicated by Mr. Wilberforce to Doctor Adam Clarke, who embraced an early opportunity of laying it before the Methodist Conference. Some temporary difficulties conspired to prevent its immediate adoption. But the impression then produced, without doubt, laid the foundation of our Mission to Ceylon and India; and was thankfully hailed by Doctor Coke as an advance of no small importance towards the attainment of his fondest plan of an Oriental Mission. It presented to him an opening, unsought for, and unexpected; and marked the outlines of a course more easy of pursuit, than the one in reference to that object which had been usually in his view.

At that time, the East India Company, who had the sole sovereignty of the Continent, tenaciously adhered to a more timid policy, with respect to Christianity within their territories, than they have since discovered to be necessary; and on that policy most of the European inhabitants of India had formed their modes of thinking and feeling on the subject. Ceylon, being more immediately under the control of his Majesty's Government, a more liberal toleration of Christian Misionaries was to be anticipated in that island, than could have been successfully expected, from the tone of feeling, as well as line of policy then ascendant on the Indian Continent. From a letter which I had the privilege to receive from the Doctor, there is reason to think that this encouraging consideration very materially weighed with him in his selection of the Island of Ceylon, as the sphere of our first Missionary attempts in that quarter of the globe. It may be added, that the "*Christian Researches*" of Doctor Buchanan, tended more fully to mature his design; while various conversations with gentlemen who had been resident in Ceylon, and especially with a medical friend, then recently returned from India,* finally determined him in his views of Ceylon, as being the most proper place for the commencement of an Asiatic Mission.

The sanctified affliction of its members, and especially of its public officers, have frequently contributed to advance the interests of the Christian Church. Men, who have been the most eminent for piety and zeal, would often have contracted a degree of inanity, however incompatible with their prevailing virtues, but for the chastening hand of providential bereavement or affliction. These events seemed to have a voice, speaking to them, in counteraction of the effects of abounding comforts; and saying, "*Arise, and depart, for this is not your rest:*" and adding, "*Whatso-*

---

* Surgeon Morton, R. A. the friend and father-in-law of Dr. Morrison, the celebrated Chinese Missionary.

ever thy hand findeth to do, do it with thy might; for there is no work, nor device, nor knowledge, nor wisdom, in the grave, whither thou goest." The plan of our mission had been long meditated. A remarkable opening had been presented under the most favorable circumstances. And yet, even the mind of Doctor Coke required the excitement of a heavy affliction, to determine it to contend with the difficulties of an immediate undertaking of the work.

In the beginning of the year 1811, it pleased Divine Providence to dissolve a union which had been unusually happy, by the death of Mrs. Penelope Coke, to whom the Doctor had been married about six years. The susceptible heart of our widowed friend received no common wound in this bereavement; his suffering was extreme; but he was enabled to bow with submission to the will of God, and was more than consoled by the assurances which he had, that his loss was the endless gain of his departed lady. By the advice of his friends, the Doctor complied with several country invitations, during the ensuing spring, which enabled him to prove the sympathy of many under his heavy trial, and also insensibly introduced him again into the active duties of his ministerial office. It was under these circumstances he paid his last visit into Norfolk; a visit which will long be remembered by many. His preaching was marked by the sanctified influence of deep affliction; and his gospel-message was attended with unction to the multitudes who crowded to hear him, as he pursued his route through that county.

The Diss circuit being at that time my appointment, I had the pleasure to meet Doctor Coke there, at the house of my superintendent, the Rev. Isaac Bradnack; whose missionary labours in the West Indies have made his praise to be heard in all the churches, and secured to him the Doctor's particular and unalterable friendship. When the Doctor, in the year 1793, had planned a mission to Western Africa, my father was one of the persons to whom he applied to embark in the undertaking; and as he had known my family for many years, he kindly expressed the pleasure he felt at seeing me fully given up to the Christian ministry. The transition to the missionary ministry was perfectly natural with Doctor Coke. And having the peculiar privilege to pass some time with him alone, we conversed on various Missionary subjects with the most lively interest.

It may be supposed, from what afterwards occurred, that the conversation was not forgotten by the Doctor; but there is reason to believe, the Asiatic Mission was not as yet in his immediate contemplation at that time; or he would have mentioned it. In July, in the following year, I was, however, surprised with a letter from the Doctor, asking my consent to go with the Rev. William Ault, then in the Stockport circuit, on a Mission to the island of Ceylon. My heart, which had imbibed a portion of the missionary fervour, from my excellent and respected superintendent, immediately replied to the proposal in the affirmative, and became instantly susceptible of a strong attachment to the preacher, though then unknown, with whom it was intended to associate me in the new work.

After consulting my invaluable friend Mr. Bradnack, and obtaining the consent of my parents and friends; who, with much natural reluctance, allowed me to act in the matter as my impressions of duty might dictate, and as my providential way might open; the appointment of the Conference was made the criterion of my decision; and the Doctor received my most cheerful consent to go with Mr. Ault to Ceylon, subject to that condition. Even in this stage of the proceeding, it was certainly not the intention of Dr. Coke to embark personally in the Ceylonese Mission. His plan was, to make a first attempt, by sending out two Missionaries; and it was a satisfaction to him that he had succeeded so far in his preliminary arrangement. I shall ever esteem it an honour (and I hope for the indulgence of the reader while I express my feelings), that I was the second individual to whom Dr. Coke was directed to apply to become a labourer in the Ceylon Mission; and I devoutly bless God, that he so graciously influenced my mind, that, without hesitation or "*gainsaying*," I was led to comply with the missionary call. To His name be all the praise! The Mission was proposed by the Doctor at the ensuing Conference, but was postponed, from the want of pecuniary means to carry it into execution.

In the latter end of the year 1812, Doctor Coke was called to endure another severe stroke, in the death of his second wife, an eminent woman, to whom he had been married but one year. If possible, this trial still more than ever detached his mind from earthly ties. A few weeks after Mrs. Coke's decease, the zealous Mr. Ault wrote to the Doctor, with the view, it should seem, of ascertaining the degree of interest he still cherished in the proposed Mission. From Dr. Coke's answer, which is now before me, within a mourning border, I am happy to present the following extract:

Leeds, Feb. 18, 1813.
" MY VERY DEAR BROTHER AND FRIEND,

" I have a Ceylonese Mission most closely at heart; more so than ever. I hope you will go to Ceylon, if the Conference consent. I have now on my list several who are willing to pay £5 per annum for seven years for the support of a Ceylonese Mission. I made a visit to Doctor Buchanan about three months ago; but it was only for a few hours; and his ardour to represent to Government and Parliament the state of religion among the blacks in the West Indies, engrossed almost our whole conversation. I intend to write to him in a few days: perhaps I may make him another visit. ＊＊＊＊＊＊. As soon as I have further information, you shall hear from me again. Go, if it please God, at all events, with the leave of the Conference. I am a little roused out of the deep affliction which seized me on the death or glorification of my dear wife. ＊＊＊＊＊＊.

"Your afflicted friend,
"T. Coke."

"Rev. W. Ault,
Congleton."

While we may observe, from the above extracts, that the mind of the Doctor was still intent on the establishment of the Mission, it does not appear that he had it in contemplation himself to engage in the undertaking, even at this date. Had it been a part of his project, there can be no doubt, from his frank and communicative disposition, that on such an occasion, and to such a correspondent it would have been disclosed, or, at all events referred to. But it is probable, that in a very short time subsequent to the date of this letter, he received those impressions of mind, which resulted in a full determination sacredly to consecrate his remaining days to the introduction and establishment of the Asiatic Mission. He by no means overlooked the difficulties of various kinds, which were connected with such an undertaking. To him, in his advanced age, some of them wore a very forbidding aspect; but the clearness with which his path of duty appeared to open before him, and, above all, his internal conviction of obligation to pursue it, rendered him immoveable in his solemn purpose; and inspired him with an assurance, that difficulties, however formidable, should not prove to be insurmountable, and that every hindrance, under the Divine blessing, should be removed out of his way.

Having thus embarked, at least in intention, in the arduous work, he found, as he advanced in his plan, both a necessity and an opening for a very considerable augmentation of the missionary strength, with which he had, in the previous year, intended to have made a commencement. This extension of his plan was worthy his benevolent ardent mind! Its object was the salvation of MILLIONS sunk in pagan vice, darkness, and peril! In our extensive Connexion, he doubted not, that he should meet with TWELVE men, like-minded with himself in the behalf of the heathen world. With this number, it was his wish to go himself, and lay the foundation of his long-desired Mission.

He had hitherto, indeed, been the principal agent in the pecuniary concerns of the Methodists' Missions. Until just before, when the Conference sanctioned a public annual collection for those missions, scarcely a pound had been expended in that laudable work, but had been obtained by his own personal application. Many fears were entertained, that his relinquishing these his home-labours would prove fatal to the foreign interests of the work. But Doctor Coke possessed a confidence that Divine Providence would still provide a supply for the support and perpetuity of that work, in which he felt he had been engaged, and was engaging, solely from the purest desire to promote the glory of God. And the event has proved, that his confidence was not misconceived nor misplaced. His resignation of this general collectorship was instrumental in calling forth the aid of hundreds of local collectors. When he relinquished the responsibility of procuring the means required for the support of our missionaries, the whole Connexion, by degrees, were led to reply, "*Let it devolve upon us, and upon our children.*" At length the Institution was regularly organized, which is now denominated, "THE GENERAL WESLEYAN METHODIST MISSIONARY SOCIETY;" and, in the hands of the able and active agency, thus brought into co-operation, the annual supplies to our Mission Fund have been raised from £3000 to an amount bordering upon £30,000. When it is considered, that this augmentation has taken place in little more than eight years, and is mainly owing, as a secondary cause, to Dr. Coke's determined espousal of Mr. Wesley's original plan of an Eastern mission, we may see in the past, as well as in the present state of our missionary treasury, an eloquent and forcible elucidation of a Scripture proverb, which says, "*There is that scattereth, and yet increaseth; and there is that withholdeth more than is meet, but it tendeth to poverty.*"

On the subject of India in general, and the peculiarities of an Indian mission in particular, the Doctor sought information from those who were most conversant with Indian affairs; among whom the name of Dr. Buchanan deserves to be particularly mentioned; both on account of his abundant means of rendering assistance to such an undertaking, and his ready willingness to afford his opinion and advice upon points which it was of the utmost importance properly to understand, and judiciously to arrange. Nor will it be any disparagement to the judgment of our venerable friend, in the estimation of thinking men, to be informed, that he invariably preserved minutes of the conversations which took place during the interviews which he had with Dr. Buchanan; and that several memoranda founded thereon were made the rule and directory of his missionary conduct.

While attending the District Meeting in London, in

the month of May, 1813, I had my first personal interview with Doctor Coke on the subject. Having invited me to breakfast with him, he unfolded his plan. I rejoiced in the unexpected honour and happiness of being one of his associates in the Mission; and unreservedly assured him of my continued determination, by Divine assistance, to make any sacrifice which might be involved in my accompanying him to Asia. He had, as has been seen already, secured the consent of Mr. Ault; and my ardour was not lessened by the sacred pleasure which he displayed in the prospect of obtaining the whole of the number which he desired should constitute his first party of fellow-labourers.

I was present afterwards, when in the District Meeting, the Doctor communicated his views and wishes to his brethren in the ministry, and requested their consent and support. The kind and affectionate endeavours which, by some, were then used to dissuade him from personally engaging in the Mission, were of no avail with him. It was in vain that some of the senior preachers urged upon him his advanced age, and other considerations, as reasons why he should abandon his intention. His mind was too deeply interested in the great object of the Mission, to be capable of giving up that part of his plan which provided that he should himself accompany it. He viewed it as imperative upon him to make this additional sacrifice in behalf of that cause which he had for so many years so laboriously and faithfully supported; and he earnestly besought the concurrence of his brethren, with the assurance, that their consent would add even years to his life, while, on the other hand, he believed their refusal would infallibly shorten his days. The surviving preachers, who were present, will well remember the affecting scene.

With an eye to the then approaching Conference,

Doctor Coke diligently employed the interval in endeavouring to procure for the project a favourable opinion throughout the Connexion, as well as in attempts to obtain candidates for the appointment, in case it should meet with the approval of the Conference. In both o these respects he greatly succeeded. Many wished him every degree of success which his own enlarged heart could desire, and accompanied them with their blessings as he pursued his route. He had the satisfaction to find several fully disposed to embark with him in his new enterprise. Of this class was Mr. Clough; who, I believe, was the third of the party in the order of engagement; and whom on his way to preside at the Irish Conference, Doctor Coke took with him as his travelling companion from his native place in Yorkshire. The disinterested devotedness which Mr. Clough has shewn, in his multiplied labours and persevering application, as well as the progress he has made in oriental learning, and the well-earned rank he holds in the esteem of all who know him, whether personally, or by character, rendered it unnecessary that any thing like commendation of him should proceed from my pen; but I cannot deny myself the pleasure of expressing, on this first mention of his name, the respect and regard entertained for him by myself and family, the result of more than five years' intimate acquaintance with him both in public and private life, and during nearly the whole of which period, he was a member of my domestic circle, and my only immediate associate in the missionary work.

From the Dublin Conference, Dr. Coke received the most complete encouragement to proceed in his Mission. Two of their number, the Rev. James Lynch, and the Rev. George Erskine, offered their own personal services; and were gladly accepted; and to them was also added a third, in Mr. John M'Kenny; who, at that time, resided in Dublin, and had not been wholly devoted to the regular itinerant ministry.

At the British Conference, which was that year held in Liverpool, Doctor Coke stated the plan which had so long been revolving in his mind. He proposed, that twelve preachers, whose consent he had previously obtained, should be appointed to the Eastern Mission,* and offered to accompany them himself, and to introduce them to their several stations. Independently, however, of the reluctance which it may be supposed the Conference would feel at the idea of parting with their long-respected secretary, there were a number of other considerations which induced them to pause before they would give their sanction to the proposed measure. In addition to these, which I need not detain the reader by enumerating, there appeared to be one obstacle which was almost insurmountable—it was of a pecuniary nature. The Connexion had already many important and expensive missions in other parts of the world; and the financial difficulties, which then embarrassed their missionary department, seemed to forbid, as unjustifiably sanguine, the immediate prospect of supporting twelve additional missionaries in a new and expensive scene of labour.

Doctor Coke was, of course, fully aware of the existence of this difficulty, and hence was well prepared successfully to encounter it: for, on its being urged, he nobly offered to defray the whole of the introductory expenses of the Mission from his own private fortune!—A rare instance of individual generosity, and of devotion to the cause of missions! To this the Con-

---

* It may be recorded, to the honour of the preachers, as a body, that Doctor Coke, at that time, had no difficulty in procuring labourers for his new and untried field of employment. I have in my possession, a list of several names in the Doctor's hand-writing, above the number who were actually engaged in the Mission.

ference could not, of course, consent; but they accepted his proposal to guarantee the sum necessary for the outfit of the Mission, in the event of its not being otherwise raised.* The principal objection to his favourite design the Doctor had thus the happiness of fully obviating; and, with that amiable spirit of acquiescence, which was so characteristic of him, when he could confide in the principles and motives of those who offered him their advice, he submitted to the curtailment of his plan; that only seven missionaries should be appointed to accompany him in the first instance; that one of these should be stationed in the colony of the Cape of Good Hope, and another in the island of Java; the remaining five to be for Asia; and that, on the part of the Conference, any further supply of missionaries to that quarter of the globe should be decided upon, according to the openings and reception with which this smaller number might be favoured.

This amended plan being proposed to the Conference, received its official approbation; and the following of the twelve, who had offered their services for the Ceylonese Mission, received the honour of appointment:

1. WILLIAM AULT; who had been in the ministry as a regular itinerant preacher for five years; in several respectable circuits in England:

2. JAMES LYNCH; who had been highly respected in the same ministry in Ireland for the same length of time:

3. GEORGE ERSKINE; who had, with much acceptance and usefulness, been similarly situated also in Ireland for four years:

---

* In a letter with which the Doctor honoured me, of this date, he says, "I have engaged to raise the whole of the money for the outfit of the Mission—TO BIND, OR FIND."

4. WILLIAM MARTIN HARVARD; who had been an itinerant in England for three years:

5. THOMAS HALL SQUANCE; who had reputably and usefully filled the same station for two years:

6. BENJAMIN CLOUGH; a preacher from Bradford, in Yorkshire: and,

7. JOHN M'KENNY; a preacher from Dublin. The Cape of Good Hope being the station of Mr. M'Kenny's choice, he received that appointment.

Though Doctor Coke had not obtained the grant of all the preachers who had expressed a willingness to accompany him, yet from the moment the subject had received the decision of the Conference, we never heard him repine, or express any dissatisfaction in consequence. His ardent and affectionate soul received, with thankful submission, the smaller number which had been allotted him; and he immediately wrote to us, informing us of the result, and requesting us to meet him in London as soon as possible. The following copy of the letter I received from him on this occasion, is inserted as a memorial of his anxious solicitude to bring into association those who had cast in their lot with him:

Liverpool, August, 1813.

" MY VERY DEAR FRIEND,

" The appointment for Asia is as follows, as finally *decided* in Conference. [Here follow the names already given.] * * * * Meet me in London as soon as you can. I shall be in London about Wednesday or Thursday in the next week, God willing. You shall want nothing. God will be with us. Meet me as soon as you can; you know how to find me. My love to all our Canterbury friends. You shall all come together as soon as possible. I am,

" Your most faithful friend,

" T. COKE.

" P. S. Bring your books, and every thing with you. We shall sail in January (God willing); the best time.

" 2nd P. S. You shall have plenty of time to see your parents and other friends."

In the foregoing letter, the reader will scarcely know whether he should most admire the ardent zeal and anxiety which the Doctor displays to accomplish his object, or the great and marked submission to the Divine will with which he made his arrangements. It was to him a point of no small importance, from powerful reasons connected with the Mission, that he should be early in London to receive his missionary sons. He earnestly longed to enter immediately upon his voyage, even by the first India fleet; and yet no less than twice, with reference to these circumstances, he provides, " God willing."—*So that ye should say,* **If** *the Lord will, we shall live, and do this or that.*

How suitable and becoming such a disposition in a short-sighted mortal! How worthy such a submission to the control of Heaven, in a good man, about to enter upon *so eventful a work !*

CHAP. II.

Doctor Coke's application to preparatory duties—Portuguese Studies—Decline of the Portuguese power in India—Subscriptions for Ceylon—Recommendatory Letters—The subject considered—Doctor Coke's successful applications—Earl Bathurst—Right Hon. Lord Teignmouth—Mr. Grant—Mr. Stevens—Mr. Wilberforce—Dr. Buchanan, &c. &c.—Piety and simplicity—Interesting scene—Interview in London—Doctor Coke's last circular letter—Replies—Missionary motto of the Rev. Doctor Carey—The Ceylon Missionaries encouraged and animated—The Rev. Walter Griffith—Thomas Thompson, Esq. M. P.—Joseph Butterworth, Esq. M. P.—The late Reverend John Barber—Portuguese Teacher—Search for a vessel—Cabalva, Captain Birch—Lady Melville, Captain Lochner—Outfit—Printing-press and types—Missionary Ordinations—Marriages of Missionaries—Dismissal from the Committee, preparatory to the voyage—Meeting at Portsmouth—Mr. Clough's Account of Doctor Coke—Kindness of friends at Portsmouth and Portsea, &c.—The Rev. Jon. Edmondson—The Rev. Messrs. Aikenhead, Fish, and Beal—The only meeting of the entire Missionary family—Missionary emotions — Rev. Henry Moore — Xavier — Doctor Coke's last Sermon at Portsea—Mrs. Ault's distressing illness—Division of the party—Embarkation at Portsmouth Point.

DOCTOR COKE having thus, under the sanction of the British and Irish Conferences, engaged those who were to be his Missionary companions to meet him in London, proceeded to apply his attention more rigorously than ever to those preparatory duties which devolved the more especially upon himself; and in his application to these, he manifested most clearly how well he was suited to the formation and introduction of a foreign mission.

He had long applied his mind to the study of the European Portuguese language, which he had understood from Dr. Buchanan, was spoken throughout the whole of the Asiatic coast and islands. This application became constantly increased, in proportion as the time appeared to draw near, in which he might in that language proclaim to the heathen and nominal Christians of India "the unsearchable riches of Christ;" and so intense was his desire to become familiar with this preparatory language, that I do not remember to have seen, from that time, any book in his hand which did not tend, in some way or other, to assist his acquirement of the Portuguese.

Helps in the study of the Singhalese or Tamul languages were less easy of access. Indeed, a teacher of either of them was not to be procured in London; and to this, as well as to his attaching more than perhaps a due importance to the Portuguese, as a medium of intercourse with the Asiatics, may be attributed the Doctor's unwearied and persevering application. It is true, that the Portuguese language is spoken throughout India. But neither is it exactly the same as that which is spoken in Europe, nor is it used to that extent in general which would admit easily of a free communication of religious sentiments. This is particularly the case with respect to the heathen aboriginal natives of the Indian continent and islands.

The degenerated state of the Portuguese language, as it is at present found throughout Asia, is, indeed, but a melancholy vestige of the general influence which was formerly possessed in the East by that once enterprising and successful nation. Had that influence been more generally consecrated to the dissemination of pure and undefiled religion among the Indian pagans, over whom it was exercised, it is more than probable it would have been continued unto the present day. But it is at the will of Divine Providence, that " nations and empires rise and fall, flourish and decay:" and the subserviency of a nation to the purposes of God in the spread of the everlasting gospel is intimately and evidently connected with its political ascendancy and greatness, and is the strongest pledge of its universal prosperity. In the order of events, the influence and language of Portugal in India has almost entirely given place to those of our own highly-favoured country. May Britain long continue the foremost and the most enterprising among the nations of the world, in the honourable and glorious cause of religion and truth; that, by her instrumentality, *the ends of the earth* may be made to *see the salvation of God!*

But the attentions of Doctor Coke to preliminary studies did not cause him to lose sight of the funds necessary for the support of the Eastern Mission. Before he left Liverpool, he commenced soliciting subscriptions; and it was in that town the spirit of zeal for this new undertaking first evidenced itself, in the liberal donations of the friends of religion for that specific object. I have seen the names of those liberal persons, as entered by the Doctor in his primary subscription book: and though it is not in my power to remember correctly the names of those who thus generously contributed to the support of this important mission, when as yet it was in its infancy, they have a just claim to all that personal satisfaction which the reflection must naturally yield them.

The Doctor's intimate knowledge of the world, and his familiarity with all that is essential to the favourable introduction of a mission to a foreign land, pointed out to him the indispensable importance of furnishing himself with every possible aid in the way of recommendatory letters to men of power and influence abroad, from their connexions in this country. His station in the church, as well as his learning and talents, and the celebrity of his previous undertakings of a missionary nature, all tended very successfully to open his way, and to favour his views with respect to several of the first characters of our nation.

The powers that be are ordained of God. It is the natural desire of every pious and reflecting Christian, not only to render a cheerful obedience to the laws of the State in the discharge of the customary duties of civil life; but when his line of duty may assume, in some cases, a character which may appear different from that of common life, it is then his sincere wish to give every reasonable assurance and security to those by whom he is governed, that, though unusual in its character, the object of his pursuit is, at least, perfectly harmless and innocent, and such as becomes a good subject of civil government.

In this respect we cannot but be struck with the marked sense of propriety which was so observable in the proceedings of the primitive preachers of Christianity, the holy and successful apostles of our Lord. There was a constant " rendering unto Cæsar the things which are Cæsar's;" an invariable deference to the political establishments of the various countries through which they passed, whatever testimonies they found themselves obliged to bear against the idolatry and depravity of their several inhabitants. Indeed, they appear to have considered political rank and eminence as demanding from them an acknowledgment of deference and respect.

Independent of any sense of Christian propriety, they knew too much of men and things, rashly and rudely to evince among any people a contempt for the authorities to which they had been accustomed to submit. And, so far as it implied no dereliction of the principles of their holy calling, they were always disposed to render unto all men their dues; not only *tribute to whom tribute,* and *custom to whom custom,* but likewise *fear to whom fear, and honour to whom honour.*

It was, probably, from a motive like this, that St. Paul, on his arrival at Jerusalem, whither he had gone by special revelation from God, waited *privately upon those of reputation*, explaining to them fully the object of his mission; lest those, who would otherwise have proved favourable to his undertaking, should, from an involuntary misconception of his character and intentions, be the occasion of throwing serious hindrances in the way of his general usefulness; and lest he should, in consequence, *by any means have run in vain, or laboured in vain.*

It has been the custom of the church in all ages to provide its public messengers with credentials of office, and testimonials to character. In the case of Christian missionaries proceeding to foreign stations, to be furnished with such testimonials, it is a duty they owe to themselves, to the civil authorities, beneath whose protection they wish to live, and to the all-important work in which they have so solemnly engaged themselves. As it respects the latter, would it not appear an unconcern almost bordering upon criminality, to neglect any circumstance which might rationally be expected to facilitate the object of their mission? It is, indeed, within the bounds of possibility for the Divine Being to open the way for his servants by miraculous interposition; but his ordinary method is, to aid them in the use of those means which his goodness places within their own reach.

In respect to the local authorities of their contemplated spheres of action, when we consider the watchful care which those exalted characters must necessarily exercise over their charge, as they are entrusted with the government of distant colonies and settlements, and the anxiety which they, of course, must feel on the entrance of a stranger into their colony, coming there as a public character to acquire a public influence; it will appear a duty of no small importance to furnish such personages with all that kind of satisfaction with respect to office and character which would remove every unpleasant surmise, and prevent any unnecessary uneasiness on that head. They may conjecture the stranger to be either a person of good principles, or of bad ones. If the latter, every degree of influence he may acquire in the colony or settlement will be an increasing evil to the limited society in which he labours to acquire and maintain that influence; and if the former, the question naturally recurs to the mind, why should he not be provided with testimonials to that effect?

With reference to himself, there is every reason connected with his own comfort, and the peaceful discharge of a duty, arduous under any circumstances, why a Christian missionary should endeavour to provide against every thing which, on his first appearance on a foreign shore, might tend to give a doubtful cast to his sacred pretensions, or afford an opportunity to the enemies of his work to suggest sentiments unfavourable to his ministerial reputation.

To these reflections it might be added, that it is among the encouraging promises made to the church militant, that, in these her latter days of increase and prosperity, even kings shall become fostering fathers, and queens nursing mothers, to the infant branches of her extending family. This promise, without considering it in too literal a sense, certainly seems to warrant the expectation, that, beneath the agency of Divine Providence, the great, honourable, and influential men of the earth, shall be cheerfully disposed to grant important facilities towards diffusing the knowledge of Divine Truth, and in protecting and befriending the humble instruments which the Almighty may condescend to use for that purpose. It is our happiness, that we live in a period of time when this promise, thus explained, has had, and continues to have, many a noble and illustrious fulfilment. Foreign countries have produced dignified, and even royal and imperial, promoters of the Christian cause ; and our own Government is always cheerfully disposed to affix the broad seal of its official sanction to any judicious attempt to communicate the blessings of the Gospel to our heathen fellow-subjects in the several extremities of the empire.

How significantly does this encouraging fact bespeak the rapid approach of the universal ascendancy and influence of the religion of Christ! God, who rules among the nations, is openly preparing his moral apparatus for the speedy production of a world which shall be *full of the knowledge of the Lord, as the waters cover the sea.* Once, it is true, *the kings of the earth stood up, and the rulers were gathered together, against the Lord, and against his Christ ;* but now the scene is changed : a glorious reverse is presented to our astonished and joyful observation; and the time is not distant, when every civilized government will regard it as a duty of imperative obligation, to render every aid within its power to promote the dissemination of the Gospel by missions to the heathen ; interwoven, as they are, with the eternal interests and happiness of man, daily communicating blessings to all who are willing to receive them. By these, the standard of the Redeemer shall wave triumphant, when the noise of war, and the din of arms, shall have ceased from the earth ; and when monarchies and republics, whatever be their pretensions to fame and immortality, shall only be remembered with honour, and celebrated with commendation, in proportion as they have been active and honoured agents in the accomplishment of the final and universal wellbeing of all mankind.

In this respect, our Mission to Asia was peculiarly favoured. Our venerated leader was a man well known both to the good and to the great. The members of the Government, during several years, had received many proofs of his excellent character and views. As the official organ of our Missionary Committee, he had obtained important interpositions from the leading members of his Majesty's government, in behalf of our interesting and important missions in the West Indies. Nor did he in vain request their favourable countenance to the Mission to the island of Ceylon. Earl Bathurst, the Secretary of State for the Colonial Department, honoured him and his party with a letter of introduction to his Excellency the Governor of the island; and to this document were added letters to other distinguished characters, both at Bombay, and other parts of India, from the Rt. Hon. Lord Teignmouth, Mr. Grant, Mr. Stevens, Mr. Wilberforce, the Rev. Dr. Buchanan, and other public-spirited and liberal men. These favours were received with gratitude by the missionaries, and by all who felt an interest in their success; and their incalculable value and usefulness to us were particularly felt, in the subsequent trying circumstances through which it pleased God that we should be made to pass, on our way to the fields of labour.

If this precautionary and preliminary measure manifested Doctor Coke's judgment, and knowledge of missionary affairs, the manner in which he endeavoured to accomplish it, illustrated his piety, Christian simplicity, and devotedness to God. He was too well acquainted with the plans made known by Divine Revelation, not to know, that all success, and more especially that which is connected with religious concerns, must depend entirely upon the Divine blessing and sanction; and he had been too long a learner in the instructive school of experience, not to feel that human agents derive their sole efficiency from the Supreme Director of the universe. There he had learned, that the hearts of all men are in the hands of God. He regulated himself accordingly. Disclaiming any inherent power properly and successfully to devise and arrange the minutest circumstance in his new undertaking; with a cautious fear, lest he should err from the path of duty, he sought in all things direction and assistance from *the Father of lights*.

Every request the Doctor made to any great personage, for the favour of a recommendatory letter in behalf of the mission, was formed in the spirit of prayer. Many of these letters of request were written by him in his carriage, as he travelled from place to place. My esteemed friend, Mr. Clough has informed me, that, when travelling with the Doctor, whenever he had finished any important letter concerning the Mission, he was accustomed to pull down the blinds of the carriage, and say, " Come, Brother Clough, let us offer this letter to God, and pray that he may give it success."

I remember, on one occasion, being present with him in London, when some favourable and encouraging letter, affecting the Mission, was received by him, from a certain nobleman. The joy of his heart, as it beamed through his countenance, I must not attempt to describe. With the utmost simplicity, he hastened to an adjoining room, in which the missionary party were engaged in sealing some circular letters, and said to them, " I have just been favoured with a most delightful letter from Lord ——. Come, let us unite to praise God, and to pray for blessings on the head of his Lordship." We then fell upon our knees; for we deeply participated in his joy and gratitude; while the Doctor, as the head of his missionary family, offered fervent praises to God, and ardently prayed for the choicest favours to fall on the liberal-minded subject of his prayers, and on all the kind and exalted individuals who had, in a similar manner, assisted to open our way. Who could have refrained from admiring and remembering such a scene? It was thus that Doctor Coke acknowledged the Lord in all his ways, in reference to the Mission; and we have all most blessedly proved, that the Lord did signally direct his paths.

As my family and friends chiefly resided in London, I arrived there several days before Doctor Coke, who called upon us one morning, accompanied by Mr. Clough whom he introduced to our acquaintance. In a few days, we were joined also by our highly esteemed and lamented brother, Mr. Ault, who has since been removed to his eternal reward; and likewise by Mr. Squance; the Irish preachers, from some cause of delay, did not arrive in London until a considerable time afterwards. For several days, we were employed with the Doctor, he in signing, and we in folding and directing, letters to the friends of missions, on the subject of our missionary establishments generally, and of the projected one to India in particular. As this was the last public effort he made to solicit subscriptions for that sacred cause, a copy of the circular may prove acceptable to those whose grateful hearts desire to cherish a deserved recollection of his ardent and unabated services.

"*London, Sept.* 14, 1813.

" DEAR SIR,

" Permit me to recommend most earnestly to your consideration, our plan for the instituting of missions in Asia. I have, for above fourteen years, had a very ardent desire to visit Asia: Providence and grace have now opened the way. Our late Conference, after most mature deliberation, have chosen six missionaries to accompany me to that part of the globe; besides one whom they have appointed for the Cape of Good Hope; which last missionary I am to leave at the Cape in the course of our voyage. Two of the missionaries are to travel with me as my personal companions and attendants; one is to be stationed in Java; and three are to labour in the island of Ceylon. We have every reason to believe that considerable help will be obtained in those countries for the support of the missionaries, when they have respectively entered on their fields of action. But the outfit will be very expensive. Let me, therefore, intreat you to grant us pecuniary aid on this important and extraordinary occasion. I need not urge upon you the innumerable arguments which have been published to the world in behalf of Asia, and particularly in favour of sixty millions of British subjects covered with heathenish darkness. Those arguments must have been too well known by you, and must have too much warmed your hearts to need a repetition.

" Ceylon is most advantageously situated as our first grand out-post for the Asiatic work. It contains, within the British territories, according to Dr. Buchanan, five hundred thousand Christians, almost all of whom are as sheep without a shepherd. About a million of Pagans are mixed with these: the whole are an uncommonly docile people. The female sex are not immured within walls, as upon the Continent, and polygamy is prohibited by law. The Portuguese language, which four of the missionaries as well as myself are now learning, and of which the remaining three will soon enter upon the study, is spoken by a very large proportion of the inhabitants, as well as along the coast of the Indian continent. The Malabar language is also spoken in the island by a great number of the inhabitants, and will open to us, under grace, the whole western coast of India. Ceylon is within a few days sail of the kingdom of Travancore, where the Syrian Christians dwell. Those who have read that most excellent work of Dr. Buchanan, his "Christian Researches in Asia," must have been much instructed and entertained with his account of the Syriac Christians, who have derived the ordination of their Bishops and other ministers from the Church of Antioch, one of the primitive churches. But this numerous body of professors are in want of pastors. Ceylon also is within thirty-nine miles of Tanjore, where the great Mr. Swartz and his associates laboured and left behind them about fifty thousand Christians; who are also, by the accounts which they themselves have transmitted to Europe, destitute, in a very considerable degree, of ministers of the gospel. I myself, with my two associates, and with the three other preachers who are to be settled in Ceylon on the itinerant plan, shall devote most of my time to the work in Ceylon: and if I live, though I have now devoted my life, under God, to the service of Asia, I shall be happy to make a visit to my favoured native island, to report to you the success which God shall be pleased to give us. In the mean time, I promise you, that we will lose no opportunities of sending you written accounts, from time to time, of every important circumstance relating to the progress of our missions.

"And now, let me again intreat you to help us with your pecuniary aid. You may certainly consider the undertaking as of an extraordinary nature, and will, I hope, as far as prudence will justify, help us in an extraordinary manner. To urge to you the love of Jesus will be unnecessary: your own hearts will suggest to you every motive on that head, with a strength and with an affection which I am incapable of expressing.

"I subscribe myself, with great respect and love,

"Dear Sir, your affectionate brother,

"And humble servant,

"T. Coke."

To this letter Doctor Coke received many answers; some of them very pleasing and animating: and others of a different complexion. But it is due to the writers of each class to inform them, that none but those which bore a favourable aspect with reference to Ceylon—none but those which tended to encourage our views of the Asiatic Mission—were suffered to make any considerable impression on the mind of the Doctor, or on the minds of his companions. These were often read and carefully treasured up by him, as so many concurring testimonies of approbation from the different members of the universal church. Those of a contrary description were only considered as they related to their writers.

It is thus that the great Apostle of the Gentiles teaches us to disregard all the difficulty and discouragement to which we may be exposed, in the way of our Christian duty—to direct our views to the bright side only of a subject—in favour of which sober and enlightened reason has already given its unwavering decision—to *run with patience the race which is set before us, looking unto Jesus, the Author and Finisher of our faith; who, for the joy which was set before him, endured the cross, despising the shame, and is set down at the right hand of the throne of God.*

Doctor Coke and his party, whatever may have been their variations of feeling with respect to their intended undertaking; and however they were affected by a variety of external circumstances, which it would be foreign from our present design to particularize; yet, in their convictions of duty and their anticipations of ultimate success, they remained unchanged, except by the increasing strength of their convictions and anticipations. They were not altogether without friends, and friends too of much discernment and influence, who deeply participated in both: in their pious conversations on the subject of their future field of labour—in their judicious remarks and valuable counsels, they fanned the trembling flame of Missionary zeal: and being persuaded that such a design would meet with the blessing of God, and that what he had promised to his faithful servants in such circumstances, he was able also to perform, they incited them, in the memorable language of the zealous and enterprizing Carey, to "*expect great things,*" and to "*attempt great things.*"

It would be endless to enumerate those of this description, who, it would be expected might be found in so large and blessed a city as London. The Rev. Walter Griffith, President of the British Conference that year, undertook a journey to attend the Committee at our dismissal, for the express purpose of adding by his presence, the weight of his personal sanction to our important undertaking. Thomas Thompson, Esq. M. P. of Hull, and Joseph Butterworth, Esq. M. P. of London; both of them gentlemen of liberal views and Christian principles; fully entered into the object of our Mission, aiding it by their obliging advice, and favouring us as individuals with evidences of their personal esteem and good will. Nor should there be an omission here of the venerated name of the late Rev. John Barber, the President of the British Conference for the succeeding year. Among the Preachers in the Connexion, there was no one who more favourably appreciated the views and feelings of Doctor Coke and his companions, who more ardently wished them prosperity in their arduous work, or who more affectionately administered to their comfort and usefulness, than that excellent Christian Minister.

The various congregations in London belonging to our Connexion manifested considerable interest in the intended Mission, as well as the members of their several Societies. The Brethren of the Mission, with their honoured leader, were met by crowded auditories wherever they were called to preach during their stay in town: and the Missionary prayer-meetings, which were held at the different Chapels in both the East and the West London circuits, with especial reference to the new Mission, were attended by numbers, who found them highly profitable, and deeply interesting.

The days of the Missionaries, during their residence in London, were chiefly employed in close attention to the Portuguese language. The Doctor had engaged a professor of several languages, a Catholic clergyman from Portugal, to wait upon him at regular seasons, to improve his method of reading and speaking the Portuguese; while every morning, at nine o'clock, the Missionary family, for the same purpose, attended the instructions of the same gentleman at his own apartments. From this gentleman they received many kind attentions ; and notwithstanding he was a member of a religious community distinct from their own, they will not fail to cherish for him all that respect and esteem which the nature of his services to them demands.

Of Doctor Coke's progress in the Portuguese language, we have frequently heard the Professor speak in terms of high admiration and surprise. It was an instance which he had rarely known, of a person at so advanced an age acquiring so great a familiarity with the peculiar idioms, and attaining such a facility in the pronunciation, of a foreign language. It was a pleasing evidence of what the human powers are capable, when pressed into the service of a cause which the mind is resolutely determined to promote; and the Professor has often expressed as great an admiration of the fervent, zealous and heavenly spirit of his aged pupil, as of his general talents and literary acquirements.

The Portuguese studies, however, of the Missionaries, were occasionally interrupted by visits to the East India Docks, and other places, in search of a suitable vessel to carry them to their desired field of labour. On these occasions, the parental regard which the Doctor bore to his companions, and the filial affection they entertained for him, induced the whole of them generally to accompany him. Those were delightful days, when, enjoying the society of our Missionary Father, we followed him as he led us to various parts of the town, on the preparatory business of the Mission!

In this way we examined several vessels before we met with any which promised to be suitable. At last, directed, we doubt not, by a Divine superintending Providence, we fixed upon the *Cabalva*, commanded by Jonathan Birch, Esq.; and the *Lady Melville*, commanded by John Lochner, Esq. These vessels were regular Indiamen, of 1200 tons burden. The division of our party was a measure to which we submitted with great reluctance. An unusual degree of affection had prevailed among us; and we had not contemplated such an arrangement: but as it appeared unavoidable, it was at last decided, that Messrs. Ault, Lynch, Erskine, and Squance, should sail in the *Lady Melville;* and that Mr. Clough and myself should be the companions of Doctor Coke in the *Cabalva*.

This important engagement having been accomplished, we were busily employed in procuring our outfit of clothes and other necessaries for our long voyage. Herein we erred, and suffered considerably through inexperience, from which those who have followed us have, I hope, derived advantage. For though our outfit was much more expensive than that of subsequent Missionaries, yet of articles suited to the torrid zone we were very deficient, as we often experienced, when afterwards perspiring in India beneath the weight of European clothing. On our arrival there, we felt it binding upon us to send home to our Missionary Committee a list, approved by our whole party, of such articles as are indispensable to an Asiatic Missionary: and by it I believe our colleagues have since in general been supplied.

There appeared something remarkable in the circumstance of two of our small party, (Mr. Squance and myself,) being acquainted with the management of the printing-press. n my making the proposal to Doctor Coke, he instantly saw the propriety of attaching to our Mission so powerful and effective an auxiliary. I accordingly received his authority to procure the requisite articles; and with the assistance of a few friends, furnished a convenient little office, on a very economical scale. A suitable supply of printing-paper was also purchased; and many of the standard books of the Doctor's private library were selected as the foundation of a public one, which it was intended to unite to the printing and translating department of the Mission. The provision of a printing-press, &c. however casual and adventitious it appears to have taken place, I have no doubt will be seen to have been most evidently providential; and, in the progress of the narrative, the reader cannot but perceive how essentially it promoted the interests of the Mission, as well as the general cause of Christianity, in the island of Ceylon.

As an especial ordination to the Missionary ministry is the custom of our Connexion, arrangements were made for investing us with this final preparation for our new work. Several of the principal congregations in London were desirous of having this service performed in their respective places of worship: and, in compliance with their request, it was deemed expedient to make the following arrangement: Messrs. Ault and Lynch to be ordained at Lambeth Chapel; Messrs. Erskine and Clough at St. George's in the East: and Messrs. Squance and M'Kenny, with myself, at our Chapel in Great Queen Street, Lincoln's-Inn-Fields. The ordination-services were interesting and solemnly impressive. Christians of different denominations assembled with our own congregations on the several occasions; and many fervent supplications were then offered up to God for our assistance and success.

Three of the party were to be married men; their intended wives, with the true Missionary spirit, having most cheerfully and zealously consented to accompany them in their perilous employment, and to share their sacrifices and toils for the sake of the perishing heathen. Mr. Ault was married at Prestbury, in the county of Chester: and Mr. M'Kenny, in Dublin. Previously to their departure from London for that purpose, they with the other Missionaries favoured Mrs. Harvard and myself with their company, at the celebration of our union. We had a particular wish that Doctor Coke should perform the ceremony; and, at our request, the polite Rector of our parish kindly gave his consent: we were accordingly united in London by our venerable leader, in the presence of our affectionate Missionary companions, and friends. It has transpired, that ours' was the last marriage the esteemed Doctor ever celebrated; and the solemn engagements of the day were so interesting, that the remembrance of them will, I am persuaded, long be cherished by the surviving members of our families.

We soon received information that our vessels had left Gravesend, and were shortly expected to reach Portsmouth, where they were to wait for convoy; and where we were directed to join them. In the prospect of our speedy departure from London, we were summoned to attend the meeting of our Missionary Comtee, in order to receive our final instructions and dismissal. There were a number of circumstances which conspired together to render our dismissal at this time very memorable. It was an affecting occasion! After the instructions had been given, several of the senior Preachers addressed to us very important and suitable advice, regarding our Missionary object and conduct; particularly Mr. Griffiths and Mr. Barber. We were then, by fervent prayer, solemnly dedicated to God, and placed beneath his providential and gracious care and blessing; and at the conclusion of the meeting withdrew, with many endearing and encouraging expressions of affection and esteem from our respected fathers in the ministry.

As our work of preparation was now concluded, and the time of sailing drew so very near, it was not considered proper that we should risk our passage by any longer stay in London: it was also the wish of Doctor Coke that we should, as soon as possible, free ourselves from every remaining entanglement, and be in a state of actual readiness for embarkation. We had freely offered ourselves to the Missionary cause; and it became necessary that we should now submit to the painful duty of separating from our affectionate families and friends.

It may easily be supposed, that this would be no small sacrifice to the parties immediately concerned; but the minds of all were rendered equal to the task; and, after a weeping farewell with some whom we shall never again meet until the resurrection of the just, we took our departure from them, and proceeded to Portsmouth; which place we reached on Saturday, the 12th of December, and there held ourselves in preparation to embark, whenever we should receive the promised notice from our respective commanders.

The meeting of the Missionary party at Portsmouth was animating and interesting on many accounts. Our venerable leader had not been without his anxious fears, lest the tender intreaties of our friends, the endearments which our prospects in our native land presented, and other causes, might affect the fortitude and resolution of, at least, some of his intended companions, and lead them to abandon the undertaking, in which he had been so anxious to engage them. But, when arrived at the place of appointment, he found *not one* was missing; that we *all* surrounded the supper-table with him on the night of Saturday the 12th—all his fears and anxieties were for ever dissipated, and he displayed a tranquil joy, and a serene satisfaction, which never afterwards forsook him. I prefer recording, nearly in the words of Mr. Clough, the circumstances of our departure from London, and assembling at Portsmouth, to any sketch which I find myself able to give;* as he was the intimate travelling companion of the Doctor at this time. He observes:

"1813. Dec. 10.—We left London, and proceeded to Portsmouth, where we were to embark. I have seldom seen the Doctor more lively and happy than he was that day. He considered it as the commencement of his Mission: and the thought, that he had so far succeeded in obtaining the consent of the Conference, with six Missionaries to accompany him (and that these were all either gone, or were on their way to Portsmouth), afforded him unspeakable pleasure. His happy soul, during the journey, would frequently break

* Mr. Clough's entire "*Account,*" may be seen in the Methodist Magazine for 1815. Vol. XXXVIII. pp. 65—68.

forth in praises to God, who had thus far opened his way to the East. When he had collected his little party at Portsmouth, and we were all assembled round him, he rose from his chair, and, lifting up his heart and hands to God, broke forth in the following language : ' Here we all are before God ; six missionaries and two dear sisters; now embarked in the most important and most glorious work in the world ! Glory be ascribed to his blessed name, that he has given you to be my companions and assistants in carrying the gospel to the poor Asiatics; and that he has not suffered parents, nor brothers, nor sisters, nor the dearest friends, to stop any of you from accompanying me to India !' At this time he seemed as though he had not a dormant faculty. Every power of his soul was now employed in forwarding the work in which he had engaged !"

Doctor Coke had appointed us to meet him at the Bush Tavern, where we were also met by the Rev. Messrs. Edmondson, Aikenhead, Fish, and Beal ; by whom we were welcomed, and received with much kind attention, and affectionate solicitude for our accommodation and comfort while in that neighbourhood. The respectable members of our societies in Portsmouth and Portsea united with their preachers in shewing us every attention; and several of them invited us to their houses until the time of our embarkation. We passed the remaining days of our residence in England, Doctor Coke at Mr. Webb's, sen.; Mr. and Mrs. Ault, at Mrs. Methwell's ; Messrs. Squance and Clough, at Mr. Johnson's; Messrs. Lynch and Erskine, at the house of a friend, whose name I am unable to recollect; and Mrs. Harvard and myself, at Mr. John Keet's. The obliging and affectionate services of these much respected friends have made impressions upon our minds which will never be erased; and I gladly embrace the present opportunity of recording our expressions of grateful remembrance.

Before our separation, the Missionary party assembled to a family breakfast at the Bush Tavern. Surely, never did such a number of individuals, previously unknown to each other, more fully imbibe each other's spirit, and mutually engage each other's affections, through attachment to a common cause, than the party then assembled. We seemed to possess a source of felicity among ourselves, sufficient to command every requisite for the happiness of each other. But the satisfaction afforded by such a meeting was never again realized by us. It was the first and the last occasion on which the entire party was allowed to meet in this world. It pleased Providence to deny to us a repetition of the pleasure, to remind us, that even in our most pure and laudable pursuits and enjoyments, we are not exempt from disappointment.

During our stay at Portsmouth, the missionaries were employed on the Sabbath-days in preaching in the chapels of our connexion; large congregations attended, and manifested considerable interest in our undertaking; in the week days we were fully occupied in writing letters, and in making those necessary arrangements for our voyage which had been purposely deferred to the eve of our sailing.

As our departure from England did not take place so soon as we had expected, a valuable opportunity was afforded of receiving letters from our families and friends, as well as for more fully deliberating upon the important cause in which we had embarked. We had the pleasure to learn, that our relations and connexions had been enabled to resign us to God, and to the work of our choice; and that we were interested in their good wishes and prayers. As some of our friends were not previously reconciled to this sacrifice, our unexpected detention in England was accompanied by this pleasing circumstance, that it enabled us to become acquainted with their cordial acquiescence, at a much earlier period than we otherwise could have been.

Whether we indulged in retrospective or prospective regards, we felt no disposition to repent of our engagements. When standing on the beach, and, while looking on the ocean which rolled before us, an involuntary impatience would arise, to engage immediately in the employment to which we were dedicated. The fervency of our affections on this momentous subject was not the ebullition of fanaticism, which calculates upon the end without a due regard to the means necessary to effect it; it was the warmth of a *zeal* actuated by *knowledge* :—a *knowledge* of the *sure word of prophecy;* founded on the fidelity of God, and of the omnipotence of his providence and grace, when concurring to spread the word of life.

The encouraging letters we received from several judicious and valuable friends and ministers served to confirm us in these impressions and purposes. A well-timed present made to us by the Rev. Henry Moore is worthy of especial notice. It consisted of copies of an interesting tract, which he had translated from the French of Monsieur Esprit Flechier, Bishop of Nismes, intitled, " The Character of a true Missionary; in a Funeral Oration on Francis Xavier, Apostle of the Indies." The copy given to me I have carefully preserved. This present was most suitable, on account of the almost prophetic outline which it drew of the exemplary character and unwearied labours of our own Founder. Xavier and Coke present admirable models of zeal, ardour, and sacrifice, to all who succeed them in the missionary work. It was our peculiar privilege to have the latter as a living copy. I extract from " Mr. Clough's Account of Doctor Coke," the following description of his singular devotedness at this period:

" We stayed several days in Portsmouth before we went on board; during which period the whole attention of the Doctor was fixed upon his work, and he was unwilling to attend to any concerns which were not immediately connected with it. From morning to night his eye was fixed upon it, as the eye of the racer who continually keeps the prize in view. He would frequently address himself to me in language like the following: ' Brother Clough, what we are now doing I am certain is of God ; and therefore what our hands find to do in this cause, let us do it with all our might !' Here I may mention a circumstance which took place a little before we left London. As we were travelling in a coach, upon some business relative to the Asiatic work, in one part of our conversation I presented a small paper for him to read, which was not altogether connected with that object. ' Brother,' said the Doctor, ' I beg your pardon ; but excuse me: I AM DEAD TO ALL THINGS BUT ASIA.' Though I wished him to read the paper, yet I admired his unremitting zeal in so holy a cause. I confess it was one of the most powerful and instructive lessons to me, and necessary to be observed in my future life and conduct. I need not add any thing more about him while at Portsmouth. There are several who had an opportunity of observing his conduct and spirit, both in public and private, at that time, who are better able to do justice to such a combination of talent, holiness, and zeal."

The Doctor's last sermon in St. Peter's Chapel, Portsea, was peculiarly remarkable. It included a summary of his views in relation to the progress and triumph of the

Christian faith; and has since appeared to me as a spiritual manifesto, with which he opened his last missionary campaign. The chapel was greatly crowded. From the text, *Ethiopia shall soon stretch out her hands unto God,** (Psal. lxviii. 31,) the Doctor enlarged on the incalculable importance of the Missionary work; on the various openings for Missionary labours, which had presented themselves in different parts of the Pagan world; and on the assured success which shall attend all such labours, (notwithstanding any temporary difficulties) while prosecuted in the faith and spirit of the gospel.

Mrs. Harvard and myself had the happiness of accompanying the Doctor in his carriage, and of being present during the delivery of this animating discourse. The effect it had upon our minds may be easily conceived; it was that of abundant and joyful confirmation in our holy purpose. We beheld the yielding mists of error and wickedness breaking away from the moral horizon of the Pagan world; and the recovered slaves of besotted superstition and impurity raising up their adoring hands to the dawning splendour of the gospel-day! The prospect was in accordance with the promises of God: and it appeared to us perfectly easy for the omnipotent Saviour to fulfil all his gracious engagements to his church. We *staggered not at the promise through unbelief;* but said, *Even so, Lord Jesus; come quickly! Amen.*

Circumstances of a painful nature tended to afflict

---

* It is a singular fact, that a sermon preached by Doctor Coke at Birmingham, many years before, from this text, first directed the attention of that most excellent man, the late Rev. S. Pearce, of Birmingham, to the destitute state of the Heathen world. The Baptist Mission to India was formed shortly after; into the views of which he entered with the most devoted interest, and continued its indefatigable Secretary till his lamented decease.—*Vide Memoir of his Life, by the late* Rev. A. Fuller.

us, while waiting for the fleet; particularly the distressing state of Mrs. Ault's health, which deeply preyed upon the spirits of her affectionate husband, and which, by sympathy, we all shared. Her indisposition, which commenced shortly before their marriage, it was hoped would be but of short continuance.—Even after her arrival at Portsmouth, her health seemed to have improved; and, with grateful feelings to God, we had begun to look forward to complete recovery. Our hopes were not of long duration.—In a few days her complaint assumed an appearance which baffled the exercise of medical skill; and the only possibility of her recovery, in the opinion of the physician who was consulted, arose from her intended removal to a warmer climate. But apprehensions were entertained, that her reduced frame would yield to the complaint before that period could arrive.

At length, on Wednesday, December 29, we received directions to prepare for embarkation early the next morning. We met at the house of Mr. Keet, senior, at Portsmouth Point, where we were received with the most marked attention by that worthy family, and several other friends, who met us there. After uniting in prayer, we formed ourselves into two parties, and proceeded to the beach. Owing to poor Mrs. Ault's illness, she was obliged to be conveyed in a post-chaise. After an affecting parting, we entered our respective pilot-boats, and were conducted on board the two ships, then lying at St. Helen's, exchanging the signal of affectionate *adieu* with our companions on the water, and our friends on the shore, until we were out of sight of each other.

CHAP III.

Commencement of the Voyage—Sea-sickness—Scrutiny of motives and object—Doctor Coke—Extract from Madame Guion—Portuguese Vulgate—The Doctor's Journal.—Mr. Clough's Account—The situation of a Missionary during a voyage—Public worship on the Lord's-day—Services in the Lady Melville—Mr. Squance—Cautious reserve with respect to the Doctor—Journal—Mr. Clough's elucidation--Sabath-evening reading--Social meetings for prayer, &c; in the author's cabin—Behaviour of the Passengers—Encouraging effects of Christian conversation with them—Note on Grace before Meat—Ship Newspaper—Signals—Mrs. Ault's illness—Visit from Messrs. Ault and Squance—Mrs. Ault's death—Her amiable and devout character—Her death greatly lamented—Its effect on the Doctor's mind—The health of Mr. Squance seriously affected—Visits the Cabalva—We pass the Equator—The visit of Neptune, &c.—Isles of Bourbon and France—Another mission contemplated for Mr. Squance—He recovers, and returns on board the Melville—Doctor Coke's attentions to the spiritual interests of the Soldiers on board—Pleasing results—Melancholy cases—Asiatic Journal for June, 1820—Effects of intoxication—A singular interview—The Doctor's hopes in reference to the Soldiers—Separated from the fleet, and rejoin—" *O cabo dos tormentados* "—Volcano—Second approach to the Line—Illness of Mrs. Harvard, and of the Author—Dr. Coke's anxiety and prayers—They recover—the Doctor discovers symptoms of illness—Solemn and affecting parting—His Death and Funeral.

THE commencement of our voyage was marked by nothing unusual to persons in similar circumstances. With the exception of the venerable Doctor, we were all more or less affected with sea-sickness; a complaint which is perhaps, for the time, one of the most distressing affections to which the human system is liable. Mrs. Harvard's share of this illness was so considerable, that she was, in consequence, a close inmate of our cabin for several weeks, During this indisposition, the recent parting from our dear friends and country frequently passed in review before us; nor could we, without momentary pain, look back upon all those endearments which crowded around us in our native land, and which, for aught we knew to the contrary, we had sacrificed for ever.

It was then, perhaps, more seriously than before, that we scrutinized the character of the work to which we had devoted ourselves, and the motives by which we were influenced, in engaging in it. Fluctuations of mind may be expected in the present state of imperfection; but our convictions of duty were invariably the same: and, being satisfied that we had followed the Divine direction, the result was an establishment of purpose. By the active and persevering example of our venerable leader, a regular course of study and employment was marked out for us. And whatever difficulties it presented to us, from the novelty of our circumstances, it was far otherwise with him. Doctor Coke was, in the most harmless and honourable sense of the word, a " citizen of the world;" for he was always at home, if he could but find employment suited to his sacred office and pursuits. This was a subject on which he frequently conversed; and, in illustration of his views, I remember he once gave us this favourite quotation from Madame Guion :—

> " O thou, by long experience tried,
> Near whom no grief can long abide:
> My Love!—how full of sweet content
> I pass my years of banishment!
>
> " All scenes alike engaging prove,
> To souls impress'd with sacred love:
> Where'er they dwell, they dwell in Thee,
> In heaven, in earth, or on the sea.

> "To me remains nor place, nor time,
> My country is in every clime;
> I can be calm, and free from care
> On any shore, since God is there.
>
> "While place we seek, or place we shun,
> The soul finds happiness in none;
> But, with a God to guide our way,
> 'Tis equal joy to go, or stay.
>
> "Could I be cast where Thou art not,
> That were, indeed, a dreadful lot;
> But regions none remote I call,
> Secure of meeting God in all.
>
> "My country, Lord, art thou alone;
> Nor other can I claim, or own:
> The point where all my wishes meet—
> My Law, my Love, life's only sweet!
>
> "I hold by nothing here below:
> Appoint my journey, and I go:
> Though pierc'd by scorn, oppress'd by pride,
> I feel thee good—feel nought beside.
>
> "No frowns of men can hurtful prove
> To souls on fire with heavenly love:
> Though men and devils both condemn,
> No gloomy days arise from them.
>
> "Ah! then to His embrace repair;
> My soul thou art no stranger there:
> There, love divine shall be thy guard,
> And peace and safety thy reward."

These lines exhibit the principles by which his devoted mind was influenced and regulated in his great work: and, it need not be added, how essential the ascendancy of such principles is to the proper discharge of those self-denying duties which such a work demands. We were thus favoured with a constant model of cheerful piety, and industrious zeal, worthy of our closest imitation. The diligent and critical perusal of the Portuguese Vulgate, a copy of which in several volumes he had procured with some difficulty and expense, with occasional epistolary correspondence, formed his general occupation. These were varied by excursions on the quarter-deck, and by the exercise of that lively and interesting talent in friendly and enlightened conversation, for which he was always so deservedly celebrated.

An extract from the Doctor's Journal, written at the commencement of our voyage, will record the ardent and devout feelings of his mind at that time.

" In the ship in which I have sailed there are above four hundred souls. About fifty of the sailors are Lascars, and chiefly, if not entirely, I am afraid, (for I have been talking with some of them) Mahometans. The gospel-door, as it respects that people, seems entirely closed. Their religion was established by the sword; and I fear that the sword must go through their nations, before they will bow to the sceptre of Jesus.

" I have a most charming study. It has two large windows that open from the stern to the sea; and my elbow-chair and my table are placed in the most convenient situation possible. I have seen, I think, seventeen ships of our fleet sailing after us. Here I employ all my time, and nearly the whole of it in reading and writing Portuguese, excepting my hours of meditation; which, indeed, I can hardly except; for my chief study is my Portuguese Bible. O how sweet is the word of God! I have loved it since I came into this ship more than ever I did before:—

> " Jesus gives me, in his word,
> Food and med'cine, shield and sword."

The following testimony from Mr. Clough's Account of Doctor Coke, is too expressive and valuable to be omitted :—

"When we had arrived safely on board, I was ready to conclude, that every anxious thought had taken its flight from the Doctor. I procured the carpenter to fix up his bed. After he had taken proper refreshment, he retired to rest, and slept as comfortably as if on shore. The next morning he arose, and commenced his usual engagements, as one " 'midst busy multitudes alone." The ship's company began soon to notice him, as being a singular character. When we came into the Bay of Biscay, and had to contend with gales of wind and tempestuous seas, the Doctor seemed alike unmoved, and pursued his labours of prayer, study, reading, and writing, with as much settled composure of mind, as though he had been on land. Now it was, that the Doctor, who had been, from the singularity of his habits, almost a suspected person, began to gain the good opinion, attention, and respect of all the passengers. His polite and easy address, and his attainments in literature, were conspicuous traits in his character: and these, together with the sacred office he sustained, attracted the veneration of all."

Notwithstanding we were all employed as our circumstances would admit, yet the inactivity of our life, compared with what we had been accustomed to in England, and the absence of those public and social religious services with which we had been favoured in our native land, were often sources of depression to us; and, indeed, to a certain extent, a cause of spiritual declension. Persons about to enter on similar stations, have need to be *prepared* for the loss of most of those devotional excitements which are so abundantly enjoyed in Christian association and communion. Without such a calculation, there is great danger lest a spirit unfavourable to ardent piety should imperceptibly usurp an influence over the soul of the isolated individual. It will be obvious, thus influenced, how every additional day will increasingly unfit him for the arduous task of retaining his integrity, and of surmounting the evils to which he will be exposed.

In such circumstances, religious worship is to a Christian mind truly delightful. At an early hour the usual flag was hoisted at the mizen, indicating that the harbinger of another Christian Sabbath had gained our horizon, and had risen to bless our race. Among the crew and passengers the customary labours and pursuits were suspended, except those which were indispensable, and the usual clothing exchanged for the Sunday suit. A large awning was generally spread; and chairs for the passengers, and planks for the crew and soldiers, were placed on the quarter-deck, with a table and chair in the centre, behind the capstan, for the person officiating. Flags of various colours were hung over the side of the vessel, to prevent the sun from proving inconvenient; and nothing was omitted by the officers which could promote the convenience of those who assembled. The other ships in the fleet, I believe, in general adopted the same measures. It was pleasing on a Sabbath morning to behold so many floating congregations of Christian worshippers; and to see the flags of the different vessels floating in the breeze, in honour of that Divine command which ordains, *the seventh day is the Sabbath of the Lord thy God.*

At the appointed hour the ship's bell warned us to prayers, and every one took his proper station. Beneath that canvas canopy, often have we *worshipped the Father in spirit and in truth;* edified by the Service arranged by the pious reformers of our Church; while the Doctor, with his large folio Portuguese Prayer-Book* in

---

* The Doctor used the Portuguese Prayer-Book while hearing the Prayers read, by way of familiarizing himself with devotional expressions in that language.

his hand, maintained an intercourse with Heaven in a language not his own; his venerable lips repeating, "*Oh Senhor, tem misericordia de nos.*"*

This was the only public service which we had on board our vessel. In the Lady Melville, the remainder of our party had an opening for a sermon in the evening, in addition to a service similar to ours in the morning. It is due to the character of that active and valuable Missionary, Mr. Squance, to insert the mention which Doctor Coke has made in his Journal of this opening:

"Mr. Squance, I must here observe, gave us a pleasing account of the influence of religion in the Lady Melville, among the cabin passengers. There were eight officers of very respectable rank in the army in the ship, who had (as far as I could learn from his modest narrative) taken a liking to his manners, address, and conversation, so far as to offer him their large cabin on the second deck, to preach in on Sunday evenings. The cabin at those times was crowded; and good, I doubt not, was done."

To this may be subjoined the more detailed account contained in the official letter sent to the Missionary Committee after our arrival in India:

"Those of our own company who were on board the Melville, began morning and evening prayers on their entering into the ship, and also class-meetings every Sabbath. This they always found a soul-reviving and strengthening means of grace. They had from one to three persons who met with them. Their evening meetings were generally attended by several soldiers; and, for a few Sabbath evenings, their cabin was very well filled. On Sunday, January 30,

---

* "Lord have mercy upon us."

several of the military and ship officers sent a note, informing them, if agreeable, they would attend the evening prayers. To this request the brethren cheerfully acceded. Brother Squance, after reading a chapter, spoke about twenty minutes, on Heb. ii. 3. After the conclusion of the meeting, they expressed thankfulness. On the next Sabbath evening, as the cabin was too small, the military officers requested them to accept of their large cabin, as several more ladies and gentlemen intended to attend the lecture. The captain of the ship, with most of the passengers, and several of the ship's officers attended. The next Sabbath evening, as one of the military officers was unwell, the brethren were requested to stand in the steerage. This was what they anxiously desired; as all the soldiers and sailors who wished to hear might there have an opportunity. From this time (Feb. 6) each brother preached in his turn during the voyage. For these opportunities, the brethren were truly thankful to God. They also commenced the duty of visiting the sick, and continued this practice till they left the ship. They found this also to be profitable to themselves."

While we rejoiced that our companions in the Melville were thus highly favoured, we felt that in the Cabalva we were rather differently circumstanced.—At that time, there was comparatively but a small portion of favourable feeling towards missionary enterprize in India. Many serious apprehensions were entertained for the result of those attempts; and the public character of our venerable leader—a Missionary of no common stamp—might possibly have occasioned a greater degree of cautious reserve with respect to himself, than it can be supposed would be excited by individuals less conspicuous and less known. Here therefore, was a call for a patient and cheerful resignation and submission, to what appeared unavoidable. But it was not a submission of apathy, or unconcern for the spiritual interests of our daily associates. The Doctor fully expressed his own feelings, and those of his two companions, when he entered in his Journal— " We have among us some Portuguese, natives of India; I wish we may be useful to them. In the dining-room our number is twenty-six, inclusive of the Captain and his two first officers. They are very polite— but, oh! we want to save souls!"

In accordance with this ardent desire to promote the best interests of men, Mr. Clough relates :—

" On the second Sabbath of our voyage Doctor Coke proposed to give a short lecture upon some passage of Scripture, the next Sunday, after the Captain had read prayers. This offer was not refused; but the weather being unfavourable, we were prevented from having service in the intended manner. However, the Doctor's offer was not afterwards adverted to; and this was a subject of rather painful reflection to him; but he observed to us, ' I believe our Captain has his reasons for it.' Since the Doctor's death, Captain Birch informed me, that his instructions from his employers were, that he should 'go on just as usual.' The Captain added, ' It has frequently been a matter of pain to me, to hinder so excellent and valuable a man from doing all the good in his power. I cannot express the respect and regard I had for Doctor Coke, since I possessed the honour and very great pleasure of knowing him.' But many of the passengers were disappointed; and frequently expressed their sorrow and regret, that Doctor Coke could not fulfil his promise."*

The politeness of Captain Birch discovered, how-

---

* This extract from Mr. Clough's Account, and the preceding paragraph, are mutually explanatory of each other.

ever a medium; and on our esteemed friend's making some reference to his Commentary on the Old and New Testament, the Captain requested to see it. Mr. Clough immediately produced his copy; and, on the Doctor's proposal, the company sat one Sunday evening, and heard him read a part of his excellent and admirable *General Preface* to the New Testament, in which they manifested considerable interest. The Doctor was too judicious to read a greater portion at that time than was likely to be agreeable; and the consequence was, that on the succeeding Sunday evening, the Captain, in a very obliging manner, requested the Doctor to continue his reading; the whole of the company coinciding as before. This request was politely repeated every succeeding Sunday evening, until the *General Preface* and *Introduction* had been gone through. By a prudent division into suitable portions of the excellent matter they contain, the conclusion of many of our Sabbaths was rendered interesting and profitable.

In addition to this, our regular meeting for singing and prayer, which was generally held every evening in my cabin, must not be forgotten. The Doctor never absented himself from these meetings; and Mrs. Harvard and myself esteem it an honour to reflect, that in his last days we were so favoured as to have so distinguished an individual as our daily guest. Often have we made an arm-chair fast to our sofa, that he might not fall from the violent motion of the vessel; in which he has sat, with clasped hands, placidly and cheerfully worshipping God; secure in the conviction, that the eye of Omniscience was upon us for good.— On these occasions we felt a union of spirit with the universal church, and realized the enjoyments of heaven upon earth. Our fellow-passengers were too generous to consider this as an interruption; notwithstanding our cabin formed a part of the roundhouse or cuddy*. They would sometimes listen to our evening song, and kindly compliment us on our singing. At their own request, some were occasionally admitted. I cannot, even now, without deep interest, look back on those devotional concerts.

Our general intercourse with the other passengers was of the most agreeable nature. An universal inclination to oblige pervaded the entire party. This disposition was infused through the whole circle by the dignified, conciliating, and engaging manners of our amiable commander; whose friendly attentions caused our days even at sea to glide rapidly away. Among other kindnesses, there was one which should not be silently passed over—*the freedom with which we were suffered to pursue our peculiar path of duty.* No compromise of our sacred character was ever required of us. We were always recognized as ministers of religion; and were permitted and expected to act accordingly.† The venerable Doctor was invariably called upon to ask a blessing, and to return thanks, at our meals. He made it a point to be first at the table, in order that the company might not be induced to depart from this excellent custom; and sometimes called on Mr. Clough and myself, in turn, to take part with him in the Christian duty. The Doctor knew too much of men and things to make this a tedious

---

* The state-room, or apartment of general resort.

† There was something so honourable, gentlemanly, and polite, in this line of conduct, and so utterly unlike some of those associations (erroneously called *genteel*) into which I have since sometimes been brought, in the way of duty, both by sea and land, that I cannot possibly restrain my ardent admiration of the liberal and candid behaviour which we experienced on board the Hon. Company's Ship, the Cabalva, commanded by Jonathan Birch, Esq.

and burthensome exercise.* Though we had not those public opportunities we desired, of declaring to them the sacred truths which formed the basis of our own hopes and consolations; yet there were few of our respected fellow-voyagers with whom we did not, at different times, and at favourable opportunities, speak on religious subjects, and in some cases with gratifying effect.

Several of the party with whom we had the happiness to sail, were persons of talent and reading, and also cheerfully communicative. From the resources of their invention and research, a few of them interested their companions by the compilation of a weekly newspaper, which was always read at the dining-table on a Saturday evening. The perfect delicacy with which this otherwise hazardous amusement was conducted, reflected high honour on its managers. Doctor Coke and his family were generally present at the publication of this Saturday Evening Gazette; and, after they had taken their wine and water, retired to rest immediately, before the commencement of the usual melody of—" *Saturday night.*"

Between the two divisions of the missionary family, there naturally subsisted a mutual and strong anxiety

* I remember a large and respectable party in India on one occasion being much disconcerted, through a want of judgment in this respect. After the company had sat down to dinner, our excellent host requested a reverend gentleman present to ask a blessing; who immediately rose, and standing behind his chair, made a long prayer of some minutes' continuance. Many could not avoid feeling much concern, that the covers had been removed before he commenced his exercise. Some of the dishes were unfortunately spoiled. Several of the guests, expecting but " *a short grace,*" and resting on their hands, half-raised from their chairs, exhibited a most ludicrous but mortifying appearance, as they looked at each other, and wondered when the end would be. Should the reader be of a lively imagination, he has probably already realized the whole scene!

to be assured of the comfort and happiness of each other: and, whenever the two vessels came near enough, each party was seen, eager to discover the health and circumstances of the other. Previously to our leaving England, we had agreed on a set of general signals, as it respected health, &c. The *white* handkerchief was to be the token of health: the *coloured* one, of the reverse. It was with pleasure that from the Cabalva we were in the general able to suspend the signal of health and peace: but it was not so with the Lady Melville. Mrs. Ault's trying situation precluded the use of the cheering white handkerchief; and we all felt the tenderest sympathy on her account. As she had lived to reach the tropical climate, and had arrived very near the Equinoctial line, we were not without hopes of her recovery. But her constitution had rapidly sank beneath the ravages of the consumption; and all the intelligence we could obtain of her by signal was of a melancholy kind.

Towards the end of the month of January, the Missionaries on board the Lady Melville had the pleasure to see Mrs. Ault rise from her long confinement. From the time she went on board, until then, she had been violently afflicted with sea-sickness, and was in consequence much reduced; yet she sat up again for a short time on the next day; but was quite sensible of her rapid decline, and was happy and resigned to the Divine will. On the fifth of February, during a calm, Mr. Ault (having been kindly accommodated with a boat by Captain Lochner,) accompanied by Mr. Squance, paid us a visit. The interview, as may be supposed, was both pleasing and painful. Mrs. Ault was still alive; and her sanguine and affectionate husband even then indulged some faint hopes that the torrid zone, under the Divine blessing, would restore her.

Our friends returned to the Melville with our best wishes. But these were not to be realized. God who *doth all things well*, had otherwise determined. Five days afterwards, as we sat at breakfast, an officer came in, and informed us, that the Lady Melville had hoisted her flag half-mast high, as the signal of death. The company, who had known of Mrs. Ault's illness, concluded that the signal was to announce her decease. The vessel was too far off to allow any communication, and the weather was unfavourable. We retired immediately to our cabin, where we wept the loss of so excellent a missionary sister, and shared the grief of her widowed husband. In a few days Mr. Clough and myself took advantage of another calm, to visit our friends in the Melville. Mr. Ault was much resigned, though greatly afflicted at his heavy loss. To him it was inexpressibly consolatory that his valuable wife died triumphant in the faith, and that her resignation was most entire.

The happy and prepared state of mind evinced by Mrs. Ault, did not prevent her departure from being a subject of long-continued regret. To all it was, doubtless, a matter of mournful reflection; and to none more so than to Mrs. Harvard; who had often expressed the pleasure she anticipated from a more intimate acquaintance with her in a foreign land; where she expected she would be almost the only female friend and companion with whom she could be favoured, under the peculiar trials and difficulties which might befal them.

This painful dispensation corrected still more our views and prospects; and tended, if possible, to unite us more closely to each other in the bonds of sympathizing affection. This was especially the case with our venerable leader, Doctor Coke. It was evident, from the very commencement of our acquaintance, that for us who had so fully entered into his views and intentions respecting an Eastern Mission, he had conceived almost a parental regard. He seemed ever to identify our comfort with his own; and had often assured us, that all the pecuniary resources of his own private fortune were as much at our service, while in this great work, as at his own. The inroad upon our party, made by the decease of the excellent Mrs. Ault, showed how closely we were entwined around his heart, and how inconsiderable he considered the sacrifice of any thing which might be necessary to the preservation of the comfort and lives of his missionary children. He formed himself after the model of the first Founder of Christian missions; of whom the Evangelist records, that, *having loved his own which were in the world, he loved them unto the end.*

As the month of February advanced, the health of Mr. Squance appeared to be considerably affected. The change of climate produced in him an excessive languor, and other very distressing symptoms. His case was in some respects similar to that of Mrs. Ault's. From repeated colds, taken when engaged in the ministerial work in his native country, and from neglecting to attend to the early symptoms of disease, (a neglect which is so common and destructive to young ministers) he had contracted a cough, from which, probably, he will never be wholly free, until his arrival in that land where the inhabitants shall no more say, *I am sick!* With him therefore the entrance upon a new climate could not fail of being a matter of some concern, especially from its first effects upon his constitution. Though his weak frame often exercised his Missionary companions with painful fears on his account, it was no cause of uneasiness to himself. He was happy in the consolations of religion, in the affectionate esteem of his associates, and in the reflection, that he had obeyed the call of Providence, by engaging in the Mission: and, in consequence, he was enabled to leave events to Almighty God.

The Doctor could not, however, be at rest, while another of the Missionary family remained in doubtful circumstances, and absent from his own immediate eye. He was aware of the hospitality which he experienced from Captain Lochner; and had been informed of the almost fraternal attention of his medical man, Mr. Wright; but he too greatly feared the tendency of the disorder, to be satisfied without daily reports of its progress, which could not always be obtained while he continued in a separate ship. Our own polite and generous Captain soon perceived the concern of the Doctor for the precarious state of Mr. Squance's health, and in the most handsome manner immediately removed every difficulty. The missionary invalid was in consequence invited to pay us a visit for a short time, which he did on the 5th of March, and was accommodated by Mr. Clough in his cabin; the attention of whom, to the comfort and recovery of his sick companion, could not have been exceeded by the nearest relative.

Mr. Squance from care and quietness soon derived considerable advantage, and was able to join our little parties in my cabin. He was, however, restrained from singing and public prayer, and all violent exertions of the lungs. In these respects our venerable leader was remarkably watchful over him. On one occasion, when we had been singing in his absence, he was grieved even to warm displeasure, under the impression, that Mr. Squance had been permitted to join in the ensnaring and prohibited exercise:—but on an explanation being given, his natural flow of kindness and friendship again pusued its wonted course.

Early in February we crossed the Equinoctial line,

in about 27 degrees, west longitude. The usual ceremonies were performed by the sailors on those who now crossed the line for the first time. One of them, personating Neptune, drawn by his *tritons*, paid a visit to the Captain, and obtained full permission to enfranchise such of the crew as had not previously been made free of his dominions. The ceremony was by no means a desirable one; and the passengers were of course not expected to submit to it. A low-minded captain, in some inferior line of maritime service, may *sometimes* be met with, who will rank his *passengers* with his *crew* on such an occasion; but this will never be suffered by any commander of respectability. The sailors, however, expected a gratuity from the passengers, in order to defray the expenses of their merriment; and when we had Neptune in our cabin, for the purpose of giving him our donation, we endeavoured to direct his mind to higher things.

On approaching the Isles of Bourbon and France, Doctor Coke, from an apprehension that an Indian climate would not agree with Mr. Squance's constitution in its weakened state, contemplated landing him to commence a mission in one of those islands; and the Mauritius was nearly decided on. Mr. Squance, being in some measure prepared for such a mission, by a tolerable acquaintance with the French language, and our general library having been furnished with several valuable French works, every thing seemed to concur. But his health had so much improved, that we began to entertain sanguine hopes of his ability to endure the climate for which he was originally intended; and on April 14, he returned to the Melville, deeply impressed with the kindness he had experienced on board the Cabalva.

I believe it is a regulation made by the Honourable

the East India Company, that each of their own vessels shall carry out a certain number of recruits for their army in India, according to their several rates of tonnage. Doctor Coke in his Journal, speaking of the ship's company, says, " Of these, two hundred are soldiers; who, excepting a very few, are, as far as I can learn, young lads from Ireland, of the Roman Catholic persuasion." To this class of men the venerable Doctor directed his peculiar attention; and, by the active enquiries of Mr. Clough, he soon learned that a few of them had attended the ministry of our preachers, and that some had even been members of our society; but, from temporal distress, or declension in piety, had abandoned their Christian friends, and finally their native land. These persons appeared to be cast by Providence in our way; and Doctor Coke appointed a suitable time to meet them for religious conversation in Mr. Clough's cabin; being the most convenient, because contiguous to that part of the ship where the soldiers were lodged.

These meetings were of a peculiar character. Several of those who had declined in their apprehensions and enjoyments of religion, and some of whom viewed themselves as outcasts and exiles from their native land, considered it as no small mercy, that God had thus met them in their flight with those valuable religious ordinances from which they had withdrawn, and that, too, in the centre of the vast ocean! Their consciences were again awakened; they were brought to a proper sense of their fallen condition, and their minds were again excited to seek for the divine mercy and salvation. It was with great pleasure and gratitude, that they witnessed the weekly return of this valuable meeting, and attended the important instructions of so aged and experienced a servant of God; and one or two others of their comrades were disposed to join with them. From the Doctor's private Journal I find the following persons composed this meeting :—" Corporal John Clinton—Corporal Charles Whiting—Watson the smith—Price, Clinton— Clark—Lowry—Jones—George Harnden — William Davis — Cornelius Vowles." Others occasionally attended, whose names were not inserted in the Doctor's list.

Those who knew our venerable friend, will suppose how much he would be interested in the spiritual welfare of these wanderers, so unexpectedly brought beneath his care. The performance of the varied duties of the ministerial office formed the work in which his soul delighted. In this work, no difficulties were to him insuperable—no condescension disgraceful—no labours toilsome. Though he had to descend by a ladder to the place of meeting, which was often, from his age and infirmities, and the motion of the ship, a perilous undertaking, yet he was always punctual; and generally returned with a smiling countenance, and a mind encouraged and refreshed.

There are few situations in which the strange and distressing vicissitudes of human life are more strikingly manifested, than in vessels which carry out recruits for our Indian armies. Many of these unpitied men have been in circumstances of ease and affluence; but, having fallen into poverty or disgrace among their own immediate connexions, choose an ignoble exile on a far distant and foreign shore; where, perhaps under some assumed name,[*] they pine away in disease and sorrow; not affording the least clue by which their mournful relatives can trace their flight, or improve their condition. I copy the following from Doctor Coke's private Journal, concealing the real names,

---

[*] Asiatic Journal, for June 1820.

"S——, taps a hogshead of rum, for drink on deck, in the presence of some of the passengers. Discovered by a Lascar—flogged. Father, a man of some substance in Scotland; himself educated at Islington and Reading; once a lieutenant in the S—— militia. O drink!"

The countenance of one of these recruits appeared familiar to my recollection. I enquired, and found it to be Cornelius Vowles. I immediately recollected the name, and took an opportunity of calling him into our cabin, that I might satisfy my mind. Some years ago, my father conducted a large Sunday-school, for the Miss More's, at Wedmore, in Somersetshire; and, as a reward to the more deserving scholars, educated some of them on the week-days, with his own regular pupils. It proved, that this Cornelius Vowles was one of my father's gratuitous scholars, and one of my early play-mates. As I had not seen him for upwards of thirteen years, I could not but be affected with our meeting thus on the wide ocean. How wider still, the difference of our present circumstances! I felt for him the remains of former friendship, and both on the voyage, and after our arrival in India, endeavoured to show him kindness. Another of the recruits was a member of a respectable family in Kent, of whom I had some slight knowledge.

Though in that part of Doctor Coke's Journal which has already been published, no reference is made to the attentions which were paid to the soldiers on board our ship, yet the Doctor appears to have borne the subject in his mind; as he adds, after noticing the success of our friends in the Melville—" As to *our* ship, I hope to have something good to say of it, when we reach Bombay." In his correspondence with some of his intimate friends, he attached considerable importance to that commencement of the Indian work, which

would, in fact, thus be made even on board the ship.—
Looking on this band of pious soldiers thus attached
to us, he promised himself powerful auxiliaries in
their future prayers in our behalf; and in their holy
and upright deportment before the Pagan Asiatics;
among whom they would shine as lights in a benighted
world.

Towards the latter end of March our vessel was
separated from the fleet, which occasioned us serious
apprehensions for the safety of our friends in the Lady
Melville; each party was apprehensive that we should
not join company again, till our arrival in Bombay.
But, in a day or two, our minds were relieved from
uneasiness, by discovering the fleet astern; the Captain
shortened sail till they came up with us. The Melville
no sooner came near enough, than we immediately
hoisted our signal of health, and gladly observed theirs'
flying out of the cabin window, in return.

During the latter part of March, and the whole of the
month of April, we were tossed about with violent gales
of wind, and sometimes by storms of considerable force.
Being in the latitudes about the Cape of Good Hope,
at this time of the year, we felt all that the Portuguese
bard has so finely described. No wonder, that the early
navigators of that nation gave so terrible a name to
that projecting part of the South African Continent, as,
" *O Cabo dos Tormentados*," " the Cape of the Tormented
Ones." In the stormy season, the winds here are tremendously violent, and the sea literally rolls mountains
high. The whole fleet on one occasion ran at the rate
of ten miles an hour; producing an awfully grand and
interesting scene. Our vessel during this run had only
two top-sails set, and these closely reefed. We seemed
to be at the mercy of one of those raging storms, in which
vessels have been known to go down head foremost, in

the midst of their progress, to be heard of no more! How supporting to the mind, in such circumstances to be able to sing:—

> "The God that rules on high,
> That all the earth surveys,
> That rides upon the stormy sky,
> And calms the roaring seas.
>
> "This awful God is ours,
> Our father and our love,
> He will send down his heavenly powers,
> To carry us above."

On Sunday the 28th instant, we passed the Isle of Bourbon. In the evening it was supposed we were only forty miles from the shore, and the eruptions of the volcano were distinctly perceived by the naked eye. The streams of this subterranean fire were issuing forth from its crater with very great velocity, shaded by immense volumes of smoke. The mountain being high, the flames first had the appearance of a large comet in the heavens, with a blazing fire in its train. It was seen the whole of the evening; the fire sometimes bursting out very fiercely, but at other times appearing but feebly and dimly. The violent tornados to which these latitudes are subject are supposed to be occasioned by this boiling fiery cavern. How many mysteries yet remain unexplained in the kingdom of nature! The following morning Commodore Craig telegraphed the fleet; but, on consulting the signal books, to ascertain the nature of the communication, it was found to be a little pleasantry relative to the volcano: "*Did you see Vulcan at work last night?*"

In our second approach to the Line, we again suffered much from the change of temperature; which was rendered the more oppressive by the frequent calms with which our voyage was retarded. Mrs. Harvard was seized with illness, in about 10 degrees south, and such was the severity of the attack, that serious apprehensions were entertained for her recovery; but by the Divine blessing on the attentions of Mr. Arnett, the surgeon of the ship, she was restored. Doctor Coke manifested in this affliction all the concern of an affectionate parent. His visits to our cabin were frequent; and if he perceived her to be enervated or depressed, he strove to animate and revive her, either by some pious reflection, or by the relation of some cheerful anecdote of his own past adventures in the Missionary work, invariably concluding each visit with prayer.

On Mrs. Harvard's recovery I was attacked with a violent fever, and about the 25th of April was confined to my bed. The disorder rendered me delirious for three or four days. The disease was most probably occasioned by my sitting in a draught of air when very warm; a circumstance which I mention, as a caution to other inexperienced travellers, for it nearly cost me my life. It was naturally a severe trial to Mrs. Harvard, but the Lord mercifully supported her mind. The passengers were remarkably kind to her; and the ladies payed her many friendly and consoling attentions. An excellent gentleman, who now holds an official situation in the Bombay Presidency, as we were on short allowance of water, presented us with half-a-dozen bottles, part of a stock which he had brought from England. From the excessive thirst which I suffered at that time, this was more valuable to us than any quantity of the choicest wines could have been.

I should not have considered my illness of sufficient importance to occupy a place in this narrative, were it not for the anxious solicitude which was displayed for its removal by our venerable and beloved friend; whose own *departure,* so contrary to all our hopes, was now so near *at hand*. It was evident, that the Doctor feared the result of my illness. His earnest and repeated prayers were constantly offered at my bed side. I remember, during an interval of relief from disordered reason, hearing him present his supplications to heaven, in language something like the following:—" Lord spare our dear Brother Harvard—spare him for thy glory—if it be consistent with thy will, do not take another* of our party—Oh Lord spare him for Asia— spare him for Ceylon—spare him for the glory of thy great name in the conversion of the poor heathen.— Amen." It pleased God to hear the prayers of his servant. My disorder experienced a favourable issue; and he rejoiced in the prospect of seeing me raised up, as it were, from the borders of eternity. But ah! how short-sighted and insecure are we in the present state! Doctor Coke never saw me again out of my own apartment! The Missionary family was to be lessened still. *Another* was yet to be taken! Death had received his commission.

On Sunday, the 1st of May, Mrs. Harvard yielding to our earnest persuasions, left my cabin for the first time since my illness, for the purpose of taking an airing on the quarter-deck. Upon her return, she mentioned to me the visible alteration in the countenance of the Doctor, which she remarked, as she observed him on the deck. In the evening the Doctor, as usual, came into our cabin and prayed. He would hardly acknowledge that he was ill, but spoke of taking some tincture of rhubarb, which he did. Our venerable friend had complained of cold, from the chilling effects of his own fine linen shirts, when damp from excessive perspiration, and had consulted Mrs. Harvard on having some made of calico, when we should reach Bombay. In the mean

---

* In allusion to Mrs. Ault's decease.

time, she begged him to use some of mine; and he took a few with him into his own cabin for that purpose.

The next morning, May 2d, Mrs. Harvard, on going to see the Doctor, found him in his cabin, sitting pensively in his elbow-chair, with his head on one of his hands. She was naturally surprised at seeing him unemployed, and expressed her sorrow at finding him so unwell. The Doctor, who always displayed a peculiar affection towards Mrs. H., from the time she consented to accompany us, appeared grieved that she had discovered his illness; and summoning his native cheerfulness, replied, that he was obliged to her—he felt rather poorly—but hoped it would soon go off. He then proposed a walk on deck; but he appeared so weak, as to be hardly able to support himself. It was apparent, that his wish was, if possible, to conceal his indisposition, lest it should occasion us pain.

The Doctor did not omit his usual visit to us in the evening; and on entering our cabin, he said to Mrs. H. on observing that she looked more cheerful than she had been; " Your countenance, Sister Harvard, is a good barometer; I need not ask how Brother Harvard is : I can always tell by your countenance."

We perceived the languor of disease, notwithstanding his evident efforts to conceal it. He sat for a short time in occasional conversation, but evidently in a state of great relaxation and debility. I was lying on our sofa-bed, very weak; and imagined the Doctor experienced a momentary dejection. To give the conversation a cheerful turn, I observed to him, how great an obligation he had conferred upon me, *in giving me so good a wife;* and how considerably my recent affliction had been lessened by her affectionate offices of tenderness. My attempt succeeded. His natural and amiable vivacity immediately played upon his countenance. He then rose, as though to embrace the opportunity of parting from us with cheerfulness; and, taking us each by the hand, with a solemn but heavenly smile, gave us his blessing, and exhorted us each to be thankful to the Lord, that we had been so happily united together! Thus closed our earthly intercourse with our venerable and beloved missionary friend and father!*

Mr. Clough accompanied him to his cabin, to see that nothing was wanting for his comfort. Being of opinion that the Doctor lay with too many clothes on his bed, he most affectionately remonstrated with him, and begged permission to take some of them off; but the Doctor declined it, and requested him not to take that trouble. Mr. C. then requested to be allowed to sit up with him; but, thanking him for the offer, he said that was not at all necessary; and that he did not doubt he should be better in the morning. After taking some medicine, he wished Mr. Clough good night; desiring him to go and pray that the medicine might have a salutary effect. Some little time after, the servant who waited on the Doctor took him in a small glass of weak brandy and water, which he drank in bed. This was the only time we remember him to have taken spirits during the voyage. No doubt he felt his system extremely oppressed, and conceived

---

* " The Rev. Mr. ———, once overhearing a man and his wife, whom he had married, violently quarreling and lamenting the day that had brought them together, went immediately to them, and returned them his marriage fees, declaring that he could not comfortably retain any advantage from an event, which they both agreed in deploring as an irreparable misfortune!" To this, the scene I have attempted to describe forms a most complete contrast. I am thankful we were so highly privileged, as to be united by such an eminent and devoted man; and that being domiciliated with us, he lived to see us happy. The idea that perhaps the happiness of our union, thus brought under his notice at our last interview, may possibly have afforded him some emotions of satisfaction in his last hours, is truly gratifying to us.

it would assist the medicine, which he had ordered for himself. He was usually his own physician, having in his early years been educated for the medical profession.

But how shall I record the events of the following memorable day, Tuesday, May the 3d? About six o'clock in the morning, Captain Birch sent for Mr. Clough, and communicated to him the distressing intelligence of Doctor Coke's death. He was discovered by the servant, on his going to call him at half-past five, which was his usual practice, lying on the floor of the cabin, in a lifeless state! Mr. Clough, having himself suffered so much from the shock, was at a loss how to give me the information, without some risk, in my debilitated state; and particularly without some danger to Mrs. Harvard. He endeavoured to draw me out of my cabin, but in vain. I was too much the invalid, to be moved at so early an hour, without some very powerful cause. When he failed in this, he came and sat by my bed-side. My wife was employed at the other end of our apartment. Immediately on his entrance, she enquired if he had seen the Doctor; a question which he evaded; but on her observing, she thought some one should go in and see him, as he was so poorly the night before; Mr. Clough, immediately wrote the following words with a pencil, on a small slip of paper and held it before my eyes—" DOCTOR COKE IS DEAD!"

I looked at him with surprise and amazement.— " Oh no," said I, " it cannot be. Do not operate on my feelings with a subject so serious." In the midst of our mutual agitation, Mrs. Harvard renewed her enquiries respecting the Doctor, and declared she would herself go and see him. With this intention, she placed her hand upon the door communicating with the Doctor's cabin; when Mr. Clough earnestly begged her to desist; adding, " It is of no service for you to go in.—The Doctor is not in a fit state for you to see him.—I must tell you plainly—DOCTOR COKE IS DEAD!" Our minds were graciously supported while hearing the awful news, the particulars of which Mr. Clough then gave us.

At length I rose from my bed, trembling from weakness and anxiety; and having been assisted to dress by Mr. Clough, walked to the Doctor's cabin, leaning on his arm. There, alas! I found the lifeless body of our venerable and beloved friend, laid on the bed. It appeared but little discomposed; a placid smile rested on his countenance; the head was turned a little on one side; while the stain, from a stream of blood which had flowed from his mouth, remained on his right cheek. Oh! what did I feel, while I stood attentively surveying the body! A crowd of thoughts in a moment rushed into my mind, like a rolling torrent. On the one hand, I viewed our friend and leader suddenly and distressingly called away from us: on the other, our situation as Missionaries, rendered thereby the most responsible and painful! I was, notwithstanding, blessed with a rising confidence in God, and could breathe out in the midst of our trial, *Thy will be done!*

Wishing to know the immediate cause of our afflictive bereavement, I requested the surgeon of the ship to give us his opinion, as to the occasion of the Doctor's death. Upon examining the body, he considered death to have been produced by apoplexy. It is supposed that he rose in the night, either to call some of us, or to reach something, and that he fell in the position in which he was found by the servant. His death took place, doubtless, before midnight; as the body was quite cold and stiff when discovered. The easy dismissal with which he was evidently favoured afforded us some consolation; since neither Captain Birch nor myself heard any struggling, or noise, which we must unavoidably have done, had there been any; as our cabins immediately joined his, and were only divided from it by a very thin wainscot.

Captain Birch kindly sympathized with us in our afflicted situation; and, unsolicited by us, had a boat prepared to carry the information to the Melville, and to bring the other members of our Mission on board the Cabalva. I wrote a note to them, to prepare their minds, and so considerate was the Captain, that though the usual time for making the signal of a decease to the fleet is nine o'clock; yet, unwilling to have their minds agitated before they had been previously prepared by my letter, he delayed having the signal made until they had arrived on board. The fleet was then telegraphed, that Doctor Coke had departed this life.* Our interview was solemn and affecting. We felt as chastened children in the presence of our heavenly Father. None knew how to speak the first, or when he spoke what to say. We were sensible of our peculiar situation, and could only exclaim, *How unsearchable are thy judgments, O Lord! and thy ways past finding out!*

After conversing together, we resolved to consult Captain Birch, as to the possibility of preserving the body, and transmitting it to Europe for interment. Messrs. Ault and Clough waited on the Captain, and assured him that no expense should be spared, were it possible to have it accomplished. The Captain heard

---

* A paragraph in the Mission Letter from Bombay, written by one of the Missionaries who sailed in the Melville, thus describes the feelings of that party on receiving my note: " When the note was read, all were as though thunderstruck: the brethren felt as if they were electrified even to stupidity, and could scarcely believe what they read. While thus exercised, sometimes gazing on the note, and then looking at each other, the surgeon of the Lady Melville entered their cabin, with a letter from Captain Birch to Captain Lochner, stating that Doctor Coke was dead. All their fears were realized, and they hastened to their brethren on board the Cabalva."

them with great attention, and expressed his willingness to do any thing in his power to meet our wishes, or to fulfil the desire of our late respected friend; but at the same time, stated difficulties so numerous and insuperable, that, after maturely weighing the subject, we thought it proper not to persist. The Captain wished us to adopt our own mode with respect to the funeral, and politely sent me a note, requesting to know how we intended to proceed; stating his desire " to shew every respect to the memory of so excellent a man."*

Five o'clock in the afternoon was the time appointed for the funeral service. The awning was spread, and the soldiers drawn up in ranks upon the deck. A coffin had been made out of some planks; this was filled with holes to admit the water; and four heavy cannon-shot tied in four bags, were fixed two at each end. The body was decently laid in the coffin, and the lid nailed down. It was then placed upon the leeward gang-way, and was respectfully covered with signal flags, as a substitute for a mourning pall. It was the first time I had been on deck since my illness, and a chair was provided for me. The ship's bell summoned the passengers and crew, all dressed as suitably as circumstances would admit, who all seemed struck with silent awe. The Captain kindly conducted Mrs. Harvard to the spot, and supported her during the solemn service. When the bell ceased tolling, I rose, and read the burial service, with emotions I shall never

* A copy of the entire note may be acceptable to the reader.
 "My dear Sir,
 " After you have determined about the burial of our worthy friend, you will favour me, by letting me know, as we all wish to show every respect to the memory of so excellent a man.
 "I sincerely condole with you all on the occasion.
  " Your's, my dear Sir, very truly,
    " J. BIRCH."
 " Rev. Mr. Harvard.'

forget, and which I could scarcely perform through weakness and agitation. At the appointed part of the service, the coffin was lowered from the gang-way, with great decorum, and committed to the deep; to be seen no more till the resurrection of the just. When the reading of the burial service was finished, Mr. Ault delivered a suitable address; and, from the sudden and unexpected death of the venerable Doctor, who the day before was walking the deck in company with them, urged the necessity and importance of habitual preparation for a future world. Mr. Lynch then read the hymn, which begins,

> " Hark a voice divides the sky,
> ' Happy are the faithful dead !' "

and concluded with prayer. The whole missionary party retired to our cabin, and after partaking of some refreshment, our friends were taken on board their own ship. The remains of the venerable Doctor Coke were committed to the deep in about 8 degrees South latitude, and 39 degrees East longitude.

CHAP IV.

Difficulty of reconciling the death of Doctor Coke, with his actual call to embark in the Asiatic Mission—Destitute situation of the Missionaries, and their painful exercises—Spend several days in searching for, and examining the deceased Doctor's papers—Disappointments—Anecdote on "Trust in Providence"—Captain Birch's generous and humane attentions—Extracts from the Author's Journal—Recommendatory letters to the Governor, and to W. T. Money, Esq.—Conversation with J. Anderson, Esq.—Divine service on board.—Exchange signals with the party on board the Melville. The statement furnished by the Author to Captain Birch, at his request, of the doctrines, discipline, &c. of the Wesleyan Methodists; the character and extent of their Missions, and the circumstances connected with the formation of the present Mission to Ceylon—Captain Birch's reply to the Author.

THE unexpected decease of the venerable Doctor Coke, viewed in connection with the immediate obligation under which he conceived himself to be laid to engage in the Asiatic Mission, may produce a suspicion as to the reality of that obligation. It may, indeed, be supposed, that the subsequent dealings of Divine Providence furnish an intimation, that he could not have been designed to undertake a work, from which he was removed at its very commencement.

With the Doctor's surviving companions there exists no doubt, that his embarkation in the Asiatic Mission was of GOD. Though he was not permitted to land on the shores of *India*, yet he had, in fact, brought his party far within the limits of ASIA—that quarter of the globe which had been so long the object of his pious solicitude—and had, in a good degree, formed the plan of their future operations, before his spirit was called to its reward.

The progress of the narrative will fully reconcile any apparent discrepancy between the opinion of the Doctor, respecting the source from whence he divided his missionary ardour, and the apparent disappointment of his expectations. It is true, he never saw the idolatry and superstition which he was so anxious to abolish; he never, on Asiatic shores, wielded the missionary weapons, he had so assiduously prepared for the intended conflict. But *it was in his heart* so to have done. He came forth, at the head of his little band, *to the help of the Lord against the mighty;* and by his death he gave such an *impetus* to the cause, both at home and abroad, as made him, like another celebrated agent of Divine Providence, a greater and more glorious conqueror in his death, than he had been throughout the whole of an active and laborious life.

The Christian's note of time for endeavouring to *do good* is *opportunity*. He must avail himself of every opening; while the result must ever remain with Him, who accomplishes his own purposes of mercy by means which baffle the calculations of men, and secure the glory to himself.

It would be difficult to furnish any adequate idea of the painful apprehensions produced by the unexpected death of the venerable Doctor, in the minds of those by whom he was accompanied. Bereft of him whom, under God, we had been accustomed to regard as our counsellor and guide; our deficiencies and unfitness for the great undertaking in which we were engaged broke in upon our minds with greater force than they had ever done before, and caused us to tremble beneath the serious responsiblity which now devolved upon us. In addition to this, we beheld ourselves most critically circumstanced, with respect to immediate pecuniary support, in the strange country to which we were hastening. No provision for such a melancholy event had been even thought of, we had reason to apprehend, before our departure from England. Our inexperience and limited acquaintance with the world also tended to increase our apprehensions. But our trouble, though great, was graciously sanctified to the production of that entire dependence on the Divine Being, so essential to the success of the work in which we were engaged. How far our bereavement tended to further the interests of the mission, it is unnecessary here to notice; but it certainly contributed, by the blessing of God, to moderate our expectations, to discipline our impetuosity, and to exercise our faith. Thus, by the most acute suffering at the commencement, preserving us in the end from errors into which we otherwise might have fallen.

A few days after the death of Doctor Coke, by the advice of Captain Birch, we took possession of his apartment, in which we passed several succeeding days, the agitation and grief of our minds rendering us unfit for any society but our own. The day succeeding the funeral was, indeed, a solemn and mournful one to us! We could hardly believe the reality of the transactions of the previous day The change, to us so eventful, was so sudden and unexpected, that we frequently started from our seats, and enquired of each other, whether it were real, or only a dream! We were, however, compelled to realize the affecting change. In the evening Captain Birch paid us a visit, sympathized with us in our painful situation, and offered his assistance in any way in which he might be able to help us. He informed us, that by law he was constituted the Doctor's executor, unless a will could be found, placing his affairs in the hands of either of us. He advised us to commence an early examination of the Doctor's papers; and obligingly said, he would have a seal put on every thing, until our minds should become sufficiently composed to enter upon the search, when he would appoint the purser of the ship to attend us in his behalf; adding, that he should be very happy if a will were found, which would remove the business out of his hands.

Our anxiety aroused us. The whole of Thursday, May 5, was occupied by Mr. Clough and myself in searching among the lamented Doctor's papers, for some document directing the disposal of his personal property; but we sought in vain : nothing satisfactory could be found. As the Doctor had stated to us only the week before his death, that he had made his will previous to leaving England, and had mentioned some of its particular provisions,* we naturally expected to meet with at least a draught of that instrument in his own possession; but in this also we were disappointed.— His agents had only provided him with a statement of his property, signed by his solicitor in London. We found also, in his hand-writing, the sums for which his own resources would enable him to draw on England : but neither of these papers, we were well aware, could invest *us* with any authority to do the same. Whatever papers belonged to the Mission, or in our opinion was necessary to conduct it, the purser was instructed to deliver up to us; and whatever of the papers or property found we decided to be strictly private, were committed to the care of the Captain, to

---

* The Doctor informed us, that he had left the whole of his property, with the exception of a few legacies to "*the Preachers' Fund;*" an institution established for the support of superannuated and worn-out ministers in the Wesleyan Connexion, and for the benefit of their widows and children after their decease. But from the insufficient securities on which his property was in several instances placed out, the fund which he intended to befriend, has not been benefited by it to the full extent of his generous design.

be by him delivered to the heirs or executors in England.

In the whole of this business it was evidently the governing principle of Captain Birch, that while he acted with a due regard to the estate of our deceased friend, he at the same time earnestly wished the Mission to be as little inconvenienced as possible by the melancholy event. Nor can it be regarded in any other light than signally providential, that our affairs had to pass through the hands of *such* an individual!

In the evening of Thursday, the Captain very kindly came and sat with us, and suggested such grounds of encouragement as our circumstances so much required. We knew that Doctor Coke had placed £.400 sterling in the Captain's hands, to be repaid him in India currency; and we imagined that we might avail ourselves of *that sum* for our immediate necessities; hoping, by rigid economy, it would be sufficient, until we could obtain further supplies from England; for we had not the least hope of obtaining any money in India. But at this visit the Captain observed, with reference to this £.400, that though he had no doubt it was designed for us as a common stock; yet, as it had been lodged *in the Doctor's own name,* and *as his own property,* he could not legally pay it to us, unless some document could be found, authorizing him so to do; as, in the absence of such a document, he must be held responsible for the sum to the executors of the Doctor's estate in England.

We received this communication nearly in silence. We saw the perfect propriety of the remark. But that sum was the last prop upon which we had leaned for immediate support! What reply could we have made? I afterwards wrote in my Journal, " We have now no resource, but as Providence may open our way! The will of the Lord be done!"—" Now," said Mr. Clough,

when the Captain had withdrawn, " it is all *trust!*"*
Captain Birch, with his usual penetration, immediately
discovered the effect this communication had produced
on our minds. He dwelt on the invariable liberality of
the Indian government; and assured us, that upon a
proper statement of our case, they would afford us every
suitable encouragement and support. He recommended
us to adopt a regular plan of proceeding, and strictly to
adhere to it. He added, that he was acquainted with
several of the leading members of the Bombay Government, and that he would use his interest with them in
our behalf. In reference to this, I entered in my Journal
the following remark : " We have, however, but little expectation from men, whose habits and pursuits are purely
mercantile; and who can hardly be expected to feel any
interest in an undertaking like ours.† But for such an
unexpected offer, we could but return our warmest
acknowledgments. We afterwards, as usual, commended
our cause to God ; feeling a desire to trust unreservedly
to him, and adopting the language of the anxious parent
in the gospel: *Lord we believe! Help thou our unbelief.*"

We employed the next day, as we had done the pre-

---

* The lively and cheerful disposition of Mr. Clough, was frequently a source of relief to us. On this occasion, he related an
anecdote of an honest and uneducated countryman, in allusion to the
above remark. The good man, a resident in one of our large manu-
facturing towns, had been often brought by the scarcity of employment into very straitened circumstances, and had experienced many
evident interferences of Divine Providence in his favour. In the
course of a conversation on Providence, the pious man observed, " It
is very easy to talk of *trusting in God* with plenty of provision in the
house, and money in the pocket ; but," added he, " I do not call that
trust, I call that *ready-money.*"

† How pleasingly we were disappointed in this respect, by the kindness which we experienced at Bombay, through the blessing of God
and the friendly interposition of our Captain, I need not anticipate my
narrative to inform the reader.

ceding one, in examining the chests, &c. of our departed leader; but with no better success. Our feelings were indescribable. Confined to our cabin, and destitute of all variety, we generally conversed on *one subject*—the forlorn situation of our Mission, especially with regard to temporal resources. By divine help, we were enabled to check the risings of distrust, and to exercise confidence in Him, who causeth light to arise *in* the darkness. The superior excellency of our undertaking, and the purity of our motives, were never-failing sources of consolation to us. We reflected, " It is the work of the Lord; and we are sincerely devoted to its interests. Why should we entertain a doubt, that God will acknowledge and prosper his own work, notwithstanding the instruments are so unworthy?"

On Saturday we renewed our search, and met with a paper which encouraged our hopes respecting the £.400 It was the copy of an account between Doctor Coke and the Asiatic Mission, in the hand-writing of his agent in London; in which, among other sums placed to the debit of the Mission, the £.400 is entered, as having been paid to Captain Birch. Though this account was not regularly signed, and hence was not legal evidence, yet it contained so strong a proof that the money was actually applied to the Mission, that we regarded it as placing the question beyond a doubt. We indulged the hope, that the Captain would, on the production of this paper, feel himself justified in advancing the sum to us. In my Journal I had written, " In this respect, we are aware that we lie at the discretion of our worthy Captain; but from his past kindness we feel assured that every thing will be done with regard to our comfort.—And if, after all, we should be disappointed, we hope to say, *Thy will be done!*"

Captain Birch in the evening paid us his accustomed visit; but we had not sufficient confidence in the paper, to introduce the matter again to him. Our departed friend, having freely mentioned to the Captain our recommendatory letters, they became the subject of conversation; and we considered it advisable to state all our circumstances to him as they stood. He evinced the deepest interest in our affairs; observed, that he was acquainted with the Right Honourable the Governor of Bombay; and promised to procure an interview for two of our number, at which our recommendatory letters might be presented. The parcel which we had for the Governor he kindly undertook to send immediately on our arrival, and to acquaint His Excellency with the death of Doctor Coke, and our situation in consequence. This, he said, would prepare our way, and lead to a longer interview than we might obtain, even if we took the parcel ourselves, from the great press of business in which the Governor would of course be involved, on the arrival of the fleet. For this friendly and judicious arrangement we returned him our sincere thanks.

In my Journal the following entry occurs:

"*Saturday*, 7th.—During the interesting conversation of this evening, Captain Birch inquired, ' if we were provided with any *letter of credit* to any merchant in Bombay, to enable us to draw our bills on England?' Here we were at a stand; as, from our knowledge of Doctor Coke's general abstraction from temporal concerns, we are led to conclude, that he did not furnish himself with such a document. And yet we can hardly believe that the Doctor's commercial friends would have allowed him to leave England without so important a provision. This, however, we are fearful has been the case, and if so, what a situation is ours! How can we, *so numerous a party*, procure support in a strange land, or offer our bills, without a security, to those who in this respect might be inclined to befriend us!

" *Sunday, May* 8.—The Captain passed a short time with us this evening. Doctor Buchanan's letter to W. T. Money, Esq. of Bombay (which was found among our recommendatory letters) was the subject of conversation. Our own opinion respecting this letter is, that it is merely one of friendship. The Captain supposes it may contain some communication from the Doctor, which will authorize Mr. Money to advance cash on our bills. Captain Birch speaks of this gentleman as a religious man; and he doubts not, that on a representation of our case, he will materially assist us. Of this our expectations are not very sanguine. But our eyes are up unto the Lord, in whose hands are the hearts of all men. Being acquainted with Mr. Money, the Captain, in the most obliging manner, proposed to wait personally on that gentleman, in the first instance, in order to prepare our way, by a statement of what he knew respecting us and our circumstances. Situated as we are, we thankfully acquiesced in the proposal. And thus far, it seems, our introduction into India is decided upon!—In the morning we had a friendly and sympathizing visit from a gentleman and his lady, passengers, going out in the Honourable Company's Civil Service. Having received from the Captain some general view of our situation, the gentleman very kindly endeavoured to remove any anxious concern from our minds, by assuring us, that should our other expectations fail, we had nothing to fear, but every thing to expect from the liberality of the Indian Government. We thanked him for his kindness, and endeavoured to confirm our hope in God.

" *Monday, May* 9.—The Captain having advised communication with the rest of our party in the other ship, relative to our intended plan of procedure, obligingly promised us a boat for that purpose, if the setting in of the *monsoon* does not prevent. We accordingly prepared a letter for the consideration of the brethren; but on application to the proper officer, we found that the boats were not in a fit state, as they had been all newly painted, preparatory to entering the harbour. We have now therefore given up all idea of communication with our dear brethren, until our arrival at Bombay; not ceasing to pray, that we may be preserved in *one spirit*, and led into *a unity of proceeding*, by the great Father of the church. We daily feel our situation more and more. *Who is sufficient for these things?*—This evening Captain Birch, as usual, paid us a friendly visit. Having read the Magazine containing the correspondence between Mr. Grant and our departed leader, on the subject of an Eastern Mission, he expressed great satisfaction from the perusal of it, and said much in praise of that much respected gentleman. He observed, that we had more friends in India to our Missionary operations, when properly conducted, than we might, perhaps, have expected to find: though there were undoubtedly many who had not given their sanction to such undertakings. And, if we *acted with prudence,* and *felt our way,* as he had no doubt we should, we might expect to meet with a very favourable reception.

" *Tuesday, May* 10.—This morning I showed to Captain Birch the sketch of the account, in which the Asiatic Mission is made debtor for the £.400 deposited with him. He advised us to keep the paper, and requested a copy of it. I told him we were aware that it could not be regarded as a legal document, but that it would furnish him with the late Doctor's intentions with respect to that sum. This he acknowledged, and said it should be allowed its full weight; that he would frequently converse with us on the subject; that we might mutually turn it over in our minds; and that upon our arrival in Bombay every thing be satisfactorily arranged, which he was fully satisfied would be the case. In the afternoon, while sitting for a little air on the poop-deck, apart from the company, the Captain kindly came up and sat with us. His first observation was: " I think you perplex and concern yourselves a great deal too much. You will do much better than you fear. I will never leave you destitute. I will see that you are comfortably situated." We thanked him for his kindness, and the conversation changed. After tea, he obligingly visited us in our cabin, and renewed the subject; hoping that we would endeavour to discard all painful views of our affairs; assuring us, that we had no room for anxiety and concern; that *he would allow us to draw upon himself, and accept our bills;* and indeed would render us every possible assistance. Such generosity I believe is seldom met with, as that which this noble-minded individual has manifested towards us! What terms could enable us to convey our sense of the interest he manifested in our comfort? We did, however, feebly express our gratitude to him, and lifted up our hearts to God in prayer and praise.

" *Wednesday, May* 11.—Nothing particular has occurred this day. We were as usual favoured with the Captain's company for a short time in the evening; but the conversation turned chiefly on the leading religious doctrines professed by our society; to a brief summary of which our esteemed friend listened with much attention.

" *Thursday, May* 12.—This morning, the gentleman who visited us on Saturday, did us the same kindness. He gave us much important information respecting the mode of living in India; and in the most friendly manner, offered his assistance in any way on our arrival in Bombay. May Providence reward him for his sympathizing attentions to us, in the time of our affliction and difficulty!* Having, since the Doctor's death, in general confined ourselves to our own apartments, we this day, for the first time, resumed our seats at the table in the state-room, and were kindly received by the company there, who appear generally to sympathize with us in our late painful loss. As might be expected, we felt considerably during the time of dinner, at the absence of the Doctor from his usual seat, which was at the head of the table, and exactly opposite to mine. I could not remove my eyes from my plate, without beholding his vacated chair, as yet unoccupied; and the view caused such emotions of mind, as to unfit me for society. In these distressing feelings my companions fully participated. We passed the evening alone; and having separated to rest, commended each other to the Lord.

" *Sunday, May* 15,—We had public service to-day upon deck. This evening the Lady Melville came so near us, that we could distinguish our dear brethren on the poop-deck, and exchanged with them the white-handkerchief-signal of health and peace. From what Brother Clough saw of them through the glass, we have been ready to fear that they are much dejected, and that Brother Squance is again unwell. But we gladly look forward beyond a few days more, when we shall form

* J. W. Anderson, Esquire, one of the Judges under the Presidency of Bombay. Both himself and his respected lady were very kind to us on our voyage. From Mr. Anderson I received the invaluable present of water at a time of short allowance. It was with the most unaffected sorrow we received intelligence of the premature death of Mrs. Anderson, a lady of great accomplishments, and of the most unassuming and engaging manners.

but one party; and whether our situation be then pleasing or painful, we shall at least be sharers in common with each other."

As Captain Birch had several times intimated a wish to be furnished with such a statement as would enable him to give the requisite information respecting us, and of our intended plan of procedure on our arrival in Bombay; we considered it highly expedient, that he should be provided with it. At the same time, we felt ourselves placed in a critical situation, as junior members of the Mission party, to attempt to furnish a statement which might involve the character of the Mission generally; or pledge ourselves to any particular line of proceeding, which might not ultimately meet with the concurrence of our senior brethren. These difficulties would have been lessened, if we could have had some previous intercourse with our brethren in the Lady Melville; we should then have been aided by their counsel, as well as relieved from the unpleasant apprehension, that we should be regarded by them as taking too prominent a part in the business.

But the urgency of the case considerably outweighed these considerations. It was necessary that Captain Birch should have the statement he requested, to enable him to give effect to his benevolent intentions respecting us, and the objects of our mission; and it was the more necessary that such a document should be put into his hands before we appeared on the Indian shore, as there were some opinions formed respecting us which needed disavowal, and others which required explanation. Of the former kind, was an idea in the minds of some, that Ceylon was only the *professed*, not the *real* object of our Mission; and of the latter description, was the circumstance of so numerous a party entering on such an undertaking, without having the usual provision for raising money. In addition to these, were some undefinable impressions, which it was desirable, if not essential, to counteract, by a candid and circumstantial communication from ourselves.

Such was the influence which we supposed these things to have on the general interests of the Mission, that we resolved to risk all personal considerations; and, whatever might be the opinion entertained of the measure, we felt it binding upon us to take on ourselves the responsibility. Accordingly, after due deliberation, I presented the Captain with the following letter:

"*Honourable Company's Ship Cabalva, May* 7, 1814.

" VERY DEAR SIR:

" THE uniform attention which you have ever paid to our comfort, since we first had the honour of entering your ship, as well as the kind offers of assistance which you have been pleased to make us, since our late distressing bereavement, justly entitle you to the information respecting our situation which you desire. With pleasure I take up my pen to give it you: a pleasure which is only affected by the ever-lamentable circumstance which has so unexpectedly rendered such information necessary.

" In the first place, then, dear Sir, it will be proper for you to know, that my five respected companions and myself are regularly accredited and ordained ministers of the Society late in connexion with the REVEREND JOHN WESLEY, of the University of Oxford; a society of Christians, known by many under the title of Church Methodists, from our zealous attachment to the doctrines and mode of worship of the Established Church of England. The concerns of this society are managed by an annual meeting of its ministers, which is called the Conference. The presidency of this meeting generally devolves upon one of the senior ministers, who is elected to the office by the Conference at the commencement of its sittings. I think our late venerable friend, the Rev. Doctor Coke, filled the office twice since the death of Mr. Wesley, and was always the principal secretary to the Conference.

" As our plan is purely an itinerant one, it is the business of the Conference to examine the character, &c. of every minister; to fix his appointment for the succeeding year, if approved of; and to adopt such regulations as the state of the societies may require, and as may appear to them likely to aid the promotion of real religion in the world. By the Conference my companions and myself have for some few years received appointments, to several numerous and respectable congregations in the connexion, who, did circumstances admit, would, I am persuaded, willingly step forward and bear their testimony to the manner in which we have been enabled to sustain the ministerial character.

" At the Conference held in Liverpool in the latter end of July and the beginning of August last, Doctor Coke urgently introduced the moral and religious state of the island of Ceylon. It appeared highly desirable that something should be done to ameliorate it. Our late venerable friend mentioned his own strong and ardent desire to visit Asia, and to take with him some Missionaries to the island of Ceylon. Upon enquiry, there were found several young ministers like-minded with himself, who offered their services, should a mission be undertaken to that island. After mature deliberation, the Conference consented to the adoption of the Doctor's plan, and appointed the present party to accompany him to the Eastern world.

" It was recommended by the Conference, that three should be stationed at Ceylon; one at the island of Java; and, in consideration of the age, &c. of our deceased friend, two were to be his companions in travel, in the event of his visiting the Continent of India, which he strongly desired to do, having his eye particularly fixed upon the natives of Rajamaul, the Syriac Christians in Travancore, and Mr. Swartz's Christians in the Tanjore country. But it was left entirely to the discretion of Doctor Coke, *which* of us should fill these several appointments; in deciding upon which, he was to act according to circumstances, and as he should discover our peculiar talent and bias of mind.

" I should here inform you, dear Sir, that the Conference commits the management of its missionary concerns, during the interval between the annual meetings, to an executive, called the Missionary Committee; which consists of the President of the Conference for the time being, and all the ministers of our connexion in and near London. These hold their meetings every month, receive communications from the missionaries in various parts of the world, and transmit them whatever assistance they need, making a full report thereof to the ensuing Conference.

" It is in this way that all our Missions are conducted. And it is with pleasure I refer you to the West India Islands, to Nova Scotia and New Brunswick, Newfoundland, and to the Colony of Sierra Leone in Africa; in which places our Missionaries have laboured with uncommon success; and though liable to suspicions as strangers, at the onset of their undertakings, have nevertheless so conducted themselves, as to procure the respect of the inhabitants, and the general good opinion of the governments of the various stations they have occupied. This has been so generally the case, that testimonials, very favourable to their Missionary character, are not unfrequently forwarded to our Committee by persons in authority abroad: and a few days since I particularly noticed a communication of that kind from the Honourable the Governor of Sierra Leone, among the papers of our late venerable friend.

" Doctor Coke being possessed of considerable property, and being extremely anxious to enter immediately upon the accomplishment of his favourite design, proposed to the last Conference, not only to introduce and establish the present Mission, but likewise to advance whatever monies might be requisite for the outfit and settlement of the Missionaries. For his reimbursement the Conference became responsible, and engaged to repay the principal with regular interest; which, as I understand, not having been present at the Conference, they intended to do in the course of the following year. There is an allusion to this in one of those letters from Mr. Holloway (who has long been the Doctor's intimate friend, and agent in pecuniary matters) which was delivered to you among the Doctor's cash papers.

" The Doctor having thus engaged with our connexion for our outfit, introduction, and support, busily employed himself in procuring proper letters of recommendation, of which he gave due information to our Missionary Committee; who, resting satisfied, without doubt, that he had provided letters of credit also, with every other necessary document, gave us their parting blessing on the 10th of December last, and commended us to God. Subsequent to this, our pecuniary resources seldom became the subject of conversation with the Doctor: we were so fully persuaded, as he had introduced other important Missions, and particularly those to the West Indies, that he was perfectly well acquainted with all that was necessary to persons circumstanced as we are, and that he had been no less careful to provide the same.

"However, it has occurred, that this subject, among many others, has sometimes been noticed in our little interviews; at which times the Doctor was extremely anxious to remove every unpleasant feeling from our minds. He has reminded us of the £400 he had deposited in your hands, as a first resource. He has also spoken of W. T. Money, Esq. as a gentleman kindly disposed, and to whom he intended to apply to become his agent; and has assured us, that it was in his power to draw upon England very largely, both upon our Missionary fund, and on his own personal estate. Often has he exclaimed, "I have given up myself and all I possess to this work—you shall never want." Had our venerable friend survived, he would have fulfilled his engagements, and we should have met with no difficulties of a temporal kind. But, alas! that which is common to all, and which we ought to have anticipated, has found its way unexpectedly into our little party; and, apparently regardless of the magnitude of our loss, has placed us in a situation at once painful and responsible.

"Permit me, dear Sir, again to refer to a point, upon which I am not unconscious of your unwillingness that I should enlarge—your great kindness to us in our afflicted and perplexing circumstances. I feel personally obliged to you, in a degree which I cannot express; and I am happy, very dear Sir, to assure you that the same emotions are ever alive in the hearts of my much respected companions. Circumstanced as we are, you have kindly offered your assistance. We thankfully accept your friendly offer. We shall hold ourselves ever obliged by the communication of any information or caution which your extensive acquaintance with Indian affairs may enable you to afford us: and take the liberty of expressing to you, our most entire confidence in your matured judgment and generous disposition to serve us.

"From a conversation which took place when you did us the favour last to visit us, I have conceived it necessary to add a few observations upon a subject, which, from a consciousness of our own sincerity, I had never once supposed would have been questioned; namely, whether Ceylon be our *real,* or only our *professed* object. I must confess, my dear Sir, I felt some degree of embarrassment, because it is a difficult matter to prove; at least, with any better evidence than our own assertion—a species of evidence, we are aware, which will be very cautiously received by persons to whom we are unknown—it will, however, be otherwise with the gentleman to whom I have the honour to submit the present statement.

"Our venerable friend was very sanguine in his expectations, so far as respected himself. From his being a clergyman of the Established Church, and so well known and respected in England, and wherever he went, he promised himself the permission of the authorities in India, to visit several places on that Continent, which I have already enumerated in this letter. With an anticipation of this, which amounted to certainty in his own mind, and with a disposition naturally noble and generous, and ready to communicate his intentions to others, the Doctor has, during our voyage, frequently made the Continent of India the subject of conversation, in a way by no means private. This, together with the wishes expressed by many benevolent persons in England, may have led to the conclusion, that we had a double design; and that, while on our leaving England, we professed to have Ceylon for our object, the Continent was in reality the destination we had in view. This, however, I assure you, is not the case.

"Possessed of the views which I have of the infinite value and benefit of Christianity to mankind, I cannot but wish that it were approved of and embraced by every human soul; and being convinced that it is the Divine will that this should be the case at some period or other, I sincerely repeat that part of the excellent prayer which he himself hath taught us, " Thy kingdom come; thy will be done in earth as it is in heaven." Hence, I shall rejoice if permitted to see the day, when the honourable the authorities of India, judging from the state of the country and every circumstance connected with it, shall consider it sound policy to permit the unrestrained dissemination of Christianity on that Continent. These observations, however, are only made by the way.

" When Doctor Coke first proposed to me to become one of his companions to Asia, Ceylon was the only place mentioned, or even hinted at, as the object of the Mission. When the measure was adopted by our Conference, it was exactly the same, only with the addition of the Island of Java and the Cape of Good Hope. And when we were dismissed by our Committee in London, it was perfectly the same. We left England, with our minds looking to Ceylon as our ultimate object. We still, of course, remain in the same mind, from the nature of the instructions we have received from our Connexion; and if the Right Honourable the Governor in Council require it, we are willing to give any security for our removal to Ceylon the first opportunity.

" The kind interest, dear Sir, which you have taken in our welfare, has led you to desire a plan of our intended Mission, with a statement of our peculiar situation. I have endeavoured to furnish you therewith; not, indeed, in so compressed a way as I could have wished, but as much so as I could possibly effect. You have here, Sir, a plain, unvarnished tale; incorrect in no point to the best of my belief; and of which I am sure you will not suffer any use to be made than for our benefit.

"Our late venerable friend was a man so exceedingly abstracted in his views, that he attended to his temporal concerns very much unlike a man of business. It is in consequence of this that we are so unprovided for in an exigency like the present. Diligently have we searched among his papers, for some document which might establish our credit in a strange land. How far we are furnished with documents of this kind among the sealed letters in our possession, we cannot with certainty say; but we hope the letters of recommendation which we have, together with the one directed to W. T. Money, Esq. will fully disclose our character and intentions, and enable us to arrange our affairs with ease and satisfaction.

"If, however, we should in this be unhappily disappointed, which we can hardly persuade ourselves will be the case, we must, submitting ourselves to the Divine disposal, rely on the respectability of our connexion in England, and on the favourable opinion entertained of it by the Government of our country; and must request permission to remain at Bombay until we can send home an account of our painful and unexpected bereavement, and receive communications from our Committee. Should our situation need this favour, and should the Honourable the Government of Bombay kindly grant it, I trust we shall ultimately proceed to Ceylon, *the real object of our Mission,* with the most grateful acknowledgements, and without occasioning any unfavourable opinion to be entertained of us.*

---

* In 1816, when the Rev. John Horner arrived in Bombay, and waited on the Right Hon. Sir Evan Nepean, the Governor, His Ex-

" I am well aware, dear Sir, of the engagements which await you, upon landing in Bombay. They will necessarily be numerous and important. Yet, I hope it will not be considered presuming or intrusive in me to hint at the essential service it will be to us, to have as early an interview as possible with W. T. Money, Esq.; His Excellency the Governor, &c. This I submit to your better judgment. If I mistake not, you were kind enough to recommend an application to Mr. Money in the first instance.

" Should you be able to confer this essential favour without too great an inconvenience to your important engagements, I am confident of the pleasure you have been so kind as to say you will feel in so doing; as well as of the satisfaction which it will yield, at a period which from the present I hope to be far, very far, distant. Allow me the liberty of expressing my most sincere and ardent wishes, for your welfare and of subscribing myself, with the greatest respect,

" Dear Sir,
" Your very much obliged, and
" obedient, humble servant,
" W. M. HARVARD."

" To Jonathan Birch, Esq.
" Commander of H. C. S. Cabalva."

To this letter we received in the course of the same day the following reply:

"*May* 17, 1814.

" MY DEAR SIR:

" I AM obliged for the ample communication with which you have favoured me. In reply to that part of it, respecting an intimation from me, about the extension

cellency was pleased to express himself in terms of decided satisfaction and approbation, relative to the first party of Methodist Missionaries who had landed in that place.

of the Mission, *I am glad you have enabled me to answer it so well.* Believe me, dear Sir, I am every way disposed to make you comfortable, and to render you assistance. And remain, with great esteem,

"Your's very truly,
"J. Birch."

"The Rev. W. M. Harvard."

I have been thus circumstantial in this part of the narrative, that the reader should, as clearly as possible, realize our situation, and recognize every individual link in the chain of mercies by which we were supported and led at that trying and important period. He will have seen how dark and perplexing were our circumstances, and how unexpectedly and gradually encouragement dawn upon our path. But *the half hath not been told.*

CHAP. V.

Termination of our voyage—Indian scenery—Meeting with the Brethren on board the Lady Melville—Difference of opinions—First Sabbath in India—Press-gang—Visited by the Rev. S. Newell—Disembarkment—Palanquin stands—Breakfast at the Bombay Tavern—Causes of disquietude—Interview with Mr. Money—Reception—Gratifying information respecting Ceylon—Ride with Captain Birch to the Governor's country seat—Native washermen—Persee women—Toddy—Native village—Persee burial place—A Fakeer—An idol—Audience with the GOVERNOR—His Excellency's condescension, and remarks on the Rev. J. Wesley—Return to Bombay.—Rev. Messrs. Hall and Nott—The Governor's house at Parell prepared for our reception—Sensations produced by the arrival of the Missionaries.

ON Saturday the 21st of May, after a voyage of twenty weeks, we were permitted to enter the desired harbour. The fleet was welcomed on its arrival by discharges of cannon from the shore; which were returned by a salute from the commodore.

Bombay Harbour is handsome and commodious; and, after so long a voyage, the effect produced on our minds by the beautiful and varied scenery was delightful beyond description. Before the anchor was dropped, we were surrounded by boats filled with natives, who with great alertness made their way on board. Of these, the more respectable were Persee merchants and agents, called *Dubashes*, and who were desirous of engaging with the Captain, or any of the officers, to dispose of the goods they might have brought with them as a private venture. The inferior Persees were anxious to hire themselves in the capacity of servants; and followed the passengers about the ship, with hands-full of characters and certificates, to which they solicited their attention. These were habited in loose linen pantaloons, and long linen coats, with bands round their waists, and neat turbans made of printed calico. Some Hindoos also offered fruits for sale.* The latter descriptions were entirely naked, with the exception of a small piece of cloth around the loins. The appearance of these dark unclothed men, climbing about the ship; the romantic appearance of the shore; the strangely constructed boats and paddles by which the fleet was surrounded; the unintelligible jargon which incessantly assailed our ears; altogether made it appear as if we had suddenly become inhabitants of a new world. The novelty of the scene, however, soon wore away; and the hope of being made useful to the idolatrous natives whom we saw around us, raised us above those feelings of disgust, which, under other circumstances, would doubtless have been excited.

Our first object was to obtain an interview with our companions in the Melville, to inform them of what we had done, and to arrange some plan of proceeding for the future. Perceiving an empty native boat, the planks of which appeared to have been sewed together, Mr. Clough and I agreed with the owner to take us on board the Mellville. We found our colleagues all well, and preparing to go on shore. This was a critical æra of our history; as, from the want of previous concert, there was danger lest we should not agree in opinion, as

* Captain Birch, having cautioned us against an unrestrained indulgence in eating fruit, which often proves fatal after the privations of a long voyage, we resolved to eat no fruit but at the table, and then very sparingly.

to the most suitable measures to be adopted on our landing. It was the opinion of Mr. Clough and myself, that it would be most advisable not to land until our business and peculiar circumstances had been represented to the proper authorities by Captain Birch; which, in our opinion, would secure us the more favourable reception. Our brethren in the Melville, on the other hand, had resolved on landing immediately, and going to the tavern. We found that the senior Missionaries considered the arrangement of our concerns to devolve upon themselves ; and, as neither party could at that time change the opinion of the other, each adhered to their own : Mr. Clough and myself therefore returned to our ship.

Messrs. Ault, Lynch, Erskine, and Squance, called on us afterwards, on their way to the shore. The difference in our opinion, however painful for the moment, had occasioned no diminution of affection. On enquiring of Mr. Ault how we could obtain money? He replied, with great composure, that there would be no difficulty on that subject; as he had found a document among the late Doctor Coke's papers committed to *their* care, which would enable them to draw on England to any amount. On his mentioning the nature of the document, we at once perceived that it would not furnish any such authority; yet we could not but perceive the goodness of God, in thus preserving our companions from the painful anxieties by which Mr. Clough and myself had been exercised.

Several of our fellow-voyagers were taken on shore by their friends in the course of Saturday, and on Sunday morning; but we remained ignorant that any on that shore would shew *us* any marks of friendship. As the bustle of the ship prevented the celebration of public worship, we found it profitable to worship God in our cabin. The sadness of our first

Indian Sabbath was increased by an occurrence which could not fail of exciting our sympathies. Our vessel was boarded by a press-gang, the officer of which required the ship's company to be mustered upon deck, according to the ship's books. After inspecting them all, he selected nearly every effective man, ordering each to prepare his chest, and go into his boat! Some of the poor fellows pleaded for exemption, but in vain. The ship's steward, who had for misconduct been put before the mast, was one of the number impressed. The whole affair did not occupy more than an hour.

In the course of the day we were unexpectedly informed that a gentleman had arrived from the shore and was inquiring for us. On entering, he introduced himself to us as a brother missionary, belonging to another religious society, and indeed to another nation. It was the Rev. Samuel Newell, one of the excellent missionaries sent out from America by the Congregational denomination, and the widowed husband of the late celebrated female missionary of the same name.* We soon felt a union of spirit; and he kindly spent several hours of the day in our company. He was surprised to find that our late venerable friend, known to him by the name of "BISHOP COKE," had, at his advanced age, undertaken an Indian voyage, and tenderly sympathised with us in the afflicting circumstances of his death. He related his own tale of woe; and a mutual sympathy was excited by the narration. Mr. Newell had visited Ceylon; and he gave us an encouraging account of that interesting island, with relation to our missionary object. We took notes of the valu-

---

* Recent accounts from India state the death of this most excellent man. As I was favoured with his friendship, and was frequently in his company during our stay at Bombay, I cannot forbear expressing my sincere regret at the loss which the Mission to which he was attached has sustained by his early decease.

able information he gave us. In the evening he took his leave.

Early the following morning, Mr. Clough and myself left the ship, and landed upon the shore of India. At the landing-place we were met by palanquin-bearers, called *Hamalls*, (a description of men answering to our sedan-chairmen,) who offered to convey us in their palanquins to any place we might wish. For this purpose they stand in rows, similar to our hackney-coach stands in London, and are paid on a similar principle; either according to the length of the journey, or for the time they are engaged. The sun was exceedingly powerful, as it was the hottest season of the year; and the rains were much later than usual. The heat and the dust, together with a most unpleasant effluvia arising from *local causes*, would have made a quick conveyance to the tavern very desirable, had not our dislike to being carried by *men*, prevailed. We pressed through them on foot, until we came to our companions, with whom we partook of a hearty breakfast, at the only tavern in the place. We found the landlord, Mr. Duncan Cameron, obliging and attentive.

After breakfast, our temporal affairs naturally ingrossed our first attention. On examination, we found that we had not sufficient cash among us to present the usual gratuities to the ship's servants. Those who had indulged the expectation of raising money by means of the late Doctor's paper found on board the Melville, were soon convinced of the fallacy of that idea; and thus, having no immediate prospect of pecuniary supplies, we found ourselves actually without the means of paying for our first meal in India! Mr. Clough and myself then communicated to our companions the measures *we* had taken subsequent to the death of Doctor Coke; and furnished them with a copy of the letter we had given to Captain Birch, with his reply to it.

They cordially approved of our conduct. As Captain Birch had presented me with a letter of introduction to Mr. Money, it was proposed that I should wait upon that gentleman, and avail myself of that opportunity to state our circumstances, and request him to assist us in our extremity. Tremblingly alive to the peculiarity of our situation, we united in earnest supplication to God, in whose hands are the hearts of men, beseeching him to open our way, and to direct us in our difficulties. I was about to leave the tavern on foot, as we had come to it; but our party, with tender affection, would not allow me to expose myself to the beams of a vertical sun on their business; but insisted upon my engaging a palanquin. I was accordingly taken by the hamalls to the office of Messrs. Forbes and Co. in the Bombay Square. Mr. Money had not yet come to the office, but was expected in half-an-hour; and I was shown into an apartment, to wait his arrival. As soon as I had taken my seat, the peculiarity of my intended application struck my view. I was about to request a commercial gentleman, to whom we were all entire strangers, to become our agent, without any communication from a correspondent in England; and to advance us money, with no other security than our assurance that it should be repaid. Losing sight for the moment of our recommendatory letters, the absence of a *letter of credit* seemed to render the success of my application impossible; and I anticipated a refusal, with a smile at our simplicity, in hoping for such an accommodation, without more adequate security. I endeavoured, however, to dismiss these distressing thoughts, and lifted up my heart to God. I presently heard the sound of footsteps; and my feelings were in a state of conflict which it would be difficult to describe. When Mr. Money entered the room, his appearance at once relieved me from my anxiety. Looking with much kindness, he enquired if my name was Harvard? and requested me to sit down, saying he was glad to see me. I took out my pocket-book, to present Captain Birch's note of introduction; when he said, "Mr. Harvard, I am perfectly acquainted with all the circumstances of your situation. Your excellent Captain has been to breakfast with me this morning: he has given me every necessary information; and I shall be very happy to advance you any money on the credit of your society at home." My feelings, as may be easily supposed, were at that moment unutterable. The disinterested kindness of Captain Birch, in having so early entered into our affairs, and the noble generosity of Mr. Money, in more than anticipating my request, filled me with an admiration and esteem for those gentlemen, which rendered me unable to express my gratitude in any suitable terms.

Mr. Money at this interview introduced a conversation, in the course of which he gave me to understand that he was a firm friend to the cause of Christianity in India; and caused me to feel that, through want of an acquaintance with his character, I had done him a great injustice, in doubting for a moment whether we should meet with his friendly aid. The only reparation for this wrong with which my own mind could then be satisfied, was immediately to state to him, in the most unreserved manner, every particular relating to the object of our Mission; and Mr. Money, in return, gave me some important advice and direction. Understanding that we had letters for the Governor, the Right Hon. Sir Evan Nepean, he recommend me to obtain an audience the next day, and deliver them myself. He further expressed the readiness with which *he* would have introduced me; but, as he was rather indisposed, he would request our worthy Captain to present me. A *peon*,* or native porter, being sent with a note to Captain Birch, the Captain soon came, and kindly undertook that service. It was arranged, that I should wait on him the following morning for that purpose.

During the absence of the peon, Mr. Money conversed with me on the state of religion in the island of Ceylon, of which he related several encouraging facts with which he had become acquainted; and put into my hand the First Report of the Colombo Bible Society, which had recently come to hand. Here I met with a feast indeed. The impulse which even the *formation* of that society had evidently given to the cause of religion in that island; the patronage which the society received from His Excellency the Governor, the Chief ustice, and all the Members of Council; and the encouragement which was there afforded to missionary efforts; all seemed to unite, with an inviting voice, to animate us to perseverance in our undertaking, and to enter upon that scene of labour as early as possible. To my mind, it was like an enchanting prospect, by which the weary traveller is sometimes gladdened, after the toil of a long and difficult ascent. It left me no cause for repining, but elated me with hope.

I hastened back to the tavern, where I communicated to my companions the particulars of my interesting interview with Mr. Money. The recital filled them with wonder and gratitude. After dining together, Mr. Clough and myself returned on board the Cabalva; Captain Birch, having with singular kindness, requested us to make the ship our home, until we succeeded in obtaining a comfortable residence on shore. My dear wife, naturally a sharer in our anxieties, partook

---

* Pronounced *pune*.

largely in our joys. We closed that day of mercies with songs of praise.

The next morning, Mr. Clough and myself met our companions at the tavern, and I proceeded to Captain Birch's lodgings, according to his appointment. The Captain had provided a *Buggy* for our conveyance; a kind of one-horse chaise, which has the back of the hood open, to admit the breeze. In this we left the fort about seven o'clock, to proceed to Malabar Point, the country residence of the Governor during the hot season of the year. On the outside of the fortification we passed through rows of tents, elegantly fitted up, in which the more respectable Europeans were residing, on account of the great heat which prevailed in the Fort. Every object was new to me, which rendered the ride very interesting. On the Esplanade there were scores of men washing, or rather bruising, the linen of the inhabitants, by beating it with violence against large stones, which are the hereditary property of the washermen, and some of which have been used for that purpose for many generations. The *washing-men* presented a sight as novel to an European as the *washing-stones*. I was no less surprised to see a number of Persee women, arrayed in pearls, jewels, and ornaments of gold, with their fine flowing mantles of rich silk, carrying large vessels of water into the town on their heads, for the use of their families. It is customary for the ladies of the most opulent Persee merchants to do so regularly, morning and evening. The manners of the East do not undergo the changes which those of European nations experience; and I could not behold this interesting scene, without being forcibly reminded of the illustration it furnished to many passages of the inspired volume.

As our road lay through a cocoa-nut grove, I had an opportunity of witnessing the agility with which the natives ascend these slender trees, entirely without the help of branches, to the height of from fifty to a hundred feet, to procure the *toddy*, or sap of the tree, which oozes from the top.*

Their mode of ascent is by tying the feet together, to prevent their slipping: the tree is then embraced with their arms, and with a worm-like motion they draw their legs after them, until they reach the top, which they appear to do with surprising ease; the toddy vessel hanging at their back. In the course of our ride, I had an opportunity of seeing something of the domestic habits of the natives. We passed through one of their villages; and, as I beheld the squalid filth and listless indolence of the inhabitants, I was led into a train of reflections on the condition of man when destitute of the gospel of Christ, which improves his civil and social character, while it prepares him for a more noble state of existence in the world of spirits.

The road which leads immediately to the Governor's residence is cut through a solid rock; and as the horse could not here keep his footing, the Captain had provided two palanquins for our conveyance up the stony height. The unwillingness with which I entered a palanquin a second time, was only exceeded by the uneasiness which I experienced during the remainder of the journey: the road being a continued ascent, and the hamalls keeping time by a kind of regular groan, I considered this noise as an expression of the fatigue they endured. I subsequently found, however, that this peculiar noise had led me to imagine the endurance of pain where none was experienced; and when I had repeatedly witnessed the ease and cheerfulness with

---

* This juice or sap is used as yeast, in the manufacture of bread. An intoxicating beverage, of which the natives are extremely fond, is also made from it.

which they carried the palanquin, I became reconciled to its use.

During our ascent, the burial place of the Persees, situated to the right of the hill, was pointed out to me. No barbarous rites are used at the interment of the dead by this description of natives; but they form their opinion of the happiness or misery of the individual in the unseen state, by circumstances connected with the decay of his body. Near the top of the hill we passed a *fakeer;* a religious mendicant, who was sitting opposite to a painted image of stone. When spoken to, he made no reply; but made his *salaam* to us, without the least alteration of countenance. These men profess to live as hermits in the midst of society. They seldom speak; and impose various restraints upon themselves, according to the nature of the vows they have made. They are supported by alms, and are held in the greatest reverence by their devotees. I was informed, that one of them had lain in one position on a plank for many years, beneath a shed close to the road. I saw the shed, which was open at the sides; but did not perceive the victim of superstition.

As the idol we had just passed was the first I had ever seen, it affected me in a manner I cannot describe. Gratitude to God, who had made me to differ, and pity for the deluded votaries of a senseless idolatry, pervaded my mind. How lamentable, that any who bear the Christian name should oppose the introduction among them of that gospel which makes known *the true God, and Jesus Christ, whom he hath sent!*

On our arrival at the Governor's residence, Captain Birch kindly introduced me to His Excellency, by whom I was received with great condescension, and invited to breakfast. The table was surrounded by several military gentlemen, and others, the principal men of the Presidency. His Excellency made many enquiries relative to the object and circumstances of our Mission; and, on learning the age of our deceased leader, expressed his surprize and admiration at his having entered upon so arduous a task at his advanced time of life. Captain Birch, having stated that I had letters for the Governor, I had the honour to present them. On reading which, he expressed great satisfaction; and promised to do every thing in his power for us during our stay in Bombay. He expressed his concern, that we should have been deprived of our venerable superintendant; but hoped we should, nevertheless, succeed in the meritorious work in which we had engaged.

The information which the Governor's letters gave him, respecting the religious body to which we belonged, led to some remarks of the most honourable kind, on the character and usefulness of our celebrated founder, the Rev. J. Wesley. His Excellency spoke from a personal knowledge of him; as he had seen " old Mr. Wesley" when he was a boy, and remembered him well. He also expressed the high sense which the British Government had ever entertained of Mr. Wesley's principles and proceedings; and added, that the great Lord North did not hesitate to attribute a considerable portion of the loyalty and contentment which prevailed in our native land, to the sound principles and indefatigable exertions of Mr. Wesley.

I must leave the reader to imagine, for I am utterly unable to describe, the emotions with which I heard so high an encomium *from such authority*, on Wesleyan principles and conduct; pronounced, as it was, in the presence of the principal men of the Presidency, from whom we had anticipated opposition to our undertaking. I knew that the principal objections which were felt against missionary efforts in the East, arose from the idea, that they were calculated to excite insubordination and revolt among the natives. These remarks from the lips of the Governor, so highly expressive of the opposite tendency of our principles and labours, appeared so well timed, and were altogether so unexpected, that I was nearly overpowered. I secretly rejoiced at my connection with such a body of Christians ; and I blessed God, that as he had, in the person of Mr. Money, raised us up a friend to provide us with *pecuniary* means; he had likewise, in the honourable testimony of the Governor, furnished us with a reputation more valuable, in our bereaved circumstances, than thousands of gold and silver.

After breakfast, Captain Birch withdrew with the Governor for some time into a separate apartment.— The particulars of that interview have never transpired ; but the disinterested efforts of the Captain to serve us, and the flattering manner in which he must have represented us to the Governor; proceeding, as I am confident they did from a real desire to further the object of our Mission; are fully known to HIM who *knoweth all things*, and whose retributive Providence will not suffer them to be unrewarded.

While the Governor and our invaluable friend were in the private apartment, Mr. Anderson, who was also of the breakfast-party, renewed the kindness which he had shown during our voyage, and entered upon an interesting conversation on Indian affairs. A military gentleman, to whom I was unknown, obligingly pointed out the peculiarities in the surrounding scenery, which is very picturesque, and was, of course, full of novelty to me. A glass, which was brought for the purpose, enabled me to see a curious species of lizard which was sporting on the rock, and which appeared to possess the faculty of changing its colour at pleasure.

In a short time His Excellency returned to the

G

virando, in company with the Captain, and addressing me in the most condescending and Christian manner, said, that there would be no objection to our remaining at Bombay until we could conveniently proceed to Ceylon. His Excellency then made some enquiries how far we were provided with furniture, and other requisites for house-keeping; and replied to the information I gave him, that we need not feel any difficulty as to a residence during our stay; adding, that he should be happy to see us at the public dinner about to be given; but, as he could well apprehend our habits to be of a retired kind, he would take another opportunity of seeing us. After expressing grateful acknowledgements in behalf of my colleagues and myself, I took my leave, and accompanied by Captain Birch, returned to Bombay. The first part of the ride was passed in silence. My hamalls loitered behind the Captain's palankeen, which afforded me an opportunity for reflection on the interesting circumstances of the morning, and the abounding kindness of Providence to us.

On hearing the Captain's voice, my palanqeen-bearers quickened their pace, and brought me alongside of his; when he communicated to me some gratifying information respecting the friendly disposition of the Governor, and of the favourable impression he had received respecting us. At this time a gentleman passed us on his way to the town. "That," said the Captain, " is the Governor's private secretary. He is now on his way to the Fort; and has directions to provide one of the first houses in the place for the accommodation of yourself and companions." This was more than could have been expected, and added to my unutterable feelings of surprise and gratitude. Before we separated, the Captain gave me some cautionary directions respecting our conduct during our stay at the Presidency; and I returned my warmest thanks to him for his kindness.

The hamalls put me down at the tavern door, and I hastened to my anxious associates above-stairs, to whom I related all that had passed. Astonishment, softened by gratitude, sat on every countenance, and involuntary tears started from our eyes. We felt thankful to the excellent and honourable men who had shown us kindness; but we were principally impressed with the interference of Providence in our behalf. We fell upon our knees; and, after praying for the Divine blessing on those who had thus succoured us, we offered our thanks and ourselves unreservedly to Almighty God, to whose service and glory we consecrated the remainder of our days. A divine blessing rested upon us, and we found it a refreshing season. God was with us.

In the course of the day we were visited by the Rev. Messrs. Hall and Nott, the colleagues of Mr. Newell, who kindly offered to render us any aid in their power. If any thing was previously necessary to confirm *our* gratitude, it was supplied by the recital of the trials and exercises through which these good men had passed, since their departure from their native land. On their arrival at Calcutta, they were detained as suspicious persons, (England and America being then unhappily at war,) and sent to Bombay, to be conveyed to England as prisoners of war. The orders which Sir Evan Nepean had received from the Supreme Government in Bengal were such, that it was impossible to show them any marked kindness, or to keep them short of the destination which had been assigned to them. Their passage was taken for England, and the day fixed for their embarkation; when, on the night before they were to have sailed, Messrs. Nott and Hall, leaving Mrs. Nott and her child in their house, repaired on board a native boat which had been provided for them, and made the best of their way to the Malabar coast.

The direction which the Missionary fugitives had taken was soon known, and one of the Honourable Company's cruisers received orders to pursue and apprehend them. They were found at Cochin, and brought back to Bombay: but as the ship had sailed in which their passage was taken, they thus avoided being sent to England as prisoners, and were ordered to reside in the Admiralty House in the Fort; a mansion which was furnished for them, but which was occasionally the residence of the Admiral of the station. They had the parole of the town; but were forbidden to go out into the country, without first appearing at the office of the Fort Adjutant. In the mean time, it was understood, the Bombay Government wrote to Bengal for further orders. The situation of these enterprising men, though exceedingly painful, might, under a Governor of a different disposition, have been much more distressing They owe much to the Christian principles and benevolent heart of Sir Evan Nepean.*

On Wednesday, the 25th, Mr. Clough and myself, as usual, visited our companions at the tavern. I afterwards waited upon Mr. Babbington, the Governor's private secretary, who gave me an order for a large boat to bring our baggage on shore, and politely offered to render us any other service. I learned from him, that the house intended for us in the Fort, had been occupied without the Governor's knowledge; who in consequence, would select another for our accommodation: we therefore deferred landing our baggage for the present. Mr. Squance, finding the heat on shore so oppressive as to render him quite unwell, was accommodated by Mr. Clough with his cabin in the Cabalva,

---

* These excellent Missionaries, of whose trials a brief outline has been given, have since succeeded in establishing a flourishing Mission at the Bombay Presidency.

while he took Mr. Squance's lodging at the tavern; an arrangement which met with the approbation of Captain Birch. By an invitation from Mr. Money, I spent an interesting evening at his house; and was afterwards taken in a *bunder boat*, or accommodation barge, from the new *bunder*, or pier, to the Cabalva.

On the Thursday, a note from Mr. Babbington was brought to me at the tavern; in consequence of which I waited upon him at his office, and received the unexpected information, that the Governor had ordered his country house at Parell, distant from town about six miles, to be prepared for our reception, and that it would be ready for us the next day. I called on Mr. Money and Captain Birch, and informed them of His Excellency's obliging arrangement, and proceeded to the tavern, to communicate it to my companions also. We immediately drew up a letter of thanks to the Governor, for his kindness and hospitality. Mr. Ault and Mr. Erskine took a palankeen, and went to see the house; while Mr. Clough and myself attended at the wharf, to superintend the landing of our luggage, and to be present at its examination at the custom-house.

In the performance of this duty the gentlemen belonging to the custom-house department manifested great politeness.* The Governor had issued an order, that all our public property should be landed duty free; and that our religious books should be exempt from the duties usually laid on books imported. I

* I cannot deny myself the pleasure of recording the names of H. Shank, Esq. the head of the customs, and of E. Godwin, Esq. the principal superintendent of police at Bombay; whose polite attention to us, whenever we had business to transact with their respective departments, will live in our grateful recollection. Indeed, the uniformly polite and hospitable reception we experienced from the different public servants of the Hon. East India Company, during our residence at Bombay, renders it difficult to particularize, where *all* have such powerful claims on our respectful regards.

paid a small sum on my library; because, being asked if *all* my books were religious, I could not answer in the affirmative; some being not strictly theological. We were by no means ignorant that our landing in Bombay had produced a considerable sensation of jealousy in the bosoms of some of the most opulent inhabitants. The expediency of an Ecclesiastical Establishment had been warmly debated in the British Parliament; and the natives were by no means unacquainted with the fact, that among its zealous opposers were gentlemen who were known to them as having formerly filled high official situations in India; and they were ready enough to draw the conclusion, that a measure, so opposed, must be attended with some disadvantages to India. They could not therefore but view with apprehension the arrival of what they considered to be a part of that Ecclesiastical Establishment, which they feared was to compel them to abandon the religion of their forefathers, and to conform them to Christianity. I believe we were the first Missionaries who had arrived from England *direct* to the Presidency of Bombay. This also might tend to excite their apprehensions.

Our arrival having thus become the subject of conversation among the natives, produced some anxiety among the European inhabitants; who, however favourably they might be disposed to judge of our character and design, could not but be apprehensive, lest the misconceptions which had gone abroad with respect to us, might be productive of unpleasant consequences, by alarming the prejudices of the natives. It is not necessary to pursue this subject. The existence of these jealousies naturally increased our difficulties, and tended to depress our minds.

The next day my companions left the Fort and proceeded to Parell, when they were introduced to the house by one of the Governor's head servants, who, by his orders, had provided their first dinner, and put them in the way of house-keeping. In the afternoon I took leave of the friendly officers of the ship, and brought Mrs. Harvard on shore. We were invited to dine by Mr. and Mrs. Money; after which we were conveyed in Mr. Money's carriage to the Governor's delightful country residence. As we passed through the country on our way, it is impossible to describe our emotions. Surrounded with mercies so new, so unexpected, so undeserved, we were encouraged fearlessly to adopt the cheering and confident language of the Apostle;— *Who hath delivered, and in whom we trust that he will yet deliver.*

CHAP VI.

Description of Parell House and Grounds—Gentoo Temple—Disgusting objects of Worship—Aversion of the Natives to the entrance of Europeans—Impositions practised by Native servants—Certificates of character—Present from Capt. Beaty—Sabbath—Attend the Fort Church—Native carriage—Visit from the Governor—Mr. Hart—Lieut. Wade—Visit to the Island of Elephanta—Its dimensions—Description of the wonderful Cave—Extracts from Maurice's Indian Antiquities—Amazing specimens of ancient sculpture—Description of the principal figure—The design of these astonishing works involved in obscurity—Tempest—The visitors to the Island exposed to considerable peril—Safe arrival—Service at the Fort Church—Lord's Supper—Letters to the Committee and our families, franked by the Governor—The party, with the exception of the Author and his wife, proceed to CEYLON, in the Earl Spencer.

THE Governor's mansion at Parell, appointed for our residence, is a handsome and commodious building, having excellent and extensive gardens and grounds attached to it. It was formerly a Portuguese church, and was connected with a monastery. Being purchased by a former Governor of Bombay, he added a beautiful upper story to it; which has this peculiarity, that the floor is raised in the centre, like the quarter-deck of a ship. This singularity is attributed to the Governor's having been for many years a naval commander. The ground-floor is made of a composition, which resembles one entire piece of marble, and which yields an agreeable coolness. This mode of forming the ground-floor, which is common to the principal houses in Bombay, is produced by adding of sugar, eggs, &c. to 'their *chunam*, or mortar. These give the floor the variegated colours and fine gloss of polished marble. The lofty pillars supporting the virando, or galleries around the house, and the noble hall, formerly the body of the church, with the grand style in which the whole is finished, gives the building the appearance of a royal palace; and, if we had been affected with any thing like fears for our safety, from the sensations which were excited by our arrival, they were more than allayed by a company of native soldiers, who were placed as guards around the house; the houses of the Governor and Members of the Council having always a guard of honour, whether the owner be resident or not.

The gardens produced the most delicious fruits, and most fragrant shrubs and flowers. Attempts were making to produce some European fruits. We saw an apple-tree of a tolerable size, but the fruit was hard and sour. The head gardener, in obedience to the Governor's orders, every morning brought us a basket of fruit and vegetables, and presented each of us with a handsome nosegay. We occupied one wing of the house, consisting of a suite of rooms communicating with a long virando. The latter we occupied as a general room, and the former as separate apartments. In the general room we transacted our affairs, and partook of our meals. Our servants slept at their own houses, with the exception of the female servant, who slept for a few nights in a lower apartment. The house having been a church, produced in her a belief that an evil spirit, which she imagined resided in some neighbouring trees, had one night paid her a visit, and *pinched her nose!* In consequence of this foolish notion, my wife found her the next morning in a violent fever. We allowed her therefore to leave our service.

Parell House is situated at the foot of a hill, on the top of which is a flag staff, and from which is an extensive view of the harbour, and the surrounding country. The bay is studded with small islands. One of which is the celebrated Island of Elephanta: on one of the others is a gibbet, from which is suspended the skeletons of two malefactors, who were executed some years ago. It is to be regretted that the beautiful scenery should be marred by such an object; it is, supposed, however, to be productive of salutary effects on the minds of the natives. From the Flag Staff Hill at low water a small isthmus may be perceived, which unites the island of Bombay to the main land. It does not appear to be more than a mile from the Governor's house. At high water there is no communication, but by a boat; but when the tide is out it may be forded ; and the tigers from the adjoining hills, stimulated by hunger, have been known to swim across in search of food; and some had been killed very near to our residence.

Though the hill is very steep, we soon gained the summit; the view from which amply repaid us for our labour. At the bottom of the hill there is a Gentoo temple, which we beheld with feelings of deep commiseration for the devotees who frequented its unhallowed mysteries. As we had determined to avoid any conduct which might tend to strengthen the suspicions which were indulged by some against us, and finding that the natives were averse to our stepping even on the threshold of their temple, we kept back. We saw enough in the exterior to excite our disgust and horror.

On the ground, carved in stone, was fixed the figure of a female, sitting in the Indian posture; but the carver had been so unmindful of *drapery*, that a description cannot be given; nor would our sense of decency allow us to take a second view. Opposite to this figure was the image of a bull, painted red, also one of their deities! Happy should we have been, to have pointed out to them a more excellent way; but our situation was peculiar: many eyes were upon us, and many misconceptions were afloat respecting us. We could only pray for them, that they might be *turned from darkness unto light, and from the power of Satan unto the living God*.

The Gentoos are particularly averse to the entrance of Europeans into their sacred temples. Even the worshippers are only admitted within certain distances of the idol, which are regulated according to the *caste*, or rank, of the worshipper. Any breach of this arrangement would, I am persuaded, from what I have seen of that people, be sufficient to produce a public disturbance, and even an insurrection, if they had not redress. Some years ago an English gentleman, in a state of intoxication, attempted to enter this temple; he was stopped by the priest in attendance, who begged him to desist, as it was not their custom to permit Europeans to see their god. The gentleman, unhappily, was not in a state to listen to persuasion; but forcing himself from them, he rushed in, and declared he would not only *see* their god, but that he would also cast an *indignity* upon him. He accomplished his threat, and uttered some imprecations against them for not becoming Christians! He was seriously alarmed when sober, on learning what he had done during the madness of intoxication; and, but for the important rank he held, and a large pecuniary present to the priests, the consequences of his sacrilegious intrusion would have been dreadful.

The second day of our residence at Parell we commenced housekeeping; and soon found that our native servants imposed upon us, not only in often supplying us with damaged articles, such as old tea-leaves dried, butter filled with black ants, stale milk, eggs, &c.; but also in charging very exorbitantly for the wretched commodities with which they supplied us. We soon remedied the former, but they baffled all our attempts to counteract the latter. We were obliged to lock up every article of food, except at meal-times. If, from motives of economy, we purchased any article ourselves, at the first hand, they would be sure to make it the more expensive plan, by their lavish manner of using it. It is the custom in India for the servants to provide every thing necessary for the house; and every week, or month, to present their accounts to their employers. We knew we could not save any thing by going ourselves to the bazaars: but, to prevent imposition, it was our custom to see the articles when brought from the market, and to settle their accounts every day, to check the charges. By this means we avoided imposition, and were better supplied. Before we adopted this plan, we had inferior meat, and other unwholesome food; when we complained, the servants thought they could easily silence our murmurings, by saying, "It is this country's custom." But we never thus interfered with them without highly offending them; which they always caused us to feel, either by spoiling our dinner, or making us wait two or three hours beyond the usual time, or both.

To defraud and impose upon persons newly arrived from Europe, who are termed by them *Griffins*, is the common practice of the native servants. By hiring some who offered themselves on our landing, relying on their *written* characters, we had (with the exception of two) a company of complete rogues; and the more honest were corrupted by the others, who would have beaten them had they acted differently from themselves.*

* As it is customary for Europeans to give a written certificate of character to servants when leaving their service, it often happens

The number of servants required in India is both expensive and perplexing. A native of one caste will not touch the work which belongs to another; and, unless you have a good head-servant to govern and control the others, they will subject you to the grossest impositions. After some time a friend procured for us a respectable head-servant, and we were then possessed of something like domestic comfort.

At the very commencement of our family arrangements we were surprised by the arrival of a gentleman's servant, who had come from town with some coolies* laden with packages; on opening which, we found half a dozen of the different articles necessary for housekeeping: plates, glass-ware, tea-ware, silver spoons, a quantity of wax candles, some jars of fine sugar, some papers of tea, &c. &c. A polite note accompanied this valuable supply, requesting us to use them during our stay in Bombay. The generous donor was Captain Beaty of the Honourable Company's marine department, a particular friend of Captain Birch. I believe he had not seen any of our party but myself. I was introduced to him by Captain Birch; and, from the representations of us which the Captain had given him, and from a respect to our religious character, he was induced to show us this mark of attention. This was but the commencement of a series of favours from this gentleman; and I cannot but regret that no reference was made to his generosity in any of our public letters from India.

that one man has a number of characters by him; and on his decease, they are frequently *sold* to others. Native servants will also from poverty, if not from less excuseable motives, sometimes *sell* or *lend* characters to each other. So that these documents cannot always be relied on as belonging to the persons who exhibit them.

* *Coolies* are a description of native porters, or bearers of burthens. These are found in every part of India.

The next day, being Sunday, as we had expressed a desire to attend the Fort Church, a wealthy Persee merchant sent a carriage, which accommodated six of us. It was of a peculiar construction, not having raised seats, as the European carriages. We sat upon an *ottoman*, which formed the floor of the carriage; and, being unaccustomed to this posture, found some difficulty in placing our legs. The church is a well-built structure, with a good organ. I was much struck with the appearance of the large *punkahs*, or fans, which extended from pillar to pillar over the pews, and which produced an artificial breeze, as they were kept in motion by the means of ropes fastened to them, and pulled by natives outside the windows. The organ had a fine effect, and its tones quite overcame my spirits. The last time I had heard an organ was in our chapel in Canterbury; and the change in my circumstances produced a momentary tear: it was not, however, a tear of regret. The service was performed by the Rev. N. Wade, one of the chaplains; the sermon was on *Divine influence*. The manner in which all the pews were furnished with prayer-books much interested me; they bore the Company's arms, with the motto, "*Auspice Senatus et Rex Anglorum*."*

At the conclusion of the service the whole congregation rose, and remained standing, until the Governor had passed out. He obligingly noticed our party, as he passed the pew in which we stood. We afterwards entered our carriage, and returned home.

It is customary to breakfast in Bombay at eight o'clock in the morning, and to dine at four or five in the afternoon. This prevails throughout the whole of India; with the exception, in some places, of a much later hour for dinner. On this account there is a meal in the middle of the day called *tiffen*, which answers

* " Under the auspices of the King and Parliament of England."

to our luncheon. This is frequently as plenteous a board as the dinner-table ; and invitations to *tiffen*, are as common as to any other meal. Ours was generally a little fruit with bread and butter. We had just sat down to our tiffen, on our return from the church, when we were informed that the Governor had arrived, and was in the garden. The rest of our company requested me to wait upon him, which I did. He kindly ordered a chair, and I sat with him for some time, conversing on different subjects. It was evident that Sir Evan Nepean was the Christian, as well as the gentleman. I begged leave to introduce my colleagues to him; he said he would himself go and see them ; and proceeding to the apartments which we occupied, he condescended to sit with us there, and conversed with each in a most friendly manner, until he rose to return to his residence at Malabar Point. In the morning, before going to church, we held a class-meeting ; and we endeavoured to spend the remainder of the day in a way suitable to its sacred character

During the succeeding week I was chiefly employed in the Fort, arranging affairs connected with the Mission. The rest of our party either remained at Parell, or made little excursions in the neighbourhood. All our mission property having been received on board the ships in Doctor Coke's name, rendered the Captain responsible for it to his executors. His private property was also intermingled with it, which tended to increase the difficulty. Captain Birch would have been fully justified, had he sold every thing by public auction, but which would have been a serious trial to us. We were grateful to Divine Providence for placing us and our affairs under the direction of so honourable and sympathizing a commander. He directed us to examine the books and papers which were in the Doctor's possession at the time of his decease, and to select such as we judged to belong to the Mission. This we did; and, on our security only, he allowed us to take possession of whatever we stated to be public property. In consequence, we obtained on our receipt, the following articles:—

> A quantity of books, (as per list.)
> A printing press complete,
> A box of printing ink,
> Four boxes of printing types,
> Two packing-cases of printing-paper,
> The Mission Library, in two large chests,
> A quantity of Portuguese Testaments and Religious Tracts.

These were lodged at the custom-house, until we could obtain a convenient place for their reception.

Mr. Hart, at that time in the employment of the Honourable Company, as superintendent of a newly-erected steam-engine; but who had been a member of our society in Birmingham, and at Lambeth near London; having heard of our arrival, called on us, and the pleasure we felt was mutual. From him and Mrs. Hart we received many friendly services during our stay.* Lieutenant Wade, Aid-de-camp to the Commander in chief, also manifested great friendship towards us, and frequently visited us.

We naturally felt great anxiety to see the singular Island of Elephanta, and to explore the wonderful cave there. Mr. Hart and Lieutenant Wade kindly undertook to accompany us; Mr. Newell, I think, was also of the party. Saturday, the fourth of June, was the day appointed for the excursion: but, as it was necessary that an official letter to our Missionary Committee should be written, and as it fell to Mr. Lynch and myself to prepare that letter, we were obliged to forego

---

* This worthy man has been recently removed, I trust, to a better world, leaving a family.

the pleasure the excursion would have afforded, and to remain at home. His Excellency the Governor had offered to frank our letter, and send it by the *overland despatch*, which was on the point of setting off; and delay was therefore out of the question.

The party proceeded to the Island of Elephanta early in the morning, in a boat provided for them by Mr. Hart. The Island is from two to three miles in circumference. Its name is derived from the figure of a large elephant, formerly an object of religious adoration, cut out of the solid rock of which the Island is composed. This statue is on the south side; and is so well formed, that from the colour of the rock, by the aid of the imagination, it may at a suitable distance be easily mistaken for a real elephant. The party experienced much inconvenience from the intense heat, especially in their ascent to the sacred cavern, which is situated about half way up the immense hill; but they were well recompensed by the view of that venerable specimen of Indian antiquity, mythology, and art.

The cave is cut out of the rocky hill, and presents the singular appearance of an entire stone chamber; being, according to the testimony of respectable travellers, about eighteen or twenty feet high, and one hundred and twenty feet square, the principal entrance being from the north. Visitors on their approach to the entrance, are sometimes alarmed by the appearance of wild beasts and venomous reptiles, which not unfrequently shelter themselves among the high grass and weeds. A Captain Hamilton, on his entrance into the cave, discharged a pistol, when a huge serpent, fifteen feet long, and two feet thick, issued from the dark recess, and compelled him and his companions to a precipitate retreat.* This circumstance must have occurred at the breaking-up of

---

* Maurice's Indian Antiquities; part ii. p. 241.

the monsoon, during which the Island of Elephanta is unfrequented for three or four months. This accounts for the passage being infested with reptiles; but when the Missionaries and their friends visited the Island, they encountered none of these unpleasant obstructions.

On entering the apartment they were filled with amazement at the immense figures which are cut out of the rock, and are arranged along the sides of the cavern, to the number of forty or fifty, each of them twelve or fifteen feet in height, and of very exact symmetry.— Although they are as round and prominent as the life, yet none of them are detached from the main rock. Some of these figures have on their heads a kind of helmet, of a pyramidical form; others wear crowns ornamented with rich devices, and splendidly decorated with jewels; while others display only ringlets of curled or flowing hair. Many of them have four hands, others have six; and in these hands they grasp sceptres and shields; the symbols of justice, and the ensigns of religion; the weapons of war and the trophies of peace. Some of these have aspects that inspire the beholder with terror; while others are distinguished by a placid serenity and benignity of countenance; and others betray evident marks of deep dejection and inward anguish. The more conspicuous figures are all gorgeously arrayed after the Indian fashion, with heavy jewels in their ears, superb collars of precious stones, belts sumptuously wrought, and rich bracelets on their arms and wrists.*

The most prominent of these Elephanta statues is the enormous bust situated on the south side, and directly facing the main entrance of the cave. Some controversies have taken place among antiquarians on the subject of this figure: some supposing that it ex-

* Maurice, sect. i. p. 245.

hibits but three faces; but our friends remarked that there were four. Mr. Maurice, in his work on Indian Antiquities, is inclined to the former opinion; but mentions also, with much candour, the opinion of the accurate Mr. Hunter, who asserts the latter. As I had not the opportunity of observing it myself, I shall furnish the reader with Mr. Hunter's description of the symbols and aspects of the three principal personages who compose this remarkable statue, as given by Mr. Maurice:— " Let us, however, consider his account of the dimensions of the august visage in the front. We shall soon perceive, from its astonishing depth and breadth, that it was intended for the image of the supreme presiding deity of this hallowed retreat; and that the sculptor wished to impress us, by the superior magnitude of the bust only, with the most awful conceptions of his unrivalled pre-eminence in every point of view. The face in the front measures above five feet in length, and the nose alone one foot and a half; the width from the ear only to the middle of the nose is three feet four inches; but the stupendous breadth of the whole figure, between the shoulders, expands nearly twenty feet. The towering pyramidical cap of the central head has in front a very large jewel; and the caps themselves of all the three are exquisitely wrought. Round the neck of the same figure is suspended a most magnificent broad collar, composed of precious stones and pearls. " The face," adds Mr. Hunter, " has a drowsy but placid appearance, which may be supposed the exact description of that absorbed state, which, it has been before remarked, constitutes the supreme felicity of the Indian deity!

" The amiable attribute of the *Preserver*, Veeshnu, is doubtless intended to be represented by the face on the right; which is arranged in smiles, and looks enamoured on a bunch of flowers, perhaps the sacred *lotos*, which its left hand holds up to view. If ever, on the other hand, the dreadful attributes of the *destroying* god Mahadeo, (Shiva or Seeva) were accurately pourtrayed, are they not evident in the monstrous, distorted, and terrific features of the remaining aspect? The eye-brows of that face are contracted into forms; the skin of the nose is drawn upwards and the *alce nostri* distended, expressing contempt and indignation. This face too is darkened by whiskers which the others have not, and the tongue is violently thrust out between the teeth. The right hand of this dreadful figure grasps a large hooded snake, (the *cobra di capello*, the bite of which is mortal) which it holds aloft, and surveys with a stern look. The snake is about a foot in thickness; and the middle finger of the hand which grasps it, three feet and a half in length. Another hand, which is now broken off, appears to have had a snake of the same hooded and enormous kind."

Mr. Maurice, who it appears had not himself visited Elephanta, suggests, " If, upon future and more accurate examination, this should be discovered to be a quadruple-faced divinity, in that case to whom can it possibly point but to *Brahma* himself, the GREAT ONE, who in the Asiatic Register is represented with four majestic aspects; as the God who not only knows, but observes, all things." It is my intention to introduce, in a subsequent part of my narrative, a more detailed account of the Hindoo theology, when this suggestion of Mr. Maurice will be more clearly understood. This immense figure must have been the principal object of adoration in this temple, though not the only one; as in the western side of the apartment there is a dark recess twenty feet square, totally destitute of any external ornament, excepting the altar in the centre, and those gigantic figures which guard the four several doors that lead to it. These figures are unclothed;

and from Mr. Maurice's account of this recess, the only conclusion is, that it was formerly devoted to that *impure worship* so prevalent in India, and the origin and circumstances of which he has so well described.

A particular description of the various other figures and ornaments in this curious pantheon, would extend far beyond my plan; and the uncertainty attending their original import leaves too much room for conjecture fully to satisfy curiosity, which on that account I am unwilling to excite. But little is known with exactness of the history and purposes of this astonishing piece of workmanship: an admirer of the arts, I can well conceive, would experience high gratification in tracing the proportion of the several figures, and in marking the delicacy with which they have been finished. But he who would endeavour to connect them with facts, and to ascertain the period of their formation, must retire from the attempt with disappointment and regret. Mr. Maurice shall be quoted to repress a design so unpromising. " One would have supposed," he remarks, "that the construction of such astonishing works, which have been called the eighth wonder of the world, would have fixed in any country an æra never to be forgotten; since not only a long period of years must have been consumed, but an infinite number of hands must have been employed, in scooping out from the living rock such extensive caverns, and forming, by the slow operation of the chisel, so many and such massive columns. It is, however, very remarkable, that no scrutiny, however rigid, no enquiry, however diligent, either among the neighbouring Brahmins, or those living upon the Continent, celebrated as they are for learning and penetration, could ever succeed in discovering the immediate sovereign who fabricated them, nor the exact epoch of that fabrication."

Our friends had nearly involved themselves in a

serious difficulty by their visit to Elephanta at so late a period of the season. It being just before the setting-in of the monsoon, the weather is subject to very great uncertainties; the monsoon itself commences at some seasons a few weeks sooner or later than at others, which renders all excursions by water rather hazardous, when within a short time of that serious change in the seasons. A violent storm of thunder and lightning, attended with rain, filled them with apprehensions lest the monsoon should have actually set in, which would have confined them to the Island; and the agitated state of the water rendered it impossible for them to return in the boat in which they had embarked. It was proposed by one of the party to write me a note, announcing their situation, and urging me to request that the ship's long-boat might be sent for their deliverance from the solitude which threatened them. This met with almost universal approbation, until the difficulty of conveying it was suggested by one of the company.— The boatmen said they would venture across to take a note; but they would not carry any one in the boat besides themselves, neither would they engage to come back again to the Island. Our friends determined therefore not to part with the boat, the only means they had of return; and as the day was nearly gone, and their stock of provisions expended, the servants were sent round the Island to endeavour to obtain a supply. A few fishermen were found, who possessed some poultry, &c. but who refused to part with them on any terms. It happened, however, that the servants had with them one of the Governor's peons, who immediately returned to the place where the party were resting, and putting on his sword and belt, repaired again to the fishermen: on seeing his uniform, they readily bargained with the servants at a fair price for whatever they wanted. A supper was soon provided, after which a few lay down to rest, while the others anxiously watched the state of the tide.

About midnight the violence of the tempest subsided, when the whole company insisted that the boatmen should push off with them. Fastening themselves to their little bark, that they might not be thrown out, they committed themselves to the waves; and by the goodness of God, they arrived at Mazagong in Bombay about six o'clock on the Sunday morning. As no other conveyance could be had they were glad to engage some hackries, or bullock carts, in which they arrived at Parell to our common joy; those who remained at home having been much exercised for the safety of the remainder, especially when the storm came on, and we found that they did not return at the time appointed.*

Most of our party were too much fatigued, by the exertions and anxieties which they had undergone, to go into the Fort that morning. Some of us, however, went to the church, being accommodated with a conveyance, as on the last Sabbath. The service was a profitable one; and at the close the sacrament of the Lord's Supper was administered. I was grieved at the small number who remained to partake of that holy ordinance; but was pleased to observe the Governor at the table.

The sacramental service was to me a refreshing and solemn season. On closing the church doors, the sexton came round, and presented each of the communicants (not excepting the Governor) with an ex-

* The Asiatic Journal, a valuable work, which presents the European public with monthly details of the principal occurrences at our Indian settlements, contains in its number for June, 1821, a very melancholy account of a far different termination of an Elephanta excursion, which occurred in the previous month of November; in which two respectable members of the party unhappily found a watery grave!

cellent Companion to the Altar. The vein of piety breathing through the little manual, the decorum and solemnity with which the whole service was conducted, and my own peculiar circumstances, all tended to impress my heart in the most salutary manner. Though far from scenes and society which had formerly interested and profited me, *I found it good for me to draw near to God.*

The next morning our official letter to the Committee, having been read and approved, was forwarded to the Governor, to be franked for the overland despatch. His Excellency sent us word, that if we wished to write to our families in England, he would also frank one for each of us, and an extra one for each of the married Missionaries. Mr. Ault and myself gladly availed ourselves of the opportunity of writing *two* letters, and the rest of our party each prepared his single letter. We were restricted to a very small sheet of paper, about the size of a duodecimo page; and our letters, when folded up, did not exceed four inches in length, and about two and a half in breadth. We felt it almost impossible to express within so small a compass all the important tidings which we wished to communicate. Our first letters, therefore, contained but a hasty and very limited account of our situation, and of the trials and mercies with which we had been visited. Some of our friends in England were dissatisfied with the brevity of our first epistles; but the cause is thus explained.

About this time we heard that it would be possible to obtain a passage to Ceylon in the Earl Spencer, a vessel going to China, but which would lie-to off Point de Galle, and land passengers. We immediately engaged with Captain Mitchell, through the agency of Mr. Money; but Mr. M. kindly remarked, that as, from the advanced state of the season, it might be attended with considerable difficulty to get a landing when the vessel arrived off Ceylon, he thought it would be improper for my wife, in her situation, to proceed with the rest of the party. I consulted Captain Birch, who was of the same opinion; and who recommended me to obtain the advice of a medical man, and then apply to the Governor in Council, for permission to remain at Bombay until after the monsoon months. Having stated these things to my companions, with their consent I made application, and obtained the necessary permission.

The Mission family, with the exception of Mrs. H. and myself, sailed out of Bombay harbour on the 20th of June, and landed at Point de Galle after a voyage of *nine days.*

CHAP. VIII.

Voyage of Messrs. Ault, &c. to Ceylon—Kind reception from the Government authorities—The Government house at Galle prepared for their reception—Condescension of Lord and Lady Molesworth—His Lordship's estimate of their character—The Rev. G. Bisset—Liberal proposal of His Excellency, the Governor, to endow schools—First Ceylon Conference—Deliberations—Wesleyan plan of stationing the preachers—Their resignation of themselves to God, and satisfaction with their respective stations—Celebration of the Lord's Supper previous to their separation—Arrival of Messrs. Lynch and Squance at Columbo—Hospitable reception by the Honourable and Reverend Archdeacon Twisleton, &c.—Introduced to His Excellency, the Governor—Invited to dine—Important assistance rendered by the Right Honourable Sir A. Johnstone, Chief Justice of Ceylon—Mr. Armour; his history and character—Preach in the Baptist Mission chapel—A Native convert—Proceed to Jaffnapatam—J. N. Mooyart, Esq.—Christian David, a pupil of Swartz—School opened—Preach in the Dutch church—Mr. Erskine proceeds to Matura—Encouraging reception—The Rev. T. G. Erhardt—Matura school opened—Service in the Dutch church—Importance of Matura, as a Missionary station—Mr. Ault sails from Galle to Batticaloe—Dangerous voyage—Reception—Acts as Chaplain—His labours among the Europeans and Natives—Mr. Clough commences his Mission at Galle—Lord Molesworth's important patronage and advice—Mr. C.'s labours among the Europeans, and efforts to benefit the Natives—Visited by Don Abraham Dias Abeysinha Ameresekera, who generously offers a residence and school-house—The Galle school opened—Native enquirers—Mr. Clough's unwearied and successful application to the study of the Singhalese language.

THE passage of our brethren who had embarked in the Earl Spencer, though speedy, was hazardous; as the vessel was carried before the wind, which blew in one continued gale, until they arrived within sight of the Island of Ceylon. The Captain was frequently apprehensive he should not be able to put them on shore; in which case they would have been compelled to proceed with the vessel to Pulo Penang, or even to

China. But on their arrival off Point de Galle, nearly the southernmost point of Ceylon, a remarkably clear day caused the signal made by the Captain to be seen on shore; and W. C. Gibson, Esq. then master-attendant of that port, immediately sent off boats for them and their chests. Messrs. Lynch, Squance, and Clough landed in a short time; but Messrs. Ault and Erskine remained, to bring away the baggage in the larger boats. They were received on the wharf by Mr. Gibson; when a series of kind services to our Mission commenced on the part of that gentleman, and his excellent lady, which have been continued without interruption.

Mr. Gibson introduced the Missionaries shortly after their arrival to the Right Honourable Lord Molesworth, Commandant of the Galle garrison; a pious nobleman, who had received intelligence of the appointment of a Christian Mission to the Island of Ceylon with no common pleasure. As they were proceeding to his lordship's residence, Mr. G. informed them, that he had a few days before received a letter from Mr. Money, of Bombay, informing him of the probable time of their arrival, and the signal which the Captain would make on coming in sight of land; in consequence of which he had been looking out for the ship. This was another proof of the lively interest Mr. Money took in our affairs, and excited their thankfulness to God. But what must have been their surprise and gratitude, when they learned that Sir Evan Nepean also had written favourably concerning them, to His Excellency, General Brownrigg, the Governor of Ceylon; who had in consequence immediately written to Lord Molesworth, directing that the Government-house in the Fort of Galle should be prepared for their reception. So signally were they favoured with the good opinion of those under whose jurisdiction they were to commence their labours.

Lord and Lady Molesworth received them with great affability, and accompanied them to the Government-house, which had been made ready for them; they then invited them to return and refresh themselves; which they did. But their fears began to be excited by the non-appearance of Messrs. Ault and Erskine, who were expected to land immediately after them; but of whom no tidings had been heard even at eight o'clock in the evening. Lord Molesworth, however, assured them there was no reason to be apprehensive for their safety; as, at that boisterous season of the year, it often happened that boats, in endeavouring to reach the land from vessels in the Galle roads, were driven (the wind and tide being both against them) several miles to the eastward. The night was to them, notwithstanding, an anxious one, and was not passed without much concern, and many fervent prayers for the safety of their companions.

Early in the morning his lordship, apprehending that the boat had been driven to the eastward, sent off two palankeens and some servants to a place called Belligamme, situated about sixteen miles from Galle, in the hope of meeting with our friends; and about five o'clock in the afternoon they arrived in safety.

It appeared, that after Mr. Lynch and his party had left the ship, Captain Mitchell detained the luggage-boat while he wrote a few letters for the shore; the ship in the mean time was driving on to sea; so that by the time they parted, the boatmen found it impossible to make Galle harbour, and in consequence directed their course to Belligamme, which was the next port.

Their situation on leaving the ship was far from pleasant. On the wide ocean—in an open boat—at the command of men with whose manners and language they were wholly unacquainted—while the darkness of the night prevented them from observing their actions :—these circumstances combined to work upon their fears; and the apprehensions they entertained for their personal safety became at length painfully active. This was particularly the case with Mr. Ault, whose nervous system had been greatly shattered, and who could not divest himself of the impression that the boatmen intended to run the boat into some creek, and rob, if not murder them. Taking his watch in his hand, he endeavoured to make the men comprehend, that if they would put them on shore, he would give it them as a present. But there was not one among them who could understand him, or make him any intelligible reply ; except one man, who had acquired a smattering of English; and who, whenever our friends appeared uneasy, or said any thing to them, (shaking his hand in the air) would cry out, "Very bad, Sir!—Very bad, Sir!" They afterwards found that the poor fellow wished to tell them, that the weather was unfavourable to their progress; and that they found it hard work to make any way.

In the middle of the night they came into the harbour of Belligamme. About half-past two in the morning they landed, and the boatmen conducted them to the house of Mr. Kunemann, the magistrate, who cheerfully rose, rendered them every assistance, and had their luggage placed in a safe store-room, until it could be removed to Galle by land; as the boat would not be able to return for several weeks; then, taking them back again to his own house, he gave them some refreshment. This respectable magistrate manifested considerable regard for religion. He said, he thanked God for the arrival of our friends, and looked upon it as a singular providence, that, by their being forced into that bay, he had an opportunity of making their acquaintance; adding a hope, that should one of them be subsequently stationed at Galle, he should be favoured with a visit. After thanking him, and praying for him, they took their leave.

At Galle, one of the Governor's servants had received orders to make every necessary provision for the strangers, at the expense of His Excellency; but for several days after their landing they dined and drank tea with Lord and Lady Molesworth. On the first Sunday, at the request of his lordship, they celebrated Divine service in the Dutch church, which was numerously attended by the Europeans resident in the garrison and neighbourhood; and in the evening of the same day his lordship intimated a desire to unite with them in their family worship. With this they gladly acquiesced; and during the several times he afterwards met with them on similar occasions, they had the gratification of witnessing the simplicity and fervour of his lordship's piety, and of hearing him express himself as greatly refreshed and benefited.

A natural openness of disposition, and a decided regard for the things of God, attached his lordship to the Missionaries. This regard was, of course, in proportion to the consistency with which they sustained their sacred character. Nor did his lordship express an equivocal opinion respecting them. In his view, (and he was a competent judge) they were men well calculated to promote the interests of that religion which he supremely esteemed. And the attentions he paid them, and the pleasure he manifested in his intercourse with them, spoke a language which the European society of Galle could not misunderstand.

Immediately on their arrival, Lord Molesworth wrote to the Governor, informing him of the same. On receiving an answer from His Excellency, his lordship informed them, that the Reverend George Bisset, brother-in-law to the Governor, and one of the colonial chaplains, would pay them a visit in a day or two, for the purpose of bidding them welcome to the island, and of making himself acquainted with the plan on which they intended to conduct their Missionary labours. Mr. Bisset readily undertook a journey from Colombo, the seat of Government, for this purpose; and, at the first interview received them in the most friendly manner; entered into conversation with them on the moral and religious state of the island, and on the means which had already been pursued for the dissemination and establishment of Christianity. He desired them to communicate freely to him their intentions and wishes; assuring them of every facility to promote their important engagements, which it was in the power of Government to afford.

Mr. Bisset, having expressed a desire to know whether any or all of them were in holy orders, the Missionaries produced their letters of ordination, and gave him some information respecting the religious body with which they were united. They also furnished him with the Minutes of the last British and American Conferences; and also with the last Wesleyan Missionary Report, which was drawn up by the late Doctor Coke; particularly pointing out to him the number of black and coloured people, who are members of the societies at our several Foreign Missionary stations. They further stated, that their immediate object in Ceylon would be to commence the study of the native languages; in order to qualify them for labouring among the Ceylonese, and to enable themselves to converse with those who did not understand English; and that, previous to their acquiring a knowledge of the language, they would readily avail themselves of any opportunity of instructing and preaching to such as might be disposed to hear them in their own language. With this statement Mr. Bisset appeared to be fully satisfied; and assured them they might expect every encouragement in so good a work.

A few days after, they had another most interesting interview with Mr. Bisset; in the course of which, he stated to them, that the Governor, with himself, and others of our respected countrymen at the seat of Government, not having any knowledge of our funds, and of the way in which they were to be supported, had been consulting on some means of assisting them, in case it should be needful: and that the only way which appeared to present itself, was to offer them a monthly allowance for teaching the English language, to the children of the principal native inhabitants, in a few of the most important towns. It was then proposed, that each of them should take the superintendence of an English school at their several stations; as this would most effectually subserve the design of their Mission; by introducing them to an acquaintance with the most respectable natives—procuring for them considerable influence—and at the same time be a most effectual method of learning the native languages.

The Missionary party made their acknowledgments to Mr. Bisset for his valuable communications, and requested a little time to make his proposals the subject of conversation among themselves. The plan appeared to recommend itself by so many important advantages, that they could regard it in no other point of view than as an intimation from Providence of the path he had chosen for them. In no other way could they account for it, that the Governor and principal men of the island should thus condescend to mark out for them the plan by which they might most effectually enter upon their Mission. They thanked the Almighty that he thus continued to shine upon their way; and believing it to be from God, and that it accorded with the instructions they had received from the Committee, they expressed their gratitude to His Excellency and Mr. Bisset, and willingly accepted of the generous proposal.

Mr. Bisset accordingly transmitted to the Governor

an account of what had passed during his visit to Galle, and that the Missionary party cordially acceded to the proposed plan. In a few days they received advice from Colombo, that His Excellency entirely approved of the design and spirit of the newly-arrived Missionaries; that he thought fifty rix dollars* could be allowed per month for each school; and that, as Colombo was already fully supplied with English masters, he considered Jaffna, Manaar, Batticaloa, Galle, and Matura, as the most eligible places for such establishments. Having given our friends this information, Mr. Bisset with great candour informed them, that this was only the Governor's *opinion;* and desired them to consider themselves at perfect liberty to occupy any, or none, of the places mentioned, as might be most congenial with their own views, and with the spirit of the instructions they had received from their society in England. As he was on the point of returning to Colombo, he recommended them to weigh the matter well, and to avail themselves of any information they could obtain, before they came to a final determination; requesting them to inform him of the result of their deliberations in a few days.

On the ensuing Sabbath they again performed Divine service in the Dutch church; one of the party read the morning prayers, and another delivered a short sermon; and on the morning of Monday, July 11, they held a consultation on the affairs of the Mission, which, in their letter from Galle to the Missionary Committee, they term "a little Conference." The first question they considered, was, " Shall we separate so widely, and to so many places?" Many serious objections

* The sterling value of the Ceylon rix-dollar is very variable. I have known it as high as eleven rials to the pound; and have also sold bills on England at fifteen and a half rials. Perhaps thirteen rials may be the average. The rix-dollars of the Cape of Good Hope, and of Ceylon are circulated at a different average.

presented themselves to this measure; but after mature deliberation, they came to a determination to separate to Jaffna and Batticaloa, on the one hand, for the Tamul language; and to Galle and Matura, on the other, for the Singhalese. Thus, in effect, the arrangement which was subsequently adopted, of dividing the island into two districts, the Tamul and the Singhalese, was the basis on which the Missionary party originally proceeded. Manaar was by this arrangement left unoccupied for the present; as, from Mr. Squance's state of health, it was considered necessary that he should not be appointed to a station alone. They could therefore occupy but *four* stations, until their number received some addition.

They then proceeded to the consideration of a question not less important, and attended with no less difficulty than the former: " Who shall go to these several places?" It is one of the excellencies of the Wesleyan Methodist economy, that the appointment of its ministers to their several stations is regulated by themselves. Possessing the best acquaintance with each other, and therefore the most capable of judging of the qualifications of each for particular spheres of action, they are enabled to suit the labourer to the soil which he is to cultivate; as well as to vary the degree of talent and exertion, according to the effects produced by previous endeavours. From this plan the most beneficial consequences have resulted. It, however, requires the constant exercise of pious and disinterested principles properly to carry it into effect.

" This," they write, " being by far the most important question, we humbled ourselves before God, and prayed for resignation and Divine direction. We looked at the places and languages, and the disposition and talent of each brother. We foresaw that those who learned the Tamul could not at any future period change with the brethren who would have to learn the Singhalese, nor the latter with the former. We agreed to fix our stations by ballot; when brothers Lynch and Squance were chosen for Jaffna; brother Ault for Batticaloa; brother Erskine for Matura, and brother Clough for Galle. We felt truly resigned to our appointments; not a murmuring word, nor we believe a thought, of the kind existed. At this instant our feelings were most acute. We found ourselves at last about to separate to various and distant parts of the island. We embraced, and wept, and prayed for each other. God had given us the spirit of love in an unusual degree. We agreed, that brothers Squance and Lynch should set out on the Thursday following; and that brothers Ault and Erskine should remain at Galle till they received instructions how to proceed to their destinations."

I have preferred that these excellent men should in their own words inform the reader of the particulars of their first meeting. The piety, simplicity, and mutual affection which they manifested, will be worthy the imitation of all their successors, and of every one engaged in a similar work. Nor is the *promptitude* with which they addressed themselves to their work less worthy of admiration. On the Friday their attention is directed to certain places, as eligible for Missionary stations. On Monday they fix their appointments; and on Thursday commence their journies to their stations. A missionary, whose soul is properly alive to his work, looks upon his individual station as a sacred charge committed to his trust; and esteems the time as comparatively lost, during which he is detained from entering upon it.

Before their departure the Missionaries resolved upon celebrating the Lord's Supper; and the morning of separation was the time appointed for this impressive and farewel service. Lord Molesworth, on learning their intention, requested permission to communicate with them, which he did. At five o'clock in the afternoon of Thursday the 14th of July, Messrs. Lynch and Squance paid a visit of leave to Lord and Lady Molesworth; concerning which, they observe, " that on this occasion, his lordship, with his lady, evinced the most powerful sympathy, and could not repress their emotions when they took leave. But how to part with our dear brethren," they add, " we knew not. The motion towards it, and the word ' Farewel,' were more than we could bear. We could only embrace, and silently pray for each other. Surely, they who are joined to the Lord are one spirit."

Messrs. Lynch and Squance reached Pantura, about sixteen miles from Colombo, on Saturday. Here they were met by two servants, sent by the Honourable and Reverend T. J. Twisleton, D.D. the senior colonial chaplain,* with a letter, conveying the most friendly invitation to his handsome seat at St. Sebastian's, during their stay in Colombo. They accordingly were conducted by the messengers to Dr. Twisleton's house, and were entertained with the most hospitable politeness by the Doctor and his lady. During their stay at Colombo they were peculiarly favoured with the friendship and society of several truly pious persons, of the Episcopalian and other denominations. They were introduced to, and formed a pleasing intimacy with, the Reverend Mr. Chater, a Baptist Missionary, who had been for some time settled in Colombo; having removed from the Burman country, his original appointment. In the evening they had the honour of dining with His Excellency, Governor Brownrigg. When they were introduced to him, he received them with the most perfect

* Now the Venerable the Archdeacon of Colombo.

affability; observing, that he considered them an acquisition to the colony; and expressed his sorrow at the public loss of so valuable a character as the late Doctor Coke. Our friends returned their warmest acknowledgments to the Governor for his hospitality and kindness to them; and expressed their hope, that by the blessing of God their future usefulness would abundantly repay, in satisfaction to His Excellency, the liberal and generous patronage he had extended to their infant Mission * The Governor's kind and condescending expressions were warmly seconded by his lady; of whose manner of receiving them, they write, that " it evinced the lady, the friend, and the Christian."

Having been favoured with letters to the Honourable Sir Alexander Johnston, the Chief Justice of Ceylon, Messrs. Lynch and Squance waited on him at his residence at Colpetty. Sir Alexander and his lady also gave them a cordial welcome to Ceylon, and wished them the utmost success in their undertaking. Sir Alexander entered minutely into the plan they had adopted; and while on many accounts he wished the whole of the Missionaries had remained together for some time, until they had become more familiar with the customs and habits of the natives; yet, on the whole, he highly commended the principles on which they had acted; and manifested considerable pleasure on finding them actuated by a spirit which would command respect from the natives, and in the end be productive of consequences highly gratifying to the friends of the Mission.

The manner in which our two brethren were received in Colombo was highly encouraging and gratifying to

* It is peculiarly gratifying, that the result corresponded with this hope. In the flattering language used by Governor Brownrigg, in his address to the Missionaries, on his quitting the Ceylon Government in 1820, and which will be found in the Appendix, the reader will perceive that the Governor's opinion had undergone no change.

themselves, as well as to their associates in the South, to whom they regularly wrote an account of their proceedings. They continued at Colombo upwards of a fortnight, receiving from the Honourable and Reverend Dr. Twisleton and his family every attention and assistance which benevolence could suggest. Here they met with Mr. Armour, the master of the principal school in Colombo, under the superintendence of Dr. Twisleton. Mr. Armour had been a member of the Methodist society in Ireland, and was, on his subsequent removal to Gibraltar, appointed a class-leader. In India he retained his piety, and rejoiced in being brought once more into connexion with the Wesleyan body.

Mr. Armour had been especially patronised by the Reverend Dr. Twisleton; who, in consequence of his indefatigable application and religious character had procured his discharge from the army, in which he had for many years been a non-commissioned officer, and obtained his appointment to the situation of master of the principal school at Colombo. From the year 1801, he had filled that situation with credit to himself, and satisfaction to his employers; aiming, not only at the mental improvement, but at the eternal welfare of his pupils. To qualify himself for more extensive usefulness, he had, by dint of patient application, become familiar with the Dutch, French, Tamul, Portuguese, and Singhalese languages: in the two last of which he was so proficient, as to be regularly licensed by the Government to exercise the office of preacher to the Singhalese and Portuguese Christians.

Possessed of such acquisitions; united with pious zeal in the cause of God, sincere attachment to the doctrines and discipline of our society, and an intimate knowledge of the customs and prejudices of the various classes of natives; a more valuable auxiliary to the Mission could scarcely have been met with; and

Messrs. Lynch and Squance regarded him as a fellow-labourer, and a brother. He communicated to them important information relative to the state of Christianity in Ceylon; together with much valuable assistance in their studies of the native tongues. At his request, they enclosed a letter from him to our Missionary Committee; which, for the Christian spirit which it breathes, and the information it conveys, is worthy of preservation.*

Messrs. Lynch and Squance were earnestly importuned to preach while at Colombo; and as Mr. Chater, the Baptist Missionary, kindly offered to introduce them to his pulpit, they occasionally preached in his neat chapel, situate in the Pettah. The congregations on these occasions were both numerous and respectable. Many of the Dutch inhabitants who understood English attended, as well as several of their own countrymen, some of whom were of considerable rank. The Commandant of the garrison not only gave permission to the military to be present, but attended himself, and afterwards expressed his high satisfaction with the discourses. The affectionate and Christian conduct of Mr. and Mrs. Chater laid the foundation of a sincere friendship between them and the Missionaries. It afforded mutual pleasure, that their difference of sentiment, with relation to some of the circumstantials of religion, did not operate as a barrier to that interchange of benevolent offices which Christianity enjoins, and which the spirit of its Author produces. *He that is not against us,* saith our Lord, *is on our part;* and, *By this shall all men know that ye are my disciples, if ye have love one toward another.* These are sentiments worthy of a place in the breast of every Christian, and especially of every Christian Missionary.

* See Appendix.

The anxiety of our brethren to reach their appointment in the province of Jaffnapatam, led them to break through the barriers which the kindness and hospitality they experienced in Colombo had created to prolong their stay. On the first of August they resumed their journey. A case of singular conversion from Mahomedanism to Christianity had recently occurred in Colombo. The convert was baptized in the Fort Church, by the name of Daniel Theophilus; and it was stated to have been the first conversion from Ismalism which had been known in Ceylon. The subject of this change was a man of strong mind, and of considerable learning; and hopes were entertained, that his public renunciation of his former faith, and open acknowledgement of Christianity, would have a powerful effect on others, and be productive of similar results. The change in his religious profession had called down upon him the indignation of his relatives and former connexions, some of whom were fully bent upon his destruction. He was in consequence taken under the immediate protection of the Government, by whom he was committed to the care of Messrs. Lynch and Squance, to be taken with them to Jaffnapatam, that he might be further instructed in the doctrines and duties of the religion he had embraced.

Mr. Armour, whose school required his attention, could only accompany them a mile from the town: but the Honourable and Reverend Dr. Twisleton and the Reverend Mr. Chater kindly conducted them ten miles on their journey. Mr. Lynch observes, " Dr. Twisleton's friendship was truly singular; not only while we were at his house, but after our departure. Mrs. Twisleton kindly sent with us a plentiful supply of every necessary for our journey, together with many other articles, which have saved us considerable expense in furnishing our house." The disinterested benevolence of this honourable and generous clergyman forms a prominent feature in the early history of this Mission.

The road by which Messrs. Lynch and Squance travelled, though destitute of the milder beauties of nature, and affording no traces of the habitations of man, did not fail to awaken feelings of interest; and the circumstance of its being occasionally infested by elephants, bears, and a small but rapacious species of tiger, kept alive in their minds a sense of the necessity of Divine protection. They escaped the perils of the desert, and arrived at Jaffna in safety.

On their arrival, they first proceeded to the residence of T. N. Mooyart, Esq. the sub-collector of the Province, to whom they had been furnished with letters of recommendation previous to their leaving Colombo. He received them rather as friends, whom he had long expected, than as strangers from a distant land. Though of a disposition the most affable and benevolent, Mr. M's. views of religion were undecided, and his mind far from recognizing its supreme importance. But his intercourse with the Missionaries, thus providentially introduced to his society, was productive of the most salutary results. Their pious conversation and consistent deportment impressed his mind with a high opinion of their moral worth. In them he saw a loveliness in religion, which engaged his affections; while a careful perusal of the works of Messrs. Fletcher and Wesley, under the Divine blessing, informed his judgment, and determined his choice. He became a member of the Wesleyan society; to the Missionaries of which he acknowledges his obligations, as the ministers of God to him for good; but with a Christian philanthropy, the fruit of genuine faith, he regards every disciple of the Saviour as his brother. His house is open to Missionaries of all denominations; and those of the American

Presbyterian, of the Church of England, and of the Wesleyan body, have had the pleasure of meeting each other under his hospitable roof.

Here they received a highly gratifying visit from Mr. Christian David, a native Malabar Christian; a convert, and formerly a personal attendant of the late celebrated Missionary, Swartz. Under the immediate patronage of Governor Brownrigg, he had been induced to settle in Ceylon, and was appointed preacher to the Malabar Christians in the Province of Jaffna. When Surgeon Moreton* was at Jaffna, he presented Mr. David with several of Mr. Wesley's Sermons and Tracts; and among others, with " The Character and Principles of a Methodist." From these, he had formed a high opinion of the Methodist societies, and received the Missionaries of that body as angels of God. He told Mr. Lynch, that he had for more than ten years, prayed that some Missionaries might be sent to Ceylon; and he regarded their arrival as an answer to his prayers. He received every encouragement from Messrs. Lynch and Squance, who took him under their care; and he, in return, manifested a strong attachment to them, and afforded them every aid in his power in furthering the objects of their Mission. He was especially valuable in procuring for them assistance in the study of the Tamul language; and often accompanied them in their excursions to the adjacent parts, for the purpose of interpreting their addresses to the natives.

The liberal assistance offered by the Ceylon Government, by the establishment and endowment of schools for the children of the natives, under the superintendence of the Missionaries, has been already stated. This plan was designed to embrace two objects; to

* Surgeon Moreton of the Royal Artillery. This gentleman, a member of the Wesleyan Society, very zealously exerted himself to promote the best interest of the native Ceylonese, during his residence in that Island.

benefit the native children, and to assist our Mission, by lessening the burthen of expense. That the latter was included in the benevolent proposal, is evident from the circumstance, that a *double* monthly allowance was made to the school at Jaffna, because it was to be the residence of *two* Missionaries. Messrs. Lynch and Squance, immediately on their arrival, proposed to hire a place, and commence the school. They were, however, by the judicious counsel of Mr. Mooyart, prevailed upon to postpone their design, until a place could be procured suitable for a school in so hot a climate.

As Jaffna was wholly destitute of the means of public instruction in the English language, the Missionaries were requested to perform Divine service in the Fort church, which they did; alternately reading the prayers and preaching. Every Sunday morning a small congregation assembled. Their preaching *extempore* at first excited some disapprobation, but it was not of long continuance. Some pleasing indications of usefulnes appeared, and they were encouraged to open meetings for religious worship on the Sabbath evenings, and the week-days also. The Mission at Jaffnapatam, was thus commenced under very auspicious circumstances; and Messrs. Lynch and Squance soon indulged sanguine hopes, that they should be able to form a society of serious persons from among their European congregation.

Towards the latter end of July the necessary arrangements being completed, Mr. Erskine left Galle for his appointment at MATURA. As the distance was not more than thirty miles, nothing worthy of particular notice occurred on his journey. In his way through Belligamme he visited the friendly magistrate, Mr. Kunemann, who had shown him and Mr. Ault so much kindness on their landing at that place. He expressed his ardent hope, that some spiritual good would be afforded to Belligamme, from the residence of Mr. Erskine at Mattura. On his arrival at his station, he received the most respectful attention from the local authorities, both native and European; especially from J. H. Granville, Esq. the collector, whose polite and very valuable aid merits particular acknowledgement. The marked attentions paid to the newly-arrived Missionary by Don David Illangakoon, the *Maha Moodeliar,* or chief headman of all the Singhalese, whose principal residence is at Matura, could not fail to produce a favourable impression on all the subordinate head-men, and the natives in general. With the Reverend J. G. Erhardt, a German Missionary, connected with the London Missionary Society, Mr. Erskine formed a close and beneficial friendship.* The proposed English school was commenced without delay; and the children of the higher class of natives attended with evident pleasure. Mr. Erskine applied himself to the study of the Singhalese language with much assiduity; on Sundays he performed Divine service in the Dutch church in the Fort. His congregation at the English services was not large, as the European garrison consisted but of few troops; but he felt much satisfaction in his work. Good impressions were produced on some of his hearers; while he industriously prepared himself for his labours among the native Singhalese.

Matura, from its local situation, is of high importance as a Missionary station. It comprehends a district, from east to west, of upwards of forty miles, and extends thirty miles into the interior. The native population is considerable; and it may be regarded as one of the principal strong-holds of the reigning super-

---

* The Rev. Mr. Erhardt, on the subsequent dissolution of his connection with the London Missionary Society, was, through the intervention of Archdeacon Twisleton, appointed to a clerical situation on the Continent of India.

stition of Budhu. Within this district some of the most celebrated temples are situated, attended by the most learned priests in the island; and it is inhabited by a greater number of native families of wealth and influence than are to be found within the same limits throughout the island. The absence of European society, indeed, will always in the first instance be regarded as a privation by the Missionary stationed there: though privations of that description, under the Divine blessing, frequently become advantageous, rather than detrimental, to the interests of a Christian Mission. It would have been extremely desirable if *two* Missionaries could have been spared for such an extensive and important district, as the line of operation might thereby have been extended. In this comparative solitude Mr. Erskine found a sacred pleasure while engaged in the work to which he was devoted, and indulged encouraging expectations of ultimate success.

The distance from Galle to BATTICALOA, the station to which Mr. Ault was appointed, is not more than one hundred and fifty miles farther than Matura; but the country intervening is so infested by wild beasts, as to render it highly dangerous to travellers, except protected by a very strong guard; Mr. Ault was therefore compelled to wait for a conveyance by water. Through the medium of Mr. Gibson, Mr. Ault engaged with the serang, or Mahomedan master of a *dhoney*, a kind of sailing barge, to convey him to his destination, and embarked on Sunday, July the 31st. It was expected that the passage would be made in three days; but the dhoney was upwards of eight in reaching the destined port; during which time Mr. Ault suffered so much, added to the afflictions he had already endured, that his whole constitution was shaken, and he was ill-suited to enter upon the arduous duties of his station. The following is extracted from a letter which he wrote to Mr. Erskine, a few days after his arrival at Batticaloa.

"I left Galle on Sunday, July 31st, and passed Matura about four the same afternoon. We anchored off Dondera, near Matura, on Sunday night, where we continued the whole of Monday, and Monday night. I should have been very glad to have called upon you, but could not. I had a very unpleasant voyage. Thrice were we obliged to anchor in the open sea; once we were becalmed; and once encountered a contrary wind. Two days we were without water; and the water I took on board was stolen from me. Our indolent crew would not sail in the day-time: they said—' the wind was too strong:' and in the night they refused, saying, ' it was not good to run upon the rocks!' so that there were but a few hours, early in the morning, in which they would sail; and even then I was obliged to awaken them. It appeared as though the conclusion of the voyage was an object of no consequence with them. They fished along the shore by day, and cooked and slept by night. We had plenty of smoke and sulphur, and noise, and filth: but for several days made no progress! We lost an anchor in a gale of wind, but providentially no further damage was done to the vessel. Our food as well as water fell short, as I had provided little more than would be sufficient for three days. I have some of my things broken, my books are wetted, and nearly all spoiled. I have been twice in the sea, but happily escaped with life. I fell overboard from the dhoney; and, on landing at Batticaloe in a small canoe, it swamped. I jumped out and reached the land in the best way I was able. But I must cease my complaints. Here I am, through much mercy, at my appointed station."

Batticaloa is a small island, little more than three miles in circumference. It has a neat, compact fort, with a few houses, and is considered the most healthy station on that side of the Island of Ceylon. It is resorted to by the invalids from Trincomalee, who generally recover after a short residence. The district to which it gives name is a very important one, having a constant trade with the interior, and contains a large population. The inhabitants are chiefly of Tamul origin. There are many Roman Catholics among them, and some Mahomedans; but the bulk of the population is devoted to the Hindoo superstition. Though the climate is generally salubrious, yet, from the drought which had prevailed during the two years previous to Mr. Ault's arrival, the inhabitants had begun to suffer from sickness; the heat was so excessive the day he landed, that the thermometer stood at 94 in the shade. Some slight shocks of an earthquake had also been felt about a fortnight before.

These circumstances, in the debilitated state to which Mr. Ault was reduced—his mind lacerated by his bereavement, and his body weakened by disease—must have tended to depress his spirits, and to make yet further inroads on his declining strength. To add to his difficulties, no suitable residence could be procured for him; the few houses in the place being occupied principally by the sick from Trincomalee, which at that time was also very unhealthy. The Batticaloa hospital was also full of poor invalid soldiers, who were dying daily.

Under such disadvantages did Mr. Ault enter upon his station. The day he arrived, he waited upon S. Sawers, Esq. the collector, who had received a letter respecting him from His Excellency the Governor; and who, prompted by his generous disposition, received him in the most friendly manner, and offered him every possible aid. By this gentleman, in his official capacity as collector, Mr. Ault was materially assisted in the object of his Mission, and invited to become an inmate of his family, while he expressed regret, that an apartment could not be afforded him. The difficulty of obtaining a residence, was, however, removed by the friendly interposition of J. Atkinson, Esq. magistrate for the Batticaloa district; with whom, and Mr. Sawers, Mr. Ault resided several days after his arrival.

Mr. Ault opened his school in a large store-room which had been obtained for the purpose; and applied himself to the work of instructing those children who applied for admission. On Sunday mornings he read prayers, and preached to the officers and soldiers of the garrison, and to the other Europeans who were disposed to be present. His congregation was seldom less than one hundred and fifty; and his generous hosts, the collector and magistrate, were among his constant hearers. In the morning the soldiers were regularly marched to church; in the evening he conducted another service, at which their attendance was voluntary; and he had the pleasure of witnessing the desire to hear the word of God which many of them manifested; while a few applied to him at an early period, under serious concern for salvation. Though encouraged in his labours among his own countrymen, he did not suffer his attention to be warped from the interests of the idolatrous natives. He laboured hard at the Tamul language; and soon commenced itinerating among the native huts in the neighbouring country.

At GALLE, Mr. Clough continued the English service in the Dutch church every Sunday; and a private house in the Fort was, at the joint expense of some of his hearers, fitted up for preaching on an evening during the week, and for conversation on spiritual subjects with those under serious impressions. The condescending attentions of Lord Molesworth, tended greatly to encourage him, and to acquire for him that influence among the people, which was productive of great advantage to the interests of religion. His lordship often appeared in company with the missionary on public occasions, and was seldom absent from the cottage in which their religious meetings were held. Whether it were a sermon, or a prayer meeting, Lord Molesworth was generally present. The effect produced on the European inhabitants was very pleasing; and the military especially were sensible of the influence of his lordship's example. Mr. Clough had frequent opportunities of conversing with several of the officers on religious subjects, and many of the private soldiers manifested a high value for the means of grace. A small class was formed of the more seriously disposed: though some turned back, several remained stedfast; and some in death bore witness to the power of religion.

The district of Galle is one of the principal stations in Ceylon. The Fort is well filled with inhabitants of various classes, but principally of Dutch and Portuguese extraction. There is a Mahomedan mosque in the garrison; the only instance of the kind in the whole island. Many European families reside in the suburbs, in groves of cocoa-nut trees, surrounded by a very large population of Singhalese and Mahomedan natives. The natives of Galle are not surpassed by those of any other district in the island for docility and gentleness of disposition; but they are enveloped in the darkness of paganism, and are avowed worshippers of evil spirits. To these, the more immediate objects of his mission, Mr. Clough's attention was anxiously directed. As a residence in the Fort would afford him but comparatively little influence over the native population, he wished to live entirely among them; to study their language, and to exert himself for their spiritual welfare. At length an opportunity was afforded him to attain the object of his wishes. He received a visit at the Government House from Don Abraham Dias Abeyesinhe Amarasekara, the *Maha,* or *Great Moodeliar,* of Galle, a fine looking man, of good understanding, and of a liberal mind; and who from his rank was possessed of unbounded influence throughout the district. After the usual compliments, he addressed Mr. Clough in English, in nearly the following words: " Reverend Sir: I am come to offer my children to your protection and instructions: I have heard you are desirous of establishing a school for the sons of our native head-men. I have, Sir, a good house, ready-furnished, near my own residence, which is much at your service. If you would please to see if it suits you, I shall think it an honour to have such a reverend gentleman living so near to me; and will assist you in all things in my power."

Mr. Clough, after acknowledging the liberal offer of the Moodeliar, went to view the premises, which are about a mile from the Fort, and only a stone's-throw from the house of the generous proprietor. They are situated in a very retired and romantic spot; and appeared in most respects to be so eligible, that Mr. Clough did not hesitate to accept of the liberal proposal. He immediately had his luggage removed; and was thus, without any expense to the Mission Fund, placed at once in a situation of comfort and respectability; and in circumstances of all others the best calculated to promote his improvement in the language, and his usefulness among the natives. His school was soon commenced, and attended by some of the most intelligent boys on the island.

The generous proprietor manifested the greatest anxiety for his comfort; furnished him with a small horse, and afforded him assistance, whenever his aid could render him any service. The patronage and friendship of the Moodeliar had an astonishing influence on the surrounding natives. Curiosity was powerfully excited; and in his new residence Mr. Clough was visited by learned priests, and persons of various classes, who came to enquire respecting the religion he professed. With these, through the medium of an interpreter, he had frequent opportunities of conversing *concerning the faith in Christ;* and had the pleasure, in some instances, of seeing them depart evidently impressed with the result of their enquiries.

By the assistance of the Moodeliar, a highly competent Singhalese teacher was procured; under whose instructions Mr. Clough applied himself with laborious perseverance to the study of that language; employing every interval from the duties of his school, to qualify himself for preaching to the natives, *in their own tongue, the wonderful works of God.*

CHAP. VIII.

The Author's residence at Bombay—Derivation of name—Teak wood—Birds, reptiles, and insects--Climate—Population--Various classes of inhabitants—The GENTOO superstition—Mode of worship—Distinction of caste—Pagodas—Festivals, fasts, processions, &c.—The Gentoo female character—The swinging ceremony—The MAHOMEDANS, their mosques and worship—Marriage and funeral processions—Juvenile merchants—Language—PERSEES—Worship, &c.—Refuse to extinguish fire—Processions at marriages, funerals. &c.—Superstitious notions founded on the decay of the body—Conversion from their idolatry difficult—JEWS—PORTUGUESE ROMAN CATHOLICS—Opulence—Chapels—Superstition and idolatry—Mendicants—ARMENIAN CHRISTIANS—Wealth and respectability—Their various establishments—Their history—BRITISH and AMERICAN CHRISTIANS—Miscellaneous information.

HAVING conducted the reader to the several stations in the Island of Ceylon, to which my fellow-missionaries were appointed, and narrated some of the most interesting events connected with their entrance on their respective spheres of labour, I shall proceed to give some account of my residence at Bombay, where circumstances appeared to justify me in remaining for a short period.

As the Governor's house at Parell was generously lent us, under the expectation that our stay at the Presidency would be short, it would have been highly indecorous to have occupied it after the departure of my companions. Several days were spent in endeavouring to meet with a suitable residence; at length one was found in a pleasant and healthy situation, about three miles from the Fort; but the rent was so extravagantly high, being 160 sica rupees (about £20 sterling) per month, that I was deterred from engaging it. On stating the circumstances to Mr. Money, he sent for the proprietor, and induced him to lower his demand to 100 rupees (£12. 10s. per month ;) which, though a large sum, was really moderate ; as the house was sufficiently large to contain the Mission property, types, press, paper, library, &c. which had been left in my care. For the reception of these, I must otherwise have hired a *go-down,* or warehouse, for which a considerable rent would have been demanded. Previously to taking possession, the owner required me to sign an agreement— that our *pigs* should not injure the vegetables, nor our children eat the fruit: this I did most readily, as our establishment at that time included neither.

As European gentlemen reside in India but for a limited period, they seldom build houses, or become land-owners. The houses in Bombay, and its environs, are generally the property of wealthy natives of different classes, who find this mode of employing their money productive of very considerable profit, in the enormous rents they obtain from Europeans. Several noble mansions, the residences of native merchants, are also found ; some of them exceedingly magnificent, surrounded by plantations, laid out in a most tasteful style, and decorated with valuable pictures. But few lofty houses are to be met with ; the generality of those occupied by Europeans consist of a ground-floor only, with a yard before and behind ; the whole surrounded by a wall, or fence, containing offices and out-houses, which are called " the compound." The houses are substantially built of stone and lime, and plaistered on the outside, which is usually white-washed, or coloured. Glass windows are seldom seen ; Venetian blinds are substituted, as they admit both the air and light. The floors, it has already been observed, are composed of a description of stucco, called *chunam ;* and, when properly made, is extremely hard and durable, and admits of a beautiful polish. The houses built by the generality of the natives for their own residences are very unpleasant to Europeans, from the closeness of the apartments, and the smallness of the windows, which appear to be made for no other purpose than to admit a small portion of light.

The country-houses are called *bungaloes*, and are raised a few feet from the ground, that cellars and store-rooms may be formed beneath. The situation of the latter has obtained for them the name of *"the go-down."* The *bungaloes* possess also a great accommodation in the *virandos*, which are made before and behind; and which sometimes completely surround the house. They are enclosed with Venetian shades, and form a most pleasant apartment, especially in the cool of the evening. The kitchens, or *cook-rooms*, as they are called, are placed at a distance from the house, to avoid the smoke and heat. None of the houses are furnished with fire-places, though in the rainy season a fire would be extremely welcome.

The Island of Bombay is seven miles in length, and twenty in circumference: it received its name from its Portuguese proprietors, and is composed of two words in their language, which signify the *" The Good Bay;"* in allusion to its spacious harbour, which is sufficiently extensive to receive any number of ships. The anchorage is excellent; and so secure is its situation, that vessels may ride in safety even in the most violent gales.

The extensive commerce and abundant wealth of this settlement are well known. The warehouses overflow with the produce and manufactures of Arabia, Persia, and China; its merchants employ an immense capital in the various branches of European and Oriental trade. Ship-building is also brought to very great perfection by the native Persee mechanics: several large vessels have been constructed by them in their commodious docks; and the teak-tree, or Indian oak, which grows in abundance in the interior, is supposed to be more suitable for that purpose than any other wood in the world; it being more elastic than the English oak, and possessing an unctuous quality, which preserves the iron-work of ships built with it from rust. The country also produces abundance of excellent and valuable timber of other descriptions, in the manufacture of which into various articles of furniture the native carpenters evince considerable skill.

Several kinds of REPTILES and venomous insects infest the whole island. The scorpion and the centipede intrude into most houses; the latter, (so called from its numerous feet) grows to a formidable size, and has the faculty of inflicting a wound with each of its feet. Swarms of ants infest the houses, especially in the country; and the white ant is particularly injurious to the timbers of the roofs and floors of houses, the internal parts of which they sometimes devour so completely, as to render them unsafe. A species of lizard, called the *blood-sucker*, is frequently met with, and excites considerable apprehensions in the minds of the inhabitants. Frogs are numerous, and very large. A respectable author mentions his having seen one which, when extended, measured twenty-two inches, and weighed between four and five pounds. Large grasshoppers, or locusts, spring about the gardens in considerable numbers, uttering a loud cricket-like note.

The BIRDS are distinguished for their richly-variegated plumage; the crow is remarkable for its carrion-eating propensity, and its bold and intruding disposition; often taking food from the tables, and will not be easily driven away. A curious insect flies about at night, called the *fire-fly;* it emits a light like that of our glow-worm; and if, in a dark night, a swarm of them settles on a tree, it appears as if it were on fire. A few of them placed in a wine glass will enable a person, with no other light, to distinguish articles on a table.

Of SNAKES there is a great variety, and the bite of most of them is mortal. An author of high repute has given the following description of the principal:—
" 1. *The cobra de capella,* which grows from four to eight feet long: their bite kills in fifteen minutes. 2. *The cobra manila,* is a small blueish snake, of the size of a man's little finger, and about a foot long, frequently seen about old walls. A species of this is found in Bombay which kills much sooner than even the former. 3. *The palæira,* a very thin, beautiful snake, of different colours: its head is like that of the common viper, but much thicker than the body: one was observed that was four feet long, and the body not much thicker than a swan's quill. 4. *The green snake* is of a very bright green colour, with a sharp head; towards the tail it is smaller than in the middle: the largest part of it is no bigger than a tobacco-pipe. 5. *The sand snake* is small and short, but not less deadly than the others. 6. *The copra de aurelia* resembles an earthworm; is about six inches long, and no longer than a small crow-quill. It kills by entering the ear, which causes madness and death. 7. *The Manilla bomba* is a very beautiful snake, of almost the same size throughout the whole length, except at the two ends, where it comes to a point. It is white on the belly, but finely variegated on the back. It lives in the sand, and is said to sting with its tail, which occasions contractions in the joints."

These noxious reptiles are seldom troublesome except in country places, and in premises which have been long uninhabited. Houses connected with gardens, or other grounds, must be swept daily; that snakes, which sometimes find an entrance, and lodge under the mat, the drawers, or any other place which will afford shelter, may be discovered. We once found a snake on the steps of our bungaloe, pursuing its way into the house. Had it bitten any of us, inevitable and almost immediate death would have been the consequence. The legs of bedsteads, side-boards, and similar articles of furniture, are either placed in pans of water, or washed with tar, to prevent the ants from crawling up them; but they will sometimes even swim across the water, and climb up the bed-posts. In the habitations of sickness they swarm exceedingly, unless the utmost vigilance be employed to keep them away. They appear to live in a regularly organized state of society; having scouts placed on the look-out in every part of the house—a bit of sugar falling to the ground would be covered with them in a minute. If a single ant finds any thing of which they are fond, but too heavy to carry off alone, it will leave it, return with a host of its fellows, and bear it off in triumph. It is also necessary, every afternoon, to clear the beds from musquitos, an insect in most points resembling a small gnat, the sting of which is exceedingly painful. In country places the bed-clothes should be also examined, lest snakes should be concealed among them.

The climate of Bombay was formerly so prejudicial to the constitutions of Europeans, that it was denominated "the grave of the English." By the encroachments of the sea, the atmosphere became impregnated with vapours, which together with the excessive heat, produced fatal effects on numbers, especially those newly arrived. These marshy spots are now completely drained, and embankments raised to prevent inundations, which have rendered it much more healthy. Bombay is now not more unfavourable to Europeans than Continental India. The heat is certainly great, especially in the middle of the day; and an exposure to the hot land-wind is injurious: but this is not peculiar to Bombay; and if proper caution be employed, immediate danger may be prevented. Throughout the whole of India many of our countrymen fall victims to what is called *the seasoning:* the greater number possibly suffer from irregularities, or from inattention to necessary precautions.

The rainy season commences about the end of May, and continues, with occasional intermission, until the conclusion of September A violent thunder storm, called "the Elephanta," in some seasons occurs at the commencement, and in others at the conclusion, of the rainy monsoon. It produces a most tremendous agitation of the elements. The rain descends with the most inconceivable force; and one of the *showers* which fell during our stay lasted night and day, without intermission, for nearly three weeks.* No description can convey to the imagination of a person accustomed only to the rains of this country, an adequate idea of the scene. *Drops* were out of the question—the clouds poured forth their treasures in *streams.* When a few hours' cessation permitted us to walk out, we found the roads almost washed away, and the fields covered with water.

The wisdom of Providence is very conspicuous in the rains which I have described. In countries where the evaporation is so copious and rapid, the moisture produced by the gentle showers of colder climates would be soon exhausted, and vegetation would consequently cease. But these abundant rains prepare the soil, and

* "An accurate description of the nature of the rains and inundations in this part of India, is given by Arian, lib. v. c. 9.; and one still fuller may be found in Strabo, lib. xv. 1013.—It was of what they suffered by these that Alexander's soldiers complained, Strabo, lib. xv. 1021; and not without reason; as *it had rained incessantly* during SEVENTY DAYS! Diod. Sicul. xvii. c. 94."—*Doctor Robertson's* "*Notes and Illustrations,*" *subjoined to his* "*Historical Disquisition.*"

cause the seed to vegetate, with such amazing quickness, that they are hailed as an invaluable good, as well by the tribes who feed upon the harvest, as by those who labour in the field. A failure of the rains in these countries is sufficient to alarm a whole nation; and from that sole cause, large districts in India have often been devastated by famine, and its attendants, pestilence and death! To counteract as much as possible the direful effects of a scarcity of water, large *tanks*, or ponds lined with stone, are sunk in different places; which are filled by the torrents which fall in the rainy season, and furnish a supply during the months in which there is no rain. The building of these tanks is counted by the Asiatics an act of high religious merit. It is not uncommon for opulent natives to expend immense sums of money in their structure; and by will to bequeath a part of their property, thus to enrich and benefit their country. In various parts of India these receptacles are of a size almost incredible. Besides these tanks, there are also wells, some of them public property, from which the inhabitants procure tolerably good water.

The population of Bombay is very great; the land literally swarms with inhabitants; who crowd the streets, and can hardly be prevailed on, by the loud warnings continually given by the drivers of carriages, to step aside, though exposed to the danger of being trodden under foot of the horses, or crushed by the vehicles as they pass along. The huts of the poorer classes of natives are small; a family of six or eight children, with the parents, is frequently met with, crowded together into a place not four feet hight, nor eight feet square. In Dungaree, the chief native town on the island, is many good substantial houses, which are occupied by natives of respectability; but these are situated among a vast population of the poorer tribes; among whom is to be found a vast aggregate of human sufferings. The inhabitants of Bombay are of almost every nation in Europe; and the superstitions which prevail among them are as various as are perhaps, to be met with in any other settlement on the face of the earth.—The principal are—*Of unbelievers in Christianity;* the Gentoos, with their numerous castes; the Mahomedans, with their different sects; the Persees, who are disciples of Zoroaster; and the Jews. *Of those who bear the Christian name*—Portuguese Roman-Catholics, European and Asiatic; Armenian Christians; Episcopalians, members of the English church; and Presbyterians, members of the church of Scotland.

The Gentoos, or Hindoos,

in their several classifications, are worshippers of gods and goddesses innumerable. The Reverend W. Ward, one of the excellent Baptist Missionaries of Bengal, in his valuable work on the Hindoos, has the following brief but comprehensive outline of their *theological system* and *mode of worship*, which I shall take the liberty to transcribe; referring my readers to the work itself for further valuable and authentic particulars.*

Mr. Ward observes:—" The Hindoo mythology, in its present mixed state, presents us with gods of every possible shape, and for every possible purpose (even to cure the itch!); but most of them appear to refer to the doctrine of the periodical creation and destruction of the world—the appearances of nature—the heavenly bodies—the history of deified heroes—the poetical wars of the giants with the gods—or to the real or imagined wants of mankind. The Hindoos profess to have

---

* Mr. Ward's " View of the History, Literature, and Religion of the Hindoos."

three hundred and thirty millions of gods : not that they have even the names of such a number ; but they say, that God performs all his works by the agency of the gods; and that all human actions, as well as all the elements, have their tutelar deities. Images have been introduced to fix the mind of the worshippers ; and attributes of power, and splendour, and various fables have been added. In the forms of devotion, and the addresses to the gods, all these attributes are recognized, and the contents of these fables rehearsed, to raise in the mind of the worshipper, the highest thoughts of the power of the idol."

The religious prostrations, ablutions, processions, and offerings among the Hindoos, are, according to Mr Ward, regulated on the following principle :— " He who approaches an idol, seeking the happiness of a future state, is required to fix in his mind only one idea— *that the god can save him;* and in this respect, all the gods, however various their images, are equal. But when a Hindoo is anxious to obtain any peculiar favour, he applies to the god whose province it is to bestow it. He who prays to *Brŭmha,* entreats that he may be like him, in order to absorption ; but he who is anxious that his members may continue perfect, and that he may enjoy the pleasures of the senses, worships *Indrŭ;* he who desires children, prays to the progenitors of mankind ; he who seeks worldly prosperity, worships *Lŭkshmēē*; he who prays for a shining body, supplicates *Vignea ;* the person who is anxious for strength, applies to *Roodrŭ;* the glutton prays to *Uditee;* he who pants for a crown, applies to *Vishwŭdévŭ* or *Swagumbhoove* : a king entreats *Sadhyŭ,* that his kingdom may be free from sedition : he who prays for long life, addresses himself to *Ushwinēē-koo marŭ* : he who desires corpulency, addresses *Prit'hivēē* : he who prays that he may preserve his home-stead, petitions *Prit'hivēē :* and the *regents of space;* he who seeks beauty, prays to *Gŭndhŭrvŭs;* he who prays for a good wife, calls on *Orvŭsee,* a celestial courtezan; he who seeks honour, prays to *Yugnu:* he who is anxious for store-houses full of wealth, calls on *Prucheta;* the seeker of wisdom solicits the favour of *Shiva;* those who seek union and happiness in the marriage-state, address *Doorga;* he who wishes to destroy his enemy, supplicates *Noiritu:* he who is anxious for strength of body, prays to *Vayoo;* he who prays to be preserved from obstruction in his affairs, calls on *Kooveru;* he who prays for the merit of works, applies to the *regent of verse;* he who prays for pleasure in the enjoyment of earthly things, addresses *Chundru.*

"He who desires freedom from worldly passions, he who asks for the completion of all his desires, he who prays for absorption, and the person free from all desire, worships *Brumha.* Hence it appears, that all the Hindoo gods, except *Brumha,* are considered only as bestowing temporal favours; and this god has been abandoned, and left without either temples or images! Thus, the whole system excites in the minds of the worshipper only cupidity and the love of pleasure; and to this agrees what I have repeatedly heard from sensible Brahmins, that few, if any, persons now attend the public festivals with a direct view to a future state."

The foregoing description, will impress the mind of the reader with a lively sympathy for the degraded spiritual condition of those millions of Indian natives, who are the victims of this sensual system. A more particular exhibition of a superstition so intricate and multifarious, would be unsuitable to the present work. That the generality of the natives have themselves a clear conception of their own religious system, is more than can be supposed; when it is taken into the account, that the mass of the people, by their inferiority of rank, are prohibited from reading the sacred books; and hence know little of their contents, but through the medium of their teachers who are frequently wicked and designing.

Among the many corruptions of the Hindoo superstition, may be ranked the inveterate distinction of caste; which most probably was first introduced as a civil or political distinction, but is now incorporated with their whole religious economy. The Brahmins teach, that from their deity, *Brŭmha*, proceeded the work of creation; from *Vishnoo*, that of preservation; and that *Shiva* performs the daily work of correction, or destruction. The two latter are still worshipped, especially the last; who, from a principle of fear, has the ascendency over the mind of the Gentoo; while from *Brumah* they derive the precedent of caste. They believe, that from the mouth of this creating deity proceeded the Brahmins; from his arms, the Khatru caste; the Banians, from his belly and thighs; and the Soodra from his feet: hence have arisen the different offices assigned to these castes: the Brahmins to teach; the Khatru to defend and govern; the Banians to enrich by commerce and agriculture; and the Soodra to labour, serve, and obey. These are the four principal castes. A fifth has been formed by the out-casts from all the others, who are denominated Parriars; a term which they use to designate any person for whom they have the most perfect hatred and contempt: these are employed to perform the lowest menial offices, and they seem to have a consciousness of their degradation and reproach.

The Gentoos have a number of edifices and sacred spots, where they are accustomed to offer their devotions. Their pagodas, Mr. Maurice observes, are so named from the Persian words, *pout*, an idol; and *ghada*, a temple. At the further end of these buildings the object of their worship may often be distinguished, by the glimmering of a lamp, which is always kept burning near it. Particular trees and stones, marked with red paint, are held sacred; to these the natives make their obeisance as they pass along the roads. The different sects among them frequently distinguish themselves by particular marks on their foreheads and bosoms.

The strictness with which they attend to their several festivals has often excited my surprise. No master can command his servant on those days. Many of the clerks in the public offices of government are Gentoos; and on these occasions even the business of the office must give place to their religious ceremonies. During my residence at Parell, one of these sacred days occurred; when processions were made to a sacred spot near the Governor's house. The whole population of Bombay appeared to be in motion on the occasion. We had an opportunity of observing them from the upper virando. They passed in groupes, or villages, each headed by a man playing on a kind of cymbal, to which the whole party loudly responded at intervals. The scene reminded us of the *going up* of the tribes of Isreal *to the house of the Lord;* and brought to our recollection that delightful prophecy, " And many people shall go and say, Come ye, and let us go up to the mountain of the Lord, to the house of the God of Jacob."—" And it shall come to pass, that from one new moon to another, and from one Sabbath to another, shall *all flesh* come to worship before me, saith the Lord."

Connected with their inflexible attachment to the ceremonies of their religion, the rigour with which they observe the austerities prescribed to them in their religious books, is worthy of notice. On many of these days of public procession they abstain wholly from food; and an intelligent native once informed me, that so strict are the more devout among them, that nursing-women, and even infant children, are not allowed either to eat or drink until the period of fasting is expired. They are accustomed to burn their dead in the same manner as the natives of Bengal: but the result of close and extensive enquiries enables me to state, that it is now many years since a widow in the neighbourhood of Bombay has submitted to burn with the remains of her deceased husband. It is worthy of observation, that wherever the Portuguese obtained the ascendency, false delicacy prevented them from prohibiting by law all such offences against human nature and civilized life!

The Gentoo females of the higher ranks are seldom seen in public; the inferior orders have sunk far beneath females of the same class in Christian countries. Doomed to serve and to suffer, sorrow is pourtrayed in the lineaments of their countenances. It is no uncommon thing to meet a woman carrying a heavy burden, with one child in a basket on her head, another fastened to her hips, and a crowd of others running after her; while her husband is probably engaged in cooking, nursing an infant, mending his garments, or enjoying his repose! After a day of hard labour, it is often the still harder lot of the poor native woman to suffer from the cruel blows of her brutal husband, who not unfrequently vents the rage of intoxication upon the hapless victim of his cruelty. Christianity alone recognizes the rights of woman; raises her to her proper rank in the scale of being; and enshrines conjugal affection, by associating it with the most endearing discoveries of redeeming love.*

The women of India are strongly attached to the superstition of their country; though it may be justly regarded as the source of their degradations and suf-

* Ephes. v. 25—28.

ferings. Whatever vows they make to their gods in seasons of peculiar distress, or in hope of obtaining some desired good, are seldom suffered to remain unperformed. The heroic woman presents herself at the time appointed, and, with a courage which would adorn a better cause, submits to whatever extremity of torture she had vowed to undergo, as the price of her deliverance.

Two instances which confirm this statement occurred during our residence in Bombay. The first, a respectable female, who had in a severe illness vowed, if she recovered, to go to a certain idol temple on *all-fours!* The temple was some considerable distance from her residence, and the roads were covered with mud. We saw her as she passed through the town of Dungaree, preceded by the players on cymbals; crowds of people followed; and several native peons, or police-officers, with their canes, attended the procession to keep order. The devotee, from her costly dress and decorations, was evidently a person of superior rank: a canopy of rich materials was borne over her head, and her offerings were carried by her attendants. She proceeded on her hands and feet, occasionally raising herself, to obtain some relief from the excessive fatigue.

The other instance took place at a hamall, or palankeen-bearers' village, near Bycullah. Seeing a considerable crowd collected, and a large rough machine, or car, fixed in the middle of the open space before the huts, our curiosity was strongly excited; and, on enquiry, we were informed, that a Gentoo woman was about to submit to the painful, but in their opinion highly meritorious, ceremony of swinging by the back. The machine raised for the purpose was formed of two strong upright pillars, firmly fixed to the platform of the car, and crossed at the top by an horizontal beam, or lever, which wrought upon a bolt, in the manner of a scale-beam; at one end of the lever beam was fixed a small tester, or canopy, in the centre of which a hook was fixed; at the other end a strong rope was fastened, by which the beam might be lowered, raised, and made fast, on receiving its victim.

After waiting some time, we observed the crowd in motion; and the poor woman was brought out, and laid with her face towards the ground. A large hook was then thrust into the fleshy part of her back, between the shoulders. A tremendous shout was immediately raised by the spectators, so that no cries of the sufferer could have been heard, had any been uttered. The canopy was then lowered, and the back hook fastened to its receiver in the beam; it was then raised again amidst the shouts of the multitude. A stranger to such a spectacle would suppose that the woman would have kept herself as quiet as possible, lest, by the tearing of her back, she should fall to the ground, and be dashed to pieces: but, we were surprised to see her throw about her arms and legs, as if it were a mere amusement; scattering on the crowd below a number of flowers which she had in her bosom: these were eagerly caught by the people, and preserved as holy. The attendants in the meanwhile pushed the car forward, and the motion, from the unevenness of the ground, must have considerably augmented the pain of the operation. After she had remained suspended about five minutes, and had thrown about all her flowers, she was lowered, and the strongest anxiety was manifested by the spectators to touch her; the fulfilment of the ceremony having conferred upon her a high degree of sanctity in their estimation. She was immediately borne away by her friends; and, as the people became more noisy and enthusiastic, we thought it best to withdraw. This ceremony is not, however, confined to females; it is supposed that several thousand persons of both sexes in different parts of India every year voluntarily undergo this torture.

The Gentoos possess many good qualities; but these are too often obscured and counteracted by indolence, deception, dishonesty, and cruelty. Many very respectable merchants, and estimable individuals of various classes, are found among them. We have had some Gentoos, as servants, who displayed much fidelity, and even affection. As Christian knowledge prevails, and Divine influence is communicated, we may expect that from this class of the natives of India, multitudes will be raised, as living witnesses to the power and purity of the gospel of Christ.

The Mahomedans

may be classed next to the Gentoos in point of numbers. They profess to believe in one God, and in Mahomed, as his prophet. This is the principal doctrine taught in their sacred books: but in India most of the religious opinions of this sect are also derived from tradition.

The numerous deities and festivals of their idolatrous neighbours have occasioned the adoption of many similar observances among them. Mahomed, his wife, and many of his relations, and primitive followers, have all their several high days; and by the ignorant multitude are held in as high veneration, as that with which the Gentoo regards the heroes of his Shasters.

The Mahomedan worship is characterized by a simplicity peculiarly pleasing, when contrasted with the noisy pomp and disgusting ceremonies with which the religious services of the other sects of India are celebrated. They are not generally disposed to admit strangers into their mosques; but these may under some circumstances be seen. They are generally built near a river, or large reservoir, for the more ready performance of the frequent ablutions enjoined by their religion. They invariably wash before they enter their mosques. So far as I have been able to observe (not having been inside one of these buildings) they are extremely plain; without any paintings or images. From the outside, a small recess, or niche, in one side of the inner wall, may be seen: by this *unoccupied niche*, they represent to themselves *the spirituality of the Divine Essence*, whom they believe to be every where present, but unseen by mortal eye.

The present disposition and conduct of the followers of Mahomed in India, do not present encouragement to hope for their early and general conversion to the faith of Christ. Among the numerous sects of India, none are more bigotted to their system, or more enraged with any who may be induced to abandon it. The persecution to which converts to Christianity from among them would be exposed, may be inferred from the contentions which frequently break out among the sects into which Mahomedanism itself is divided. If two of these sects meet at the celebration of a festival, or if their processions meet on any public occasion, acts of violence, ending in bloodshed, if not in death, are frequently the consequence. At the changes of the moon the Mahomedans make public processions to their mosques; which, when they occur in the night, produce a very splendid effect. Their nuptial cavalcades are always in the night, and are peculiarly interesting to Europeans; they furnish the Biblical student with a most luminous illustration of our Saviour's parable of the " Ten Virgins."

The funeral ceremonies are very affecting: the most piercing outcries and bitter lamentations are made over the deceased for several hours; and to swell the note of sorrow, hired mourners attend, who pour forth their doleful songs with all the apparent agony of real grief. The body placed upon a bier, and covered with a white cloth, is carried by six men, followed by the male relatives and friends. Attendants throw scented water on the procession as it proceeds. A priest, who walks before, repeats some sacred sentences; to which the company occasionally respond, in a kind of chorus. Such a scene is solemnly impressive in a country, where one day frequently finds the healthy man at a feast, and the next beholds him carried to the tomb!

The better-informed among the Mahomedans, notwithstanding their bigotry, evince considerable superiority and vigour of mind. Their children are educated in a more liberal manner than those of the other tribes; and polite learning is cultivated by many in more advanced life. In the European practice of medicine some have acquired celebrity, and the best native surgeons are found among them.

The natives of this sect are at liberty to follow any occupation, and discover much ingenuity both in trade and commerce. The children often engage in merchandize as soon as they are able to carry a bundle of five or six pounds: they also make expert sailors; and most of the country boats are manned by them. Their general language is the Moor, or Hindostannee.

The Persees

a numerous and respectable class of the natives of Bombay, were driven from Persia, the land of their forefathers, by a sanguinary Mahomedan persecution, or conquest. They possess a great portion of wealth and intellect, and consequently possess considerable influence. They pay religious worship to fire and water, by which they pretend the Supreme Being is represented. A few among them, it is said, have attained to great abstraction of mind, and superiority over the natural passions. They have a regular priesthood, and a species of patriarchal government among themselves. They avow their subjection to the laws of the Presidency; but they have also laws of their own, to which they all submit; and punishments are inflicted in private, for those offences which are not cognizable by the common law.

They keep regular seasons of prayer. At the rising and setting of the sun they publicly worship the orb of day. The sea-shore of the Esplanade near the Fort of Bombay, at those seasons, is crowded with bowing and prostrate Persees; the more religious among them seek a retired spot, where they may perform their ceremonies unseen and uninterrupted. I have frequently observed the man who had the charge of our garden, standing by the side of the well—by a vessel of water—or exposed to the rain—repeating his prayers aloud; when he always untied the girdle which fastened his dress. His devotions did not, however, wholly engross his attention. If any of the workmen had omitted to obey his orders, or any thing struck his recollection, as necessary to be done, he would, in the midst of his prayers, vociferate to the workmen; and when the matter was arranged, return to his unfinished prayers. In answer to my enquiries, he informed me, that " their religion allowed them to speak to any one during prayer, provided they did not open their mouth, so as to separate the upper and lower teeth; and though he was often obliged to be angry with the men for their neglect of duty, yet when at prayer he always kept his teeth closed." This may be a tradition of the common people only.

The Persees have a very great reverence for fire, by the side of which they perform their devotions in their houses. No inducement will prevail on servants of this class to carry fire; and neither persuasions or threats will induce them to extinguish the sacred element, though it be only to put out a lamp. Europeans generally have gauze hung round their beds, called musquito curtains, as a defence from those venomous little insects. The inside of the curtain having been well beaten out by a towel, the servant secures the bedclothes after the master is in bed, to prevent the musquitos from entering; otherwise sleep would be impossible. At the Governor's house, shortly after our arrival, two of our party had retired to rest, and had not put out the lamp, which, not being aware of his religious aversion, they desired the servant to do. The boy told them, " he could not extinguish his god; but that he would call a servant of another caste to do it." To prevent any further difficulty, one of them rose, and put out the lamp himself *

The Persees contract for their children in marriage at a very early age; sometimes in mere infancy. The young couple are afterwards brought up together; living alternately with the husband's family, and with the family of the wife. At a certain age an entertainment is given, according to the circumstances of the parties, frequently very costly and sumptuous. The new household is then constituted, and the married pair live by themselves. It is not uncommon for large sums of

* Some years ago, a Persee gentleman, on a visit to England, had apartments with a friend of mine; and one day, drying his turban by the fire, it suddenly burst into a flame. My friend in much alarm ran to extinguish it; but he anxiously kept her back, and desired her to forbear. In conversation afterwards, she asked him, If in his country a house caught fire, they would not endeavour to put it out? He replied, in broken English—" No, no, we not put out fire; we pull down next house, and then it not burn more "

money to be spent at these entertainments; and the bride is endowed with a profusion of pearls and jewels, as her marriage portion.

Their funeral ceremonies are very peculiar. They do not inter the bodies of their dead; but place them in a situation above ground, to decay gradually. After the flesh has been devoured by the birds, the bones are deposited in a common receptacle, by a person appointed for the purpose. The process of decay is particularly noticed; and when the ravenous birds first descend upon a corpse, they observe particularly which of the eyes is first devoured. If it be the right eye, the surviving relatives are made acquainted with the fact, as a circumstance indicative of the happiness of the departed spirit; the reverse is considered an unfavourable omen. By reason of the heat of the sun, much less noxious vapour is emitted from these bodies than might be expected; the flesh is soon shrivelled up, and the bones turn quite black.

It is of importance that the friends of Missions in Europe should be acquainted with the numerous obstacles which present themselves to the progress of Christianity in India, that the labours of devoted Missionaries may be properly appreciated, and implicit dependence be alone exercised on Him, who hath declared, that the work is to be accomplished—*not by might, or by power—but by his Spirit.* Buried in sensuality, or immersed in worldly business; the slave of a superstition which shuts from his heart the realities of the unseen state; while it administers to his pride, by placing him in a rank superior to the other tribes; the Persee will require an influence more than human to awaken his soul, and to break his fetters. The bitter and unrelenting persecution to which he would be exposed, on departing from the religion of his forefathers, must operate upon his fears, if his attention should be arrested by the imperative claims of Christianity. In such a case, he must literally *leave all* for Christ. His nearest relatives would become his bitterest foes, and cast him out from among them; while the whole tribe would make common cause against him, and probably destroy him secretly, without leaving a clue to discovery.*

The Jews

are not very numerous in Bombay, but by their countenance and dress are sufficiently distinguished from every other class of natives. No opportunity of intercourse with them was afforded me. The following extract from Doctor Buchanan's "Christian Researches," contains a correct representation of this interesting people. " At the beginning of the following year (1808) the Author visited Cochin a second time, and proceeded afterwards to Bombay; where he had an opportunity of meeting with some very intelligent men of the Jewish nation. They had heard of his conferences with the Cochin Jews, and were desirous to discuss certain topics, particularly the Prophecies of Isaiah: they engaged in them with far more spirit and frankness, he thought, than their brethren at Cochin had done. They told him, that if he would take a walk to the bazaar, in the suburbs without the walls of Bombay town, he would find a synagogue without a Sephar Tora, or book of the law. He did so, and found it to be the case. The minister and a few of the Jews assembled, and shewed him the synagogue, in which there were some loose leaves of paper in manuscript, but no book of

---

* During my residence at Colombo, a Persee boy was admitted into one of the Mission Schools, and was afterwards presented by his father for Christian baptism. The father subsequently died, affording ground for hope concerning him; and the lad continues to manifest a pious dispositions.

the law. The Author did not understand that they disapproved of the law; but they had no copy of it. They seemed to have little knowledge of the Jewish scriptures or history."*

The Portuguese Roman Catholics.

Among the various denominations of Christians in Bombay, the Portuguese Roman Catholics are the most ancient, as well as the most numerous. Their places of worship in the Fort are neat, commodious buildings, in which priests educated in Europe officiate. Several of the most opulent merchants and land-owners are of this nation and profession; these have generally a chapel supported by themselves attached to their country houses, the bells of which regularly ring at the hours of prayer. Besides these, there are several clusters of native Portuguese houses in different parts of the country, each furnished with its separate chapel, and supplied by priests from the Portuguese settlement at Goa; where native young men are trained for the ministry, according to the rites of the Romish church. The Portuguese Christians, by their neatness and cleanliness, exhibit a pleasing contrast to the external appearance of their heathen neighbours.

The common people of the Portuguese Romish Church of Bombay, are in a state of great ignorance and moral degradation. Being possessed of but little knowledge of the Holy Scriptures, their ideas of sacred things are derived from tradition and ceremonies. A closer acquaintance with them considerably lessens even the favourable impression produced by their attention to the forms of Christianity. It is to be

* The Author begs leave to refer his readers to Doctor Buchanan's interesting work, for many curious and important particulars respecting the state of the Jewish people in India.

hoped, that there are some among them who worship God in spirit and in truth; but many of their superstitions are but a very small remove from those of the heathen around them.

On a visit to one of their places of worship, we saw a large altar, with a crucifix; but the principal object of their reverence was a female idol with a child in its arms, which was carefully preserved in a small recess. In answer to our enquiries, we were informed, that a great part of the property of a Portuguese chapel in India consists of images of various sacred persons, male and female. These are regarded with high veneration by the common people; and when any of them have occasion to raise money for any particular purpose, one of these images is procured from the *Padre* (the spiritual father or minister) on certain terms; and carrying it about in a plate, covered with a white cloth, they endeavour by this means to work on the piety and benevolence of their benefactors. One of these occasional mendicants applied at our house. The image of "the Holy Virgin" was in her plate; and she informed me, that the *Padre* had lent it to her from the church;—that it was God!—and that, by the help of it, she was endeavouring to obtain money, to purchase some oil and flour, which in a late dangerous sickness she had vowed to give the church, in case of her recovery. I exhorted her to " offer to God her thanksgivings, and to pay her vows to the Most High;" though I fear but to little purpose.

The Armenian Christians

compose, according to general report, the most wealthy Christian Society in Bombay. Their respectability of character, and correctness of conduct, entitle them to honourable mention. Doctor Buchanan, in his " Christian Researches," has introduced the following remarks respecting them :—" A learned author, in a work published about the beginning of the last century, entitled ' The Light of the Gospel rising on all Nations,' observes that the Armenian Christians will be eminently qualified for the office of extending the knowledge of Christianity throughout the nations of Asia. This is undoubtedly true. Next to the Jews, the Armenians will form the most generally useful body of Christian Missionaries. They are to be found in every principal city of Asia; they are the general merchants of the East; and are in a state of constant motion from Canton to Constantinople.

" Their general character is that of a wealthy, industrious, and enterprising people. They are settled in all the principal places of India, where they arrived many centuries before the English. Wherever they colonize they build churches, and observe the solemnities of the Christian religion in a decorous manner.

" Their Ecclesiastical Establishment in Hindostan is more respectable than that of the English. Like us, they have three churches in the three capitals; one each at Calcutta, Madras and Bombay; but they have also churches in the interior of the country. Their bishop sometimes visits Calcutta; but he is not resident there. The proper country of these Christians is Armenia, the greater part of which is subject to the Persian government; but they are scattered all over the empire : the commerce of Persia being chiefly conducted by Armenians. Their patriarch resides at Erivin, not far from Mount Ararat.

" The history of the Armenian church is very interesting. Of all the Christians in Central Asia, they have preserved themselves most free from Mahomedan and papal corruptions. The pope assailed them for a time with great violence, but with little effect. The churches in Lesser Armenia indeed consented to an union, which did not long continue; but those in Persian Armenia maintained their independence; and they retain their ancient scriptures, doctrines, and worship, to this day. The Bible was translated into the Armenian language in the fifth century, under very auspicious circumstances, the history of which has come down to us. It has been allowed by competent judges of the language to be a most faithful translation. La Croze calls it *the queen of versions*. This Bible has ever remained in possession of the Armenian people; and many illustrious instances of genuine and enlightened piety occur in their history. The manuscript copies not being sufficient for the demand, a council of Armenian bishops assembled in 1662, and resolved to call to their aid the art of printing, of which they had heard in Europe. For this purpose they applied first to France; but the Catholic church refused to print their Bible. At length it was printed at Amsterdam in 1666, and afterwards two other editions in 1668 and 1698. Since that time it has been printed at Venice; but at present, in India, a copy is scarcely to be purchased at any price.

"The Armenians in Hindostan are our own subjects. They acknowledge our government in India, as they do that of the Sophi in Persia; and they are entitled to our regard. They have preserved the Bible in its purity, and their doctrines are, so far as we know, the doctrines of the Bible. Besides, they maintain the solemn observance of Christian worship throughout our empire on the seventh day; and they have as many spires pointing to heaven among the Hindoos, as we ourselves."*

* "Christian Researches," pp. 258—262. The Doctor has likewise

Episcopalians, &c.

The island of Bombay has but one church connected with our National Establishment: it is a handsome and commodious building, and in general well attended. Since our arrival in 1814, the Presidency has been constituted an archdeaconry. There is also a church for the members of the Kirk of Scotland; and a chapel belonging to the Congregationalists, or Independents, which is connected with the American Mission.

The country contiguous to Bombay is fruitful, producing considerable quantities of corn and hay; for which a ready market is found in the capital. Cocoa-nuts and rice are also supplied in great abundance. The former grow chiefly in " the woods," a part so denominated from the number of cocoa-nut-trees which are planted together. The roads through these small woods afford pleasant retreats from the excessive noon-tide heat: and a few convenient houses occupied by Europeans, and numbers of native huts, are scattered among them.

Each rice-field is surrounded by a bank, to retain the water with which it is supplied in the rainy season. An intelligent author has remarked, " The growth of this grain has a peculiarity not unworthy of notice: as it loves a watery soil, so, to whatever hieght the water rises, it keeps pace with it, even to

recorded the following gratifying anecdote. " Cacheck Arrakell, an Armenian merchant in Calcutta, when he heard of the King's (Geo. III.) recovery from illness in 1789, liberated all the prisoners for debt in the gaol of Calcutta! His Majesty, hearing of this instance of loyalty in an Armenian subject, sent him his picture in miniature. He wore the royal present suspended at his breast during his life; and it is now worn by his son, when he appears at the levee of the Governor General."—*Ibid.*

eleven, and sometimes fourteen feet; the summit of the plant always appearing above the surface of the water."

The Parell road, and a new road recently made along a most romantic part of the sea-shore, are the favorite fashionable promenades. The bazaars are well supplied with vegetables, beef, mutton, and kid; also poultry and fish in abundance. The fruits are very fine; especially the Mazagong mangoe, which partakes of almost every quality deemed gratifying to the taste. The oxen of Bombay are deservedly prized for their docility and speed; and perform much of the labour usually performed in England by the horse: they will travel with ease seven or eight miles an hour. The *hump*, a large fleshy substance, which is found between their shoulders, is frequently salted, and sent, as a delicacy, to various parts of India.

The Fort of Bombay is a continual scene of business and bustle. It has but few houses in it suitable for the residence of Europeans. In those occupied by English gentlemen, the ground floors are used as warehouses, and the upper part for domestic purposes. The family apartments are often elegant, and sumptuously furnished, affording a striking contrast to the outside appearance of the buildings.

CHAP. IX.

Peculiar situation of the Author at Bombay—Native curiosity—Conversation with a Gentoo youth—Meetings for prayer, religious conversation, &c.—Extracts from Journal—Pleasing indications of usefulness—Visit from a Portuguese lady—Interesting and affecting conversation with some invalid soldiers—Portuguese studies—Sentiments of a military officer respecting Christian Missions—Conversation with a Gentoo physician—Chinese merchant at the prayer-meeting—Lieutenant Wade, his shipwreck, and death—The Author engages a passage to Ceylon—Various incidents during the voyage—Safe arrival at Point de Galle.

THE suspicions which had been produced in the minds of the natives, and even of some Europeans, by the arrival of the Missionary party at Bombay, and the pledge I had given that the Island of Ceylon was the place of our intended Missionary labours, rendered my residence at the Presidency after the departure of my companions a period of painful anxiety. Though restrained by prudential motives from the public exercise of my office as a preacher of the Gospel, even my appearance in the streets excited considerable curiosity; and led the naturally inquisitive natives sometimes to enquire of me, in their broken English—" How long Master stop here?"—" When Master go away?"—" Will Master live here all days?"—" Master not go to other country?"—" What for Master stop in this place?"— To remain insensible to the anxiety which existed among the various classes of natives, as to my character and destination, was impossible; I therefore invariably endeavoured to satisfy their curiosity, and to subdue their apprehensions.

The following extracts from my Journal will enable the reader to form a tolerably correct idea of the difficulties of my situation, and of the opinions of the natives respecting our character:

"*June* 26, 1814.—On calling upon Pestonjee Bommanjee, a wealthy Persee merchant of Bombay, I was informed that he had retired to sleep, as is customary after dinner with the natives of rank. I was therefore requested to wait till he arose. A young Gentoo, who appeared to act as clerk to the merchant, came near to the place where I was seated; and, after many attempts to introduce a conversation, the following, in substance, and to the best of my recollection in form, took place:*

Gentoo.—What you be?—a captain or a merchant?
Myself.—I be neither captain, neither merchant.
G.—You be private gentleman then?
M.—Yes.
G.—You stay here—Bombay—or you go?
M.—I only remain here till after the monsoon.
G.—Where you go then?
M.—Then I go to Ceylon.

He fixed his eyes on me with evident curiosity, and deep interest, and proceeded—

G.—There be three gentlemen go Ceylon—Missionaries—last week?
M.—Yes; there were *five* gentlemen—Missionaries—go last week to Ceylon. I am a Missionary; and when monsoon be done, then I go too.
G.—I can't think—Missionary!—What be Missionary?—A Bishop?†
M.—No, no; he not be a Bishop: a Missionary be a man who give good advice to the heathen.

---

* The broken English I had acquired during the voyage from England, by overhearing the conversations between the native seamen and their shipmates; and on my arrival in India, I often found it a convenient medium of intercourse with the natives.

† The real cause of the alarm which was produced amongst the natives by our arrival, arose, I apprehend, from their regarding the terms, *Missionary* and *Bishop* as equivalent. They had learned from the English newspapers, that the appointment of a Bishop for India had met with considerable opposition both in and out of Parliament; and among the most strenuous opposers of the measure, were gentlemen who had filled high official situations in India. Opposition from such

G.—Give good advice, how—like one merchant he give *advice* to another merchant?*

M.—No, no; I not make you understand. A Missionary—he give *good advice.* He tell men to be good; he tell men not to get drunk; not to steal; not to tell lies; not to say bad words; he tell how they may be saved: then they go to heaven when they die—that be a Missionary.

G.—Oh! oh! that be a Missionary: I not know what was Missionary.

M.—They want a great many Missionaries in Ceylon. They be glad to have ten—twenty—thirty—forty—Missionaries: more than they can get. It cost much money for passage from Europe; and only a few persons like to come as Missionaries.

G.—Some people they no like Missionaries?

M.—Yes, it is so; some people no like Missionaries; they think they be very bad men. Other people think Missionaries be very good men.

G.—I like Missionaries very well—I think be very good men.

M.—You come to Ceylon, I be very glad to see you.

G.—Oh! I pray great deal God Almighty; I no want come to Ceylon.

M.—It is very good to pray to God Almighty; all good people pray to God Almighty.

G.—Yes; very good to pray to God Almighty.

He then went to another part of the office; but returned soon after, and re-commenced the conversation; which I insert, for the purpose of showing the strange conceptions which many of the natives entertain of distant countries.

G.—Do you know Mr. B——, and Mr. F——?
M.—No.

quarters naturally led them to the conclusion, that a Bishop would be *very prejudicial* to India. *Missionary* being a term to which they could attach no definite idea; and our arrival following so close upon the discussion of the Episcopal question in Parliament; we were regarded as forming part of that Establishment, which the fears of some led them to imagine was to *coerce* the natives into an abandonment of their religion, and a profession of Christianity! It affords me much pleasure to be able to state, that the enlightened liberality and Christian conduct of the Bishop of Calcutta, (the first Bishop sent to India from England) while they have silenced objectors, have confirmed the friends of the measure in their opinion, that incalculable benefit would result to that country from the appointment of enlightened and consistent clergymen, under Episcopal jurisdiction.

* He had misunderstood my meaning; supposing the word to mean *a letter of advice!*

G.—Europe people *too many castes* to know all. Europe people live in streets; houses numbered, 1, 2, 3, 4. You want find gentleman, you ask what number he live: then you go, you find him?
M.—Yes.
G.—What street you live in in Europe?
M.—You not know, if I were to tell you—Peter-street.
G.—Peter-street.—What, in London?
M.—No; a great way from London—much far."

He then retired; and I saw no more of him.

If zeal for the glory of God, and pity for the heathen who perish for *lack of knowledge,* ever pervade the soul of a Missionary, they may be supposed to exist in no ordinary degree, when he first beholds the countries in which superstition reigns, and when the demoralizing and destructive effects of its unhallowed usurpation over the hopes and fears of his fellow men, are daily present to his view. Such was my situation; but prudence—not produced by fear for my own personal safety, but arising from a conviction that the permanent interests of the Mission were involved in my present conduct—dictated the necessity of using the utmost caution in my conversations with the natives on religious subjects. The restraint under which I felt myself laid was painful in the extreme; nor was I without fear, that I suffered caution to prevail over imperative obligation.

The public worship of God, which we attended in the Fort every Sabbath, was frequently rendered refreshing to my weary spirit. The society of Mr. and Mrs. Hart was also a source of much pleasure; Capt. B. and Mrs. R., both seriously disposed, were also introduced to our acquaintance; and we agreed to meet once a week, for the purpose of conversing together on the state of religion in our own minds. A reference to my Journal will best shew the results of what was intended, at first, to be strictly a private meeting.

" *Sunday, July* 24, 1814.—This has been a day of

refreshment to my soul. God has spread a table for me in this land of spiritual dearth. In the evening we held our little class-meeting :* there were present four persons, besides Mrs. H. and myself. I found it very good to speak and hear of the things of God. Mr. Hart and his wife, I hope, are in earnest for salvation; Captain B. and Mrs. R. appear to be sincere seekers after God. I afterwards read Mr. Wesley's Sermon on the New Birth, and concluded with prayer.

" *Monday, 25th.*—Mrs. R. has, in a note to Mrs. H. expressed the benefit she received from our meeting last night. The Lord be praised!

" *Thursday, 28th.*—This evening we held a meeting for prayer and expounding the scriptures. Captain B. introduced four strangers, who, with Lieutenant Wade, and Mr. and Mrs. Nott, (the American Missionary, and his wife, who had taken dinner with us,) formed our congregation. Messrs. N. and H. engaged in prayer; after which, I read and expounded Mark x.; and found some enlargement.

" *Sunday, 31st.*—Captain B. and Mrs. R. spent some time with us: I read and expounded the lesson for the day. In the evening we held our class-meeting. Mr. and Mrs. T. were added to our number. Tears were shed, and vows were made.

" *Thursday, August 4th.*—We held our meeting, as usual. Twenty, including Mrs. H. and myself, were present. A gracious influence appeared to be felt by all. Matt. vi. 33, was the passage selected; and I hope some lasting impressions were produced. I felt as if I could have given my soul to the people.

---

* The weekly meetings for religious conversation and prayer, held by the Wesleyan Methodists throughout their Connexion, are termed *Class Meetings.*

"*Sunday* 8*th*.—This morning I heard the Reverend N. Wade, at the Fort church, on Evil Speaking. The sacrament was administered after the sermon. I found it to be a solemn and profitable season. In the evening more than twenty were present, to whom I read the Reverend Mr. Sellon's Sermon on Titus iii. 5. Deep attention was manifested by all; and some of the poor invalids* (twelve of whom attended,) wept. The class met after the public service—*Nine* were present.

"*Thursday*, 11*th*.—The meeting for prayer and exposition was held as usual.

"*Sunday*, 15*th*.—Owing to the rain, but four attended the class-meeting. Some conversation respecting the Lord's Supper took place; which led me to select a sermon on—*This do in remembrance of me.*

"*Thursday*, 19*th*.—We had a good meeting to-night: several of the invalids were present, to whom I trust the chapter expounded was beneficial.

Sunday, 22*d*.—A very wet day. This evening but few were present. I afterwards read Mr. Wesley's Sermon, on, *We must all appear before the judgment-seat of Christ;* and found it a solemn time.

"*Thursday*, 26*th*.—Mrs. R. spent the day with us; and interested us by a statement of the consistent conduct of our friend, Mrs. T. Being invited to a dancing-party one Lord's day, she simply but politely replied, that 'her conscience would not allow her to comply with the invitation.' The person who invited her felt

---

* These are old, worn-out soldiers, chiefly Englishmen; who, after being many years in the Honourable East India Company's service, are permitted to retire on a pension, and to settle in the country. Some marry native women, by whom they often have families. From their peculiar character and occupation, they hold little intercourse with any but themselves: and their marriages sometimes lead them to disregard even the *profession* of Christianity.

herself offended, and removed her two children from Mrs. T.'s school! In the evening our little society (for so I must now term it,) with six or seven of the invalids, met at the prayer meeting. I expounded Isaiah xii.; and I hope good was done.

"*Friday, 26th.*—The Rev. Mr. Nott dined with us. A conversation afterwards took place on the duties of the Christian ministry, and on the encouragement afforded to expect the powerful aid of the Holy Spirit, in the arduous work—a delightful as well as suitable theme in a land of heathenism.

"*Sunday, Sept. 11th.*—This has been a profitable day. In family worship 1 felt a gracious influence: after which we went to visit Mr. T., who is confined by illness. I read and expounded a passage of Scripture, and engaged in prayer. While there, an English invalid came to beg for charity. I embraced the opportunity of speaking to him concerning the value and interests of his soul. There appeared hardly any thing of the Englishman remaining in his character. He assented to all I said; but such a compound of insensibility and barbarian depravity I never before saw. Oh, India! thou hast been a land of darkness and death to many of my countrymen! On returning home, I met with a soldier who has two brothers in the ministry, and who was himself once a pious man. I prayed with, and gave him a hymn-book and some tracts, and lent him the Life of Mr. Grimshaw. In the evening we had a small but serious company; to whom I delivered a sermon on Lament. iii. 24. Our class-meeting was deferred till to-morrow evening; when, if all be well, we are to meet at Captain B.'s.

"*Monday, 12th.*—According to appointment, we met at the house of Captain B. Lieutenant W. was with us. It was a soul-reviving time.

"*Thursday, 15th.*—At our meeting this evening I expounded 2 Cor. v., and found much liberty; particularly while speaking on the certainty of our dissolution; on our appearance at the judgment seat of Christ; and on the assurance which, even in this life, the Christian may obtain of his final salvation and happiness. Mrs. H. spent the day with us, and was much affected while conversing about the things of God.

"*Sunday, 18th.*—I accidentally met Sir W. W. Bart. who manifested much politeness, and even kindness. He had previously made us an obliging offer of assistance in any way in his power. His mother, I believe, was a respectable member of our society. I this evening preached, by engagement, on *the knowledge of the Divine forgiveness;* from Mark ii. 10. While delivering this sermon I *stood* up to preach, for the first time in India. A writing-desk, placed at one end of the dining-table, formed my pulpit. May those who heard be excited to seek with earnestness the remission of sins! Mrs. A. a lady of a Portuguese family, who spoke very good English, called on me this evening previous to our meeting, for the purpose, as she stated, of *hearing me preach!* I invited her in; but was considerably agitated when she told me, in answer to my enquiry, how she heard that I held meetings at my house, that it was ' *the common talk of the island!*'*"

At one of our meetings a more than usual number of the invalids was present; and I felt my mind much

---

* My uneasiness was occasioned by fear, that in holding such meetings, I had committed an illegal act; and that, as they became more public, they might be prohibited by authority. Had I consulted some of my very kind and respectable friends, it is probable my fears would have been removed; but so apprehensive was I of being advised to desist, and so greatly did I dread complete inactivity, that I abstained from asking counsel, and proceeded as my way appeared to open.

affected while addressing myself immediately to them. I assured them of the deep interest I felt for their welfare, as my countrymen in a strange land; and thus touched a chord which produced at once confidence and gratitude in their hearts. I proposed to meet them separately on a future evening: when thirteen of them attended; and the circumstances of that evening will never be erased from my memory. After a suitable introductory address, I besought them to unbosom themselves freely to me on the momentous concerns of their salvation. I spoke to them in rotation; enquired of them their names, birth-place, time and cause of their leaving their native land; their views and feelings, at different periods of their life, relative to religion, and their present feelings and determinations. I was surprised at the frankness which they displayed. But what tales of sin and woe did I hear! What heart-rending scenes were laid open to my view! The sobs and tears of many stopt their utterance, while narrating the histories of their former days. From twenty to forty years had been added to the eternity which is past, since they burst asunder the ties of country and kindred to encounter the vicissitudes of a soldier's life in India. They had shared the fatigues of the most harassing campaigns, and escaped the dangers of those sanguinary conflicts, which have distinguished the history of our Eastern possessions during that period. But, alas! their spiritual interests had been awfully neglected; they had not heard, on the average, one sermon for each year they had spent in India!* They were evidently deeply impressed by my admonitions and advice; and seemed

* During the last few years, the number of faithful ministers in India has been increased, by the appointment of several consistent and laborious chaplains to the different settlements: from whose attentions to this class of men much good may be anticipated.

to feel that God had visited them in their exile; and some promised to turn to him *with full purpose of heart.* Most likely the judgment of the great day will arrive, before I know whether the hopes entertained respecting some of them were realized or not.

These pleasing indications of usefulness, by which my efforts were encouraged, led me to look forward with regret to the period when my departure for Ceylon would leave the little society I had collected, *as sheep having no shepherd.* The more I reflected on the circumstances which had led to the establishment of the meetings for prayer and preaching, the hand of Providence appeared the more manifest. The establishment of a Mission at the Presidency was a most desirable object; and I was not without hopes, that, in the event of my receiving the sanction of my colleagues to remain at Bombay, the permission of the Governor and Council might be obtained. Jealous of my own ability to decide in a case of such importance, I resolved to be guided by my fellow-labourers; and therefore wrote to them a full representation of every particular, and placed myself at their disposal. In the course of a few weeks I received their reply; in which they expressed their opinion to be unfavourable to my continuance at Bombay; and urged my sailing for Ceylon at as early a period as possible. My conviction, that God had opened a door for the introduction of our Mission into Bombay, remained unshaken; it was therefore with great reluctance that I took the necessary measures for leaving that island.

As the Portuguese which I had acquired previously to leaving England, and had studied during the voyage, was but very imperfectly understood by the country people, I endeavoured to gain an acquaintance with their dialect. One of the invalids (a native of Holland) afforded me a little assistance. With his aid I formed a small dictionary in Portuguese and English; and, having no books in the dialect of the country, then translated some parts of the Liturgy, and a few chapters of the New Testament; while occasional conversations with the natives corrected my erroneous pronunciation.

Our religious meetings continued to be held; and edification and spiritual advantage were professed by several. The interest excited at first among the inferior classes, spread to those of a higher rank; and we had with us, occasionally, persons of considerable influence.

"*Monday, October 3d.*—At our meeting this evening twenty-five were present; among them was Major ——, of the Hon. Company's Engineers, who heard attentively, and afterwards thanked me for the sermon, which was founded on 2 Cor. vi. 1. I found much freedom in speaking. Several were affected. May the fruit remain! A long conversation afterwards ensued between the Major and myself, on the possibility of converting the natives of India to the Christian faith. He evidently possessed a cultivated mind, with great politeness. He gave me credit for sincerity of intentions; but expressed regret at my having embarked in a cause so hopeless. He said, that he had resided in India many years; had been in various parts of the country, and witnessed the native superstitions and prejudices; and that so strong was their attachment to the religion of their ancestors, and such their fear of losing caste, that he really believed their conversion to the Christian faith was absolutely impossible. I replied, that I was fully aware of the difficulties he had mentioned; and, with him, felt, that to surmount them by mere human efforts, would be impossible: that we therefore relied on the promise of God, to accompany the preaching of *his Gospel* with the powerful influence of *His Spirit,* by which we fully expected the whole world would eventually be converted to the faith of Christ. His reply I shall long remember: ' If, indeed, Sir,' said he, ' you look for success from a *supernatural*—a *divine*—influence, I must yield my argument: I see no reason why you should despair; and wish you all the success you desire.'"

The imperfect acquaintance with the *nature* of Christianity evinced by this gentleman's reply, is, unhappily, met with too generally among Europeans in India; and may be regarded as the fruitful source of that scepticism on religious subjects, which is the boast of many; and which, while it produces the sneer of contempt in those whose impotence withholds them from offering decided opposition to the promulgation of the Gospel, has in the higher circles occasionally manifested its hostility to Christianity in vexatious and oppressive conduct towards its faithful ministers and followers.

The unhappy effect produced on the minds of the natives of India by the infidel opinions and immoral lives of Englishmen, might be illustrated by a reference to numerous instances which have fallen under my own observation; but one will suffice. During an illness with which I was afflicted while at Bombay, I was attended by a Gentoo physician, possessed of much intelligence, and evidently, in many respects, a very superior man. I occasionally drew him into conversation on religious topics; but, unhappily, was not the first Englishman with whom he had conversed on the subject of Christianity; and he had formed his opinion from his first impressions. Looking me stedfastly in the face, one day, he replied to some of my remarks,—" All Englishmen not speak like you, Sir, about this matter—I was know one gentleman—Mr. Z.—he say, Christian religion all lies—nonsense—and he call Mr. A. fool—silly—because he make prayer at Christian church."

Mrs. Harvard's expected confinement took place the latter end of September; and to the many mercies by which our residence in a foreign country had been marked, her preservation in the hour of danger, and the safety of the child, was added by our preserving God. The unabated attentions paid to her by the excellent ladies of W. T. Money, and T. H. Pelly, Esquires, will never be obliterated from our recollection. Our little son was baptized by the Reverend N. Wade, the chaplain of the Presidency; who with great readiness paid us a visit for that purpose.

Shortly after Mrs. Harvard's confinement we received a visit from Mr. Luncheon, a Chinese gentleman, who sailed from England with us in the Cabalva. He congratulated us on the birth of our son; and placed a piece of silver in his hand, as a token of the prosperity he wished to attend him through life. It happened to be the evening for our prayer-meeting, and Mr. Luncheon attended the service, and knelt during prayer. At the conclusion, he expressed satisfaction. From his imperfect acquaintance with our language, he of course had but little idea of the nature of a Christian prayer-meeting; but the service had evidently impressed his mind. Laying his hand on his heart, he said, " Oh! very good—I feel it very good :—English religion good religion. I very much glad you come to China." While on the voyage, the subject of prayer was introduced in the course of a friendly conversation; and he was asked if he ever prayed? To which he replied, " Oh, no—cannot pray in a ship—not enough room. My religion want room—much room—to pray God."*

At the moment when we anticipated an early removal

---

* He referred to the various prostrations used in the idolatrous worship of his own nation.

from Bombay to our ultimate destination, our departure was still longer delayed by a severe illness which succeeded my wife's confinement, produced by the severe cold and excessive damps which follow the rainy season.* At length, our passage was engaged in a brig which was expected to sail for Colombo in a few days. The vessel was small and inconvenient; and the solicitude of our friends induced them to urge our further stay, till a more commodious vessel could be obtained. To the interference of Mr. Money we were again indebted for a reduction of one-half from the sum originally demanded by the Captain for our passage; who at first required 1,000 sica rupees; but at length consented to convey us, and the whole of the Mission property, for 500, or rather more than £.60 sterling.

The superintendence of the little society and congregation which had been raised by my instrumentality, was committed to the charge of Mr. Hart; who with great reluctance, which was only conquered by a consciousness of the exigency of their circumstances, consented to take the oversight of them, till the arrrival of a Missionary from England.†

* The cold which succeeds the rains in India is often fatal to Europeans newly arrived. In a letter, dated December 28, 1814, and sent to our friends in England, the following remarks are introduced: "We felt the cold more sensibly last Sunday, than we did in England the preceding Christmas-day. Mrs. H. went to church; and, though wrapped in two thick double shawls, literally shivered with the cold. The effect produced on the system by the cold of India, is very different from the bracing, invigorating influence of an English winter. It insinuates itself into the intestines; and frequently occasions obstructions, mortification, and death. The best preservative from its influence is fine flannel worn next the skin. Persons proceeding to India, should not fail to provide themselves with this most essential article of clothing."

† Mr. Horner arrived at Bombay in April, 1816, having been ap-

The weighty obligations under which we had been placed by the condescension and countenance of His Excellency Sir Evan Nepean, induced us to seek an audience previous to our leaving the Presidency; and Mrs. H. and myself went to Parell House, for the purpose of expressing our grateful sense of his kindness towards us, and our missionary companions. We were denied the honour of a personal interview, from a serious accident which confined the Governor to his room. The Venerable Archdeacon Barnes obligingly undertook to convey our acknowledgements to His Excellency; and, after a conversation with me on the subject of missions, in which he appeared to feel considerable interest, presented me on my taking leave with several publications of the Society for Promoting Christian Knowledge. His evangelical sentiments and ministerial fidelity, joined with the greatest liberality of mind, will, I trust, render this clergyman a public blessing to the Presidency.

Among the many expressions of affectionate regard which were conveyed to us previous to our departure, the following extract, from a note addressed to us by Lieut. Wade, (whose religious character, and friendly attentions to myself and companions have been already noticed,) will not be deemed uninteresting; especially as the writer has since exchanged the earthly for the heavenly country :*—" Accept my best wishes and re-

---

pointed to that station by the preceding Conference. In a letter, written from Ceylon, I informed him such particulars as were likely to assist him in his work. There is but too much reason to fear, that the promising appearances in some of my hearers at Bombay, which had excited my hopes, and encouraged my labours, were blighted soon after my departure. The valuable letters of Mr. Horner, inserted in the Wesleyan Missionary Notices, will furnish the reader with the history of the subsequent proceedings at that important station.

* Lieut. Wade left India in October 1814, on his return to his gards for you both, and the assurance of my prayers to *the Giver of every good and perfect gift*, that he will abundantly reward your pious labours; rescuing by them many souls from the power of Satan, and bringing them into the kingdom of God. That you may both be partakers of the heavenly kingdom—through Him, for whose sake, for the extension of whose kingdom, and for the increase of whose glory, you have devoted yourselves in this distant and neglected land—is the sincere prayer of

"Yours, very sincerely,
"JOHN WADE."

"*January* 15, 1814, We left the shore of Bombay, and embarked for Ceylon, after taking leave of our generous friends, Mr. and Mrs. Money, by whom we were laid under renewed obligations up to the moment of our departure. BOMBAY will be identified by us with our recollections of providential interposition, and be referred to, as illustrative of generous and disinterested hospitality, while memory retains its seat.*

native country; and had nearly completed the voyage, when the vessel was wrecked off Portland Point, and he, with most of the passengers and crew, perished!

* Captain Birch, to whom we had been so greatly indebted, and who had procured our introduction to those whose friendship and services I have had occasion so frequently to mention, had several months before proceeded on his voyage to China. Previously to his departure, my companions united with me in a letter of thanks to him for his complete and entire redemption of the pledge he gave us in our bereaved and almost destitute circumstances. With that generosity of mind for which he is distinguished, he always replied to every acknowledgment of obligation, that " any little service he had rendered us had afforded him real satisfaction." The Wesleyan Missionary Committee, on the arrival of Captain Birch in England, officially acknowledged the valuable services he had rendered to the Mission, and presented him with copies of the Rev. Messrs. Wesley and Fletchers' Works, handsomely bound, as a token of their esteem.

As the vessel was detained in the harbour, it afforded several an opportunity of coming on board the next day: being the Lord's Day, we celebrated Divine service, and commended each other to the care of Him who is the *Keeper of Israel.* On Monday the vessel left the harbour; when we had a pleasing instance of fidelity afforded by two of our native servants. One of them had been entrusted with money, to purchase for our use a few articles of which we found ourselves in need; and had not returned when the vessel began to sail. Of course we had given over all expectations of seeing him again; but, after some time, a small boat was discovered making after us with all possible rapidity—it contained the Persee lad, accompanied by our Gentoo *paniwaller,* or water-boy. A rope was thrown to them; and they handed us the articles through the port-hole. We rewarded them for their integrity; and they, after many *salaams,* and shedding some tears, returned to Bombay, and we proceeded on our voyage.

The first few days we suffered the usual inconvenience from the motion of the vessel, the sea being very rough; but we were much more annoyed by the oaths and imprecations of the captain, in giving his orders to the crew. On the 23d, we found ourselves off Cape Ramas; the next day the Bednore mountains appeared, raising their majestic heads, and affording a fine back-ground to the scene before us. On the 24th, we came in sight of Cochin: it being the Lord's Day, we had Divine worship upon deck. About fifteen of the crew were Roman-Catholics; who attended the prayers on deck in clean apparel. Although they did not sufficiently understand English to derive much advantage from the service, they remained until the whole was over, and behaved with great propriety. When they retired, they each made a bow to me as they passed my chair. As the weather was generally favourable, we occasionally dined on the deck, highly gratified by the romantic prospects of the country, afforded by our sailing so near the shore. We had no opportunity of touching at Goa,* or at any of the remarkable places situated on that coast. An invalid gentleman, a lieutenant in the Indian army, who was our fellow-passenger, gave us much interesting information concerning the Marhatta tribes, who once held such predominancy in that part of India, and the wars by which their power was at length completely annihilated. The benevolent exertions now used by Christians of every denomination, to spread the Gospel of peace throughout that interesting country, afford a striking contrast, in the selection of their objects, and the choice of their instruments, to the designs of unhallowed ambition, and the *means* by which the contending parties strove for the sovereignty of the soil.

The beginning of February we reached Cape Comorin, the southern extremity of the Indian Peninsula. The weather being what the sailors call a dead calm, we cast anchor, and waited for a wind to waft us across the Gulf of Manaar to Colombo, which lies on the opposite side. This passage, we were informed, is sometimes performed in less than forty-eight hours; so that we considered our voyage as nearly accomplished. It, however, pleased Divine Providence, that we should not reach our destination so soon as we expected. One evening, while quietly lying at anchor, one of those tremendous squalls arose, which are common on the Indian coast at that season; and such was the force of the wind, and the violence of the sea, that the most serious apprehensions were entertained by the Captain, that the vessel would part her cable, and the anchor be

* GOA belongs to the Portuguese. It will always be memorable, as having been the scene of the most abominable cruelties, exercised by that flagitious people on the natives, under a pretended zeal for Christianity. The infamous Inquisition has, within a few years, been entirely abolished.

lost. To prevent this, all hands were employed to bring the anchor on board; which, having accomplished, they let the vessel drive before the wind, and we were soon out of sight of land.

The losing sight of land gave us no uneasiness for the first three or four days; though, as the captain endeavoured to steer in a north-east direction, we expected before the expiration of that time to fall upon some part of the Ceylon coast: but when a whole week had elapsed, and no land appeared, we began to be apprehensive that the vessel was driving too much to the leeward, in the direction of the Maldive Islands. Tremendous thunder-storms, which at intervals broke upon us, accompanied with heavy rain, added to the uncomfortableness of our circumstances; especially as all the ports, and openings for light and air, were necessarily closed. Mrs. Harvard and myself, with our little boy, the nurse and her child, and a native servant girl, were all confined below, in a small apartment about nine feet long, by six broad! The expedients to which we were compelled to resort while confined in this place, were productive of the most unpleasant feelings at the time; though, when placed in happier circumstances, the remembrance of them has provoked our smiles.

A second week arrived, and passed away as the former, in anxious suspense, and constant efforts to descry some object by which to shape our course, and so to free us from the distressing ignorance of our relative situation. Sometimes, what appeared to us to be a flight of birds, has enkindled hope that we were approaching land; but, after many hours' sailing, the disappointment which succeeded, has only served to give additional poignancy to our distress.

The characteristic apathy of the natives renders them more capable of patient endurance under privation and suffering, than of active exertion in seasons of danger.

Our crew appeared perfectly resigned to their situation, and manifested no discontent at the short allowance of provisions on which they were placed; but the adverse winds, and incessantly fruitless sailing from point to point in search of land, at length overcame their patience; and it was with the greatest difficulty that the Captain and mate could keep them to their duty, which was unintermitted, owing to the roughness of the weather. It was truly affecting to see the poor half-clothed men exposed to the chilling rains, shivering with the cold, while engaged in working the vessel; knowing, as we did, that the daily portion of food they received was scarcely sufficient to support life, much less to enable them to endure such labour. As they had no drink but a small quantity of water, the ship's store of spirits being exhausted, I gave up for their use a few small boxes of wine and spirits, which I had purchased at Bombay for my Missionary companions in Ceylon. It was with feelings of the truest enjoyment, I beheld the first allowance served out to the poor fellows, as they were working on the deck in a drenching rain: it revived their spirits, and recruited their wasted strength. The superstition of the Roman Catholic seamen suggested a new expedient. They imagined we should have a favourable change, if a subscription were entered into for the benefit of their new church at Madras. A sum was soon collected among them, to which the Mahomedans contributed; at the suggestion of the Captain, I also gave a donation.

A mutinous disposition which manifested itself among the ship's company about this time added much to the dangers of our condition. It originated in some supposed injury they had received from the mate of the ship. The mate was a country-born Portuguese; and the complaint was founded on some dispute relative to the money collected for the Madras Portuguese church. The violence manifested by those who considered themselves aggrieved, was so great, that bloodshed would have ensued, and the safety of the vessel and passengers been endangered, but for the prompt interference of the captain, who promised the complainants ample redress; and, as he ordered the mate into immediate confinement, the tumult was stilled. He requested me to act as judge when the weather should permit an investigation. During an interval of calm, a chair was placed for me on deck, the crew summoned, and the delinquent brought forth.

The captain, with great warmth, espoused the cause of the crew, and accused the mate of almost every thing that was infamous; protested, that he had more than once saved him from an untimely end, but that he should now most certainly be punished as he merited. Having concluded his accusation, he immediately proceeded to pass sentence upon the culprit—that he should be suspended from his office as mate, and hanged at the next port we came to. This appeared very rough justice, and I was heartily glad when I had liberty to leave *the bench*. I afterwards strove to soften the captain's mind towards the poor man, but in vain. He protested he would never more forgive him—that many a better man had been executed—and that it was a duty he owed to society to bring such a wretch to justice. He concluded by saying, " I am sorry I cannot attend to *your reverence's* recommendation!"

The commencement of the third week found us in equal ignorance, and under increased despondency. To add to our distress, it was now evident, that the captain was himself as completely at a loss, with respect to the course he was steering, as any of his crew.

While we remained within view of the coast, and the sun continued visible, by the help of " Horseburgh's Directions," the situation of the vessel was regularly announced without any reluctance; but it was now complained, that the *sun* could not be clearly observed ; and our situation could not be ascertained. Our stock of provisions grew very short. When the stock of water was nearly exhausted, and the daily allowance served out was exceedingly small, the crew generously sympathized with Mrs. Harvard and the nurse; and, that they might have the more, the poor fellows cheerfully relinquished a part of their own allowance. This was an alleviation of their privations, and attached us greatly to the men; but unless we speedily made land, we knew that the store of water would be wholly exhausted. We endeavoured to strengthen ourselves in God, by remembering his past merciful interpositions in our behalf.

The third week since our last sight of land was drawing to its close, and still nothing presented itself around us, but one complete circle of sky and water ; and every day some fresh article of food was announced to be entirely consumed. The coop contained but a solitary duck, so nearly starved, as to be unable to shake off the swarms of ants which covered its beak and eyes. This the captain had ordered to be killed, " lest it should die." On the 22d of February the vessel was pronounced by the captain to be to the *eastward* of Ceylon, and in the latitude of 7 deg. 43 m. It was supposed we had sailed past the island, and were entering the Bay of Bengal. The wind was so strong from the northward, that we could only steer a north-east course. The inhospitable Andamans*, seemed to be the land to which we were steering ; and the captain feared to tack about, lest the wind and current together should drive us across the line.

* ANDAMAN, or ANDEMAN Islands, in the East Indies, situated about 80 leagues from Tannasserim, on the coast of Siam. They are but little known. Only the East India ships touch at them, and are supplied by the natives with rice. The inhabitants are by some represented as an harmless inoffensive race of men, and by others as cannibals. Long 92 deg. east, lat. from 10 to 15 deg. north.—*Encyc. Perth.* vol. ii. p. 105.

Our fellow passenger, the military officer, remarked to the captain, that in his opinion the vessel would carry more sail, and lie nearer to the wind. This was deemed a high offence; as it implied a suspicion of his ability to direct the vessel; and, under the influence of anger, he hoisted all the sail he could, and brought the ship so much up, that she laid nearly on her side; at the same time swearing, that if other people did not value their lives, he did not care for his :—he would show that he was not afraid to carry sail, &c. This so alarmed the lieutenant, that he ran on deck in his undress, being confined to his bed, and begged the captain to shorten sail, promising never to interfere with the course of the vessel again. The captain, notwithstanding, kept up as much sail as he could with safety; but an hatchet was brought on deck, that if a sudden squall arose, he might be prepared to cut the ropes. We thus made as much *northing* as the wind would possibly allow us; and as a change of the moon was near, we hoped that the wind would then alter, and so enable us to tack about and drop on the island, which was supposed to lie to the south-west. But in the middle of the same night, we were aroused by the long-desired cry of " *Land!*" and by boats which came off to us at day-light we learnt, with wondering gratitude, that the land to which we had been thus providentially directed, was Point-de-Galle, in the Island of Ceylon!

The misunderstanding between the captain and our fellow passenger was plainly over-ruled by Divine Providence to become the means of our deliverance: for, had the vessel made any less *northing* than it actually did, we should, probably, have passed the island in the night; as, with all the northing it did make, we only reached the southern-most point of the island; and had we passed the land in that latitude, and then proceeded on the mistaken notion we had entertained of gaining the eastern coast of Ceylon, our destruction on the Maldives would have been almost inevitable. The night being so light and clear was also greatly in our favour; for, though we were driven near to the most rocky part of the island, the vessel did not strike, nor sustain any injury.* This concurrence of circumstances which human skill could not influence, impressed us with a sense of the Divine goodness.—*It was the Lord's doing, and marvellous in our eyes.* The captain's astonishment, on discovering that we were off Point-de-Galle, was equal to our own. " I'll break my quadrant," said he, (uttering at the same the most horrid oaths and blasphemies) " as soon as I get on shore, and will have a new one. Some of the men must have let it fall, and injured it, for it has misled me, indeed!" He was indeed deceived; having mistaken S. W. for S. E.; but his egregious ignorance of navigation was the cause of his deception, and of the dangers and privations to which we had been reduced.

Before we came to anchor, the captain committed the charge of the vessel to the mate he had so solemnly threatened to destroy! It was now evident, that the displeasure he had manifested towards him was merely assumed, in order to quiet the tumultuous disposition of his crew. This became more apparent, when he ordered two lanterns to be fastened to the rigging, and caused several of the men to be tied up and flogged by candle-light. One of them, a poor Caffre, died in a few days afterwards, and was thrown into the sea!

* In the month of April 1822, a vessel bound for England, in her passage from Colombo to Galle, was lost by running on the rocks very near the spot where we first made the island. Mr. Clough was on board at the time; but he and the rest of the passengers, as well as the crew, providentially escaped.

CHAP. X.

Arrival at CEYLON—Interview with Messrs. Clough and Squance—Point-de-Galle—Bay, scenery, &c.—Description of Mr. Clough's residence—Prayer-meeting—Visit from the Guard Moodeliar—Lord Molesworth—His Lordship's character and affecting death—Loss of the Bengal Indiaman by fire—Service in the Dutch church—Illness of Mr. Squance—Receives kind attention from the Hon. Chief Justice—Preaches by an interpreter—Necessity of adopting such a medium of instruction—Narrative of the Conversion and Baptism of PANDITTA SEKARA, a learned Budhuist Priest—His subsequent appointment to a situation under the local government—Meeting of the Mission party at Galle—The Author's appointment to Colombo—Letter from New South Wales—Mr. Ault's illness—Journey of the Author and his family to Colombo—Rest houses—Caltura—Slow travelling—Met by Mr. Armour—Cinnamon gardens—Relative of the late Queen Charlotte.

FROM the deck of our little vessel, now safely anchored in Galle roads, we surveyed, with feelings of deep interest, the island which we had so long regarded as the scene of those labours, to which we were devoted by duty and inclination. We looked back upon the past with gratitude, and to the future with hope.

Boats, laden with provisions, and various kinds of fruit, soon surrounded our vessel in considerable numbers; the owners of them came on board, and found a ready market for their commodities. We purchased some trifling articles of an interesting native lad, who spoke tolerably good English, and who pleased us much by his quickness of intellect, and obliging manners. Not having any Singhalese coin in our possession, we engaged to pay him in the after part of the day; but he left the ship, and though we used every effort to discover our little creditor, our enquires were unavailing;

nor did we see him afterwards. The wrong which he thus sustained from us, though wholly unintentional, gave me considerable pain.

Our first and immediate business was to forward a note to W. C. Gibson, Esq. to whom we had letters of introduction, acquainting him with our arrival, and requesting him to furnish us with the means of coming on shore. It was my intention to have paid Mr. Clough, my fellow-missionary, an unexpected visit; but, being informed by Mr. Gibson of our arrival, he hastened to the beach, accompanied by Mr. Squance, who was on a visit to Galle for the benefit of his health, and came off to the vessel in the first boat. We recognized each other long before the boat gained the vessel; and testified our mutual joy by signs, till the more intelligible language of speech could be employed.

The meeting was most affecting; but the sensations of my fellow-labourers were peculiarly overpowering, as they had long since regarded us as entombed within the bosom of the ocean. Information had reached them of the time of our sailing from Bombay, and of the smallness of the vessel in which we had embarked, by the captain of a much larger vessel, which left Bombay harbour a few days after us, bound to Colombo; and with whom our attentive and anxious friends had engaged, in case he met with us at sea, to take us on board. The larger vessel arrived nearly a month before us; and every succeeding day strengthened the conviction, that the bars of the great deep had closed on us for ever!

POINT-DE-GALLE* is so named from the projecting rocks on which the Fort is built. It is one of the most populous Forts in the island, and, besides a considerable number of Europeans, comprehends a vast society of natives. The bay is commodious, and capable of re-

---

* In the Singhalese language, *Gal* signifies *a stone*.

ceiving vessels of three or four hundred tons. The ships of the East India Company, and other large vessels which call here on their voyage from Continental India to Europe, anchor in the roads. During the war, Galle was a rendezvous for vessels from Calcutta, Madras, and Bombay; where at regular seasons they obtained convoy, and then proceeded on their homeward voyage.

The scenery, on entering the bay of Point de-Galle, is singularly beautiful. The crowded Fort, to the left, presents a fine contrast with the opposite shore, which appears to be without inhabitants. Mr. Gibson's handsome bungaloe rises from a hill on the right, like a Chinese pagoda from the midst of surrounding jungle; while the stupendous Kandyan hills, and Adam's Peak,* proudly rising above all, furnish a most imposing background to the enchanting view.

On reaching the wharf, we found that the kind foresight of Mr. Clough had provided me a conveyance, and that his excellent friend, the Guard Moodeliar, had furnished a palankeen for Mrs. Harvard and the child. We soon arrived at Mr. Clough's residence, and partook of a hearty meal; the privations we had so long endured having prepared our appetites to enjoy, with inconceivable relish, the wholesome and excellent provision which was set before us. Our repast consisted of

* *Adam's Peak* is the highest and most conspicuous mountain in Ceylon. Mr. Cordiner states, that " it is of a conical form, situated about sixteen miles E. by S. of Colombo; and distinctly visible to those who sail on the S. W. coast, for a distance of one hundred and fifty miles." This mountain is highly venerated by the Ceylonese; and many fabulous stories are in circulation respecting it. The bigoted worshippers of Budhu formerly considered it so highly sacred, that no Christian could breathe its atmosphere, and live. But this opinion must have been shaken; as, during my residence on the island, it was visited by several English gentlemen. One of the first who gained its summit informed me, that the natives regarded him with evident surprise on his return from his hazardous enterprize alive, and in good health!

Singhalese rice, and egg curry;* and though I have frequently partook of the same dish, both at my own, and at other's tables, I never met with any which appeared so excellent. Contrasted with the meager and limited fare to which we had been so long restricted, we considered it a delicacy of the highest order.

When we had satisfied the pressing claims of hunger, we had time to observe more particularly the situation of Mr. Clough's residence. A poet's imagination could scarcely conceive of a spot more suited to the residence of a Christian Missionary. It is built between two gradually sloping hills. A native village rises behind it, and is connected with it by an agreeable serpentine walk, which comes to the back door of the house. Immediately in front is a spacious lawn, on which the tenants of the adjoining wood frequently fed and sported, and conveyed to the minds of delighted visitors an idea of the security which reigned in the primitive Eden. A few paddy-fields,† and the spacious bay, formed the distant prospect. The house itself appeared the sacred habitation of devout peace and retirement. A refreshing breeze continually passed through it; and the silence which reigned in the sweet sequestered spot was seldom interrupted but by the warbling of the birds, and the humming sounds from the interesting native-school which adjoined the house.

In the afternoon of the day we landed, Messrs.

---

* *Curry* is a dish in high request among all the natives, and most of the Europeans in India. It resembles an English stew; but has rather more liquid. The *curry* is formed of aromatic seeds, onions, ginger, saffron, &c. *Ox's oil*, as the natives term it, *ghee*, or native butter, is sometimes introduced. Fish, flesh, and fowl may be curried. Singhalese rice is peculiarly suited to curry: chillies and a lemon improve it; as does also a native sauce called *samball*.

† Native corn-fields. The rice-grain, before it is beaten and cleared from the husk, is called *Paddy*.

Clough and Squance introduced us to the circle of their acquaintance in the neighbourhood. The story of our perils and escape was a prominent feature in the conversation; and called forth many expressions of sympathy and wonder from our auditors.*

Towards evening we had the honour of waiting on Lord and Lady Molesworth, by whom we were received with that courtesy and kindness for which they were so distinguished. His lordship apologized for not inviting us to abide at his house; stating, that he was on the eve of quitting Ceylon for England, and had in consequence considerably reduced his establishment. The unequivocal proofs of attachment to our Mission, which his lordship had manifested from the first arrival of my companions, has been already noticed; and I endeavoured to express the high estimation in which we held the countenance he had afforded it. We were also introduced to Mr. Gibson and his excellent lady, and were welcomed by them with the most cordial reception. I afterwards accompanied Mr. Clough to the prayer-meeting, held in an unoccupied house in the Fort, which had been fitted up for public worship by the contributions of some who had received benefit from Mr. Clough's ministry. A considerable number attended; including a few English soldiers; the fervour of whose prayers, and hearty "amens," at the close of the several petitions, led me to hope that they had been

---

* To add to the impression made on our minds by the deliverance we had experienced, the wind by which we had been so violently and unexpectedly driven *towards the island*, changed immediately upon our landing, and blew with equal violence *from* the shore! Our vessel was, the same morning, driven from her anchorage, and beat several miles out to sea; so that it was two days before she could again make the bay. Some may attribute this circumstance to *chance;* but the Christian reader will recognize, with me, the controul of HIM *whom the winds and the seas obey.*

taught to pour out their hearts before the Lord. I selected the hymn, commencing,

'God of my life, whose gracious power,'

and found enlargement of soul in singing the praises of our great Deliverer.

On our return to Mr. Clough's residence, we were surprised by a visit from the Guard Moodeliar, accompanied by his wife and family, and attended by a retinue of servants, some of them bearing *chules*, (flambeaux, formed of the dried branches of the cocoa-nut tree). The procession had a very novel, and at the same time a very grand appearance, as we viewed its approach to the house. In the conversation which arose, the Moodeliar shewed great independence of mind, and generosity of disposition, unaccompanied by ostentation; indeed, the whole of his deportment impressed me with a high opinion of his character. He repeated his desire to render us every service in his power; and after a short stay, the family returned in the same order in which they came.

The next morning, before breakfast, Lord Molesworth paid us a visit on horseback, unattended. He alighted, left his horse at the garden gate, and entered the virando. With the greatest condescension, he commenced a conversation on various topics relating to the establishment of Christian Missions in the East; and by the excellence of his remarks, and the practical nature of his observations, led me to form a high estimate of his wisdom and piety. He had resided a considerable time in India, and had acquired an extensive acquaintance with the prejudices and manners of the natives; and with the objections produced by those European residents who were opposed to the establishment of Missions among them. The standard by which his lordship measured the moral qualifications

of Missionaries was high, but it was scriptural; and if
some of his remarks appeared severe, that severity was
justified by the immense injury which the cause of
Missions must sustain in India, by the absence of
either piety or prudence in their agents. My fellow-
labourers and myself can never forget the lessons of
wisdom which we derived from his lordship's conversation, or cease to regret that the Mission was so soon
deprived of his patronage and advice.*

* Lord and Lady Molesworth, with a considerable number of other passengers, embarked for Europe in the Arniston Transport. When off Cape Laguellas, on the coast of South Africa, the vessel was unfortunately wrecked; and our noble friend, his lady, and most of the passengers and crew were suddenly hurried into eternity. It has been stated by some of the survivors, that in the awful crisis which immediately preceded the sinking of the vessel, his lordship displayed the calmness of the Christian, and endeavoured to impress on the minds of his fellow-sufferers the importance of preparing, by penitence and prayer, to meet their God. Had his lordship remained in Ceylon a few weeks longer, he would have received from Europe the appointment, which it was the object of his voyage to solicit. His valuable life would thus have been preserved, and the important services he had rendered to our infant Mission, have been continued. *Be still, and know that* I AM GOD, silences our complainings, and furnishes a reply to the vain speculations which man, in the plentitude of his ignorance, forms respecting the ways of the Almighty.

Mr. Clough, whose knowledge of Lord Molesworth was more intimate than that of any of the other Missionaries, bears the following testimony to his character, in a letter to the Rev. John Barber; dated Galle, January 8, 1815. " It would be ungrateful and unjust, not to mention his Lordship's unremitting kindness and attention to me, while I have been labouring in this place. Not content with general countenance, he has condescended to offer his assistance and cooperation with me, as far as lay in his power, whenever I might consider them necessary. Hence, I have had his superior wisdom to consult; and have invariably found him, not only willing, but greatly pleased, to do any thing for the furtherance of the work of God, and particularly as relating to the natives. Both officers and men have a bright example in the conduct of his Lordship. He never absents himself from church, except in a case of absolute necessity; and has even attended my lecture at a private house in the Fort on week-day evenings. I may say, he has been to me a friend, a father, and a guide."

In the way from Mr. Clough's house to the Fort, our attention was arrested by the great quantities of cloth, and other merchandize, together with large pieces of half-consumed timber, masts, and spars, which were scattered along the beach. They formed part of the materials and cargo of the Bengal Indiaman, of 1,200 tons burthen, which, a short time before our arrival, took fire when on the eve of sailing, and was, with a most valuable cargo, totally destroyed. The ship was crowded with cabin and steerage passengers: among the latter was a number of invalid soldiers; several of whom met death in this most terrific form. Most of the surviving passengers and officers afterwards embarked in the Arniston, and perished with Lord and Lady Molesworth on the South African coast.

The first Sabbath morning after my arrival, I occupied Mr. Clough's pulpit in the Dutch church, and preached to a respectable and attentive congregation from Psalm clxiv. 15, *Happy is that people whose God is the Lord.** Several respectable families of that nation still reside at Galle; but having no resident minister, they assemble for worship in their church, previously to the English congregation, when a sermon and prayers are read by one of their elders in their own language. The Dutch clergyman on the Colombo station, who receives a settled stipend from the English Government, pays an annual visit to Galle, to baptize the infants, and administer the ordinance of the Lord's Supper; when any question relating to their church discipline is referred to his decision.

The disease which compelled Mr. Squance to leave

---

* The Dutch church is a commodious building, in a good state of repair. It is furnished with an organ; and the walls are adorned with several well-executed monuments, principally in memory of persons who had held high official situations in the island when in possession of the Dutch.

his station at Jaffna, was at first of a most alarming aspect. Sir Alexander Johnstone, the Chief Justice, being on the northern circuit at the time of his attack, felt so deeply interested in his recovery, as in the most condescending manner to urge his return to Colombo with him; a change of air appearing likely to prove beneficial. Mr. Squance accepted the invitation, and experienced so great benefit from a few days travelling, as to be able on the road to address a Tamul congregation, through the medium of an interpreter. The congregation was collected, and the interpreter, obtained, by the influence of the Chief Justice; whose opinion in favour of this mode of imparting instruction to the natives, was on that and other occasions decidedly expressed. This was one of the first attempts made by the Wesleyan Missionaries in Ceylon to address a native congregation; and, but for the mode then adopted, they must have resided among those to whom they were especially sent, without employing any direct effort for their salvation, until they had acquired a knowledge of their language. Objections to this mode of conveying instruction exist in the minds of some persons; though it is by no means contrary to the customs of the East. The high sanction which it obtained from the recommendation of Sir A. Johnstone, and the success which has followed its adoption, will fully justify the Missionary who avails himself of this channel of communication, until, by a laborious application to the study of their language, he is competent to address the natives in their own tongue.*

---

* The Rev. S. Laidler, one of the Missionaries belonging to the London Missionary Society, in a letter addressed to the Rev. Doctor Waugh, dated Bangalore, May 16, 1820, says—"Considering the blessings which followed the labours of Brainerd, though he never learned the language of the Indians, but spoke through the medium of an interpreter, I judged that it would be inexcusable in me, if I did not make

The modesty of Mr. Squance led him to decline the benevolent invitation of Sir Alexander Johnstone, to occupy an apartment at his seat at Colpetty. But the kindness and condescending solicitude of the Chief Justice, were daily continued until he was fully recovered; while he found a home, in every sense of that comprehensive word, in the house of Mr. Chater; who, with Mrs. C. assiduously attended him during a dangerous illness which seized him shortly after his arrival at Colombo, and under the influence of which he continued a considerable time. Mr. Clough was summoned from Galle, to attend what was supposed to be the death-bed of his fellow labourer; but by the Divine blessing on the unremitting attentions of J. Scratchley, Esq. surgeon of the Royal Artillery, he was at length so far restored as to be able to return to Galle with his affectionate friend; the quietude he enjoyed in his residence, and a close attention to the prescribed diet, produced a most salutary effect on his debilitated frame. He, however, on my arrival, had still the appearance of an invalid.

During Mr. Clough's temporary residence at Colombo, a circumstance took place, which, from its singular importance, forms an interesting era in the history of the Wesleyan Ceylon Mission. PETRUS PANDITTA SEHARA, a learned priest of the Budhurst religion, and whose attachment to his faith was strengthened by the honours and emoluments connected with the priesthood, was induced to abandon those honours and emoluments, and to become an outcast from his tribe, that by following Christ, he might obtain a better inheritance in the future world!

Influenced by a desire to become intimately acquainted

some effort to impart instruction in the same way, till I am able to address the natives in their own tongue: particularly as God had given me a servant, who, while at Madras, had received a religious education, and is able to read the Tamul fluently."

with the superstitions of the natives, that he might be the better prepared to expose their absurdity and sinfulness, Mr. Clough took every opportunity of being present at their religious services, and endeavoured on such occasions to engage the priests in conversations on religious topics, in the hearing of their followers. A celebrated *banna maddua,* at which the priest was carried in great pomp on the shoulders of his followers, furnished the first opportunity for converse with Petrus Panditta Sekara. The conversation which then took place communicated a ray of light to his understanding, and the discovery which it made powerfully affected his heart. He sought to Mr. Clough for further information respecting the religion of Christ; and his deportment at every succeeding interview strengthened the hope, that his enquiries were not dictated by vain curiosity, but were the result of an increasing desire to arrive at truth.

The reputation which he had gained for superior knowledge and sanctity, had raised him to a high pitch of consequence among the votaries of Budhuism; and there is sufficient reason for believing that his moral characer was in reality upright and unblamable. Various marks of distinction had been conferred on him. He had resided for a considerable time with the King of Kandy; and at his inauguration as a priest had the honour of riding on the king's own elephant. Mr. Clough, in his interesting narrative of this extraordinary conversion, says concerning him, " He is every where celebrated for his extensive acquaintance with the literature and religion of the island, and for his profound knowledge of the Oriental languages." About two months after Mr. Clough's first acquaintance with him, he made known to him the entire revolution of sentiment which his mind had undergone; professed his firm conviction of the Divine origin of Christianity; and expressed a wish openly to renounce Budhuism, and to make a public profession of his faith in Christ.

As such a step would inevitably subject him to the privations of poverty, if it were not immediately followed by direct attacks by the enraged idolaters upon his life; Mr. Clough made Governor Brownrigg acquainted with all the circumstances of the case. His Excellency forwarded an immediate answer, that if the priest, from conviction, embraced the Christian religion, protection should be afforded him, and a small allowance made to preserve him from want. The Governor's letter conveyed encouragement both to Mr. Clough and his interesting pupil; for whose baptism at Galle, preparations were then made.

The perils to which the young convert was exposed during the absence of Mr. Clough, (who had been summoned from Galle to Colombo by the serious illness of Mr. Squance) are thus described by Mr. Clough : " I had not been absent a week, before the report, that Petrus Panditta Sekara was about to renounce Budhuism, was spread throughout the district, and at length came to the ears of the high-priest himself; who was so alarmed at the intelligence, that he assembled fourteen of the head priests, and despatched them to prevail upon him, if possible, by some means or other, to abandon his intention to embrace Christianity ; stating, that if a priest of his rank and importance in the religion of Budhu renounced his religion, it would not only disgrace his own character, but greatly injure their faith. However, he continued immoveable ; and the matter spread so rapidly, that before the fourteen priests left him, the number had increased to fifty-seven ; who all used every possible method to prevail on him to abandon his intention. His family also joined their endeavours to the priests' ; some weeping, some expostulating, and others threatening to put an end to their existence, if he so disgraced them. Many head-men of the district came to him with large presents, observing, ' If *you* forsake the priesthood, it will ruin our religion in this country.' But their united efforts were ineffectual. To preserve his life, he was compelled to flee from his temple in the country, to the house of an European in the Fort of Galle, where he met a letter from me, directing him to proceed to Colombo without delay. On this occasion, Lord Molesworth, Commandant of the Fort, behaved, not only like a friend, but as a Christian, who had the cause of God at heart. He took him into his own house; and when he came off to Colombo, gave him money sufficient to bear his own expenses, and those of the men who went with him as a guard."

The news of his abandonment of idolatry reached Colombo before him, and excited interest among the Europeans of all ranks. On his arrival, he experienced the kindest reception from the friends of religion ; but was especially indebted to the Honourable and Reverend T. J. Twisleton, whose pious and appropriate instructions, while they illustrated the excellence, established the claims, of the Christian religion on his approval and choice. The entreaties and remonstrances of his relatives followed him to Colombo, in letters which evidently deeply affected him: but he shewed no infirmity of purpose : while he loved his family with a strong affection, his love to Christ enabled him to bear their reproaches, and to reject their persuasions.

" A day or two before his baptism," observes Mr. Clough, " I called upon him, and found him very cheerful and happy, ' I dreamed,' said he, ' last night, that my robes were covered with all kinds of filthy reptiles. I was so disgusted at the sight, that I went to a river, and cast them in, never to touch them again. When I awoke this morning, I found myself without clothes, and my robes folded up and thrown on the far side of the room. Now, thought I, God has sent me this dream, to shew me the bad state I am in, and to confirm me in all my former resolutions. I am only sorry that I am forced to put the robes on again."

On Christmas-day, 1814, the once idolatrous priest of Budhu was publicly admitted into the visible church of Christ on earth, by the ordinance of baptism; which was administered at the Fort church, in the presence of a large congregation, by the Reverend G. Bisset; Messrs. Clough and Armour attending as his sponsors.* As the instance was remarkable, and, viewed in all its bearings, was calculated to produce a peculiar influence on the minds of both Europeans and natives, it was deemed desirable that a connected and authentic statement of the whole case should be published, and Mr. Clough was requested by the Governor to draw up such an account; on receiving which, His

* The Rev. G. Bisset very obligingly furnished me with a copy of the entry made at the time, in the Registry of Baptisms of the English church at Colombo. The original is in the hand-writing of the Hon. and Venerable Archdeacon Twisleton.

" BAPTISM, 1814: Dec. 25, *Petrus Panditta Sekara,* a converted priest of Budhu; who was induced to embrace the Christian religion through the mild, clear, and persuasive arguments and exhortations of the Rev. Mr. Clough, a Missionary of the Wesleyan persuasion, who had been residing at Galle; and had taken frequent opportunities of viewing the idolatrous rites and ceremonies in the temple of which the convert was a leading priest.

" This newly-converted Christian had received from Mr. Clough the valuable present of a New Testament in Singhalese, which circumstance, not only caused him to read it throughout, with a mind bent on the search after truth; but induced him at a numerous meeting of priests of Budhu, to take the Testament with him, and lecture them during a whole night from the Gospel of Matthew, which they heard with no less astonishment than attention."

" *A true copy of the Colombo Baptismal Register.*

" *Witness my hand this* 27th *day of May,* 1817.

" G. BISSET,
" Assistant Colombo Chaplain."

Excellency was pleased to prefix a suitable introduction, and ordered the whole to be inserted in the " Ceylon Government Gazette." This interesting document will be inserted in the Appendix; but the following allusion in the Governor's introductory remarks to the event of which the day chosen for the baptismal ceremony is commemmorative, while it proves the general interest excited, and manifests the pleasure it communicated to His Excellency's own mind, deserves a place in the narrative itself.

" From the natural influence of his character and abilities," observes the distinguished writer, " such an example promises to be of signal use in the propagation of Christianity. The causes which led to his adoption of the Christian religion, and the probable consequences of his conversion, were noticed, with much effect, by Mr. Twisleton in his sermon; and they furnished a most appropriate conclusion to a discourse delivered on the anniversary of HIS nativity, who was destined to be *a light to lighten the Gentiles.*"

The conversion of this distinguished heathen, and the circumstances of destitution to which his renunciation of Budhuism would have inevitably reduced him, but for the Governor's interposition in his behalf, brought to our view the difficulties we should encounter, in the cases of those who might, like him, cast away their idols, and so literally forsake *all* for Christ. The Wesleyan Methodist economy makes no provision for native converts, *as such:* indeed, in no country, except India, is such a provision necessary; and even there, to hold out pecuniary support to the natives, as a bounty, on renouncing heathenism, and professing Christianity, would present a temptation to their proverbial cupidity, and furnish ground to suspect that their profession of Christianity resulted, not from a conviction of its truth, but from respect to worldly advantage. The more the subject was discussed, the more we were led to admire the prudence and piety which have led the members of some Christian Missions to supply the native convert with the means of providing himself by industry with *the bread which perisheth;* while they direct and encourage him to seek that *which endureth to everlasting life.* He is thus preserved from want, and protected from danger; not in a state of indolence, but as the price of his own labour. The subsequent establishment of a printing-office at Colombo, connected with our Mission, enabled *us* to furnish employment and protection to a few.

The literary qualifications of Petrus obtained for him the situation of Singhalese translator to the Government, at a fixed salary; and, as his return to Galle would have placed him among those most incensed at his abandonment of their faith, it was deemed advisable that he should remain at Colombo, under the care of Mr. Armour; and that his studies should be directed with a view to his becoming, at a future period, a preacher among his own countrymen, of *the Gospel of the grace of God.* Mr. Clough, in his interesting narrative, observes—" I flatter myself that this man will be capable of doing as much good among the natives, as *fifty European Missionaries.* Many of the priests are so shaken by the conversion of their leader, that they also appear inclined to embrace Christianity. But they are deterred by the certainty, that when they cast off their robes, they lose *all,* even their freehold estates, if they have any.*"

Mr. Erskine, who had entered upon his work at Matura, no sooner received information of our arrival, than he hastened to Galle to bid us welcome: an illness

---

* Petrus was possessed of property to a considerable amount; and forfeited all, by embracing Christianity.

with which Mr. Lynch had been attacked at Jaffnapatam, rendered a visit to the south of the island necessary to his health. The whole of the Missionaries, with the exception of Mr. Ault, were thus unexpectedly brought together; and we improved the opportunity, by conferring on the state of the Mission. My appointment was fixed for Colombo, the capital of the British territories in Ceylon.

A letter from *New South Wales* was read at this meeting. It stated the wish of the writers (friends to the Wesleyan Methodists in that colony,) to open a correspondence with our Mission; and requested, in case any of the Missionaries should become seriously affected by the climate of Ceylon, that they would visit their more salubrious climate; and, while seeking a restoration of health, at the same time afford them an increase of spiritual instruction. Mr. Clough had recently experienced an attack of illness, by which it was feared his constitution was greatly weakened; it was therefore proposed that he should avail himself of this invitation, and visit New South Wales. It has often afforded me satisfaction that I strongly objected to this measure, which was abandoned. He was ultimately appointed to Colombo; where he fully recovered, and rendered the most efficient assistance to the concerns of the Mission.

Intelligence of Mr. Ault's alarming indisposition also reached us at this meeting. A letter to him was immediately forwarded, in which we unitedly recommended him to leave his station, and to reside for some time either at Galle or Jaffna, in the hope that a change of air would facilitate his recovery. The removal of Mr. Erskine from Matura was also considered necessary; and, as the health of Mr. Squance was yet unequal to the labours of Galle, it was determined that Mr. Erskine should join him at that station.

The subject of preaching by the medium of interpreters was submitted to the meeting; and, after much conversation, it was agreed to commence that mode of preaching immediately. The lawn in front of Mr. Clough's house being a most eligible spot for the purpose, a congregation was collected, and Mr. Lynch, the senior Missionary, delivered a sermon; which was interpreted in sentences by a respectable Mohandiram of the Magistrate's Court, named D'Alvis, who had become decidedly pious, and joined our society. Several of our own countrymen attended the service; and while the singularity of the mode excited the curiosity of both Europeans and natives, the attention with which they listened, led us to hope that in some a higher principle would eventually be produced.

Mr. Armour obliged us with a friendly letter of congratulation previously to our departure from Galle, and made us an offer of part of his house at Colombo, until an eligible residence could be procured. Mr. and (Mrs. Chater—also offered us similar accommodation.— But as we were not personally acquainted with either of these friends, I left my fellow-labourers to determine which of their invitations should be embraced. They decided on our residing with Mr. Armour; and that I should supply Mr. Chater's pulpit, agreeably to his wish, during his expected absence from Colombo on domestic affairs. With this arrangement I most cheerfully acquiesced; and preparations were made for our immediate departure.

It being deemed advisable that we should travel over-land to Colombo, our luggage was placed in a dhoney, provided for us by the kindness of Mr. Gibson; and, as a more pleasant mode of conveyance could not be obtained, owing to the Kandyan war, we agreed with some natives to convey us, and a few lighter articles of luggage, in *bandies*, or bullock-carts. The vehicle in which we travelled was furnished with a covering of cocoa-leaves, to shelter us from the rain and sun; and every thing being in readiness, our cavalcade, consisting of five bandies, each drawn by two small oxen, moved forwards; Mr. Lynch, accompanying us, on his return to his station at Jaffna.

Owing to the slow movements of the oxen, and the many stoppages made by the drivers, we did not on the average travel more than two miles an hour. We halted at Gindurah, about two miles from Galle, and took some refreshment; during which, our bandies and luggage were ferried across the river. Mr. Lynch found considerable difficulty in settling with the ferrymen for their services, owing to his not being acquainted with Singhalese, nor they with Tamul or English. We here discovered, that not having engaged a native servant previously to leaving Galle, was an omission which would expose us to much inconvenience and delay throughout the journey. As the singularity of our appearance had brought a considerable crowd together, Mr. L. loudly enquired of the spectators, " Can any one among you speak English?" But the only response produced by his enquiry was a loud laugh from the spectators, who appeared heartily to enjoy our embarrassment. We found, at last, that one of our bullock-drivers could speak a little English; and he became our interpreter with the boat-men.*
Having acquired his small stock of English words from the lowest characters of the British soldiery, we were frequently disgusted with the vulgar and profane terms he employed. Mrs. Harvard having occasion to ask him a question, his reply was unwittingly couched in

---

* The establishment of *Mission Schools* along this line of road has considerably remedied this inconvenience. Scarcely a village can now be found between Galle and Colombo, but furnishes its readers in the English language

language so abhorrent, as wholly to preclude her from further conversation with him.

The night was considerably advanced before we arrived at Hicgodde. A pupil of Mr. Clough, a respectable Singhalese youth, who had returned to his village in order to prepare accommodations for us as we passed through it, met us some distance from the place. He was accompanied by several others, bearing *chules*, which afforded us a cheering light; and his father having sent some arrack for the drivers, they proceeded with more spirit. On reaching the *Rest-house*,* we were received by the father of the youth,† with marks of considerable respect. Olla-leaves were hung about the door in a tasteful manner, and a hot supper prepared, of which we partook with keen appetites, and thankful hearts.

From Hicgodde we proceeded to Amblangodde. The rest-house here, being pre-occupied by the officers of a military detachment, we were supplied with refreshments by a native headman, of which we

* India does not afford to travellers the accommodation of *inns*; but in Ceylon their absence is supplied in some measure by the erection of buildings on the public roads, at suitable distances, called *Rest-houses*. These are, in general, furnished with a few chairs, tables, and bedsteads; and are under the care of some subordinate native head-man; who supplies the requisite articles of food at a moderate charge. It is customary when travelling, to send a native servant a stage in advance, to give the necessary orders, that the accommodations required may be in readiness. The attention of this young man obtained for us this convenience at Hicgodde; but at the subsequent stages of our journey our situation was often very unpleasant.

† This good man, two or three years afterwards, was on our recommendation appointed to the situation of a Government Catechist-master: and his son (the young man above referred to,) having given evidence of his consistent piety, and competency for the work, was by the Wesleyan Methodist Conference of 1819, appointed to travel as a Native Singhalese Missionary. There is ground for hope, that some other members of this family have embraced the truth.

partook in the street; and went forward to Gosgodde, where we slept in an olla bungaloe, built for the accommodation of the inspector of cinnamon on his visits to that district; great quantities of which are cultivated in this neighbourhood. At Bentotte the Moodeliar, who was intimately acquainted with Mr. Clough, had ordered every accommodation to be prepared against our arrival: among the refreshments were oysters of a most delicious flavour, for which this place is much celebrated. We had not the opportunity of thanking the Moodeliar for his attention to our comfort, he being absent from the village on public business.

A short distance from Bentotte we passed the noble river of that name, and arrived at Caltura late on Saturday night. R. Sneyd, Esq. the Collector of the district, had shewn Mr. Lynch much attention when passing through from Jaffna; and had engaged him to spend a Sabbath with him on his return. Mr. Sneyd had retired to rest when we arrived; but his butler quickly prepared tea and coffee, which in our circumstances of fatigue were very refreshing.

Caltura is pleasantly situated at the mouth of a fine river, and is constantly cooled by the sea breezes. It is hence very salubrious, and is a favourite resort for invalids from other stations. The Dutch Governors spent the time they could spare from public business in this delightful town; and a house was erected for their residence, which now bears the name of the King's House, and was the place of our temporary abode. The following morning we paid our respects to Mr. Sneyd; whom we found to be a gentleman possessed of general information, united with great urbanity, and unremitting in his endeavours to promote the welfare of those under his care. We were invited to dine, and experienced the most hospitable and kind reception In the course of the day Mr. Lynch addressed a numerous native congregation from the door of the Government House; when one of the Collector's cutchery interpreters rendered the sentences into Singhalese, as they were delivered.* The interpreter, who was a young man, had received his education under Mr. Armour at the Colombo Seminary, and was not unacquainted with the theory of Christianity. He appeared to feel much pleasure while engaged in interpreting the discourse; and the assembled natives listened with considerable attention.

On the following morning we proceeded on our journey; and, crossing the river shortly after, arrived at Pantura. Here we crossed another river, narrower than the former; and were then within fifteen miles of Colombo. We were anxious to gain our ultimate destination that night; but the distance was considered by our drivers too formidable to be accomplished in so short a time: the oxen were therefore unyoked, and we proceeded to the rest-house for refreshment and repose. Throughout the whole journey, the drivers manifested much greater regard to their own interest than to our convenience; and evidently wished to consume as many days as possible. Their insensibility rendered remonstrances unavailing. They moved slowly along, or halted, just as they pleased. I was frequently com-

---

* The *Cutcherry* is the counting-house, or, more properly speaking, the Treasury, of the district. The Collector has the sole management of the cutcherry; where all the native head-men of the district who hold situations under Government attend daily to make their reports, and to receive their orders. Respectable young men, aspiring to Government offices, obtain admission into the cutcherry, as "volunteers," to be initiated into public business; and by their talents and assiduity to recommend themselves to the notice and patronage of the Collector.

pelled to alight, and enter the arrack shops which are scattered along the road, to induce them to proceed; and when my efforts failed, was obliged to act as driver to the whole cavalcade, till they thought proper to relieve me.

The last stage of our tedious journey was commenced early the following day, when we proceeded at a considerably quicker pace than any which had preceded it. The drivers were probably stimulated by the fear of our representing their former behaviour to the *Peacecalloonaansey*, an officer of considerable authority, one of whom resides in every principal town in Ceylon; and whose displeasure would be severely felt by a *cooleykaree*, or labourer.

About half-way between Pantura and Colombo we halted for breakfast, and agreed with the tenant of a small hut for some boiling water. I retired behind the trees, for the purpose of making those alterations in my dress which our approach to the principal town rendered necessary. We had scarcely finished our slender meal, when we perceived a carriage approaching us from Colombo: it proved to be Mr. Armour, in his family bandy,* who, with kind regard to our convenience and comfort on entering into Colombo, had set off to meet us. We directed the bandy-drivers to follow with our luggage; and Mr. Lynch, Mrs. Harvard, and myself entered the conveyance furnished by our attentive friend. Passing through Galgisse, (leaving Mount Lavinia, the Governor's delightful residence, on our left,) we entered a road made through the celebrated cinnamon groves in the neighbourhood of Colombo. The reports which we had heard in England of these

---

* A light and commodious caravan, generally on springs; and constructed so as to admit a small family to sit within it.

gardens, and the effects which were said to be produced by the powerful effluvia attributed to the trees, led us to expect that we should, at least, experience some inconvenience when surrounded by such numbers as we now beheld. We were therefore a little surprised that no perceptible effect was produced on our olfactory nerves, though we were in the midst of thousands of trees. But the fact is, the scent is only produced by piercing the leaf, or bruising the bark of the tree; and unless this be done, there is nothing by which the scent can distinguish a grove of cinnamon from a plantation of any other trees.

The approach to Colombo by these gardens is exceedingly pleasant: the trees do not rise higher than seven or eight feet; and when there is any breeze, the waving of the branches produces a coolness which is most refreshing. The road is kept in a state of good repair at a considerable expense; and the gardens, uniting beauty with convenience, furnish the respectable inhabitants of Colombo with most agreeable morning and evening rides.

Quitting the cinnamon gardens, we entered Marandahn, a Mahomedan village in the immediate vicinity of the Colombo Pettah.* A mosque of considerable grandeur meets the eye at the entrance of this village: the road through which is shaded by rows of palm and cotton trees; at intervals the eye rests on the stately jack-tree, which rears its magnificent head above every other, as if to assert its indigenous pretensions to the

---

* Supposed to be derived from the Singhalese word, *Peta;* which signifies *the outside.* Ceylonese towns in the immediate neighbourhood of fortified places are usually thus designated; and being principally occupied by the natives, are in other parts of India called *the Black Town.* The Ceylon appellation, certainly, seems the most preferable, because the least invidious.

soil. As we passed along this pleasant grove, Mr. Armour directed our attention to a house in which a Mahomedan prophet had professed to fast *forty days*. To prevent the imputation of imposture, his followers had procured the seal of a magistrate to be affixed to the door, at the commencement of the stipulated period; and at the termination it was broken with great solemnity. As the tiles of the house were merely laid on the roof in the Indian manner, without mortar, or any other cement, it was evident that food might have been conveyed to the inmate with perfect ease, without violating the seal.

A short distance further we passed the residence of the Count Ranzow; a near relative of the consort of our late beloved monarch, George the Third. He has a numerous family of daughters, some of whom are married to respectable young men of the island. He is said to have passed through scenes of varied suffering; but his affinity to the illustrious house of Brunswick cannot fail to procure for him the sympathy of every British heart.

With feelings which it would be difficult to express I entered the Colombo Pettah, the appointed scene of my future missionary labours. A consciousness of inability caused me involuntarily to shrink from the mighty undertaking. But a conviction of duty, and the hope of sufficient aid, united with pity for the deluded votaries of idolatry by whom we were surrounded, kindled an impatience to commence the work which had brought me amongst them.

On arriving at Mr. Armour's residence, which is situated in the Grand Pass,* we were received by Mrs. Armour, a Tutecorene lady, who manifested

---

* The principal road from Colombo to the interior of the island.

much pleasure at our safe arrival. The other members of the family were introduced; and each vied with the rest in expressions of kindness, and in the performance of a thousand little offices, which while they tended to promote our comfort, illustrated the amiableness of their dispositions, and powerfully conciliated our regard.

CHAP. XI.

Interview with Archdeacon Twisleton—Visit from the Chief Justice—Submission of the Kandyan territory to the British Crown—Audience with His Excellency the Governor—Death of Mr. Ault at Batticaloa—His epitaph—Mr. Lynch preaches his funeral sermon before the Governor—Baptist Mission church—Arrival of Mr. Clough—Village preaching—Singhalese interpreter—Weekly meeting of preachers—Dutch church—Malabar Christians—Purchase of estate—Public subscription—Captain Schneider—Sunday School—Levee—Lady Johnstone—Colombo theatre and Orphan House—Mission printing press—Government press—Day school—Ava priest—Head printer—Illness of the Author—Kindness of the Catholic Missionaries—Journey to Galle—Preaches in an idol temple—Visits the Government schools—The Ava priest embraces Christianity, and is baptized.

THE kind offices of Mr. Armour procured for me, the day after our arrival, an introduction to the Hon. and Rev. T. J. Twisleton; of whose valuable services to our Mission I had heard so much from my companions; and for whom, though a stranger to his person, I felt a strong and grateful attachment. The affability with which he received me, and the interest he evidently felt in the important objects of our Mission, impressed my mind with a reverential regard for this most excellent clergyman; who, unshackled by the prejudices which confine so many within the narrow circle of their own sect, rejoiced at the prospect of a wider spread of the gospel of Christ by our means; and cheerfully wished us success in extending the boundaries of the Redeemer's kingdom.

The church newly-erected by the Government for the Tamul Episcopal Christians in Colombo, was generously offered for our religious services; but as Mr. Armour had previously hired a house for that purpose, and had commenced a Portuguese service, the offer was respectfully declined. A suitable residence in the Main Street of the Pettah was also engaged by Mr. Armour, to which the Mission property was immediately removed; but, as the house had been long unoccupied, we continued to reside with Mr. Armour's family until the necessary operations of cleaning and ventilation were completed.

That no time might be lost, and as little expense incurred as possible, Mrs. Harvard and myself daily superintended the people employed. One morning, while thus engaged, we were thrown into some little consternation by a visit from Sir Alexander Johnstone, the Chief Justice, on his way to the Supreme Court at Hulfsdorp. A couple of chairs comprised the whole of our household furniture; and our dress and appearance were by no means suited to such an interview. But the kindness of our visitor at once removed our embarrassment. He expressed the most lively pleasure at our safe arrival after the dangers of the voyage from Bombay to Ceylon; and, after some general remarks, and a pleasant allusion to the employment in which he had surprised us, took his leave; having first given us an invitation to spend that evening with him and his family at his seat at Colpetty.

An event, which furnishes an important era in the history of Ceylon, took place a short time previous to our arrival at Colombo. The king of Kandy by his cruelties had long rendered himself the object of terror to his oppressed subjects. At length one of his prime ministers incurred his displeasure; and, dreading the effects of his wrath, took refuge in the British territories. The enraged and sanguinary monarch, disappointed at losing the object of his meditated revenge, seized the wives and children of the fugitive, and put them to a cruel death. The feelings of nature prompted to revenge: and, as his own arm was too impotent to reach the author of his woes, he applied to the British Government, and offered, if a small military force were granted him, to employ his powerful influence to reduce the Kandyan dominions to the British crown; but as no direct outrage had been committed by the Kandyan monarch on any British subject, the Governor, while he sympathized with the bereaved and justly indignant applicant, did not consider himself authorized to sanction such an attempt. But when, a short time after, the inhuman king, as if infatuated to his own ruin, presumed to seize some British subjects; and cruelly mutilated them, by cutting off their ears, nose, and tongues; the rights of outraged humanity, and the honour of the British crown, alike demanded the interposition of the Government. An expedition was sent against the unnatural monarch, which was accompanied by the ex-minister; whose wrongs impelled him to exert all his influence against his late master; and whose knowledge of the country, and acquaintance with the disaffected chiefs, enabled him to render the most important aid to those entrusted with the command.

The British troops were hailed as deliverers at every stage of their progress; the Kandyan dominions submitted to the British crown; and the tyrant, by whom every tie of humanity and justice had been violated, was delivered a prisoner into the hands of the Governor. Thus was the whole territory gained almost without the loss of a single life; and a way opened for the introduction of the Gospel among those idolators, between whom and the means of salvation a barrier seemed to exist a few months before, which would require the lapse of ages to remove. *The Lord reigneth!* and it is not the least interesting employment of the Christian, to trace the operations of His government, in preparing and hastening forward the period, when *all the kingdoms of this world shall become the kingdoms of God, and of his Christ; and when* HE *shall reign for ever and ever!*

His Excellency Governor Brownrigg, having been absent some time from the seat of government, receiving the submission of the Kandyan chiefs, and making the necessary arrangements for the proper administration of justice in the newly-acquired territory, returned to Colombo a few days after our arrival; when we had the pleasure of witnessing his public entry, attended by a long train of the civil and military authorities and principal inhabitants. The British standard was hoisted at the Government House, and the royal standard of Kandy placed beneath it; to indicate the subjugation of that kingdom to the British crown. The scene was interesting to the politician; but much more so to the Christian Missionary; before whom it presented a new and interesting field for the moral culture of faithful labourers.

Our arrival having been mentioned to His Excellency, he was pleased to honour us with an invitation to spend the evening at the Government House. After the kindest and in many instances minute inquiries respecting our voyage, journey, and present situation, His Excellency, in the presence of a very numerous assemblage, gratified us by the assurance that he considered our Mission an invaluable acquisition to the island—heartily wished us the most extended success—and tendered us his protection and assistance whenever they might be necessary. It is almost superfluous to say, that such liberality and condescension, while they inspired gratitude towards the honourable individual by whom they were expressed, increased, if possible, our attachment to the Government he represented, and our thankfulness that we were placed beneath its sway.

The march of a conquering army may frequently be traced by the graves of the warriors who have fallen in the conflict. We were called to mark our progress by a tomb. Our highly esteemed companion, Mr. Ault, who had for a considerable time laboured under severe disease, at length yielded to its power; and was called to repose from labour in the Paradise of God. No European was with him at the time of his dissolution; but he was attended by a native Malabar, who at his desire read a chapter from the Scriptures; having made a few pious remarks on which, he turned in his bed, and resigned his spirit into the hands of his Redeemer. His remains were followed to the grave by the European inhabitants, and by most of the Dutch descendants and natives of the station. The burial-service was read by his friend, Mr. Sawers; and the native and burgher inhabitants of Batticaloa marked their sense of his worth, and testified their respect for his memory, by the erection of a monument over his grave, which bears the following inscription:

SACRED

TO THE MEMORY OF THE

REVEREND WILLIAM AULT,

Wesleyan Missionary.

This Stone is placed over his Mortal Remains by the Protestant Burghers of Batticaloa; as a Testimony of the Esteem and Regard with which they were impresed by his

EXEMPLARY PIETY, MORAL GOODNESS,

AND THE

RELIGIOUS INSTRUCTION

Which he imparted to them during the short period that he was permitted by PROVIDENCE to remain among them.

Obiit 1st April, 1815.

Lady Brownrigg, when informed of Mr. Ault's decease, wrote a letter of condolence to Mr. Lynch, as the senior Missionary, expressive of her ladyship's deep regret for the loss the Mission had sustained; and accompanied with a hope, that the scene of his labours, thus left destitute, would be filled up as soon as possible. A very pleasing testimony to the character of our deceased brother also appeared in the " Government Gazette," in the article which announced his death.*

The Baptist Mission chapel was offered by Mr. Chater for a funeral service; and it was at first arranged, that the friendly offer should be accepted; but we were unexpectedly favoured with an invitation to occupy the Fort Church on that occasion, accompanied with an intimation that His Excellency the Governor, and family, intended to be present. The succeeding Lord's day evening was fixed on for the service; and the church was ordered to be lighted at Lady Brownrigg's expense. We were honoured with an invitation to dine at the Governor's house on that day: Mr. Clough, who had joined me at Colombo, and Mr. and Mrs. Chater, were also of the party. The funeral sermon, which was delivered by Mr. Lynch, was heard with deep attention; and the brief outline given of Mr. Ault's religious experience and ministerial character evidently excited considerable interest in the crowded assembly. Many were present who had previously entertained groundless prejudices against our doctrines; in several instances these prejudices were removed, and esteem took the place of suspicion. It was even intimated to us, that the church would be readily granted us for *a regular Sunday evening service.* But we did not consider ourselves at liberty to make such an engagement;

* See Appendix.

especially as the Fort is principally inhabited by Europeans, and we were desirous of devoting the evening of the Sabbath to the instruction of the native population.

Mr. Chater's request, that I would supply his pulpit in his absence, was readily complied with. Mr. Clough and myself attended his ministry after his return, and frequently accepted invitations to preach for him. But the *close* principle on which the Baptist Mission church was then formed, prevented our being invited to join them at their sacramental services. It has sometimes happened that we have been requested to preach previously to the administration of the Lord's Supper; and, though considered qualified to expound to them their Lord's will, have been tacitly required to retire while they acted in obedience to it. This innocent inconsistency has provoked our smile, but never occasioned any breach in our friendship; nor would it be introduced into this narrative, but for the opportunity of stating that the more liberal practice of *open* communion has since been adopted by them.

The Government " Seminary" at Colombo, which was conducted by Mr. Armour, contained many Singhalese youths who had acquired a sufficient knowledge of the language to act as interpreters between us and their countrymen; and as native congregations could be readily collected in the government schools, we formed the plan, with Mr. Armour's assistance, and under the sanction of the Hon. and Rev. Principal of Schools, of supplying a few of the country places around Colombo with preaching by interpreters on the Lord's day. Two or three of the government proponents were by authority associated with us; and a meeting was held every Friday, for the purpose of fixing the appointments for the ensuing Sabbath—to enquire into the character of the preachers—to afford them advice—and to receive any communication respecting the proceedings of the preceding Sabbath. These meetings always commenced and concluded with prayer; and were productive of considerable benefit to those who attended them. Thus, under our immediate superintendence, twelve or fifteen of the villages in the vicinity of Colombo were regularly supplied with public religious instruction every Sabbath.

When this plan was explained to the excellent Chief Justice, he expressed his cordial approbation of its tendency; and lent us his powerful influence to carry it into effect. For this purpose he directed that Mr. Philipsz, the principal Singhalese interpreter of the Supreme Court, should accompany me whenever his aid was deemed necessary. Being a most respectable native chief, Mr. P. was a valuable acquisition. His being Interpreter to the Court gave him considerable influence over the natives; and order, respect, and attention invariably prevailed in every congregation in which he officiated. The school at *Cowillawatte* was one of the first places to which Mr. P. accompanied me. A pulpit formed of chunam, or mortar, and having the appearance of solid stone, was prepared for the preacher. The *ability* of the interpreter could not be questioned; but a deep consciousness of the high importance of the subjects he was thus made the medium of communicating to his countrymen, literally overpowered his feelings, and it was with the utmost difficulty he performed the functions of his office. As he evidently suffered much on every repetition of the attempt, his request to be permitted to discontinue his services was complied with; and his place was cheerfully and efficiently supplied by Mr. Dias, the Second Interpreter of the Supreme Court, who came forward for that purpose, and was my " companion in travel" every Sabbath, for several months. Zeal, undisciplined by prudence, impelled us to exertions in these itinerant labours which were too violent to be lasting. In company with my interpreter, I have frequently travelled beneath the beams of an Eastern sun, twelve or fifteen miles in one day—addressed three congregations—and returned in the evening to preach in English in the Pettah. My colleague, Mr. Clough, was no less regardless of himself. The leading of the singing also devolved on us, which was even more laborious than preaching. The abundance of the harvest, and the paucity of labourers, is the only apology to be made for efforts which cannot be wholly justified; and which at length inflicted injuries on my constitution from which probably it will never wholly recover. Mr. Dias was, at length, incapacitated by illness from continuing his very valuable aid; and a young man from the Seminary was engaged in his room.

The acquisition of the English language being regarded by the young chiefs, and the more respectable class of natives generally, as highly desirable, we resolved on commencing a service in English on Tuesday evenings, in the house in the Outer Pettah, with an immediate regard to their advantage; and that every facility might be afforded to their imperfect knowledge of our language, the discourses were invariably formed of familiar expressions. The place was usually crowded, and the attention and seriousness with which every part of the service was regarded, encouraged us to commence a prayer-meeting on Saturday evenings in the same place. At this service Mr. Armour occasionally prayed in Portuguese, and the whole closed with a short, familiar address. This service was also well attended; and of many we had ground to hope, that they had *believed our report;* and that *the arm of the Lord* was *revealed* in their emancipation from the bondage of idolatry.

We had for some time contemplated the establishment of a *Sabbath evening* service; but were withheld by an apprehension that our justly-respected friend, Mr. Chater, would regard it as likely to diminish his congregation. The idea of rivalry was never cherished by us; but we feared lest we should sacrifice our duty at the shrine of false delicacy. We therefore determimed, with Christian candour, to open the matter to Mr. Chater; and that we might be removed as far as possible from the immediate scene of Mr. Chater's labours, we obtained the use of the Dutch church, in which, with a full conviction that the numbers and moral necessities of the inhabitants justified the attempt, a Sabbath evening service was commenced. To no circumstance connected with the Mission can I refer with greater satisfaction than to our conduct in this affair. At this distance of time and place from the scene of the transaction, my deliberate and conscientious decision is, that had we abstained from the attempt, we should have criminally compromised our principles and duty.

The Malabar Christians are supposed to have sprung from the Syrian Christians in the Travancore country; and considerable numbers have settled in Colombo and Jaffna. Christian David, (of whom mention has been already made) being on a visit to Colombo from Jaffna, introduced his brethren resident in Colombo to our notice, and joined with some of the principal members of his denomination in a request to us for a weekly service in our house, until their new church could be completed. We set apart Thursday evenings for this purpose; and preached to them every week, by the medium of an interpreter, until the opening of their own church; when Archdeacon Twisleton engaged to preach to them once a fortnight, and we supplied their pulpit the alternate week.

The congregations which assembled at our old house at last increased so considerably, that accommodation could no longer be afforded; and the purchase of the premises, for the purpose of altering and enlarging them, became necessary. By the agency of Mr. Armour, the purchase was completed, and, after a careful examination of various proposals, and the estimated expense of carrying each into effect, we finally determined to pull down the old erection, and to rear an entirely new chapel, after the model of Brunswick Chapel, Liverpool; the plan of which had been presented to Doctor Coke, by its architect; and which the Doctor had brought from England, from a conviction, that its form and internal arrangement were admirably adapted to a hot climate.

In the preliminary arrangements we were highly indebted to the scientific and active co-operation of Captain Gualterus Schneider, of the Engineer department; by whom the workmen were engaged, the materials procured, and the building superintended, till its completion. To have attempted any remuneration adequate to the value of this gentleman's services, would have been as repugnant to his generous mind, as it was above the reach of our resources; but I had the pleasure to present to Captain S. on the behalf of the Mission, a silver cup, bearing a suitable inscription, as a memorial of his services, and the sense which we entertained of their high value.

The expense of the purchase and building rendered it very desirable to obtain, if possible, some pecuniary assistance from the inhabitants of the settlement towards its liquidation. The novelty of a public subscription in Ceylon appeared, indeed, to forbid too sanguine hopes of the success of such an application. We first made our application to His Excellency the Governor by letter, in which we stated the object of the building, the cost of its erection, and our wish to relieve the Missionary Fund, which must otherwise be burdened with the whole of the expense: and concluded by humbly hoping that our subscription would be favoured with His Excellency's sanction. On the same day we received a reply, couched in the most encouraging language, and enclosing a handsome donation. A similar application was made to the Hon. Chief Justice, who generously favoured us with a donation of the same amount. Archdeacon Twisleton added to his former kindness. Each member of His Majesty's Council, without exception, presented us with a donation. The Reverend G. Bisset also expressed his good will, by aiding the subscription with his name and influence; and these were followed by many of the principal inhabitants both civil and military.

A considerable part of this success must be attributed to the warm interest which Archdeacon Twisleton took in our undertaking. In several instances, he prepared the way for our personal application; and on one occasion took our subscription list with him in his carriage, and returned it with additional subscriptions to a considerable amount. The Reverend J. D. Palm, (minister of the Dutch Reformed Church) introduced us to several of the principal members of his congregation, and thus afforded us material aid. The burgher inhabitants, with the chiefs and inferior orders of the natives, influenced by the example of their superiors, gave liberally towards the promotion of our object; some in their own names, and others in the names of the younger members of their families. As our delighted eyes glanced through the long list of generous contributors, gratitude to them, and to HIM by whom they were influenced, swelled our bosoms.

The benefits which have flowed to the children of the poor in England from the streams of knowledge conducted by the Sunday-school system, and the facilities which such schools afford for the communication of religious instruction, induced us to attempt the establishment of a Sabbath school in Colombo. No institution of the kind had hitherto been introduced into Ceylon; and the publication of the plan was most favourably received, both by the classes of inhabitants it was intended to benefit, and by our benevolent countrymen in high official stations, who were interested in their intellectual and moral improvement. In many instances the subscription towards our building was materially assisted by the anticipations formed from the new school. The day of the opening was announced by a hand-bill printed at the Government Press;* and His Excellency, to mark his approbation, ordered a copy of the bill to be inserted in the " Government Gazette" the following week. A gratuitous admission of our subscription list was also granted, with such additions as it received from time to time, till the building was completed.†

The birth-day of His late Majesty (Geo. III.) the friend and patron of every institution to promote the education of his subjects, fell on Sunday, and was fixed on as most appropriate for the opening of the first Sunday school in Ceylon. An anxious crowd surrounded our house in the morning; some to apply for the admission of their children, and others to witness the opening of the school. Within a short time after the opening, we had enlisted upwards of twenty Singhalese and native-born teachers, and more than

* The author avails himself of this opportunity to correct an error which unintentionally appeared in this hand-bill. It stated our new institution to be the "introduction of the Sunday-school system into *India.*" The Baptist Missionaries, whose praise is in all the churches, had, twelve years before, established a Sunday-school at one of their stations on the Continent of India.

† A copy of this list, &c. is preserved in the Appendix to this Work.

two hundred and fifty children, who sat together, without any distinction of *caste;* including a considerable number of females, whom Mrs. Harvard took under her peculiar care. These were joined by a number of girls belonging to a native school at Colpetty, supported by Lady Johnstone; who every Sabbath caused the most diligent of the scholars to be conveyed to our school in a native cart; which, followed by their brothers on foot, formed a procession highly gratifying.

His Majesty's birth-day was celebrated on Monday, with every demonstration of loyalty. In the preceding week we were honoured with an official invitation to a ball and supper, to be given at the Government House on the occasion; every respectable European receiving a similar mark of attention at the national festivals: but while we acknowledged in suitable terms the respectful regard which the invitation conveyed, we were permitted to decline being present at the festivities; and from the same person who obliged us with the invitation our apology was commended, on the ground of consistency of character. Mr. Clough and myself attended, with many of our countrymen, to pay our personal respects to the representative of our venerable King, and thus to express the loyalty in which we yielded to none. We took our place in a retired part of the room, and were far from expecting any particular mark of attention from the Governor; but on His Excellency's approach to our part of the circle, the condescension with which he noticed us, rendered our taking a more public station necessary. His Excellency made several commendatory remarks respecting our Mission—especially enquired what success had marked the opening of our school the preceding day—and expressed a hope that we should have health and encouragement to prosecute our important work. This distinguished public reception was highly gratifying to our personal feelings; but every personal consideration was forgotten, in the contemplation of its probable effects on the character of the Mission, in the estimation of our countrymen and the natives throughout the island.

The house becoming too small for the increasing number of our scholars, our attention was directed to the theatre, which had been fitted up for a select company of performers from the civil and military departments; but had been for several months totally unoccupied. The premises were at the disposal of the Hon. Robert Boyd, one of the Members of Council, who had particularly sanctioned our Mission; and who, on its being mentioned to him, that the theatre would be suitable for the Sunday-school, gave us immediate possession; with liberty to take down the scenery and decorations, and otherwise to adapt it to our purpose. The dressing-room was appropriated to the female department; the younger boys were placed in the pit; and the stage was occupied with our table of office, surrounded by the boys of the higher classes. We occupied the theatre in this way for many months; until some of the young men of the settlement determined on reviving their former amusements, we were politely requested to provide another place of accommodation. Lady Brownrigg then kindly interfered in behalf of the school, and the Dutch Orphan House in the Pettah was obtained for our use.

The Dutch church, which was fully at our service, we were obliged to vacate from the effect of a powerful echo, and the heavy expense of lighting up so large a building: and the house in which our public religious meetings had been subsequently held being about to be pulled down, to make way for the new erection; we removed to a building belonging to the late A. Cadell, Esq. Paymaster-general, and formerly used as a workshop, which he allowed us to fit up for the reception of our congregations. Though the appearance of the place was by no means attractive, some of the most respectable inhabitants attended, and good was evidently done. A class was formed, and met weekly at our house in Main Street; the members of which frequently expressed their respective feelings in their "own tongues." Dutch, Portuguese, Singhalese, and English, were often spoken at these meetings, Mr. Armour acting as our interpreter. Some of these first members of our little society at Colombo are now employed as schoolmasters, class-leaders, and local-preachers, in connection with our Mission.

Our printing-press and types, with the rest of the heavy baggage, having arrived from Galle, I applied myself immediately to the work of fixing and arranging them for use. We first printed the spelling-book of the Sunday-school Union, in three parts, for the use of our Sunday-school; and several thousand copies of that useful work have been distributed through the island. An abridgement of the Wesleyan large Hymn-Book was next provided for the use of our English congregations: this was followed by editions of Bishop Hopkins's Exposition of the Ten Commandments, and Fletcher's Address to Earnest Seekers of Salvation; well calculated to impress the mind with the requisitions of the law, and the provision of the gospel. The Governor's lady ordered several copies of the latter pamphlet for private distribution. The typographical execution of these works was greatly superior to any printing previously produced on the island; we received in consequence many applications to print for the inhabitants, and complied in every case consistent with the character of a "Missionary Press." The Third Report of the Colombo Auxiliary Bible Society, with the Anniversary Sermon preached on the occasion, was executed at our press, and gave such satisfaction to the committee, that favourable mention was made of it in the Report of the succeeding year. At the desire of the Hon. Chief Justice, we also reprinted Doctor Baldæus's Account of the Religious State of the Province of Jaffnapatam;* towards the expenses of which he generously presented us with 100 rix-dollars.

The printing-office established by the Dutch Government, which was taken possession of by the British on the surrender of the island, had continued in nearly the same state of disorder in which it was then found. Overtures to purchase our press for the use of Government were made to us; but our responsibility to the Missionary Committee, whose property it was, blended with our conviction of the vast utility of such an agent, when properly directed, for the dissemination of religious knowledge, obliged us to decline the offer. I was then requested to undertake the superintendance of the Government press, at a fixed salary. This being incompatible with my character as a Missionary, was also declined; but I readily offered to attempt a renovation of the office; which was, in consequence, placed under my control, and the workmen received positive orders to follow my directions. I devoted an early hour every morning to this task; and, as walking to and from the Fort would have incapacitated me for the subsequent duties of the day, I hired a triacle,† not having at that time any conveyance of our own.

For several mornings, each successive visit discovered only the arduous task I had undertaken. Whole founts

---

* A further notice of these publications will be inserted in the Appendix.

† A machine resembling a chaise, with a third wheel in front, (from which its name is derived,) and which acts as a rudder, to direct its course. A cooly walks in front, to steer the vehicle; and another behind, to push it forward.

of type were rendered unserviceable, by large masses of broken matter cast among them; and the materials which were in use were so intermixed, as to render correctness, (to say nothing of neatness) utterly impossible. This state of things was caused by the habitual intoxication, and consequent neglect, of the head printer; by whom great expense had been incurred, but who had criminally neglected the duties of his department. By the persevering application of two workmen, who were desirous of carrying my directions into effect, and who were always in attendance upon me at my morning visits, a gradual improvement was produced; materials which had not been brought into use for years were made serviceable; habits of cleanliness and order were formed among the workmen; at my recommendation, the head printer was discharged with a pension, and one of my assistants appointed to his situation. The Government printing-office was thus rendered efficient and respectable. As a pecuniary recompense was declined, the thanks of the Government were conveyed to me in a letter from His Excellency's private secretary; and I had an ample reward, in being able to evince a willingness to render any service in our power to those whose condescension and patronage had laid us under such lasting obligations.

A new line of employment, which promised considerable usefulness, as well as pecuniary profit, by which the expense of the mission would have been lessened, was presented in an application made to us by a military officer proceeding to a distant province, to undertake the charge and education of his children during his absence. After some deliberation, we acceded to his request. A gentleman connected with the civil department, who accompanied him, also requested permission to send his children for daily instruction. These were followed by many similar applications; and Mr. Clough and myself contemplated the establishment of a boarding and day school in connection with, and in aid of, the expenses of the Mission; in which, from there being no such school in the island, we should have met with considerable success. We each attended the school on alternate days; and wrote to England for the opinion of the Missionary Committee, as to the propriety of our undertaking. But their decision was unfavourable to the prosecution of our plan. A laudable fear, lest we should be too much involved in *secular* concerns, produced an immediate communication, directing us to abandon the undertaking, so far as the boarding department was concerned.*

Our dwelling-house being situated on the main road from the country into the Fort, gave us frequent opportunities of conversing with the natives on their way to and from the town. The result of these interviews was often encouraging; and in one instance were productive of consequences which cannot be remembered without genuine pleasure. A Budhuist priest (known by the title of the AVA PRIEST) was introduced to us, by a note from the Rev. G. Bisset. He possessed much acuteness of intellect, enriched by scientific and literary research; was highly respected by his disciples; and had attained to the honourable distinction of *Maha Nāiaka*. His equipage was more splendid, and his whole appearance displayed a greater degree of style, than we had before observed in any native. The motive by which he was *first* influenced in desiring our acquaintance, can only be known to the " Searcher of hearts :" but he hesitated not to declare himself an Atheist in

---

* The day-school, I believe, continues in connection with the Colombo station; and, in addition to the children of several European families, its list of pupils has comprised some of the children of the most respectable native chiefs.

principle; and asserted his ability to disprove the existence of God. Perhaps the *enmity of the carnal mind* against the being and perfections of the Creator of heaven and earth, was never more awfully displayed than in the impious expressions and spirit of this man. As we were thus challenged by him, to support by argument the doctrine of the very *existence* of the glorious Being we professed to serve, Mr. Clough and myself agreed to hold ourselves disengaged at any time he might desire an interview. For several weeks he daily held a controversy with one or both of us; and earnestly did we supplicate the Source of wisdom to confer on us ability to confute his specious reasonings. Several of his arguments were new to us; but we were enabled to meet them, at the moment they were advanced, with counter-arguments, which not only satisfied our own minds, but which evidently shook his confidence.

In the intervals of these conversations, he occasionally sought to Archdeacon Twisleton and Mr. Bisset on the same subject; and we beheld with the deepest interest the strong holds of error, in which he had apparently entrenched himself, with the full persuasion that they were impregnable, yielding to the superior force of truth; while the victim of delusion, astounded at his past impiety, and awakened to a sense of his real danger, solicited our prayers, that God would assist him in his search for true wisdom. In order to bring his sincerity to the test, he was asked, whether he would consent to my preaching in the temple of which he was the chief priest? He expressed his entire willingness that I should do so the first opportunity; and, but for the distance at which it was situated, his offer would have been immediately accepted. His pride was now renounced, and he became a humble enquirer—a disciple, receiving with meekness instructions in the first principles of the doctrine of Christ, with a view to his admission into the church by Christian baptism, of which he was desirous.

The multifarious duties immediately connected with my work as a Missionary, and which daily demanded my time and strength, rendering me unable to manage alone the mechanical department of the Mission Press, our attention was directed to Emanuel Jantz, one of the workmen in the government printing-office, who had recently attended the public services at our chapel with great seriousness; and of whose abilities I had some knowledge, from his having assisted me in the reformation of the government office. On its being represented to the Governor, that we were in want of an assistant in our printing department, His Excellency gave directions that we should be at liberty to select any one we pleased (with the exception of the newly-appointed superintendant) from the Government workmen; and on proposing the matter to Mr. Jantz, an engagement was formed, and he was officially dismissed from the employment of Government to us.*

In November, 1815, an addition was made to our family, by the birth of a second son. Mrs. Harvard was attended by J. Scratchley, Esq. of the Royal Artillery; to whose professional skill and constant attentions she was, under a kind Providence, indebted for her recovery after a long confinement; and placed us under renewed obligations, by his attentions in our subsequent afflictions. The infant was baptized in January following, in the Fort church, by the Reverend G. Bisset. Archdeacon

---

* During my residence at Ceylon, Mr. Jantz justified the choice we had made, by a faithful attention to the duties assigned him. Had he continued in the service of Government, he would, when no longer able to fill his situation, have received an allowance for the remainder of his life. A sense of justice induces me to express the hope, that should he continue in our service, he will not, under similar circumstances, be left without adequate support.

Twisleton and his lady, with Mr. Clough, my valuable colleague, appearing as sponsors for the child; who was named *John Twisleton,* to perpetuate the recollection of their kindness. We passed the remainder of the interesting day at their residence: and I cannot but remember with gratitude, that at the birth of the child, Mrs. Harvard was attended by the Hon. Mrs. Twisleton with all the affectionate solicitude of a tender mother.

During a fever, by which I was attacked soon after, and under the debilitating influence of which I remained a considerable period, the attentions of my friends were unceasing. Among the many enquirers after me, two *Roman Catholic* Missionaries will not easily be forgotten. With the kindest solicitude they visited me; and, seated by my bed-side, sympathized with me in my affliction, and earnestly prayed for my recovery. While I continued at Colombo, we regularly interchanged friendly visits.*

My reduced frame requiring a cessation from labour, and a change of air, Mr. Squance undertook the superintendance of the press; and Mr. Erskine having urged me to visit Galle, I determined to comply with his friendly invitation. Mr. Clough's health also demanded a relaxation from active duties; and we agreed to travel together. Accompanied by Mrs. H. and family, we proceeded on our journey. Gratitude to God and to my respected brethren, for the indulgence of a temporary absence from the arduous duties of my station, filled my heart while we were on the road. We arrived at Galle in safety; and were received by Mr. Erskine with his characteristic warmth of feeling.

Unmixed pleasure is not the portion of man in this world. A week after our arrival at Galle, death entered our family, and removed from our embraces our lovely

* Appendix.

infant, John Twisleton. We buried him in the Dutch church, " in sure and certain hope of his resurrection to eternal life ;" and " sorrowed not as those without hope." *Rajagooroo,* the Ava Priest, on hearing of our bereavement, addressed a letter of condolence to me, in which he who so lately denied even the being of God, sought to encourage me with considerations deduced from the doctrine of *Divine Providence.* This fresh proof of his sincerity induced me to propose a visit to his temple, which is situated at *Dadalla,* in the vicinity of Galle. He was, however, on a journey at that time; but apprising him by letter of my desire, he gave directions to the priest next in rank to himself to receive us with respectful attention ; and, with his full concurrence, I preached by an interpreter at the door of the temple, *in front of the great image,* to a large congregation of priests and people, from 1 Cor. viii. 4, *We know that an* IDOL *is nothing in the world; and that there is none other God but* ONE !

During this interval from more severe labour, I applied myself to the attainment of a more perfect knowledge of the country Portuguese dialect ; and delivered my first sermon in that language. At the express desire of the Hon. and Rev. Principal of Schools, Mr. Clough and myself visited the government schools in the Galle and Matura districts. While on these journies we preached to large and attentive audiences, and baptized and married considerable numbers. On our return to Colombo, the Ava Priest publicly renounced idolatry ; and was baptized into the faith of Christ, by the name of GEORGE NADORIS DE SILVA ; and I had the pleasure to unite with the Rev. G. Bisset as one of the sponsors, at his baptism in the Fort church.

CHAP. XII.

Attendance of native females on Christian worship—Opening of the Malabar church—Missionary estate at Colombo—Printing of the Singhalese Scriptures—Arrival of Wesleyan and Church Missionaries—Village labours—Milagria and Galkeece—Favourable circumstances—The late Bishop of Calcutta—Pagan enquirers—An aged Naiaka—Kandyan headman—Adikar—Kandyan priest baptized—Affecting case of a converted priest—Preaching in the garrison—Arrival of Baptist and American Missionaries—Mr. Warren—Missionary union—Conference—Singular visitor—Shrewd remark of an idiot—Assistant Missionary—Madras Mission—Missionary estate at Galle—Preaching to Budhuist priests—Baptism of one—Matura station—Missionary estate at Colpetty—Native school —Opening of Colombo Mission-House—Services—Mr. Clough's translation of the Liturgy—Contributions—Death of Mr. Tolfrey— Type Foundry—Unsuccessful attempt to commence a Kandyan Mission—Providential interposition.

THE beneficial influence of the Gospel on the domestic concerns of human life, is generally admitted. We longed to witness its salutary operations among the native females who professed Christianity in Ceylon; to whose knowledge of its doctrines and experience of its blessings a barrier existed, in the prejudice which prevailed against their attendance at places of Christian worship, except at the administration of baptism, and the celebration of marriage. Mr. Armour had succeeded among a small colony of washermen, which he had taken under his instruction, in shaking this prejudice; and Mr. Clough and myself were induced to employ every prudent effort to effect an entire abolition of this injurious prejudice. For this purpose we conversed with our male hearers; urged them to bring their wives and daughters to the house of God; strengthening our appeals by scriptural precepts and examples; to which, as bearing the Christian name, they were supposed to submit in every thing pertaining to Christian worship. Mrs. Harvard generally accompanied me to the country places, that her presence at public worship might also operate as an encourgement to the native females to adopt a similar conduct. The presence of an European female on these occasions produced a considerable sensation, especially among the native women; who, stimulated by curiosity, were at first seen, during the service, cautiously approaching, and secreting themselves among the trees, that they might, unperceived, gain a look at the novel visitor. Whether convinced by our arguments, or overcome by the importunities of their wives, it is of no moment to ascertain; but at subsequent visits we had the pleasure to find several present at the preaching; who appeared much gratified by the notice taken of them by the female missionary. The numbers gradually increased; and the attendance of the women at public worship ceased to be considered a strange thing.

The change thus effected in the views and conduct of the natives in this important particular, was fully appreciated in its probable effects on the general interests of religion throughout the island; and the Rev. Doctor Twisleton in his sermon, preached at the opening of the Malabar church in July, 1815, adverted to the circumstance, with a warmth of pleasurable feeling, which evinced the interest he took in the improvement of the native character; while the liberality of his heart led him to refer, in terms of strong commendation, to those by whose instrumentality the change had been effected.

The workmen employed in the erection of our new place of worship, and other buildings, being paid by the day, were sufficiently alive to their own interest; and evidenced, by their tardy operations, a disposition to prolong the work as much as possible. We therefore removed into the dwelling-house, though unfurnished, that our presence might excite them to greater diligence. The house is situated on the east side of the chapel; on the west are rooms for the day-school, the book-binders' office, &c.; and on the north are two ranges of commodious buildings, fitted up for the Mission printing-office. We now availed ourselves of an offer made us some time previously by His Excellency the Governor, to employ any of the materials of the Government printing-office not required for the public use; and obtained a press which was lying in an unserviceable state; which, when repaired, we found of considerable use.

The Colombo Bible Society, having received Singhalese types, and two presses, was engaged in the laudable work of supplying the Ceylonese with a new version of the Scriptures in their own language. The mental derangement of the head-printer had subjected the work to considerable delay; while the Society's funds were burdened with a regular expenditure for wages and other charges. An application was made to us by the Committee to complete the work; and the terms on which we expressed our willingness to undertake it meeting with their unanimous approval, the materials were removed to the Wesleyan Mission Printing-office, which we felt to be greatly honoured by so early becoming an instrument to promote the glorious objects of the British and Foreign Bible Society. The Annual Reports of the Colombo Society contain the most gratifying allusions to the improved style of execution, and to the reduction in the expense.

Our engagements thus daily increasing, we looked with considerable anxiety towards England, for an addition to our numbers. From some accident, we had not received any official letters from our Society at home, since our departure at the close of 1813; and the consequent absence of all information concerning what measures the Conference had adopted respecting Ceylon, and what (if any) aid we might expect, frequently produced a depression of spirits. But information of the arrival of the Rev. John M'Kenny at Batticaloe, which reached us about June, 1815, afforded us heartfelt satisfaction. He had been directed by the previous Conference to leave his station at the Cape of Good Hope for Ceylon; and was the bearer of letters, containing the cheering intelligence, that four more Missionaries, appointed by the same Conference to Ceylon, might be shortly expected. The Rev. Messrs. Shroeter, Greenwood and Norton, three Missionaries of the Church Missionary Society, arrived at Ceylon, the appointed scene of their future labours, about the same time. The two last were the first *English* clergymen who had embarked as Missionaries to the Eastern world. They were all truly pious men, and well qualified for their work. Their destination was subsequently changed for Continental India; and Messrs. Shroeter and Greenwood soon left the island; but Mr. Norton and his family remained with us nearly three months; during this time our pulpit was at his service; and he frequently preached for us, I hope not without benefit to his hearers.*

Notwithstanding the acccumulation of labour by which almost every succeeding week was distinguished,

---

* Mr. Norton's station was fixed among the Syrian Christians in the South of India, where some encouraging openings presented themselves; his excellent wife died at Allepie. Mr. Shroeter died in the North of India. Mr. Greenwood is, I hope, still living in the neighhood of Calcutta.

Mr. Clough and myself continued our attentions to the native Singhalese, both in town and country; and were much encouraged by the cleanly appearance and orderly deportment of the people in several of the villages which we regularly visited, as well as by the attentive crowds of males and females which assembled to listen to our instructions. The village of *Milagria* furnished a pleasing instance of the change effected on the external appearance and manners by the introduction of the gospel, and an attendance on its ordinances. Though situated near to Colombo, in the vicinity of the cinnamon gardens, it had been for many years without any place of worship. The ruins of the old church were hidden by jungle; and as the cinnamon shrub had taken root in the church-yard, it fell under the jurisdiction of the cinnamon department.

It was with the immediate sanction of the Chief Justice that we first visited this village, and were attended by the principal interpreter of his court. With the consent of a native land-owner, a school-house, built with timber, and roofed with the leaves of the cocoa-nut tree, was erected. The expense of this building we defrayed ourselves; intending, if the effects of our visits were satisfactory, to apply to the Government to erect a church of more durable materials. For many months divine service was performed in this school-house by ourselves and the government preachers, in rotation; and the consequence was, a reverence for the holy Sabbath, and an evident reformation of manners in many of the most vicious inhabitants. Of some it was hoped, that they were not merely reformed in morals, but *renewed in heart*. A weekly meeting for improvement in sacred vocal harmony was instituted by the Mohandiram, among a few of the more serious; and a subscription towards the expense of erecting a new church was entered into by the inhabitants. We laid before the

Government a petition from them, soliciting assistance in their design; but from the rigid adherence to a system of economy, did not succeed in the application.* At *Galkeece*, another village in the same direction, and in circumstances of similar destitution with respect to religious instruction, the Governor, on our application, erected a church at his own private charge, in consequence of his country residence being situated in its vicinity. The sacred edifice stands a monument to the enlightened benevolence of the truly Christian Governor.

Our endeavours to benefit the native Christians were sanctioned by the approbation of the highest personages in church and state resident on the island.† His Excellency the Governor, and the Honourable Chief Justice continued to manifest their approbation of our village labours, and their satisfaction at the success by which they were attended. The Rev. Doctor Twisleton kindly assisted us in the work, by affording us the use of his carriage to convey us to the more distant places, and by accompanying us occasionally on these interesting excursions, introducing us to the Government Schools, and sanctioning our services by his presence. On one of these preaching and truly Missionary journies we were met

* *Milagria*, in Portuguese, signifies *miracle;* and was probably applied to this village while possessed by the Portuguese, with reference to some remarkable circumstance connected with its history at that time. The Appendix will contain some interesting particulars respecting Mr. Clough's visits to this and some other of the villages; and, would the limits of the work admit, the account might be lengthened by extracts from my own memorandums of similar visits. The Monthly Mission Papers of the Society contain, from time to time, much information of this description.

† The late excellent Bishop of Calcutta honoured us with a visit; and with pious fervour pronounced a benediction upon us and our labours. His recent removal by death from the sphere in which he was accomplishing extensive benefits among the Natives and Europeans, has called forth deep regrets from all who knew his character.

by the Governor and his suite, with Lady Brownrigg, who attended our service in a native olla church, while by the medium of an interpreter we proclaimed to the attentive crowd, *Whatsoever things were written aforetime, were written for our learning.* The Chief Justice accompanied us on another occasion to the church of a neighbouring village, and introduced us to the inhabitants, as persons who were sent *to tell them words whereby they might be saved.* For such important facilities and countenance, rendered to us by persons whose high official stations invested their approbation with the character of *authority,* and whose dignified condescension imparted a lustre to their rank, we were unable to make any suitable return; but we experienced much pleasure in forwarding to each of our kind and honourable friends an official acknowledgment from our Missionary Committee in London, of the deep sense entertained of their important assistance; and requesting their acceptance of copies of the works of the venerable Founder of Methodism, handsomely bound.*

Our labours among the nominal Christians frequently led to intercourse with professed pagans; many of them attended our public services; while others visited us at our dwelling, for the purpose of more private conversation. Among the latter were several of the Budhuist priesthood. An aged *Nāiaka,* came with great pomp and attended with a train of followers, bringing with him a nephew, whom he desired should be made a Christian. In answer to our enquiry, why he did not *himself* embrace the religion in which he wished to have his nephew instructed; he replied, that he felt he was too old to encounter the difficulties of so important a change; and on our bringing him into an argument, he attempted to defend his paganism, and departed as

* See Appendix.

confirmed an Atheist as he came. The lad remained with us, and was subsequently baptized. We employed him in the Mission printing-office, where he was taught to earn an honest and sufficient maintenance. His conduct was very orderly, and it is hoped he will become pious and useful.

During a visit to the Governor by *Eheylapola*, the Adikar whose family were so cruelly murdered by the Kandyan king, one of the attendants of the Adikar, led by curiosity, entered our premises, and appeared greatly interested while the process of printing was explained to him. He was particularly gratified on seeing his own name printed in the native character. We explained to him, that ourselves, our presses, and all our premises, were solely devoted to the spread of the knowledge of our Saviour; on which he loudly exclaimed, " *Bohomo onda!*"—a term expressive of high admiration. We presented him with a part of the Singhalese New Testament; and he departed much gratified, exclaiming, " *Bohomo onda!*" as he quitted the premises.

A short time before this visit a young Kandyan priest, named *Poonchy Ralee*, or *Little Gentleman*, had attached himself to us; and, at his earnest request, was received as a servant into our family. On hearing of his residence with us, the Adikar, who had known him in his own country, sent for him, to make some enquiries relative to himself and his new masters. On his introduction, the Adikar asked, " Well! how do you like your new situation? How do you like to live with these people *who talk about God Almighty?*" Poonchy Ralee, who understood the meaning of this piece of atheistical raillery, respectfully replied, that as yet he was but a learner—that he did not know much of the new religion; but that from what he had learned of it, he preferred it to his old system. The Adikar bid him behave himself well; and told him to follow the new religion, if he thought it the best. This engaging and affectionate youth was afterwards baptized by the name of Joseph; and accompanied Mr. Callaway to his station at Matura, where after a few months he died, affording a pleasing hope that his end was peace.

The Ava Priest, (of whose conversion an account has been already given,) manifested a strong desire for the conversion of his idolatrous countrymen. He introduced to our notice a priest of his acquaintance, possessed of considerable property; of strong natural powers, which he had improved by travel into China, and other countries; and whose acquaintance with foreign languages was familiar and extensive. His disposition was meek, and his manners prepossessing. He professed himself dissatisfied with the Pagan superstition of which he was a priest; offered himself for baptism into the Christian faith; and begged us to instruct him in the *principles of the doctrine of Christ.* The knowledge we had acquired of the deceptive character of the natives, made us habitually cautious in the admission of candidates for baptism. In this instance our examination of the motives which induced the application was more than usually severe; and his replies to our questions were given with the greatest apparent sincerity, and afforded us considerable satisfaction.

On our stating to him, that it would be out of our power to afford him any pecuniary aid, George Nadoris united with him in assuring us, that he neither desired nor needed any; as he was possessed of money to a considerable amount. We received him as a probationer, and placed him under instruction. After waiting till his probation had nearly expired, his desire for baptism became so strong, that he was unable to bear any further delay. Procuring for himself a suit of clothes, he cast away for ever the yellow robes of his atheistical priesthood; and one Sunday morning, as we were about to attend the early service, he presented himself at our door, and saluted us with a most urgent request for immediate baptism. Dressed in a blue silk coat, we scarcely knew him at the first. On enquiring what had caused him thus suddenly to change his apparel; he informed us, that he was so weary of appearing in the dress of an heathen, and so desirous of being acknowledged as a disciple of the Lord Jesus Christ, that he could restrain his feelings no longer; and hoped that, as he had in his heart cast away his former abominations, we would no longer withhold from him that ordinance, which our Lord had appointed for the admission of those into his church, who have sincerely embraced his faith and service. Under such circumstances, *who could forbid water* that he should be baptized? We complied with his request; and publicly received him the same day before the evening congregation. He was baptized by the name of *Benjamin Parks:* the first name was chosen out of respect to Mr. Clough; and the second from the same feeling towards Mrs. Harvard's father.

Hitherto our efforts on the Colombo station had been confined to the Pettah, and the country places. Our congregations in general consisted of natives, country-born people, a few Dutch inhabitants, and some of the more respectable English residents; with a few soldiers occasionally, whose regularity of conduct obtained for them permission to leave the garrison, to attend our evening service. There were, however, several hundreds of English soldiers in the Fort, to whom, from their dissipated habits, such an indulgence could not be granted; and to these we were desirous of extending our efforts for their edification and salvation. An application to this effect was made to the Governor by the Rev. G. Bisset, and permission was most readily granted us to visit the military hospital, and to preach in the Fort, whenever we thought proper. As the garrison chaplain was exemplary and zealous in the discharge of his official duties, and the Rev. Mr. Chater had a regular service in the Fort for the military, and other inhabitants who were disposed to attend; we fixed an hour which was not occupied by any other religious service, nor assigned to military duty. All appearance of sectarian opposition was thus avoided; and the soldiers had no temptation to neglect their duty, under pretence of attending the services of religion. We have reason to believe that our labours were not in vain. Some profligates were brought to God; and a Sabbath-school was opened in the Fort, which was conducted by a few of our garrison congregation.

The cause of Missions in Ceylon received early in 1816, a valuable accession of numbers, by the arrival of the Rev. Messrs. Richards, Meigs, Bardwell, Warren, and Poor, who (with the exception of Mr. Warren) were married; and, with their valuable wives, (all eminently qualified for the important station they were called to fill,) presented a pleasing scene to those who had contemplated the vastness of the field, and the paucity of labourers. This little band had been sent forth by the Congregational Missionary Society of America. They continued in Colombo for some time: Mr. and Mrs. Bardwell at length took their departure for Bombay; and their associates removed to the Province of Jaffnapatam; where they obtained from the Government the temporary grant of some church premises, which had long lain in ruins; and exerted themselves with persevering industry to promote the salvation of the natives.*

* Mr. Warren was soon compelled by ill health to leave his station; and embarked for the Cape of Good Hope, as the most probable means of recovery. An unerring Providence removed him from

The Rev. Messrs. Callaway, Carver, Broadbent, and Jackson, (of whose appointment to Ceylon by the British Conference, we had been informed by Mr. M'Kenny) had by this time arrived. As our Island Conference was near at hand, it was judged most expedient to defer the question of what stations they should occupy, until a general meeting should afford us the benefit of each other's opinion and advice. In the mean time Messrs. Carver and Jackson continued with the brethren at Galle, and Messrs. Callaway and Broadbent joined us at Colombo, where our multifarious duties rendered their aid most acceptable.*

Mr. Callaway being acquainted with the process of printing, rendered him a most valuable auxiliary in that important department of the Mission : and the hand of Providence appeared eminently conspicuous in the *time* of his arrival; as Mr. Squance had suffered

---

labour and pain on earth, to rest and peace in heaven. He died at Cape Town in the triumph of faith. The piety of his conversation, and the tranquillity with which he resigned his spirit into the hands of his Redeemer, were rendered the means of converting his attendant. His remains were interred in the burial-ground of that settlement. Mr. Warren's family is connected with the Wesleyan Methodists in America: but his truly Catholic spirit embraced the followers of the Saviour by whatever name they are designated among men.—I am concerned to learn that our friend Mr. Richards has also recently departed this life.

* The Rev. Thomas Griffith and his wife arrived by the same vessel, as an increase of help to the Baptist Mission. They were warmly introduced to our friendship by our brethren; and we had the happiness to enjoy much intimacy and union of affection with them. The talents of Mr. Griffith for acquiring languges, were not of the common stamp; and he soon gained a surprising familiarity with the Singhalese. But after repeated attacks of the epidemic cholera, he was under the painful necessity of leaving the little flock he had gathered at Point-de-Galle, and of returning to his native land. The voyage and change of climate has had a happy effect on the constitution of our valuable friend. I trust he will be long spared to labour in his own country for the cause in which his soul delights to be employed.

severely from having superintended the printing-office during my absence in the early part of the year; and in a few days after Mr. C.'s arrival at Colombo, a most severe illness compelled me to relinquish all exertions. My medical attendant feared that my constitution had received a shock which would be fatal to my hopes of active usefulness in the cause of Missions; his unintermitted attentions were, however, rendered effective by the divine blessing; and by the latter end of the year I was able to preach occasionally, though I have never been restored to my former vigour.

In the month of July the brethren arrived in Colombo from their various stations to attend the Conference; the business of which was transacted with great harmony and affection; and the daily preaching at five o'clock in the morning and seven in the evening, which was something very new to the inhabitants, excited considerable attention, and was rendered beneficial to many. Mr. Callaway was appointed to re-commence the *Matura* Mission; Mr. M'Kenny to reside at *Galle;* Messrs. Broadbent and Jackson to open Missions at *Trincomalee* and *Batticaloa;* and Mr. Carver to accompany the brethren to *Jaffnapatam.* An address from the Conference was presented to His Excellency the Governor, on the general state of the Mission, which was honoured with an encouraging and gratifying reply; and the brethren about to proceed to new stations were kindly promised by the Governor the same favour of introduction and official patronage which had been so kindly afforded to the first party.

During the sittings which the brethren held for the arrangement of our Missionary affairs, they were one day suddenly surprised by the appearance of an old Budhuist priest, who had found his way up-stairs, and who, taking his seat among them without any ceremony, explained the object of his visit, which was to request their application to the British Government, that he might be made the chief over all his sacerdotal brethren in the whole island. His application appeared to them as singular as his appearance; and they informed him they would much rather assist him to obtain an entrance into the Christian church, than to gain any kind of distinction in the pagan priesthood. He listened with much attention to what was said about our Lord, and his blessed gospel; but replied, that at his advanced age he could not think of leaving his old religion, unless we could secure him the same marks of worldly distinction which his present rank in the priesthood gave him among his countrymen. He frequently visited us after the Conference had broken up; and we sometimes entertained faint hopes of him: but he was too worldly and *material* in his views to embrace the spiritual religion of Christ.*

The Conference of that year was rendered remarkable by the admission of Mr. W. A. Lalmon to the Missionary itinerancy under our superintendance. This young man was the first preacher who was raised up to our assistance among the inhabitants of the country. His first religious impressions were received under Mr. Clough's ministry at Galle; and from the beginning he remained a steady and constant member of our society there. He was descended on his father's side from a Swiss family; but his mother and himself were natives of the island. His acquaintance with several languages rendered him a valuable acquisition as an interpreter; and his ministerial talents as a local preacher having been approved, he was received on

---

* An idiot, who accompanied Capt. Schneider as his servant, one day, when the priest was with us, uttered a very shrewd prophecy of the issue of our attempts for his conversion. Looking archly at him, he said, " *You* will not become a Christian : you are too fond of having *samball* with your *curry*."—*Samball* is a choice sauce, sometimes eaten by the natives; and the idea thrown out by the idiot was, that the priest was too much enslaved by *self-indulgence*, to encounter the difficulties and trials of a Christian profession.

trial as an Assistant Missionary, and appointed to the Matura station with Mr. Callaway. On being proposed as a candidate, he was examined before the Conference, respecting his religious experience and doctrinal views; he was then affectionately addressed by some of the brethren, and solemnly commended to the Divine teaching and protection. It is with pleasure I add, that Mr. Lalmon has since completed his probationary period of four years, with much credit to himself and satisfaction to the Missionaries; under whose superintendence he still continues to be employed.

Our brethren at Jaffna had the preceding year received a most earnest application from a small society of Christians at *Madras*, who had united on Wesleyan principles, and were desirous that a Wesleyan Missionary should be sent to reside among them. Mr. Lynch, the chairman of our district, communicated to our Missionary Committee in London their application, and other circumstances which appeared to promise a favourable opening to a Mission at that Presidency. In consequence, Madras was added to our Eastern Mission; and the Honourable Court of Directors having, on the application of our Committee, licensed me to exercise the functions of a Missionary in any part of their territory, instructions to proceed to that station were forwarded to me from England.

My heart was united to Ceylon by numerous ties. For those who were the fruit of my ministry among the inhabitants, I felt the affection of a parent; and to my fellow-labourers in the work, the attachment of a brother. Nor could I contemplate a separation from the interesting circle which, unconfined by party limits, friendship had drawn around me, without considerable regret. A sense of duty, however, overcame every other consideration, and preparations for my departure were commenced with all possible promptitude.

As the servant of the Mission, no private feeling should have induced me to postpone my departure; much less to have remained in Ceylon, contrary to the arrangements of our Missionary Committee in London. But a chain of circumstances over which I had no control, concurred to set aside the arrangement. Independently of the state of our own Mission, which on many accounts seemed to require my longer continuance in Colombo, the official authorities of the island were very averse to my departure. Archdeacon Twisleton strongly remonstrated with my colleague, Mr. Clough, against the measure; and His Excellency the Governor, and the Hon. Chief Justice condescended to interest themselves. A letter was addressed to me by His Excellency's private secretary, communicating their feelings on the subject. A vote was also passed by the Committee of the Bible Society, deprecating my removal from the duties by which I was connected with them. Gratifying as interposition from such quarters must necessarily have been to my feelings, it was, nevertheless, a source of painful anxiety. I, however, left the question wholly to my brethren; believing that God would direct them to decide for the welfare of the Mission, and his own glory. Mr. Clough laid the whole matter before the Conference. After viewing the subject in all its bearings, the brethren determined to re-appoint me to Colombo, and to appoint Mr. Lynch to the new Mission at Madras.* Application was made to the Government at Madras, to grant him permission to superintend the congregations at that station, until advice could be received from England.

Mr. Lynch was furnished at his departure with letters of introduction from the Governor, Chief Justice, and other persons of the highest consideration in Colombo,

* Appendix.

to their friends at Madras. His piety and zeal soon endeared him to the pious part of the inhabitants; while the consistency of his conduct secured to him the respect even of those who made no pretensions to religion. The Missionaries of different denominations at that settlement found in him a fellow-labourer in the common cause. Madras was to him a scene of considerable usefulness; two places of worship have been erected; and several natives, and others, have embraced the truth, and found the liberty it proclaims.*

The increasing importance of the Galle station rendered the purchase of an estate for a Missionary residence highly desirable; and one of the largest houses in the Fort, being vacant, and more eligible than any place which offered in the suburbs, a subscription was commenced, the premises purchased, and part of the house converted into a spacious place of worship. The Missionaries on this station were encouraged by very hopeful appearances of piety and ministerial talent in a second country-born young man, whom they accordingly employed as a local preacher.† Their labours among the Singhalese were also accompanied by some gratifying measure of success. For a considerable time they regularly preached in the house adjoining the Budhuist temple at Dadalla, the priests of which generally prepared it for Christian worship! They did not indeed realize *all* their anticipations; but, in the course of time, one of the priests became a decided convert to Christianity, and at his own request was baptized by the name of *Daniel Alexander*. His heathen robe was sent to England, as a present to my esteemed friend, the Rev. Isaac Bradnack; as was also a silken robe, belonging to the Ava priest, to the late venerable Joseph Benson.

In the hope that a change of air would effect a favour-

* The Madras Mission has now interesting branches at *Bangalore, Seringapatam,* and *Negapatam.*

† Mr. John Anthoniez.

able alteration in my heath, which was too much impaired to admit of my attending to the varied duties of the Colombo station, we removed, at the earnest recommendation of the Chief Justice, to a small cottage in the immediate vicinage of his country-seat at Colpetty. The obligatons under which Mrs. Harvard and myself had previously lain to that distinguished individual and his excellent lady, were here increased by a series of kind attentions, the value of which was enhanced by the mode in which they were administered. The Mission was not neglected by this necessary absence; as Mr. Callaway remained at Colombo, until my health should be sufficiently restored to resume the accustomed engagements. By the end of the year I was able to preach occasionally, and to undertake the partial superintendence of the Mission press. The intelligence and application of our head-printer, (Mr. Jantz,) supplied my lack of service, and enabled Mr. Callaway to enter upon the scene of his appointed labour at Matura; his absence from which had required no ordinary exercise of self-denial. The "yearning charity" for the souls of the perishing heathen, which first impelled him to Ceylon, was but partially satisfied, until he entered fully upon his beloved work. On his arrival at Matura, he met with a most friendly reception from all classes of the inhabitants, both European and native; and the Mission there was re-commenced under very encouraging auspices.

My residence at Colpetty had brought the dearth of religious instruction in that increasingly populous village more immediately under our view. A military school-house, in which some of the washerman caste assembled, was the only place of Christian worship in the village. The school, which had been hitherto supported by Lady Johnson, her ladyship wished to be placed under our care, as the Hon. Chief Justice contemplated an early departure for England, owing to her ladyship's declining health. We therefore regarded my temporary residence in the village, as designed by Providence to interest us deeply in the future welfare of the inhabitants; and as an eligible estate opposite to the cottage we had occupied was for sale, it afforded us an opportunity of carrying our designs into immediate execution. This was purchased on advantageous terms; and the subscription to meet the expense, was most generously aided by several of the European inhabitants at Colpetty; at the head of whom the Chief Justice and his lady must be placed. The Hon. R. Boyd, Sole Commissioner of Revenue, to a liberal subscription added the influence of his personal example, by occasionally visiting the school after its establishment. The subscription was commenced in November, and the building was opened in March following.

Our new place of worship in the Pettah, the completion of which had, from various causes, been much delayed, was at length completely finished, and was opened for the public worship of Almighty God, on Sunday, Dec. 23, at seven o' clock in the morning. The service was commenced by reading the prayers of the Established Church; after which an appropriate discourse from Psalm cxxii. 6. was delivered by Mr. Clough. An organ, which had been purchased at Galle, rendered us the assistance we had so much needed in the conduct of the singing, and excited much attention. A numerous congregation attended the opening service, among whom were many of the subscribers; who expressed their approbation both of the building and services. In the evening the place was crowded at an early hour. His Excellency the Governor, and nearly all the principal Europeans in Colombo were present. The sermon, founded on Luke ii. 14. devolved on me. A train of reflections which pressed on our minds, tended to make the engagements of this day highly interesting to us; and we indulged a hope that the truths which we endeavoured faithfully to explain and enforce, were not delivered in vain.

The building, which we designated, "THE WESLEYAN MISSION HOUSE," is of the amphitheatre form, with three rows of seats, and is capable of accommodating from five to six hundred hearers. Its appearance is neat, and the materials substantial.* A few days after the opening we were favoured with a note from the Governor, expressive of his approbation of the building and the opening services, with a renewal of his promises of patronage and support. A further donation from His Excellency was inclosed.

On opening the Mission House, we agreed to have service in English at seven in the morning of every Sabbath, and at the same hour in the evening. In the hope of exciting an interest in the minds of the natives, a service in Singhalese, to commence at halfpast ten in the forenoon, was established. Before the Singhalese sermon, an abridgment of the Liturgy, translated by Mr. Clough, is invariably read; that language being so verbose, that the entire Church Service is not read to any Singhalese congregation. The Portuguese sermon on Tuesday evenings continued to be numerously attended by the natives, Dutch, and country-born inhabitants; among whom were many females, who were much pleased with the accommodation which the Mission House afforded them.

In compliance with a custom which had its origin with the Dutch, a box was placed at each door o the chapel, to receive the contributions of those who were disposed to deposit any sum in aid of the expenses of the place. Our Portuguese hearers invariably

* A tablet to the memory of the late Rev. Dr. Coke is fixed on th right of the pulpit; and another in memory of Mr. Ault, on the left each bearing an appropriate inscription. See *Appendix*.

dropped a small piece of money into the box as they retired.* We had also a public collection on the first Sunday in every month for the same purpose.†

The progress of truth in Ceylon received, apparently, a powerful check in the sudden and lamented death of W. Tolfrey, Esq. the indefatigable and faithful translator of the new version of the Singhalese New Testament. A monument to his memory, testifying the high estimation in which he was held, and the valuable services he had rendered to the Colombo Bible Society, was erected in the Fort Church. The chasm occasioned by his removal could not be filled by any other individual; and the translation of the Scriptures in which he had been engaged, devolved on a Committee chosen for the purpose.‡

* The hymns sung by the Portuguese congregation were translated by Mr. Armour from the large Hymn Book, as they were required; and printed on slips of paper, until a sufficient number were supplied to make a complete collection. The preacher was obliged to translate the chapter he read before the sermon, as at that time there was no version in the country Portuguese. Mr. Newstead has since, in part, remedied the inconvenience. He has also, in unison with Mr. Fox, composed a very acceptable and useful hymn book, less *European* in its style than Mr. Armour's translation.

† The usual mode of a public collection in Ceylon appears rather singular to a stranger. The sexton makes it in a bag fixed to the end of a pole, which he hands round the place of worship. Sometimes in the Dutch churches a second collection is made at the same service; when a small bell attached to the bag is carried round, which announces its approach previously to its being presented for the donation. Our sexton, who was a foreigner, was anxious to introduce the *bell-bag* into the economy of our Mission House; but the first attempt in our English congregation disturbed in some degree the decorum of the service, and we prohibited its future introduction. A gentleman filling a high official station invariably attended our chapel on the collection evenings, bringing with him his numerous and interesting family, every member of which contributed.

‡ This committee consisted of C. W. Layard, Esq. the Rev. Messrs. Chater, Armour, and Clough; two learned Singhalese natives; and Petrus Panditta, and George Nadoris; with the particulars of whose renunciation of Budhuism the reader has been already furnished.

In the government of the world, one part of the plan adopted by the Almighty, is, to educe real good from seeming evil. The removal of Mr. Tolfrey from the important work in which he was so meritoriously employed, was the means of combining the talents of pious and qualified individuals of different religious denominations; thus assimilating the Colombo Bible Society into a nearer resemblance of the Parent Institution in England: the catholicism of whose plan is at once the strength and beauty of its constitution.

To the liberality of the Committee of the British and Foreign Bible Society, the Colombo Auxiliary was indebted for a most important addition to its previous means of disseminating the Scriptures in the Singhalese tongue. An order was given to the proper quarters, to supply the Society in Colombo with a complete fount of Singhalese type, suitable for an octavo edition of the Scriptures; the former edition, having been printed in quarto, was not so suitable for general distribution. On the arrival of the type from Serampore, where it was cast, it was found to have sustained such material injury on the passage, as to be wholly useless, until some of the characters, which were completely destroyed, could be replaced. A delay of some months must inevitably have ensued, but for some practical knowledge of type-founding which I had providentially gained at an early period of my life; and, at the request of my colleague, and others to whom I mentioned the circumstance, I endeavoured to replace the imperfections with type of our own manufacture. A small foundry was fitted up; and, after some improvements, became adequate to the supply of whatever types our establishment required.

We were indebted to the Baptist Missionaries at Serampore for instructions for making printing ink; and it only remained for us to be able to make our own paper, to possess all the materials necessary for printing, without depending on foreign supplies, always expensive, and frequently uncertain. Our local situation was by no means favourable to such an undertaking; but, should a Missionary be sent to Ceylon, possessed of a practical acquaintance with the process, it would form a most suitable employment for the native converts at some country station.*

To introduce the gospel to the Kandyan provinces had been a favourite design with us, ever since their subjection to the British crown. Application was made to the Government for permission for one of our number to proceed to the interior, to attempt the establishment of a school, as a preliminary measure. Mr. Erskine and Mr. Clough were each desirous of undertaking this Mission; but the provinces were not considered to be yet sufficiently tranquillized to justify the attempt. His Excellency promised to return a favourable answer to the application upon his return from a tour in the interior, if the state of public affairs would allow of the attempt. The superintending providence of God was soon discovered in the prevention of this undertaking. A few months only had elapsed, when a sanguinary rebellion broke out among the Kandyans,† which aimed at the extirpation of all Europeans; and in which the life of the Missionary might have been sacrificed; and possibly the rebellion itself charged, by the enemies of Christian Missions, upon the peaceful religion he had attempted to introduce.

* Some attempts have been made, under the sanction of the Government, to establish a paper-manufactory on the banks of one of the rivers North of Colombo; and though the experiment in the hands of natives was but partially successful, the results fully convinced me of its practicability, if placed under the direction of an European acquainted with the process.

† See Introduction, page xxxviii.

CHAP. XIII.

Apathy of the Malabar natives—Points of difference in the Singhalase and Malabar characters—Discouraging circumstances in the South —Establishment of a native school at Negombo—Opening of the Colpetty school-house—Compelled to recognize the distinction of caste—Attachment of the children to the school—Purchase of Mission Premises at Negombo—Native marriages—Plan for establishing Mission schools throughout the Island—Encouraging proofs of success—Meeting of the Mission Conference—New Stations— Schools—Execution of a Soldier—Conversion of two Budhuist priests—Sir Hardinge Gifford—J. Sutherland, Esq.—His son, Mr. J. Sutherland, placed with the Missionaries—Received on trial as a Missionary—Illness of several of the Missionaries—Singular application—Establishment of regular worship—Review—Church Missionaries.

WHILE the Missionaries at the several Singhalese stations were encouraged by the favourable appearances which have been narrated, those employed in the Malabar districts were painfully exercised, owing to the little apparent success which attended their labours. In the native bazars they generally succeeded in collecting congregations; but their addresses were listened to with the most painful indifference; and no curiosity, much less interest, was excited among the natives by the momentous subjects on which they dwelt. At *Batticaloa* and *Trincomalee* they frequently preached to English and Portuguese congregations; and on these occasions were *blessed in their deed*. The English day-school at each of these places was also well attended. At *Jaffna*, the European and country-born inhabitants afforded the Missionaries considerable hopes that an effectual door of usefulness was opened to them. Some had evidently *believed from the heart*. The general deportment of those who attended their ministry was consistent; and their regard for the means of grace excited the expectation, that more extensive good would be accomplished. The place of worship at length became too small for the congregation; and the Missionaries felt themselves justified in purchasing more capacious premises. These, by the generous contributions of their friends, were converted into a neat and commodious chapel, which was soon filled with hearers; and this also becoming too small for the continually increasing congregation, was superseded by one yet better adapted for the accommodation of the people.

Among the Pagan natives but little encouragement was afforded to hope. The Malabar differs materially from the Singhalese in the cast of his disposition, and general deportment toward Europeans. In the latter, there is a docility and curiosity which are highly favourable to Missionary efforts; but the Malabar native adds to a most inveterate attachment to Paganism, a haughtiness of spirit, and superlative contempt for Europeans; a trait of character also observable among the Hindoo natives of Continental India. Even these barriers, insurmountable by mere human exertions, shall be cast down by the power of God, and the Malabar become *obedient to the faith* of the Gospel. With the valuable American Missionaries, who had settled in the same province, our brethren held the most friendly intercourse. Fellow labourers in the same field, partakers of the same trials, and animated by the same considerations to perseverance, they naturally sought the society of each other; and found their spirits mutually refreshed, by Christian intercourse.

Though more favoured in the South with facilities of access to the natives, than our brethren in the Malabar districts, *we* were not strangers to the feelings of discouragement. Possibly, our expectations, raised in the first instance higher than theirs, by the hopeful appearances which attended our early efforts, the disappointment which ensued on not realizing our hopes to the extent we had anticipated, might be productive of as great *sickness of the heart*, as that occasioned by their *deferred hope*. Instances of native conversions were comparatively few; in many the fair blossoms which had excited our hopes, were nipped by unkindly blasts; and these, added to the disproportion between the number of natives who attended our ministry, and the few who appeared to be influenced by the truth, produced a feeling of painful despondency, which, had it been indulged, would have unnerved our efforts, and destroyed our peace. This feeling, however, did not gain the ascendancy, except during intervals of exhaustion, and temporary forgetfulness; when we found a counteracting principle called into exercise by having recourse to *the word of God and prayer*.

A new path of usefulness opened before us. One of our Sunday-school teachers had been recently appointed Interpreter Mohandiram to the magistrate of Negombo, about twenty miles from Colombo. At our recommendation he had opened a school for the children on the Sabbath, and so great was the desire to obtain instruction, that he was unable to communicate it to the numbers who attended for that purpose. In addition to the Sabbath, he devoted an early hour of some of the week-day mornings to the same employment; and was not unfrequently awoke at day-break by the noise of his little pupils, who were waiting in the virando for his appearance. On being informed of these particulars, Mr. Clough determined on paying him a visit; when he found more than seventy boys desirous of instruction. A school was, in consequence, opened; of which the brother of the Mohandiram was appointed master, with a suitable salary. This young man was the first schoolmaster we engaged: he ultimately became decidedly pious, and remains a steady member of our society. The Mohandiram was, and still continues, a Roman Catholic.

Early in 1817, the school-house at Colpetty was finished, and we had the pleasure of admitting to the benefits of the institution upwards of one hundred boys, and nearly fifty girls. The latter were placed under the immediate care of an intelligent young woman of Dutch extraction, who had been recommended to us by Lady Johnstone. One of the pupils instructed by Mr. Clough at the Mission school at Galle,* was appointed the general master, with a native assistant teacher under him. On the day of opening, Mr. Philipsz acted as my interpreter, at the express desire of the Hon. Chief Justice. We at first hoped that the invidious distinction of *caste* would not have found an introduction into the Colpetty school; but in this we were mistaken. Considerable curiosity had been excited among the inhabitants, as to what course would be adopted; and many conversations had been held among them. A *vellalah* brought us to the test; by presenting his daughter for admission as a pupil, expressly stipulating, that she should not be classed with children of an inferior caste. I hesitated to receive her upon such a condition; but finding the applicant was about to withdraw with his child, and having reason to suppose that his example would be generally followed, I concluded upon yielding to

---

* The young man whose attentions to us on our journey to Colombo, are referred to at page 244.

their prejudice, leaving the gradual influence of Christianity, the benevolent truths of which we should have frequent opportunities of inculcating, to undermine an evil which we should have failed to extirpate at once. I therefore immediately announced, that the children of different castes would be seated apart from each other; a regulation which gave universal satisfaction to the natives.*

No native school could be commenced under more favourable auspices than the Colpetty school. Directly patronized by Sir Alexander and Lady Johnstone, and frequently visited by her ladyship, who evinced the deepest interest in its success, especially of the female department, it was recommended to the approbation of the natives by no ordinary means. A school expressly for Singhalese females was an experiment, if not directly opposed to the native prejudices, at least contrary to all previous usage†. By the blessing of God, it was attended with complete success; and future generations will reap incalculable benefits from the establishment of the female school at Colpetty. The occasional visits of the Hon. Chief Justice and the Hon. R. Boyd, and the encouragement given by them to the more diligent and regular scholars, invested the institution with great advantages, and produced among the scholars most favourable results. The Mission school at Colpetty became the theme of conversation throughout the adjacent country; and numerous applications for admission into it were made to us from distant villages. One of the boys, the son of a native washerman, who regularly attended, every

* The death of the little girl a few months after led me to look back to the measure by which her admission to the school was effected with particular pleasure; especially as she had evidently derived considerable benefit from the instructions; and, it is hoped, obtained a saving knowledge of Him who said when on earth, *Suffer the little children to come unto me, and forbid them not.*

† Lady Brownrigg had previously founded one for the benefit of the Tamul Christians at Colombo.

morning walked to the school from the distance of six miles; and returned in the evening: another lad of the highest caste, whose attendance was punctual, cheerfully walked *sixteen* miles every day to enjoy the advantages of the institution.

The situation of Negombo, from its commercial intercourse with the interior, rendered it a most desirable Missionary station. Mr. Clough and myself therefore resolved on devoting considerable attention to it, with a view to its becoming a regular station on the next arrival of Missionaries from England. At much personal inconvenience we occasionally visited it, and preached to the inhabitants. A bungaloe, situated in a salubrious and eligible spot, being for sale, we purchased it for 1500 rix dollars. This was the only purchase made by us without first opening a subscription to defray the expense; but in the present instance it would not have been expedient; and, as it was sufficiently commodious both for residence and a place of worship, it soon more than redeemed its original cost by the saving of rent. While passing a few days at this place, I received the news of the arrival at Galle of the Rev. Messrs. Fox, Osborne, and Newstead, from England. Mr. Fox was joyfully welcomed by us in Colombo a few days afterwards; and his two companions remained at Galle until the Conference.

The legality of the native marriages solemnized by the Missionaries having been questioned, as we had not being regularly licensed by the local Government for that purpose, His Excellency forwarded to each Missionary the necessary qualification; issuing a proclamation, by which all such marriages were declared valid, as well as any which might be hereafter solemnized by us, conformably to the existing regulations. By the articles of capitulation the island is, I believe, still governed by the Dutch law; which, with respect to marriages, inheritances, and some other points, bears a resemblance to the law of Scotland.

So great an interest had been excited among the natives by the establishment of schools, that we received constant applications from the inhabitants of various villages to extend to them the advantages of instruction to their children, by the formation of schools among them. Disappointed in the sanguine expectations we had first indulged, of extensive and rapid conversions of adult natives to the faith of Christ, Mr. Clough and myself regarded with feelings of peculiar pleasure, the desire manifested by them to place their children under our care; persuaded that our hopes of the future must be, in a very considerable degree, founded on the cultivation of their minds, and the formation of their character. We therefore digested a plan for the establishment of a regular chain of Native Mission Schools; and submitted it, by letter, to the consideration of our brethren at the different stations.

On a subject of such magnitude, embracing so many particulars, perfect unanimity of opinion was hardly to be expected. Some of our brethren regarded the plan as impracticable; while others feared that the attempt would too much divert our attention from the ministry of the word. Impressed with a full conviction of its favourable influence on the design of our Mission, the projectors of the plan determined, in dependance on the Divine blessing, to introduce it to the Colombo circuit. They experienced also considerable assistance from the judicious arrangements and zealous co-operation of Mr. Callaway, then stationed at Matura. And by the ensuing July fourteen schools, (in which nearly a thousand native children received regular daily instruction,) were founded at these two stations only. The following extract of a letter, dated June 17, from Archdeacon Twisleton, who was at that time the Principal of Schools, will shew with what approbation the system was regarded by the Government.—" I am directed by His Excellency the Governor to express to you, that he much approves of the Missionaries *directing their attention to the establishment of schools;* and that the Wesleyan Missionaries cannot, in his conception, be employed in any manner so well calculated to produce extensive and permanent good, as in the management and superintendence of schools in which the English language and the principles of religion are taught."

Our worthy brother Fox entered heartily into the project; assured us that it would meet with the sanction and co-operation of our Committee in England; and accompanied us to several places to open schools. Our plan required, that the inhabitants of a village, when desirous of the establishment of a school, should consent to erect their own school-house, and then send us a list of candidates for instruction, before we would consent to visit them for the purpose. These conditions were cheerfully complied with; and petitions for schools crowded in upon us from all quarters, many of which we could not possibly attend to. From *Bentotte,* situated fifty miles from Colombo, we received a most pressing application. At *Pantura,* fifteen miles from Colombo, I had the pleasure of opening a school under the immediate patronage of Don Abraham de Saram, the second Maha Moodeliar,* an intelligent and respectable native chief; and appointed a young man, educated at the Seminary under Mr. Armour, to be the master. At *Morotto,* about twelve miles from Colombo, a school was also formed ; and a pious Singhalese, a native of the village, and a member of our society at Colombo, was placed in it as master. On calling over the names of the scholars at the opening of the Morotto school, they were severally desired to answer,

* Appendix.

"Yes, Sir," the meaning of the words being first explained to them. They were also informed, that it was the answer given by English scholars when their names were called over. The parents, who had crowded round the school, were highly delighted upon hearing their children speak English; and were afterwards overheard extolling the abilities of the minister; who, they said, had taught their children to *speak two English words in two minutes!*

In forming a school at *Slave Island*, a village in the vicinity of Colombo, a piece of ground for the erection of the school-house was voluntarily given us by a Moorman; and both male and female children of several of the Malay inhabitants, who are in general the most bigotted Mahomedans, were entered as pupils. At the village of *Wellewatta* the wife of the Mohandiram engaged to superintend the female department of the Mission school. The master of our *Sea Street* school was a native doctor of good reputation; and the children of his patients were most devotedly attached to his instructions. It is difficult to describe the interest which our proceedings excited among all ranks, but especially in the hearts of the untaught and indigent natives, who ardently desired their children to possess the advantages of education, which had been denied to themselves. On its been announced, that we contemplated the establishment of a school in the neighbourhood of the Colombo *New Bazar,* many of the inhabitants of that populous district were greatly affected; and were filled with surprise that any motive could induce persons to care for the improvement and welfare of their children. Some, with clasped hands and tears in their eyes, exclaimed, " Then God hath remembered us, poor destitute inhabitants of the New Bazar!"

In the month of August, as many of our number assembled at Colombo as could conveniently attend, for the arrangement of the general affairs of the Mission. By the timely arrival of the brethren already named, we were enabled to occupy two new stations, (*Negombo* and *Caltura*,*) besides considerably extending those which were previously occupied. *Bentotte* was attached to the Caltura Circuit; *Amblangodde* to Galle; and *Belligamme* to Matura.† Colombo was again assigned to me; and Mr. Lynch was requested to return to Madras, until a Missionary regularly licensed by the Court of Directors for that station should arrive from England. Two converted Budhuist priests were this year attached to the Caltura and Negombo circuits; and ninety-two persons, professing " a desire to flee from the wrath to come," were reported as members of our infant societies, inclusive of twenty-two at Madras.

The Conference presented an address to our invaluable friend, the Hon. Chief Justice, who was about to proceed to England, to which he returned a highly gratifying reply.‡ The plan of a periodical circular, to contain a quarterly letter from each station, was proposed and adopted by this Conference. A copy of this small publication is regularly transmitted to each Missionary, and to the Committee at home. Some gloomy communications which had found their way to England sug-

---

* The assistance afforded to our brethren, Messrs. Fox and Newstead, by J. Deane, Esq. Collector of Colombo, and J. Atkinson, Esq. Collector of Caltura, deserves a grateful acknowledgment. The services rendered by the latter gentleman to Mr. Ault at Batticaloa have been already referred to. The former succeeded Mr. Bisset as Secretary of the Ceylon Auxiliary Bible Society. Mr. D. sailed in the same ship from England with Messrs. Fox and Newstead; and afterwards availed himself of every opportunity to evince the high estimation in which he held them.

† By a reference to the map it will be seen, that the entire line of the Singhalese district of the island was thus comprehended.

‡ Appendix.

gested the propriety of publishing regular official statements of our proceedings at each station. From these circulars the periodical publications of our Missionary Society are in general supplied with intelligence.

The plan for establishing Mission Schools throughout the island, after mature deliberation, was cordially adopted. The Colombo brethren were appointed the General Superintendents of the Schools, and were requested to furnish the other stations, in which they had not been commenced, with the requisite instructions· Our printing office speedily afforded a supply of class-papers and suitable elementary works; and in the course of a few months between *three and four thousand* Ceylonese children were brought under the salutary instruction and discipline of *Missionary Day Schools*. In a few cases we were able to engage suitable females, chiefly of the country-born class, who were qualified to act as school-mistresses; and we then found no difficulty in obtaining female scholars, who were invariably instructed in a part of the school separated from the boys. Our female charge was peculiarly interesting. The novelty of its character, and its ultimate beneficial results on Ceylonese society, rendered a female native school a scene for pleasing anticipations. In addition to the improvement of their minds, their future usefulness and domestic comfort were consulted, by giving them instruction in needle-work, lace-making, and other female employment. Rewards of cloth were occasionally bestowed on those most expert at their needle, which they made into articles of clothing for themselves, and wore as distinguishing proofs of their proficiency. The female department of every school on the Colombo station was under the general superintendence of Mrs. Harvard; who paid them regular visits, and with much labour and anxiety contributed to the efficiency of the plan. The first rewards, consisting of pin-cushions, and similar articles, were wrought by her own hands.*

The latter days of a private of the 73rd regiment, condemned to suffer death at Colombo for striking his officer, whom we regularly attended at his own request until the time of his execution, afforded us encouragement in our efforts to benefit our countrymen, in connection with our Mission to the natives. He had been a very desperate character; but during the imprisonment which preceded his execution, he earnestly sought mercy from God through the mediation of his Son; and there is ground to hope that he did not seek in vain. His crime was committed on the 27th of September, and the awful sentence was put into execution on the 27th of the following month. The change which had been effected on his heart, and which he manifested by satisfactory proofs of penitence and reformation, excited great attention throughout the island. On his way to the place of execution, to which he was accompanied by Dr. Twisleton, Mr. Clough, and myself, he repeated, with the utmost composure and placidity, a hymn which had been rendered useful to him. He said, he preferred death to life, from the fear lest he should relapse into sin; and when we parted with him, a few moments before the fatal shots were discharged, his last words were—" Farewell! Glory be to God! I am a happy man." He was only twenty-six years of age. The circumstances of his death were improved in a sermon at our place of worship in the Fort, which was

---

* The progress of the girls in some of the schools was highly gratifying. They soon became competent to the performance of any description of plain needle-work; and to obtain for them a regular supply, Mrs. Harvard, at the suggestion of Lady Johnstone, drew up a list of prices at which needle-work would be executed at the Colpetty school, with some regulations appended. A copy of this will be inserted in the Appendix.

heard by a crowded congregation of his comrades, and afterwards printed for general circulation.

It had been the practice, from the beginning of our residence at Colombo, to deliver a sermon to children and young people on New Year's Day, at Easter, and Whitsuntide. These services, which were held in the Dutch Church at Wolfendahl, were attended by crowds who behaved with the greatest seriousness. We commenced the year 1817 with a sermon to young people in the Mission House; and it affords me satisfaction to know that the custom is still cherished by large assemblies of natives, both old and young; many of whom came from the surrounding villages to the distance of several miles. The service on the 1st of January, 1818, was rendered singularly interesting by the attendance of two Budhuist priests, who had been convinced of the evil of idolatry; and who, having passed a probationary interval, requested on that occasion to make an open renunciation of their former errors, and publicly to take on themselves the profession of the Christian faith. Their case was rendered more interesting by the melancholy fact, that they had both been baptized in their infancy, though subsequently introduced to the Budhuist priesthood by their semi-heathen parents. Their names were Don Adrian de Silva, and Don Andris de Silva. They had each previously transcribed on talipot leaves the whole of the Acts of the Apostles, which they presented to us, in token of their admiration of that history of the first Christian Missions. During the sermon they sat near the pulpit in their priestly robes, at the conclusion of which they underwent an examination respecting their faith in the Gospel; when they withdrew, and for ever laid aside the badges of their former Atheism; which they gave into my hands on their return to the congregation, as expressive of their public surrender of themselves to our Lord and his service. Don Adrian was afterwards appointed to act as a Singhalese local preacher, and Don Andris as a master in one of our Native schools.*

The beginning of the year 1818 was marked by the return to England of Hardinge Gifford, Esq. (now Sir Hardinge,) the Advocate Fiscal, or Attorney General, of the island. This gentleman, an able and public friend of Christianity, was from the beginning a well-wisher to the Mission, and subscribed towards the erection of our place of worship. For the purpose of instructing and interesting the natives in the nature and objects of the Bible Society, Sir Hardinge composed a valuable Tract entitled " A Dialogue between a Mohandiram and his Friend," which was extensively circulated with good effect. We were in the habit of visiting a native school which he had established on his own estate; and our attentions were always most obligingly acknowledged. On his departure, he expressed his ardent wishes for our most complete success.†

About the same period, the late J. Sutherland, Esq. Secretary of State for the Kandyan Provinces, another of our respected friends, was obliged by ill health to return to his native land. A short time before his departure from Ceylon, his two children, who had been sent to Scotland for education, returned to their widowed parent; and, unwilling to take them back immediately, he made arrangements for their continuance in Ceylon, till the result of his voyage should be known. After breakfasting with him one morning, in company with our mutual friend, W. C. Gibson, Esq. of Galle, Mr. Sutherland requested that I would receive his son, an intelligent and amiable youth about sixteen years of age, under my protection; engaging to pay a

* Their robes are still in my possession. I am happy to add, that these converts continue faithfully to prosecute their holy calling, under the superintendence of our Mission.

† Sir Hardinge has since been appointed the Chief Justice of Ceylon.

competent sum for his support; and expressing a hope that he might hereafter be engaged in some department of our Mission. I observed, that if employed as a Methodist Missionary, his son would be necessarily exposed to some hardships; for, however favoured we were in our exemption from direct persecution, under no circumstances was the life of a Missionary free from trials. To this he replied, that he had seen much of men and things; and that, with all its disadvantages, he should think his son honoured by a connection with the Wesleyan Mission.

Mr. James Sutherland, Jun. was accordingly placed with us. He was of an engaging disposition, and had received the rudiments of a superior education. With a correct knowledge of English, he possessed a respectable acquaintance with Latin and Greek. He manifested an aptitude for acquiring languages, and his mind thirsted for knowledge. I felt for him all the solicitude of a father, and was frequently rendered uneasy by a sense of the responsibility of my trust. From the exposed situation of our house in Colombo, and its connection with the workmen in the adjoining offices, I deemed it most prudent to place him at a station less exposed to temptation; and at my request Mr. Newstead received him under his care. The Hon. R. Boyd, the friend and agent of his father, approved of the measure, and liberally supplied all his wants. By the divine blessing on the pious and judicious instructions of Mr. Newstead, he became sincerely and decidedly religious; and has since been received on trial as a Missionary and fellow-labourer.* His respected father did not survive to behold the accomplishment of his wishes. His lamented death occurred soon after his arrival in England.

Our Missionary family was again visited with afflic-

* Appendix.

tion. Mr. Squance, at Jaffna, had a return of serious indisposition; as also had Mr. Erskine at Galle, which was so severe as to oblige him to remove from his station to Batticalao. Mr. Carver, whose valuable labours at Trincomalee had procured for him so much deserved respect, was also compelled by a dangerous illness to undertake a voyage; and Mr. Newstead's exertions and anxieties in his station had considerably impaired his health. Mrs. Fox, being near her confinement at Caltura, (where at that time there was no other European female, nor even an European medical man,) Mrs. Harvard undertook the journey, accompanied by an European nurse, whom she engaged to attend Mrs. Fox in her confinement. This act of friendship was peculiarly acceptable; but the nurse was addicted to intoxication, and the principal weight of attendance fell on Mrs. Harvard, whose health was by no means equal to the task. The consequence to her was a violent illness at Caltura; and crossing the river on her return laid the foundation of the intermittent or jungle fever; which so debilitated her system, that the medical man urged her removal from Ceylon: but she resolutely determined to abide by her husband and her work to the last. My esteemed colleague, Mr. Clough, at the same time yielded to the pressure of disease; and in the month of April embarked for Madras, to try the influence of a change of climate. At Madras Mr. C. experienced much attention,* and derived considerable benefit from the change. He did not return till the following October. During his absence, his place at Colombo was supplied by Mr. Callaway, who left his station for

* Among many others, Mr. Clough especially records the kind and liberal attentions of the Rev. W. Malkin, chaplain to the Hon. Company at Poonamalee, about thirteen miles from Madras; with whom he passed some time during this visit. This pious clergyman and his lady endeavoured in every possible way to alleviate his affliction, to sustain his mind, and to promote his recovery.

the purpose, and availed himself of the opportunity to superintend some of his own important publications as they passed through the press.

Mr. Callaway's residence at Colombo afforded me a relaxation from the regular routine of business connected with the printing office, and other departments of our establishment; and I gladly embraced the opportunity of more frequently visiting the neighbouring villages to preach in, and inspect the native schools we had founded. A singular application from a Budhuist priest, to be employed as a Missionary Schoolmaster, induced me to proceed to the village in which he resided. It was situated in an insulated spot, surrounded by jungle. To my astonishment, I found a considerable number of interesting boys whom he had taught to read *the Holy Scriptures!* He not only offered himself for Christian baptism, but promised to use his influence to induce his Pagan neighbours also to embrace the faith of Christ. I stipulated, that as a proof of his sincerity, he should convert his temple into a place for Christian worship; and secretly rejoiced in the prospect of thus dispossessing Satan of one of his strong holds. On this point he hesitated, it being public property, and requested time to consider of the proposal. I was treated by him with hospitality during my stay; and preached to a congregation he collected to hear me. It has given me concern that I never had an opportunity of repeating my visit. Nor have I since heard any tidings of my host and his connexions.

Our Missionary excursions among the native villages were now peculiarly gratifying: the schools having excited so much interest among the people in general, that wherever we went congregations readily assembled. At the school visitations, our bungaloes were generally surrounded by the parents of the children, who anxiously attended the result of the public examinations; and we invariably discoursed with them on the things of God. At length we were led to the establishment of a regular Sunday service in all the Mission Schools, which was encouragingly attended. The providence of God doubtless conducted us to this *effectual* mode of collecting congregations. Parents naturally esteem those who aim to advance the interests of their children.

The number of native places of worship in connection with our Mission, having increased beyond our means of supplying with preaching, we had recourse to the labours of local preachers. A few of our schoolmasters were deemed capable of delivering an extemporary sermon; and when the country congregations could not be otherwise supplied, the masters were directed to read from a collection of sermons provided for them by Mr. Clough. Mr. Clough's Singhalese translation of the Liturgy is invariably read in all the schools at the commencement of the service.

We now, with thankfulness to the Author of all good, considered the Mission as fully established. Substantial places of worship had been erected in all the principal places in the island, and nearly a hundred smaller ones were attached to the different stations. In these *God was worshipped* by many of the natives *in spirit and in truth*. The immediate effects of Christian preaching on the native congregations, were not, of course, equal to those produced on a people better acquainted with the truths of the gospel; but though not the same in extent, in their nature they were the same. A few of the adult hearers were brought under a deep concern for salvation; some afforded satisfactory evidence of genuine conversion; and many were led into those habits of reverence for divine ordinances, and regard to moral and social duties, which are the invariable results of an introduction of the Gospel.

On Whit-Monday Mr. Callaway preached in the

Colombo Mission House, to a crowded assembly of young people collected from the surrounding country. After the service a heathen brought his nephew forward for baptism. His whole family resided in a very dark region near the Kandyan boundary. The boy was placed under instruction; and suitable advice was given to his Pagan uncle, who paid much attention, expressing a willingness to learn the way to be saved. He intimated, that if a school were established in his village, many of the inhabitants would gladly embrace Christianity; and was informed that Cornelius should pay them a visit. When Cornelius reached the village, most of the men were absent in their corn-fields; but the women who were at home, heard his word gladly; and he left them under an engagement to visit them again. On his journey, our young friend passing through a very populous part of the country, perceived an encouraging opening for a school, at a benighted place called *Peypiliana*. The inhabitants cheerfully engaged to erect the school-house; a suitable man offered himself from the Seminary; and I promised to embrace an early opportunity of establishing the school.

About the middle of the year, Ceylon was favoured with another supply of labourers in the field of Christian Missions, by the arrival of four excellent Episcopal clergymen. The Rev. Messrs. Lambrick, Mayor, Ward, and Knight; sent by the Church Missionary Society in England. The brethren of the Wesleyan Mission gave them a cordial welcome; and warm expressions of good will were interchanged. Mr. Lambrick subsequently received an appointment to a military chaplaincy in Kandy, which afforded him considerable facilities in the study of the native languages. Mr. Mayor fixed his residence in the vicinity of Galle; Mr. Ward selected Calpentyn, a station to the north of Negombo; and Mr. Knight proceeded to Jaffnapatam.

Messrs. Lambrick and Knight were unmarried. The wives of Messrs. Mayor and Ward appeared to possess much of the spirit and qualifications requisite for the important sphere in which they were to move; and well-founded expectations were raised, that extensive benefits would result to the natives of their own sex, from the influence of their pious instructions and example.

The Church Mission has since been re-inforced, by the addition of the Rev. Mr. Browning, who has an interesting establishment in Kandy; and Mr. Lambrick is now entirely devoted to his Missionary work. Mr. Knight's efforts in the north, have been succeeded with pleasing prospects of much ultimate good. Mr. Ward has joined Mr. Mayor in the southern Mission. Their station, which is a few miles from the sea-coast, has been laboriously cultivated by them; and it is gratifying to know that they rejoice in the work of their hands.

CHAP. XIV.

Pleasing results of the Native schools—Colpetty school—Juvenile piety—Mrs. Harvard's visits to the female schools—Happy deaths—Remarks on immediate effects of Missionary effort—Success from the Lord alone—Hallibowitta school—The Author's illness and removal from Ceylon—Missionaries meet at Galle—Commencement of the voyage—Landing at Falmouth—Retrospect and conclusion.

THE pleasing results of our School System; to which the Divine blessing had imparted a success beyond any thing we had ventured to hope; had, from the beginning of its adoption, diffused a most *beneficial* and *animating* influence among the members of our Missionary family. The order and regularity it had introduced into our itinerant plan; the ready access it afforded us to the parents of the children; and the interest it gave us in their affections; together with the native talent it elicited, and the various energies it employed; combined to impart a character of permanent efficiency to our Mission, which we could not contemplate without gratitude to God, and anticipations of unbounded advantage to future generations.

These anticipations were not enthusiastic; the *means* (under the Divine blessing) being fully commensurate to the *end*. Already several thousand native children received daily instruction in the principles and duties of Christianity, under the constant superintendance of Christian Missionaries; and (to say nothing of the effect of other efforts used by ourselves, and the Missionaries and ministers of other denominations) how salutary an influence must be produced by the example and prayers of these children on the domestic and social circles! How many idolatrous parents will be led to renounce idolatry, and embrace Christianity with the heart, won by the pious exhortations and prayers of their own offspring! And when the children now under instruction become themselves heads of families, they will teach *their children* to *set their hope in God; and not be as their fathers, a stubborn and rebellious generation.* Thus God will have in perpetuity a seed to serve him. *One generation shall praise his works to another, and declare his mighty acts.* The mild and benevolent truths of Christianity silently conveyed into the families of the natives by these schools, will, in innumerable instances, have an effect more certainly destructive upon their idolatrous practices, than the most direct and pointed attacks, however skilfully and zealously attempted.

In some of the schools, a few of the children manifested deep concern for their eternal welfare; and meetings were held by these pious children, for conversation on religious experience and prayer, which the masters conducted. A meeting of this description was instituted at the Colpetty school, which was visited by Mrs. Harvard and myself for the first time, about a year after its commencement. On entering the school, we found about thirty native boys assembled, who rose to receive us. I desired them to resume their seats; and proceeded to question them on their experimental knowledge of religion. A deep seriousness prevailed throughout the assembly; and their answers to my questions were distinguished by a modesty and diffidence which was highly pleasing. The measles had previously occasioned a considerable mortality in the village; and this circumstance had been attended by a most salutary influence on many of their young minds. I inquired of one boy, who had recently recovered, whether, during his illness, he thought he should die; and, on his replying in the affirmative, asked him, whether the apprehensions of death had made him afraid? He answered, " that since God had given him power over temptation, and taken away the love of sin from his heart, he did not fear to die." Others replied to similar questions to the same effect. About six professed to have found *peace with God through our Lord Jesus Christ;* and, upon inquiry, it was ascertained that their general deportment was consistent with their profession.*

On visiting the female schools, Mrs. Harvard occasionally met with incidents equally pleasing. Groups of Singhalese girls would crowd around her, listening with the deepest attention, while she talked to them of Jesus and his salvation. She seldom lifted her eyes upon her auditory, without observing some of them in tears. Two boys and two girls, who were removed from our schools by death, gave very hopeful proofs of having been trained in them for heaven. Detailed accounts of the progress of the schools, and the particular instances in which the instructions were accompanied with a more than ordinary influence, are contained in the periodical publications of the Society; in which also are frequently found gratifying statements of Missionary usefulness among the adult natives.

The labours of Missionaries among the heathen, ought not to be wholly estimated either by themselves

---

* Three things are worthy of observation. *First,* That this little Society was formed by the pious care and zealous attention of our friends Cornelius, and Mr. Coopman, (a respectable and useful local preacher.) *Secondly,* That for the first nine months this class was entirely conducted by them, and never met by a Missionary. Hence their meeting cannot be attributed to any servile principle, but appears to have been produced by a genuine concern for salvation. *Thirdly,* That none of the boys were more than fourteen years of age, and the greater part from eight to twelve. Surely, out of the mouth of these comparative babes God perfected praise!

or others, according to the *immediate* effects which may arise from them. From the peculiarity of their circumstances, these may not always bear a due proportion to their wishes, nor indeed to the results of less ardent exertions, in circumstances more favourable. The chief source of satisfaction is, the reflection that we are doing our utmost in the good cause—that we are endeavouring to do it in the best way, and that God has promised that no labour shall be lost in his work. It is well to remember that we are undermining the moral citadel of Satan; and that the mine which must in its operation prove fatal to the interests of the enemy, may well deserve all the protracted and unseen preparation which the assailants may have devoted to it. Success, in any measure whatever, is from the Lord alone. Recognizing this principle, I always felt disposed to be thankful for the smallest degree of present success; and for any chain of circumstances, which rationally promised it as an ultimate consequence of present labour.

Our limits forbid any thing like an enumeration of all the instances of native conversion with which our efforts were encouraged. Some even of the Kappoa description were brought to confess their deeds, and to forsake their curious and diabolical arts. Several of the Budhuist *priests became obedient to the faith*. Many adult natives of the general mass, and a few honourable individuals among them, felt it to be their happiness to obtain an enrollment among the disciples of Christ; cheerfully submitting to the discipline of his church, and conscientiously engaging to regulate themselves by the precepts of his holy word.

But an unexpected termination was about to be put to my Missionary career. After organizing a school at the village of *Kallibowilla* near *Peypiliana*, a sudden attack of illness obliged me to stop on my way home at the house of a friend. It was hoped that the immediate assistance I obtained would counteract the influence of the disease; but it was too obstinate in its character to be eradicated. For some time my recovery was considered hopeless; and, though it pleased God that the sickness should not be unto death, yet my constitution was so broken up, as (in the opinion of my medical attendants,) to render an immediate return to Europe necessary for the preservation of my life. Mr. Clough arrived from Madras at this juncture, and communicated to the other Missionaries, at their respective stations, an account of my situation, and the opinion of the medical gentlemen as to the necessity of my removing from Ceylon to Europe. With their consent, a passage for my family and self was engaged on board the Princess Charlotte, Capt. Rennoldson. Mr. Fox, having recently sustained the loss by death of his estimable wife, his little girl was consigned to our care, to convey her to Mrs. F.'s friends in England.*

The propriety of sending from England a person properly qualified to superintend the printing department of our Mission, had been long urged by me upon our Committee in London, as necessary to my emancipation from a mode of employment, which, however important as an auxiliary to the Mission, was imposing an additional weight on my constitution, and was more *secular* in its character, than was consistent with my feelings as a Missionary in a heathen country. At length my wishes were partly realized; though not in time for the preservation of my health. A short time previous to my leaving Colombo, a person sent from England to manage the printing department, arrived at Colombo; a circumstance which afforded me the most heartfelt satisfaction.

The preparations for our removal from Colombo being now completed, another, and that a severe trial,

* Appendix.

yet remained—to quit the scenes of so many interesting events, and to tear ourselves from persons who had manifested towards us so strong an attachment, and to whom we felt ourselves united by no ordinary ties. The last day we remained at Colombo was spent with our invaluable friend, Archdeacon Twisleton, and his family, at his residence, and we left the town in his carriage. The Governor and his lady condescended to take a most friendly leave of us. His Excellency added to his former kindnesses, by furnishing me with an introductory letter to his friend, the Under Secretary of State in London.

As we were likely to be detained at Galle, waiting for the vessel, for some days, a general meeting of the Missionaries who could conveniently attend was convened, that some arrangements, rendered necessary by my departure, might be made. At this meeting, John Anthonietz, and Don Cornelius de Silva Wijasinghe, were received on probation as Missionary Itinerants. An address from the Missionaries thus assembled was presented to the Governor, on the suppression of the Kandyan rebellion, which was most favorably received.*

The Mission appeared, from the statements made at this meeting, to be in a state of progressive improvement. At the request of my brethren, I preached a farewel discourse before them in the Galle Mission-House, selecting for my text, Isa. xli. 6, *They helped every one his neighbour; and every one said to his brother, Be of good courage.*

The spirit of genuine catholicism, by which the various denominations on the island were distinguished, had often contributed to our mutual comfort, and furthered the cause of our common Saviour.† My com-

---

* The Address, and His Excellency's gratifying Reply, were both inserted in the Government Gazette shortly after.

† Appendix.

mission was opened at Colombo, in the chapel of the Baptist Mission there; during my residence on the island, I had frequently preached in the Presbyterian and Episcopalian churches; and my last sermon was delivered in Portuguese, at the chapel of my valued friend, Mr. Griffiths, the Baptist Missionary at Galle, from Heb. iv. 9. *There remaineth therefore a rest to the people of God.* During our stay at Galle, we resided at the hospitable mansion of Mr. and Mrs. Gibson, and received from them every attention which friendship could suggest.

Our voyage commenced on the 9th of February. On the 12th our fourth child was born. Mrs. Harvard was much favoured in the recovery from this confinement; and the beneficial effects of the voyage, were soon pleasingly visible in her appearance. As our vessel carried a number of invalid soldiers and their families, I formed and superintended a day-school on the quarter deck, for the benefit of all the children on board. It was often a gratifying employment to visit the sick on board, some of whom died on the passage, affording hopes that they had not heard in vain. And on the Sabbath we generally had prayers and a sermon on the deck. May the seed thus sown, appear in some future day. On our voyage home, we touched at St. Helena and the Cape of Good Hope; and we landed at Falmouth in the latter end of July.

In arranging the materials for the present Narrative, I have necessarily been led to retrace the steps which led to my employment in that field of honourable exertion. Possessing a heart alive to the endearments of friends and country; both of which were renounced when I entered upon the work; though my body and soul have frequently bent beneath the weight of the duties it imposed; and though I returned to my own country with a constitution shattered, and the prospect of a premature grave; yet, calmly reviewing all *the way which the Lord hath led me,* I reckon that the trials and sufferings I have endured, are not worthy to be compared with the comforts I enjoyed, and the prospects by which my soul was animated in the Missionary cause. With a deep conviction of my insufficiency for a work so arduous, I count it the highest honour of my life that I was permitted to embark in it. Neither discouragement, disaffection, nor disgust, occasioned my return. Nothing but a conviction that my life could (humanly speaking,) be preserved by no other measure, induced me to abandon my post.

A missionary spirit, I trust, still animates my bosom; and, were my bodily strength restored, I would gladly embark again in the same glorious undertaking; in which case I would prefer the island of Ceylon to any other field of missionary labour of which I have any knowledge. But bereft of that strength, I would animate my Christian brethren, of every denomination, who are able to sustain the labour, to go forth *to the help of the Lord against the mighty.*—To those who are engaged in preaching among the heathen *the unsearchable riches of Christ,* and to the promoters and conductors of Christian Missions in general, I address the animating exhortation of the Apostle, *Be ye stedfast, unmoveable, always abounding in the work of the Lord; forasmuch as ye know that your labour is not in vain in the Lord!"*

APPENDIX.

No. I.—*Introduction*, p. xxix.

THE circumstances which led to the dethronement of the last Kandyan king are, happily, of a cast seldom paralleled in the history of mankind. The sad relation needs no poetic colouring, in order to interest the tender emotions of the reader, to whom I shall take the liberty of presenting it on the authority, and in the language, of Dr. Davy. Having noticed the origin of a misunderstanding between the king and *Eheylapola*, his first Adikar, in consequence of which the latter resorted to arms in self-defence, and fled to the British territories, after having been defeated by the king's forces, the Doctor proceeds: " Hurried along by the flood of revenge, the tyrant, lost to every tender feeling, resolved to punish Eheylapola, who had escaped, through his family which remained in his power: he sentenced the chief's wife and children, and his brother and his wife, to death; the brother and children to be beheaded, and the females to be drowned. In front of the queen's palace [and between two celebrated temples] as if to shock and insult the gods as well as the sex, the wife of Eheylapola and his children were brought from prison, where they had been in charge of female jailors, and delivered over to the executioners. The lady with great resolution maintained her's and her children's innocence, and her lord's; at the same time submitting to the king's pleasure, and offering up her own and her offspring's lives, with the fervent hope that her husband would be benefited by the sacrifice. Having uttered these sentiments aloud, she desired her eldest boy to submit to his fate; the poor boy, who was eleven years old, clung to his mother, terrified and crying; her second son, nine years old, heroically stepped forward; be bid his brother not to be afraid—he would shew him the way to die! By one blow of a sword, the head of this noble child was severed from his body: streaming with blood, and hardly inanimate, it was thrown into a rice mortar; the pestle was put into the mother's hands, and she was ordered to *pound it*, or be *disgracefully tortured*. To avoid the disgrace, the wretched woman did lift up the pestle and let it fall. One by one, the heads of all her children were cut off; and one by one, the poor mother—but the circumstance is too dreadful to be dwelt on. One of the children was a girl; and to wound a female is considered by the Singhalese a most monstrous crime: another was an infant at the breast; and it was plucked from its mother's breast to be beheaded. When the head was severed from the body, the milk it had just drawn in, ran out, mingled with its blood!

" During this tragical scene, the crowd who had assembled to witness it, wept and sobbed aloud, unable to suppress their feelings of grief and horror. *Palihassane* Dissave was so affected that he fainted, and was expelled his office for shewing such tender sensibility. During two days the whole of Kandy, with the exception of the tyrant's court, was as one house of mourning and lamentation; and so deep was the grief, that not a fire (it is said) was kindled, no food was dressed, and a general fast was held. After the execution of her children, the sufferings of the mother were speedily relieved. She and her sister-in-law, and the wife and sister of *Pusilla* Dissave, were led to the little tank in the immediate neighbourhood of Kandy, called Bogambarawave, and drowned. Such are the prominent features of this period of terror, which, even now, no Kandyan thinks of without dread, and few describe without weeping. Executions, at this time, were almost unceasing; the numbers put to death cannot be calculated; no one was perfectly secure,—not even a priest, not even a chief priest; for *Paranataley Anoonaika Cunnansi*, a man in the estimation of the natives, of great learning and goodness, fell a victim to the tyrant's rage. To corporal punishments, imprisonments, &c.—those minor causes of distress,—it is unnecessary to allude; in the gloomy picture they are as lights to shades.

" Disgusted and terrified by the conduct of the king, the chiefs and people were ripe to revolt; and only waited the approach of a British force to throw off their allegiance.

" Acquainted with what was going on in the interior, it was impossible for our government to be unconcerned. His Excellency Lieutenant General (now General Sir Robert) Brownrigg prepared for hostilities, which seemed to be unavoidable. He had stationed a force near the frontier, in readiness to act at a moment's notice; and he had made arrangements for invading the Kandyan provinces should war break out.

"Cause for declaring war soon offered. Several of our native merchants, who in the way of trade had gone into the interior, were treated as spies, and sent back, shockingly mutilated;* and very soon after, a party of Kandyans passed the boundary, and set fire to a village within our territory. The declaration of war against the Kandyan monarch immediately followed this act; it was made on the 10th of January, 1815. On the day following, our troops entered the Kandyan territory; they found the *Three* and *Four Korles* in a state of revolt, and they were soon joined by *Molligodde*, the first Adikar, and many of the principal chiefs. Almost without the least opposition, our divisions reached the capital; on the 14th of February our head-quarters were established there; and on the 18th the king was taken prisoner. Forsaken by his chiefs, he fled on our approach into the mountainous district of *Doombera*, accompanied only by a very few attendants. Driven by heavy rain from a mountain where he concealed himself, during the day, he descended and took shelter in a solitary house in the neighbourhood of *Meddahmahaneura*, not aware that there was a force at hand lying in wait for him. The party was a zealous one, composed of natives of Saffragam, headed by a staunch adherent of Eheylapola. As soon as intimation was given of the king's hiding-place, the house was surrounded, and the monarch seized. He was sent to Colombo, and from thence to Vellore; where he is still in confinement." [1821.] *Travels*, p. 321—325.

No. II.—*Introduction*, p. xxxii.

THE VEDDAS. The following communication from the Rev. Mr. Roberts, Wesleyan Missionary at Batticaloa, contains the most recent information of this singular people, which has yet been published:—

"In the course of my journey to Trincomalee in the month of January last, I only saw one Vedah; the reason for this

"* Ten were thus treated:—their noses were cut off, and some were also deprived of an arm, others of their ears. Two only of these unfortunate men survived to reach Colombo, presenting a most miserable spectacle,—the amputated parts hanging suspended from their necks: the other eight died on the road."

I suppose was, that the waters being much out near the coast, they had retired farther than they usually do into the interior. But on my return to Batticaloa I met with nine of these wretched sons of Adam, three men, four women, and two boys. They were exceedingly shy, and had it not been for an old Vedah, who informed me he had several times seen Europeans before, they would have been altogether inaccessible. Without any hesitation he accompanied me to the shed where I had to spend the night, and seemed much gratified with the attentions he received. After some conversation I inquired if he had any family; he replied in the affirmative. Where are they? ' In the jungle." Here I observed he was a little discomposed, but his fears were soon silenced. I wish you would bring your family here. ' They will not come.' Why? ' They have never seen a white man; they are much afraid, and besides this they are at a great distance.' But after using many persuasions and the promise of a gift, he set off into the jungle with a promise soon to return.

"After the lapse of a considerable time I heard some loud shrieks, apparently made by persons in great distress. On inquiring of the coolies as to the cause of the noise, they said the Vedah was bringing his family, and they were much afraid. I immediately went into the jungle in the direction of the noise, but the poor distracted creatures no sooner saw me than they gave a dreadful scream, and again rushed into the thicket. The Vedah said I must remain in the hovel, or they would never come near; upon my promising to remain in the place, he set off again after his distracted family. For a considerable time I heard him call aloud in the forest without receiving any reply; at last they answered, and begged he would not take them again; he answered, that they would not receive any harm, and that the great man had promised to give them some good thing. At last they consented to come, on condition that he walked first, and that they were allowed to remain at a distance.

" I, of course, remained in the Bungaloe, and the family, consisting of the father, mother, son, and daughter, stood before me. A short time after this another family made its appearance, who had probably heard the noise. They, however, on seeing some of their tribe so near, appeared less timid, and joined themselves, though not without caution, to the group. I have often heard it asserted that they have a language of their own: differing materially from Malabar or Singhalese. I called the old man, and asked him what language they used: he replied, 'Singhalese and Tamul.' Have you no other? 'No.' But in what language were those people conversing? 'Singhalese.' I found upon examination, it was nothing more than corrupted Singhalese, which my boy in the first instance could not understand. I suppose the difference does not amount to more than that which exists between the dialects of the Northern and Southern counties of Britain.

"Their Tamul was equally barbarous. They pronounced it very short, and made one word serve for many purposes. But thinking they still might have a language peculiar to themselves, I requested the old man to tell me the names of different things in all the languages they knew; these I found agreed invariably either with Tamul or Singhalese.

"I observed one little boy apparently much agitated, and succeeded, through his father, in quieting his fears; but in putting out my hand to take hold of him, he cried out and ran into the jungle with the swiftness of a deer: upon inquiring the cause of his alarm, the father replied that the Moormen sometimes stole their children, and they were seldom heard of again; two of his children had been taken from him in this way, but they had died of grief. I asked him to place one under my care, assuring him I would be the child's father, and give him plenty of rice and curry, and good clothes. 'Alas!' said the father, "what can I do; two are gone, and if you were to take one, he would die as the other did, and I should see him no more.'

"I was much surprised to see them have some tattered clothes about their bodies, as I had heard they were in a state of complete nudity. I asked where they procured the cloth: the answer was, that the inhabitants of distant villages gave it in exchange for honey, wax, and elephant's teeth. Some of them had a quantity of glass beads about their necks, which had been acquired in the same way. I offered the old Vedah a piece of bread which I had brought from Trincomalee, which he ate without any hesitation, but the others refused to taste, stating they were much afraid. On pulling out my watch I observed that it excited considerable attention, and I prevailed on them to come near to hear the beating, and they were much astonished and afraid, particularly so, when they observed the rapid revolution of the seconds hand; this led them to retire to their former place.

"I inquired of the old Vedah, where they slept? 'On the trees.' But where do your wives and children sleep? 'On the trees.' But how can they climb! 'It is their nature.' Do you marry? 'We do not marry: we take a woman, and when we are tired of each other, we part and seek another.' What do you eat? 'Such things as we can get!' And what are they? 'Roots, deer's flesh, honey, and fish, when we can catch it.' Do you ever catch elephants? 'Yes.' How? 'We shoot them with the bow and arrow, and follow them till they fall.' What religion are you? 'I do not know what you mean.' Where do people go after death? 'We do not know.' How many Vedahs are there in those forests? 'We cannot tell.' Are there 500? 'Yes, more.' Are there 1000? 'We cannot tell.'

"It was now become quite dark; and observing some of them very impatient, I began to think what would be the most acceptable as a present: I had neither beads or knives with me, so I ordered the boy to bring a large cotton sheet, and divide it into pieces, and present them to the two oldest women; this, I saw, was a most acceptable present. The rest of the group began to look rather anxious, but I gave to them some fanams, with which they were also pleased, as they could purchase salt and other articles to be had only for money. Upon my telling them they might go, they immediately retired into their much-loved jungle.

"I shall not soon forget the wildness of expression in their features, particularly in the eye; their hair was disordered and brown with the sun. I could think of no comparison to mark the difference betwixt them and my coolies, than that which exists betwixt a wild beast just brought from the forest, and one that has been tamed. Their state is alike calculated to excite the attention of the Philosopher and the Divine. By comparing the poor Vedah with the Malabars who live in villages, he sinks almost to the brute. For his subsistence he has to depend upon the productions of the jungle, such as roots, plants, and fruits, or the uncertainties of the chase; and lives and dies like his shaggy companions of the forest."

Missionary Notices, Jan. 7, 1823.

No. III.—*Introduction*, p. xxxvii.

Through the kindness of Archdeacon Twisleton, I obtained a copy of the " *Statement of Portuguese Cambawadda, Jowan Mendoze, of the village of Wohakatto, in the Audagodde Corle, Matala District, about eight miles N. West of Nalande.*"

" I am head of the Church, but not a Padri. I am called, in consequence, Saint Christian. There are about two hundred of us professing the Roman Catholic Religion. I have a Singhalese Testament written by a Portuguese Padri, (a native of Portugal) named Jacob Gonsalle. I have also several prayers written upon olas.

" After the expulsion of the Portuguese from the Kandyan country, by Raja Singha, some prisoners were captured, who were not permitted to quit the interior, but had lands granted them: the following villages were appropriated for their residence, viz. *Waauda, Calogalla,* and *Wahakotto;* about the same time a number of Malabar Christians established themselves at a place called *Galgamma,* in the Seven Corles, three days' march from Putlam, where there is now a fine large church, with about two hundred people professing Christianity.

" The village of *Waauda* is situated in the Seven Corles, and *Callogalla* is in Toompany. The people of *Wahakotto* are the descendants of Portuguese, as were the former inhabitants of Waauda and Coloogalla, who were deprived of their lands, and driven out of the country, in consequence of joining and assisting the Dutch in the invasion of the interior. Such of them as could not effect their escape were murdered; and there now remains no vestige of them or Christianity in those parts of the country. On the borders of the Lake at Kandy, at a place called *Bogambera,* was the principal church, and twelve Padries were attached to it. King Koondasala, who was third successor to Raja Singha, would not allow the Roman Catholic Religion to be exercised in his dominions, and caused the principal church of Bogambera, as also the inferior ones throughout the country, to be destroyed, and ordered the Padries to quit it.

" King Kierty succeeded Koondasala, and it was during his reign that the Christian inhabitants of Waauda and Caloogalla were expelled. Shortly after this event, a great famine and plague raged in the interior. The King, attributing the cause of those calamities to the persecution of the inhabitants of the last named villages, ordered the images which had adorned the church of Bogambera, and had on its destruction been deposited in his stores, to be given to the people of Wahakatto, with permission to rebuild their church, and enjoy their religion.

The younger brother of Kierty (name unknown) succeeded him, who allowed them the full enjoyment of their religion, as did the late King; and they have not been interfered with since the reign of Kierty.

The Kandyans call them Portuguese. They are considered on a footing with the Vellalahs, and perform the same duties as people of that class.

No. IV.—*Introduction*, p. xlv.

The following is the Singhalese pronunciation of a few of their domestic phrases. (*a* as in *hat*.)

Bread	*Poo'-peh*	Salt	*Loo'-no*
Butter	*Doon'-tell*	Rice	*Ha'-rl*
Fish	*Ma'-loo*	Tea	*Tey*
Beef	*Da'-dey-mas*	Sugar	*See'-nee*
Fowl	*Kook'-oo-lang*	Spoon	*Hen'-deh*
Chicken	*Kook'-ool-pe'ttoa*	Large	*Loe'-koe*
Cock	*Kook'-oo-la*	Small	*Poon'-tchee*
Hen	*Kee'-kel-ee*	Little	*Tik'-ka*
Drake	*Ta'-ra-wa*	Table	*Mey'-cey*
Duck	*Ta-ra-wee'-a*	Chair	*Poot'-too-a*
Eggs	*Bee'-joo*	Stool	*Baunk'-oo-a*
Milk	*Kee'-ree*	Sofa	*Lo'-e-baunk'-oo-a*

The accentuation of some of the principal proper names, &c. incidentally occurring in the work, may also be acceptable to the reader:—

Amb-lan-god'-de	Ma'-tu-ra
Bat-ti-ca-lo'a	Mo-han'-diram
Baz-za'r	Mo-de-li'ar
Bel'-li-gam-me	Mor-rot'-to
Ben-to'tte	Ne-go'm-bo
Cal'-tu-ra	Pan'-tu-ra
Co-lom'-bo	Trin-co-ma-lee'
Col-pet'-ty	Vel-lal'-lah
Cha'-li-a	Wel-le-wat'-te
De-wel'-lah	Wol-fen-dahl.

No. V.—*Introduction*, p. 1.

THEY SACRIFICE TO DEVILS. The remarks of the learned Dr. Whitby on this passage are so just and pertinent, that they are here inserted, with a view of confirming the application which has been made of them to the awful state of the heathen world at large. " Here Le Clerc saith, ' The Greek word doth not necessarily signify devils or evil spirits; for the heathens did not always sacrifice to evil spirits, if we consider what were their true thoughts.' But the wisdom of God did not think fit to consider the *speculations* of some of their philosophers; but what was indeed their practice, and what the object and directors of their worship were, and who was gratified by it. They pretended to own a supreme deity; but the spirits which spake in the oracles they consulted, which moved their idols and resided in them, and set up, and promoted their whole idolatrous worship, were doubtless *evil spirits;* and so the primitive Christians engaged to force them to confess themselves to be, even before those who paid homage to them. The pulling down of this idolatrous worship is, in our Saviour's language, *the casting out of the prince of this world.* (John xii. 31. and xvi. 11.) The converting the Gentiles from this idolatry to the worship of the true God is *the turning of them from* THE POWER OF SATAN *unto God;* (Acts xxvi. 18.); *the delivering them from the power of darkness,* (Col. i. 13.), who before walked according to THE PRINCE *of the power of darkness,* (Eph. ii. 2.), and were *led captive by* SATAN, at his will. (2 Tim. ii. 26.) The Psalmist, according to the Septuagint, saith that *all the gods of the heathen* ARE DEVILS. (Psal. xcvi. 5.) And of the Jews who sacrificed to them, it is said *they sacrificed to* DEVILS *and not to God;* literally, *to evil, wasting, and destroying spirits.* The Jews said the same of the Gentiles, that they were sacrificing *to* DEVILS *and not to God;* (Baruch iv. 7.); and so they are also styled, 2 Chron. xi. 15. and Rev. ix. 20.; and so all Christians ever did expound *this place;* and with good reason, it being absurd to think St. Paul is here dissuading Christians from having fellowship with good angels."

On the same subject, in reference to the primitive superstition of the Ceylonese, a quotation from Mr. Bisset's first Sermon before the Colombo Auxiliary Bible Society may be deemed a confirmation sufficiently authentic:—

" Nor is there much greater reason to expect a more scrupulous regard to the obligations of sincerity and truth, from those who, through default of Christian instruction, have relapsed into the superstitions of *their ancient idolatry*. The chief part of their worship appears to be an adoration of *malevolent spirits* upon the most servile principles of fear. It is not before *such altars* that a life of integrity, innocence, and truth, or a contrition for past offences, can be supposed an acceptable oblation. Gifts, offerings, and voluntary privations, may well be considered the most grateful sacrifice to those *malignant demons;* and while the deluded victim of superstition hopes to bribe the forbearance of their vengeance, instead of purifying his morals, and correcting his vicious passions, he deadens every feeling of guilt by lulling all apprehension of punishment." *Sermon,* p. 14.

" The chief adoration of the uninformed Singhalese is addressed to *the vindictive deities or demons, worshipped in the Dewallahs.* The word *Dewallah* is a compound, signifying the residence of an inferior deity. The account given by Robert Knox is in this, as well as in most other instances, perfectly correct. He says with great gravity—' Indeed it is sad to consider how this people are *subjected to the Devil*; and themselves acknowledge it to their misery, saying *their country is so full of devils and evil spirits*, that unless in this manner they should-adore them, they would be destroyed by them.' " *Ibid. Notes,* p. 32.

No. VI.—*Introduction,* p. lvi.

Not only is it probable that the Chinese *Foh,* and the Ceylonese and Siamese *Budhu,* are the same person; but the learned Jesuit, Father le Comte, in his entertaining Letters, traces the origin of *Fohism* in China to a communication with the island of Ceylon; from whence the Siamese also profess to have received their popular superstition. Having given an interesting account of Confucius, Le Comte adds: " The Chinese report that he had frequently this saying in his mouth, *It is in the West, where the true saint is found:* and this sentence was so imprinted upon the spirit of the learned, that, sixty-five years after the birth of our Saviour, and nearly 500 years after the death of Confucius, the emperor MIM-TI, touched with these words, and determined by the image of a man that appeared to him in a dream, coming from the West, sent ambassadors that way, with strict orders to continue their journey till they should meet the saint whom heaven had acquainted him with. It was much about the same time that St. Thomas preached the Christian faith in the Indies. Now, if these Mandarines had followed his orders, peradventure China might have received benefit from the preaching of this apostle. But the danger of the sea, that they feared, made them stop at the first island,* where they found the idol *Foh*, who had corrupted the Indies several years before with his damnable doctrine: they learned the superstitions of the country; and, at their return, propagated *idolatry* and *atheism* in all the empire. The poison began at the court; but spread its infection through all the provinces, and corrupted every town.

" Nobody can well tell where this idol *Foh*, of whom I speak, was born; (I call him an idol and not a man; because some think it was an apparition from hell.) Those who, with more likelihood, say he was a man, make him born above a thousand years before Jesus Christ, in a kingdom of the Indies, *near the line;* perhaps a little above Bengal. They say he was a king's son. He was at first called *Che-kia;* but at thirty years of age he took the name of *Foh*, and was on a sudden possessed, and, as it were, filled with the divinity, who gave him an universal knowledge of all things. From that time he became a god; and began, by a vast number of seeming miracles, to gain the people's admiration. The number of his disciples [priests] is very great; and it is by their means that all the Indies have been poisoned with his pernicious doctrine. Those of Siam call them *Telapoins,* the Tartars *Lamas* or *Lama-sem*, the Japoners *Bonres,* and the Chinese *Hocham.*"

London 8vo. edit. 1738, *p.* 200 *and* 326.

The following sketches of *Chinese Fohism,* in so many respects resembling the *Budhuism of Ceylon,* is subjoined, from the pen of a highly respectable Protestant Missionary, whose very recent death cannot but be deplored by the friends of the Mission cause.

" The Chinese, however, are more generally (at least since the introduction of Budhuism) believers, with the Pythagoreans and Indians, in the doctrine of the transmigration of the soul from body to body; a doctrine which

* Dr. Robertson's Observations on Chinese Navigation already quoted, p. 24, seems to fix Ceylon as the Island here mentioned.

hangs in terrorem over the serious and thinking among them. It is affirmed that some will have to pass through 'eight hundred millions of different bodies!'

"Perfect stillness, silence, and an entire extermination of the passions, feelings, and even thoughts, is considered by the followers of *Foh*, as the perfection of virtue, and the only sure passport to their imaginary paradise.

"Their system of morals, as explained by the learned, contains much that is good. Many of the duties of relative life are set forth with as much clearness, as could be asserted from a people who know not the true God.

The *Elysium* of the West, which the followers of *Foh* look for, is such as the deluded imagination of an Asiatic would naturally paint. Fortified palaces—groves of trees, producing gems—pools of fragrant water, yielding the lotus flower as large as the wheel of a cart—showers of sweet odours, falling on a land, the dust of which is yellow gold—myriads of birds of the most exquisite plumage, singing on trees of gold, with the most harmonious and ravishing notes of a hundred thousand kinds, &c. &c.

"The sufferings of the *Tartarus*, which their terrified imaginations have figured, are represented in pictures as the punishments in purgatory and Tartarus were exhibited in the Eleusinian and other heathen mysteries; with this difference, however, that these are exposed to public view—those were seen by the initiated only. Red hot pillars, which the wicked are caused to embrace—devouring lions, tigers, snakes, &c.—mountains, stuck all over with knives, on the points of which the condemned are cast down, and seen weltering in gore—cutting out the tongue—strangling—sawing asunder between flaming iron posts—the condemned creeping into the skins of those animals, in the form of which they are destined to appear again on earth—boiling of the wicked in caldrons—the wheel, or apparatus, by means of which all the operations of the metempsychosis are performed—horned demons, with swords, spears, hatchets, and hooks—wretched mortals, alternately shivering with indescribable cold, and burnt to coals with devouring fire:—these, with numberless other such things, are represented with gross and disgusting minuteness.

"But it would be endless to mention the different parts of their complicated system, in which scarcely any thing but darkness, confusion, or absurdity, is palpable. In this gloomy labyrinth, to look for a system of religion suited to the condition of man, and adapted to make him wise, and virtuous, and happy in this world, and eternally blessed in that which is to come, would be as vain as to seek the reviving light of the sun in the thick darkness of midnight."—*The late Dr. W. Milne's Retrospect of the Ultra Ganges Mission*, p. 34. 8vo. *Malacca*, 1820.

No. VII.—*Introduction*, p. lviii.

PRESERVED IN THE PRINCIPAL TEMPLE OF KANDY. "The tooth of Budhu," remarks Dr. Davy, "is, by the Budhuists, considered *the most precious thing in the world*, and the palladium of the country; the whole of which is dedicated to it. It was brought by the daughter and nephew of the king of Kalingoonratte, when in danger of falling into the hands of a neighbouring monarch, who made war for the express purpose of seizing it." In the rebellion in 1817, this sacred relic having been clandestinely obtained by the insurgents, it became a mighty instrument in forwarding their nefarious plans, and in inspiring their adherents with confidence of the ultimate success of their cause. Its subsequent recovery by our government naturally produced an opposite effect on their minds. From the author of the preceding observations, the following description of the relic is also inserted. " Through the kindness of the governor I had an opportunity (enjoyed by few Europeans) of seeing this celebrated relic, when it was recovered, toward the conclusion of the rebellion. It was of a dirty yellow colour, except toward its truncated base, where it was brownish. Judging from its appearance, at the distance of two or three feet, (for none but the chief priests were privileged to touch it,) it was artificial, and of ivory, discoloured by age. Never a relic was more preciously enshrined. Wrapped in pure sheet-gold, it was placed in a case just large enough to receive it, of gold, covered externally with emeralds, diamonds, and rubies, tastefully arranged. This beautiful and very valuable bijon was put into a very small gold *karandua*, (a kind of dome or casket,) richly ornamented with rubies, diamonds, and emeralds: this was enclosed in a larger one, also of gold, and very prettily decorated with rubies: this second, surrounded with tinsel, was placed in a third, which was wrapped in muslin; and this in a fourth, which was similarly wrapped; both these were of gold, beautifully wrought, and richly studded with jewels: lastly, the fourth karandua, about a foot and a half high, was deposited in the great karandua. Here, it may be remarked, that when the relic was taken, the effect of its capture was astonishing, and almost beyond the comprehension of the enlightened. *Now, the people said, the English are indeed masters of the country; for they who possess the relic have a right to govern four kingdoms: this, for 2000 years, is the first time the relic was ever taken from us.* And the first Adikar observed, 'That whatever the English might think of the consequence of having taken Kappitipola, Pilime Talawe, and Madugalle, (the three principal rebel chiefs) in his opinion, and in the opinion of the people in general, the taking of the relic was of infinitely more moment!" *Travels*, p. 367—369.

No. VIII.—*Introduction*, p. lxiii.

NESTORIAN MISSION. " The first writer who mentions the introduction of Christianity into the island of Ceylon, is Comas Indicopleustes. He found in the sixth century Christian churches established in Ceylon, as well as in most of the cities of India which he visited. These churches were subject to the Nestorian Primate, from whom their priests received ordination. It does not appear from Ribeyro's account, that any remains of Christianity existed at the time of the Portuguese settling in Ceylon, A. D. 1517. This French translator thinks the natives had all relapsed into idolatry; but that some traces of the old Christian government were to be observed in the discipline of their heathen priesthood. I have therefore said that Christianity was first established in Ceylon by the Portuguese, because we know very little of the Nestorian churches, founded by the Persian Missionaries or merchants: and it seems probable, that during the nine intervening centuries, between the time of Cosmas and the settlement of the Portuguese at Colombo, they had fallen into complete decay."—*Notes to the Rev. G. Bisset's Sermon*, p. 28.

No. IX.—*Introduction*, p. lxix.

DECAY OF CHRISTIANITY IN CEYLON. " The consequence of this lamentable want of religious information has been an alarming relapse into idolatry: for, so congenial to every proper feeling of the human heart is the spirit of religion—so intimately connected with the hopes and fears of man is the belief of a Supreme Being, and a controlling Power exalted far above the reach of mortal strength—that if the true faith be neglected, false religions will prevail: if the Divine grace and quickening spirit of Christianity be suffered to languish, superstition and idolatry will take an easy possession of the vacant breast. But, whether from this deficiency of Christian instruction, the uninformed native has degenerated into a mere outward profession of Christianity, or taken refuge in the ancient superstitions of his country, the general effect upon the public morals has been alike pernicious. In the one case, a sluggish indifference has stifled every spark of vital principle.—Where there is neither hope of future reward to animate, nor dread of consequent punishment to deter, what bar is there to the indulgence of every vile and vicious passion? what restraint to the perpetration of every crime, wherever immediate detection and punishment are not apprehended?"—*Sermon by the Rev. G. Bisset, p. 11.*

No. X.—p. 157.

His Excellency Governor Brownrigg.

Extract from the Missionary Notices for Nov. 1820.

" CEYLON. The following Letter from the Wesleyan Missionaries in Ceylon, to His Excellency Sir Robert Brownrigg, Governor of that Island, and his Excellency's kind and condescending answer, will be read with pleasure by all those who, with Christian solicitude and good will, have watched the rising interests of that Mission from its commencement.

" *To His Excellency, General Sir Robert Brownrigg, Bart. and G. C. B. Governor of the Island of Ceylon, &c. &c. &c.*

" MAY IT PLEASE YOUR EXCELLENCY,

" We have learned with the most sincere concern, that this favoured Colony is likely very soon to be deprived of your Excellency's residence and paternal government; an event, which we beg leave to say will be very sensibly felt, not only by ourselves, but by every member of our Mission family, resident in the Island. Previous to your Excellency's departure, we feel particularly desirous of communicating some additional assurance, that every respectful feeling of esteem and gratitude which we have had the honour and happiness to cherish in our hearts towards your Excellency, from our first arrival in the Island, continues unalterably the same, with the exception, that succeeding occurrences have tended very greatly to increase and strengthen them; and we earnestly intreat you will favourably receive this as our humble apology for troubling you on this trying occasion.

" We are, indeed, sorry that, in consequence of our members being so widely dispersed over the Colony, most of them will necessarily be deprived of the happiness of uniting with us at this time; yet such is our union and oneness of feeling, especially in the grateful, respectful esteem we ever feel for your Excellency, that we beg, as an additional favour, you will kindly allow us to include all their names with those of our own.

" As this may be the last opportunity we shall ever be favoured with of addressing ourselves to your Excellency in this country, we wish to record in the most lasting manner possible, that your condescending, kind, and friendly demeanour towards us, during the whole of our residence in this Island, has invariably been such as to render your Excellency's name and government ever dear to us all; and we feel assured, that neither time nor circumstances will ever erase from our hearts those grateful feelings which have been created by unnumbered acts of voluntary kindness. It would be exceedingly difficult for us to retrace minutely the many pleasing occurrences to which we now refer, and which, by your Excellency's kind influence, have continued to accompany our efforts from the commencement of our Mission; yet we frequently recur to them with pleasure and delight; and the recollection of the many past favours which we have received, fills our hearts with the sincerest gratitude, and naturally excites in our minds very anxious feelings at the prospect of your Excellency's approaching departure. Notwithstanding, however, we shall, to the latest period, feel a gratifying pleasure in associating your Excellency's name with the success which has hitherto blessed our labours in Ceylon. We must beg your condescending indulgence for the freedom we take, in expressing our sentiments in so familiar a manner; but almost every thing connected with present circumstances gives rise to reflections in our minds, which are exceedingly difficult to be expressed.

" Before we conclude our present communication, we cannot deny ourselves the pleasure of presenting to your Excellency our sincerest congratulations upon the great and lasting satisfaction it must afford you when retiring from the Colony, to leave it in so tranquil and improving a state; not but that your Excellency has had difficulties to contend with, and difficulties of the most trying and painful nature; yet, by the continued smile of a kind Providence upon your great and persevering exertions, the disquietude that threatened us is completely calmed, and we not only enjoy peace and quiet in all our borders, but so far as our knowledge of the state of the Colony extends, the cheering countenance of civil and commercial interests, and much moral and religious improvement; but here we can speak with more confidence, and from our peculiar situation, reserve would ill become us.

" From the most correct accounts we have been able to collect, it appears that even the nominal profession of Christianity was but in a languid state among the natives, on your Excellency's arrival in this Island. The opportunities of improvement, and the means of instruction for the native population, were exceedingly inadequate, and by no means answerable to the claims they had upon the attention of the Christian world; circumstances which, wherever they exist, will be lamented by reflecting minds. But the period to which we now refer, was a happy era to the native inhabitants of Ceylon. The first great and effectual attempt that was made in their behalf, was the establishment of the Auxiliary Bible Society under your Excellency's immediate patronage and support, for the purpose of publishing the Sacred Scriptures in their own languages. The Society has been enabled to extend its active and spirited operation into almost every part of the Island. It has already sent abroad about 3000 copies of the New Testament; and 3500 more will shortly be ready for publication. In addition to this, it has printed about 22,000 copies of smaller works, extracted from the Scriptures, which have been every where distributed. Hence, not a town, not a village, and, in some districts, scarcely a family but has experienced its good effects. Such efforts, when viewed in connexion with other benevolent and Christian exertions, such as, the repairing and erection of large and convenient schools in the most populous neighbourhoods, for the instruction of the native youth; together with the erection of a number of commodious places of worship for the accommodation of the native Christians, to excite and encourage among them an increased attention to the visible forms of Christian devotion; must place in a very pleasing light your Excellency's ever watchful care and anxious concern for the moral and religious improvement of the inhabitants of this large Island: And we cannot but add our sincerest wishes that those plans so well laid down, and so prosperously begun, may be fully accomplished; and this we are confident will call forth the thanksgiving of generations yet unborn.

" But we must again beg your Excellency's kind indulgence while we mention another interesting fact closely connected with the improvements, moral and religious, which, for several years, have been going on under your government. We now refer to the liberal sanction and extensive countenance which the cause of Christian Missions has invariably met with from your Excellency; and it is only from a fear of being tedious, that we deny ourselves the pleasure of taking such a view of this subject as we conceive it highly deserves. When our Mission arrived in this Island, we laboured under some of the most painful disadvantages. The loss of our venerable leader, the Rev. Dr. Coke, was an event of itself almost sufficient to have discouraged us from proceeding in our work, considering its arduous nature, and our great want of experience for such an undertaking—And not having anticipated such an event, we were necessarily unprepared to meet it. Thus situated, we landed in Ceylon; but though strangers, with little to recommend us, except the goodness of the cause in which we had embarked, your Excellency honoured us with the most condescending welcome in the colony; pointed out to us our respective spheres of labour, and at the same time favoured us with many other encouragements which we cannot now enumerate, but which will ever live in our grateful remembrances.

" After a trial of several years under such favourable circumstances, it is very natural to expect that considerable success would have resulted from our attempts. On this head we have met with several things which have been cause of regret, and which, perhaps, had it been in our power, we should have ordered otherwise; notwithstanding, it is with pleasure we can state that we have had to encounter nothing hitherto, in any of our operations, that has amounted to a discouragement, but, on the contrary, we can assure your Excellency that we have met with many things to encourage us, and to satisfy our minds that our undertaking is approved of by the great Head of the Church. Hence we feel as much encouraged to prosecute our work as ever we did. We have now fourteen Missionaries resident on the Island, besides several interesting young men, both native and country-born, who promise to be very useful. Several of our brethren have attained a competent knowledge of the native languages, and are devoting almost their whole attention to the improvement of the natives, by preaching to them, and instructing them both in public and from house to house. They also spend much of their time in making useful and necessary translations either of the Sacred Scriptures, or of little works of a religious kind. We hope also that the literature of the Island will, ere long, be considerably advanced by their publications, both of Dictionaries and Grammars of the language, as well as some translations of the native books which are in a state of forwardness, but which have never yet appeared in any European language. As our great object is to instruct the natives in the principles of Christianity, we endeavour to make all our pursuits subserve this desirable end: and as our holy religion can only be properly embraced by the natives of India from the clearest conviction of its great superiority over every other religious system, we are sensible that these changes can only be accomplished, under a Divine direction, by the regular diffusion of instruction among them. This persuasion led us some time back to resolve upon the establishment of Christian schools, to bring forward the children in the knowledge of their own language; and in a considerable number of these schools, the English language is taught with the most flattering success. But while we endeavour to make the rising generation acquainted with the first rudiments of learning, we study at the same time to accompany these instructions with such others of a religious kind, as we are convinced will answer the designs of our Mission. And on your Excellency's leaving the Colony, it may not be uninteresting to be informed, that we have so far succeeded in these attempts, as to have established in different parts of the Island, about 72 schools, which include 4591 children, all under daily instruction; and every child thus instructed, is seen and examined by a Missionary, at least, once a month. From this system of schools, conducted on such plans, the most moderate calculation will be in favour of their proving greatly beneficial, especially to the rising generation: and though it becomes us to speak with diffidence, when we pronounce an opinion on what is still future, we cannot but entertain the most pleasing anticipations of the result of such a combination of effort as is now displayed in this Island by the Bible Society, Tract Societies, and Missionary Societies, all of which are actively employed in dispersing abroad the light of Divine truth, and helping forward the great attempt which contemplates nothing less than the complete triumph of our holy religion over every prevailing system of heathenism. It is an effect which is not confined to the Island of Ceylon. The spirit and disposition are predominant in almost the whole Christian world; and it will, we have no doubt, be a soothing reflection to your Excellency in a future day, that during your Excellency's residence and government in a heathen country, you had an opportunity of taking so public, so honourable, so Christian a part in the great work. May it please a merciful Providence to prolong your Excellency's continuance in this life for many years, and may your Excellency be favoured to hear from these distant regions, that every hope, every wish you may have formed with respect to the moral and religious improvement of the native Singhalese, has been very abundantly accomplished.

" We shall not cease to recommend your Excellency, and also your amiable family, to the continued protection of a kind Providence when on the great deep; and shall constantly implore Him who has the uncontrolled command of winds and seas, graciously to vouchsafe every blessing and protection necessary both for a safe and pleasant voyage; and we beg to repeat the assurance that the most grateful and respectful esteem of our whole Mission, will ever continue to accompany your Excellency's name.

" Repeating our intreaty that you will excuse our troubling you at so great a length, we have the honour to remain, with the greatest respect and esteem, your Excellency's greatly obliged, ever thankful, and ever humble servants.

" Signed on behalf of all the Wesleyan Missionaries in Ceylon,

" B. Clough,
" G. Erskine."

" *Mission-house, Colombo,*
Jan. 25, 1820."

THE GOVERNOR'S ANSWER.

" *To the Brethren of the Wesleyan Mission.*

" Gentlemen,

" It is with a lively sense of satisfaction that I have received your respectful and affectionate Address.

" From the first moment of my entering upon the government of this Island, I considered the religious improvement of the people to be of paramount importance. It is, therefore, most gratifying to me to hear you, Gentlemen, who have devoted your lives to the promotion of Christianity, speak in high terms of my co-operation, and to know that the measures of my government, in aid of your Missionary labours, have been sanctioned by the testimony of your warm approbation.

" On this ground nothing can be more acceptable to my feelings than your strong expressions of gratitude, however they may attribute to me a degree of merit which I am not entitled to claim. The chief ends that I have had in view, were the happiness of the people confided to my care, and the honour of my own country, to which I was responsible for the sacred trust.

" It was, therefore, my bounden duty to foster and encourage the attempts of those who came forward with their voluntary assistance towards both of these great objects, by communicating that which it is our glory to spread, as well as to enjoy, and labouring to enlighten the people of this foreign land, by a diffusion of that religious knowledge, with which Providence has blessed our own.

" That I was influenced by motives of another kind, that I felt the full obligation of propagating, for its own sake, the Divine truth of that religion which has been throughout life the source of my consolation and hope, I would rather choose to be collected from my conduct, than received upon any assurance of my own professions.

" But it is unnecessary to dwell upon my sincere zeal for a wide extension of the Christian faith, as if it were independent of other motives; because it is, in fact, inseparably connected with the duties of my political office; it is the surest foundation upon which I could hope to build the permanent welfare and happiness of the people, whom I have been deputed to govern.

" It would be to me a subject of most afflicting regret, if I were to leave this Island, after presiding over it in the name of my king for almost eight years, without a conviction that some desirable improvement had been commenced under my temporary rule. I hope and trust that I may take my leave of Ceylon, without any cause for such a mortifying reflection; whatever may have been the progress hitherto, I confide in the goodness of Providence for producing hereafter, effects corresponding with my laborious and persevering exertions for the public good.

" If I were to quit my government without some public expression of my respect and esteem for the Brethren of the Wesleyan Mission, I should be insensible alike to the general claims of their meritorious conduct, and to the gratitude which I owe them for their zealous aid in promoting those objects which I had so much at heart.

"From the beginning, Gentlemen, of your settlement with a few Missionaries in this Island, until the present moment, when the number of your Brethren is augmented to fourteen, your exertions have been principally directed in that course, which is, I think, for the attainment of your Christian purpose, the most secure and direct.

"The numerous schools established under the vigilant superintendence of your Mission, forming a most extensive system of public education, cannot fail to produce a most beneficial effect upon the morals and habits of the rising generation. There can be no doubt that even among the native people who call themselves Christians, the earliest application of religious instruction will be most likely to make a deep impression upon the youthful mind, which has not been hardened by the prejudices and corruptions of a maturer age, and to convert a nominal profession into a sincere reception of the Christian faith. But when our observation is turned to that large part of the native population which yet wanders in heathen darkness, the superior advantages of early education are still more striking snd apparent.

"The native adult, who professes Christianity, is not unwilling to hear, though little disposed to retain lessons of religious and moral instruction.

"But avowed heathens are averse even from listening to the teacher, who would convince them of their errors. The strong hold of superstitious idolatry is then only accessible by a pre-occupation of the children's minds with a better knowledge; and it is remarkable, that however the Budhist, or Hindoo, may themselves revolt from the pious attempts of Missionary conversion, so desirous are they of improving their young families, that they gladly send them to the Wesleyan schools, and freely permit them to learn the first rudiments of Christianity. The prevailing wish also to have their sons acquire the English language as a means of advancement, stimulates this general disposition with the powerful excitement of personal interest. This favourable state of opinion upon the subject of education, gives among all castes of natives a fair opening, of which the Wesleyan Mission has taken full advantage; and from their numerous schools it is but reasonable to expect the most beneficial results.

" The great influence of the press is exercised with more or less effect over every civilized country in Europe; but here where it was so much wanted, it was utterly unknown. It was rare that any publication ever appeared in a language intelligible to the people, except a Regulation of Government. The children had nothing to learn, their parents had nothing to read. But the Wesleyan Missionaries have established a press, from which there is such a continual issue of elementary works of devotion, morality, and science, that the native population is at length gradually admitted to a participation in the riches of European knowledge.

" The first and last object of human learning is the knowledge of salvation, attainable through the Holy Scriptures; and to that it is natural for a Missionary union to turn their chief attention, and apply their most strenuous efforts. Supported by the friends, and encouraged by the patronage of the Colombo Auxiliary Bible Society, it is from the Wesleyan press that the Scriptures are now given to the Singhalese, and will, ere long, there is reason to hope, be supplied in abundance to every native of Ceylon.

" Thus much I have said to shew the grounds for my belief, that this Island is already much indebted to the Wesleyan Mission: it will be still more indebted, when their system of education is completed, when a sufficient number of scholars have been trained up to superintend the pious work, and the Missionaries themselves can settle and live among the natives, converse freely with them in their own language, and give them all the benefit of present example, enforcing the pure doctrines and precepts of the Gospel.

" Now, Gentlemen, I take my leave of you, thanking you for your kind assurance of esteem, as well as for your prayers for my safety: in return I wish you most sincerely an ample share of prosperity and happiness, with the fullest success in the great object of your Mission.

" That your efforts may be guided by Providence to a joyful termination, is indeed a wish that I shall always cherish with a warmth in proportion to the fervent interest which I feel, in whatever may contribute to the security, comfort, and blessing of the island of Ceylon.

" ROBERT BROWNRIGG."
" *King's House, Colombo,*
   Jan. 30, 1820."

p. 260.

From the Ceylon Government Gazette, Wednesday, April 19, 1815.

" DEATH. At Batticaloa, on the first instant, after a tedious illness of three months, *The Reverend* WILLIAM AULT, one of the Wesleyan Missionaries, who arrived about a year ago. His sincere piety, his ardent zeal, indefatigable industry, and modest unassuming manners gained him the esteem and respect of all at that station, both Europeans and natives. Possessing rare qualifications for the meritorious and useful work which he had undertaken, his success, in the short space of eight months, in raising among a numerous body of natives, but nominally reformed Christians, at that place, a respect for, and a decent observance of at least the external form of religion, was truly remarkable. And although he had not to boast of having made any converts from either the Heathen or Mahometan Faith, to that of Christianity, yet, by the establishment of eight schools for the education of Hindoo children; and by his talents and address having so far overcome the scruples and prejudices of their parents, as to introduce the reading of the New Testament as the only school-book to the more advanced scholars, he has laid the foundation for a most extensive propagation of our Faith."

The above (written by an eminent civilian, who honoured our deceased brother with his intimate friendship) expresses the estimation in which Mr. Ault was held at the place of his immediate labours. The following document, which explains the object for which it was issued, Mr. Ault having died intestate, places on record the favourable opinion formed by the Supreme Court of Judicature of the character of the Mission generally.

In the Supreme Court of Judicature, in the Island of Ceylon. GEORGE THE THIRD, by the Grace of God of the United Kingdom of Great Britain and Ireland, King, Defender of the Faith.

In the matter of the Goods of the late Reverend Mr. WILLIAM AULT, Missionary, deceased.

As the Court is anxious to shew the sense, which it entertains of the great benefit which the inhabitants of the country have derived from the establishment of the Wesleyan Missionaries on this Island, and the confidence which it reposes in the Society of which they are members. IT IS ORDERED, that the Registrar do consult with the Reverend Mr. HARVARD, as to every point which relates to the Estate of the late Mr. AULT now under his official administration, and that he do adopt in the course of his administration of the said Estate, such measures as may be deemed by the Reverend Mr. HARVARD most agreeable to the Wesleyan Society itself, as well as most consolatory to the feelings of the relations of the said Mr. AULT; and as it appears, upon the suggestion of the Reverend Mr. HARVARD, that it will be attended with considerable convenience to the Missionaries here, as well as to the relations of the late Mr. AULT, if the proceeds of the sale of the late Mr. AULT's effects should be forthwith remitted through the Wesleyan Society to his said relations. IT IS FURTHER ORDERED, that the Registrar do forthwith take such steps as may be necessary for carrying the said suggestion into effect.

WITNESS THE HONOURABLE SIR ALEXANDER JOHNSTONE, Knight, Chief Justice at Colombo, the twentieth day of May, in the year of our Lord, One Thousand Eight Hundred and Sixteen, and of our Reign the Fifty-sixth.
T. W. VANDERSTRAATEN,
Acting Registrar.

No. XI.—p. 159.

THE REV. ANDREW ARMOUR. In introducing to their friends some extracts of letters from this deserving individual, the Wesleyan Missionary Committee in their *Monthly Notices* for February, 1816, have given the following summary of his previous history:

" The highly esteemed friend from whom the Committee received the following letter, is a convincing proof of the power of the Lord to save, and the happy influence of vital goodness. The pious soldier has sometimes, by the gracious providence of God, been the instrument of planting the Redeemer's standard in distant lands, and of holding forth the word of life to the perishing heathen. The account which he gives of himself in a former letter will be gratifying to our readers:—" From the year 1787 to 1792, I was a member of your society, and in the army. In the last mentioned year, on going to Gibralter, I was made the instrument of establishing a society, which, I am happy to understand, remains till this day. From Portugal I sailed for India, in the year 1798; since which time I have not had the smallest correspondence with your society. In 1800 I arrived here, where, since the beginning of 1801, I have been at the head of the high school at this place, and have thus an opportunity of qualifying myself, in some degree, for the work dearest to my heart—that of preaching the Gospel.

" For a number of years, different circumstances seemed to combine together to thwart my wishes in this respect; but in the year 1810, Providence began to open the way before me; and ultimately, in 1812, by the removal of the last surviving Dutch clergyman on the island, every obstacle was removed. I was licensed to preach in Singhalese, and to that long and greatly neglected people, the Portuguese, so called. In these languages I preach as the Lord enables me; and though I cannot yet boast of much fruit, I have great reason to believe that my poor labours are not altogether in vain. It is all my desire to spend the remainder of my days in spreading the fame of the Saviour, whose grace made me happy in a humble station, through the instrumentality of the people called Methodists. I beg, therefore, that you may still consider me as belonging to your Society. Remember me when you lift up your hearts to the mercy-seat of our common Lord."

" Letter from Mr. A. Armour, to the Missionary Committee.

" *Colombo, September* 1, 1815.

" I had the pleasure of writing a few lines to you shortly after the arrival of your Missionaries at this place; giving you to know a little of my own history, and requesting that you would consider me, as still a member of your society, and devoted to the interest of your Missionaries. Your little band has suffered considerable diminution since they left England; but our loss we have no doubt, is the infinite gain of those deceased. With regard to the surviving Missionaries, the Lord has hitherto helped them:—and they all bid fair for being useful in this country. I cannot say, however, that I am without fear concerning them;

nay, I do fear that intense labour will soon injure their constitutions. And how are they to be kept from labouring? Only by their getting more help. For my own part, 1 am labouring according to my poor abilities, in concert with the Missionaries, and intend so to do as long as I live.—I feel it good to be united to the people of God: and God does meet with us, even in this benighted and thirsty land. We have hopes that the cause of religion will prosper in this place; but still we have great reason to complain of our little success. Dear Brethren and Fathers, pray for for us; for much we want your prayers. Oh! pray that the power of religion may continue among the few who seek his face in this part of the world, and that the same may emanate from them to all around. And, Oh that you might think it expedient to send us more labourers: be assured of this, that you will never be able to send a sufficient number! Oh! what a field for missionary labours in this island! No doubt your own Missionaries will give you a better idea of it than I am able to do. Give me leave, however, to assure you, that the fields are white abroad to the harvest. Yes, I think the natives are, at the present time, more ready than ever to receive the Gospel;— but, alas, for hundreds of thousands of them! for how are they to hear without a preacher?

" I recommend myself, along with your infant cause in this island, to your favourable notice, requesting above all, a special interest in your prayers; and beg leave to subscribe myself,
" Dear Brethren and Fathers,
" Your unworthy brother in the Lord,
" A. ARMOUR."

" Extract of a Letter from Mr. ARMOUR to the Secretary, the Rev. JAMES BUCKLEY.

" *Colombo, Nov.* 16, 1816.
" MY DEAR BROTHER,

" I received your letter of the 17th of December last, on the 17th June this year: and beg leave to assure you and my very dear Fathers and Brethren of the Committee, that the same proved a very great blessing to my soul; a blessed and timely stimulus to my humble exertions in the great work of spreading the savour of a Saviour's name.

" The kindness of my dear Fathers and Brethren, in

taking so much notice of me, fills me with inward shame; for I am surely not worthy of so much notice.

"Yes, my dear brother, from my long acquaintance with the Methodist connexion, I know that the end, the sole end which the Methodists have in view, is the conversion of sinners of every clime, and of every sort, from the error of their ways, and to save immortal souls from death. Any other end than this would be an unworthy one. To this great end the Methodists have evidently contributed much, since the time that the venerable Wesley began his missionary career: even the enemies of Methodism cannot deny this. And still the great work goes on: it is the Lord's work, and he will accomplish it. Blessed be God for the days which the world now witnesseth. Blessed be God that the heathen can no longer say, that no man careth for their souls; for lo! the Missionaries of the cross are going forth in every direction, preaching repentance to the heathen world, and remission of sins through the atoning blood of Christ. And here is work enough for the whole Christian world. Alas! my brother, what are all the exertions of Christendom, when compared to the wants of the heathen. I speak from experience. Men do not learn Christianity intuitively: man by nature knows not God.

"On the 13th instant, I returned from visiting a place about 34 miles from Colombo, and only about six or seven miles from the sea-beach. My visit was in consequence of the inhabitants having petitioned Government to grant them a school, and afford them the means of Christian instruction. Poor creatures, on my coming to speak with them, I discovered with sorrow that scarcely any one of them had so much as heard that there is a God; and any of them that had heard of a Supreme Being, had been taught to disbelieve every thing of the kind. But my dear brother, it is not the ignorance of the Ceylonese which most discourages the Christian Missionary; it is rather their credulity, superstition, and want of firmness. I do not know, that ever a Christian minister has been contradicted in his endeavouring to teach the Singhalese: they rather seem to take it for granted, that what he says is right and true, so far as it regards Christian nations. But they have among them cunning and designing men, who are too successful in making the untutored Ceylonese believe, that the white man's religion does not answer them. Nor is it the priests of Budhu that stand most opposed to Christianity. Budhuism of itself is evidently tottering; and were it not in league with *devilism*, I think that it would soon fall to the ground: but this is now actually the case. The priest of Budhu, while he denies the existence of an all-creating power, acknowledges the existence of innumerable demi-gods and demons. Houses, called Dewallas, are erected, in which the effigy or portrait of the devil, to whom the place is dedicated, is generally placed. A person generally known by the name of Kapoorawla, (the termination *rawla* is one of respect) pretends to have power over, or interest with, the supposed devil. The priests of Budhu support the fraud, and these Kapooas support Budhuism.

" These devils are supposed to be going about, seeking to work mischief on the bodies of men; and hence it is that every sickness and every adversity that befalls them, is supposed to be through the agency of the devil. The Kapoa is applied to: he persuades them to this belief, and that the devil must be pacified with sacrifices and offerings. The patient makes his offerings and sacrifices, and the Kapooa enjoys them: and if the patient get better, the devil is supposed to have been appeased; but if he dies, the devil is supposed to have been implacable. Nor do the Kapooas and designing priests rest here. After the death of a person, whose sickness proved incurable, the surviving relatives are given to understand, that the devil, not being propitiated, is determined to take revenge on the survivors; and that their house will be haunted, &c. unless they make further offerings and sacrifices. And thus the Kapooas find a means of subsistence, by avowedly serving the devil in this manner. Sometimes a priest of Budhu takes upon him to act the part of exorcist, pretending to propitiate and expel the devil. If not, the priest begins where the Kapooa leaves off; pretending to have power in the invisible world; they will tell the surviving relations, that they have procured, or can procure a happy transmigration: and thus they in their turn must reap their reward.

" Thus it is with the Singhalese, and thus it will be, I greatly fear, till by dint of missionary exertions, the darkness of such abominable superstition shall be dispelled.

" Blessed be God, the day begins to dawn, and nothing shall be impossible with God. But O my dear brother, let the people of England, who long to see, and would rejoice to see the conversion of the heathen world, assist their Missionaries with their earnest prayers. Let the Missionary Societies join the Missionaries themselves, and devoutly pray, Help, Lord, for vain is the help of man. And let every possible aid be afforded to the Missionaries, in order to give efficiency to their labours and endeavours: in order to meet with ultimate success, suitable means must be afforded.

"So far as I am acquainted with your Mission in this island, I consider Galle to be the best station as yet: I do hope, however, that your Committee will receive favourable accounts from all the stations. I return you many thanks, my dear brother, for the two sets of magazines which you had the goodness to send me, and wish very much to send you something from Ceylon; but at present I do not know of a single thing that would be acceptable to you.

"Present my hearty affection to all my dear Fathers and Brethren composing your Committee: God knows that I sincerely love and highly esteem them every one. And that Heaven's best blessings may descend on you, is the earnest prayer of,

"My very dear brother,
"Your's, affectionately,
"ANDREW ARMOUR."

No. XII.—p. 239.

PETRUS PANDITTA SEKARA. The following Sermon by this early convert, in which he gives an outline of his own change, has been considered as likely to be more interesting to the reader, than the account referred to in the narrative; especially as some extracts from that document have been already made. The style of the Sermon is peculiarly eastern; and its simplicity rendered it especially suitable to his own countrymen. It was one of the first he composed.

SERMON.

"*Brethren, if any of you do err from the truth, and one convert him, Let him know, that he which converteth a sinner from the error of his way, shall save a soul from death, and shall hide a multitude of sins.*"—JAMES V. 19, 20.

"Beloved brethren, to err from the truth, is to err from the true religion. The Apostle James says, If one could convert a heathen, he would save a soul from death: that is, he whose soul was in danger of being lost, by continuing in a wrong way, is led into the right way, which leads to eternal life, and is saved. The multitude of his sins is covered, or prevented from being brought against him.

"Beloved brethren, there are a great number of religions in the world, but of which one only can be the true religion, for all cannot be true. Therefore, that must be the true religion, which admits a Creator, and one only everlasting God. Now, if one, with a hope of saving his soul, turns his back upon the religion of this eternal God, and worships another, his labour may be compared to a famished foolish kid, that endeavours to suck the horns of its mother, instead of the teat. Some religions deny the everlasting God, who created the world. But how, it must be asked, can a rational person believe them to be right? No man can see the soul; yet, from the motions, feelings, and other actions of the man, there can be no doubt of his having a soul. Therefore, my friends, cannot you be convinced, from this wonderful world, and the various parts of creation, namely, the heavens, earth, sea, sun, moon stars, men, &c. and their regular organization, that there is a God, and all thes are in his works; and likewise, can't we consider that these things cannot be made by themselves, and that it is impossible so to be.

"If the world was created by itself, and not created by God, how is it possible that the wonderful events thereof should remain invariably the same, without the interposition of God? Will ever a puddy field be ploughed properly, by the oxen alone, without a husbandman? If the creation is of itself, there must be much changeableness in the world, and a want of regular system and order. As, for instance, the members of a man, such as the nose, might come in the place of the ear, and the ear in place of the nose; the chin in the place of the mouth, and the mouth in the place of the chin.

"Friends, certainly God created the world, and the many things therein. He is an *eternal Being;* he knows the events of the *past, present,* and the *future* times: he knows the thoughts of all the inhabitants of the world. If any one doubt that it is nothing but the mere obscurity which is the cause of his heathenish faith. The chicken in the egg could not see the sun, moon, and the world, being covered with a shell, and its eyes not been open; likewise, my brethren, you can't know and acknowledge the everlasting God, or believe in the Saviour, as you are covered with the shell of heathenish faith; and as you have not the light of understanding. Your eyes are not open: therefore we should rejoice and be thankful to God, and those preachers who lay before us such a just and cheerful religion of a Holy Trinity; consisting of God the Father, God the Son, and God the Holy Ghost. Who can be averse to embrace this religion, offered by those who have some efficient knowledge thereof? Surely none. The Apostle Paul says, in his Epistle to the Romans, chap. i. verse 16, "*I am not ashamed of the Gospel of Christ, for it is the power of God unto salvation, to every one that believeth; to the Jew first, and also to the Greek.*"

"Beloved brethren, I myself was one of the principal preachers of the Budhist religion, in this island of Ceylon; and during my priesthood, I not only acquired some proficiency in the Palic Sanscrit and Singhalese science; I also spent good part of my time in preaching and learning the religious books of Budhu, and of some other religions. It is well known to you, that I was much esteemed among the Budhists for my preaching; and was respected and rewarded by royal favours, and by chief ministers of state; yet I found in that religion no REDEEMER to save our souls from death; no CREATOR of the world, or a beginning to it. Consequently, I had some doubt always in my mind, as to its reality; and had some suspicion that the world and its thousands of wonderful parts, was the creation of an Almighty God. While I was reflecting on this, a conversation took place between me and the head priest of *Saffragam* district, called *Attedassa Teronansey*, of the temple of *Kottembulwalle*. He asked me, who could believe that a child (as it is said in the Christian religion,) could be conceived in the womb of a virgin? To which I answered, If the world, and all its curious things, which we see about us, were created of themselves, it is no wonder that a child should have been conceived in the womb of a virgin. Upon which the priest was somewhat displeased with me. While I was in this condition, I happened, through the blessing of God Almighty, to speak with the pious Rev. Mr. Clough, since which, I have maintained a friendship with him, and have continued to attend and converse with him concerning the Christian religion. By this means, the obscurity and doubts which were over my mind, were perfectly cleared off, and the light of the Christian faith filled my mind in their stead, as easily as colours are received into fine white linen when painted; so I consented to be baptized. While I was in doubt, a large *Mandowe* was erected, in the place called *Galwadogodde*, at *Galle*, for the performance of a very great ceremony of Budhu's religion; there were assembled twenty-eight preachers, (or priests,) including myself, and an immense crowd of common people of both sexes. During that ceremony, I read over two chapters of the Gospel of St. Matthew before the multitude, and spoke to them upon that subject in a friendly manner. Some time afterwards, the people of *Galle* district, hearing that I was at the point of leaving the priesthood, and of being baptized, gathered into a large body, and spoke in such a manner against my intended baptism, that scarcely any man could have resisted them: in consequence of which, I was in a state of perplexity for some time, being strongly inclined to be baptized, on the one hand, and to comply with their request on the other. But after my arrival in Colombo, all the hesitations and agitations of my mind were completely done away, by the sweet and admirable advice I received from the Hon. and Rev. Thomas James Twisleton, the chief chaplain in this island. Just as darkness vanishes by the appearance of the sun, I was enlightened, and was actually baptized, without regarding the aversion and abuse I was likely to undergo from the people of the Budhu's religion; giving up my relations and friends, the teachers of my former religion and the situation I was in, and the lands and other property which I obtained from the Budhu priesthood. Thus I embraced Christianity, and became a member of Christ's church, which circumstance is perhaps known to every one of you. Beloved brethren, your principal object must be, to seek the means of obtaining a happy and eternal life. You are labouring, both day and night, to support this uncertain life, yet you never think of the means of saving your soul. If you labour so much for this uncertain and temporal life, how much more ought you to labour for the salvation of the immortal soul? Are we not sinners by nature, and under the curse of God? Yes. And why do not we think of the means of being saved? We being sinners by nature, God took compassion on our sad state, and sent his only Son, Jesus Christ, into the world, to suffer punishment, and to be crucified, and to die for our sake, and to save us from our sins: He also rose the third day from death, and ascended into heaven. Now we have received the Gospel wherein are contained his own doctrines, which he delivered while he was in this world, for the direction of mankind, and for their salvation. The holy Gospel is the way to lead every man to salvation. We have many evidences to convince us of its truth, not only by the Holy Scriptures, but also in the profane histories of the ancient heathens. There is no other way of salvation except this very way by the

Gospel. Many persons in this world are worshipping images, made of wood, clay, &c. with a view of being saved by them; yet they do not consider that the images cannot hear their prayers, nor see their homages, neither accept a single thing of their offerings; consequently, those labours and services are of no use. They lead men to break the second commandment of our Creator, the Lord God. And can they be blessed of this? There are some persons who deny the existence of God, and say, Where is he? who saw him? and many such foolish words; but it is the height of stupidity; for there is no man who can judge in what way the power and grace of God is bestowed. We ought only to consider that we are sinners, and to obtain our salvation through Christ, the Son of God. There is no profit in their entertaining such false and vain thoughts; for they resemble a foolish physician, who is brought to cure a wounded man of an arrow received in a battle, who, instead of applying his remedies, quietly sits inquiring, who was the person that shot him? from whence the arrow came? what is the name of the archer? and many other long and foolish particulars, and so lets the man die. My brethren, do not entertain such vain thoughts as this foolish physician; look out for immediate remedies for salvation, pulling out the arrow of sin from you. It plainly appears to a good Christian, that the ceremonies of devils prevailing in this country, are the ways leading to death. Some one of you say, If you forbear from doing evil works, there is no need of worshipping God. But I do assure you, that no man can be saved, though he do good works, if he do not worship the Godhead, consisting of God the Father, God the Son, and God the Holy Ghost; as the man will never grow fat, though he dress and ornament himself with much good apparel and jewels, unless he also eat food. Therefore, I conjure you to do good works, from a complete Christian faith in your hearts. We must be saved by faith in Christ; by loving God, keeping his commandments, praying to him, studying his religion, and repenting of our past sins: he who errs from this way, errs from the truth. Britannia, the Queen, sent her children to shew the right way to the children of her sister Ceylonia. As a learned physician cures the leprosy with good remedies, we have good doctors to cure our false faith, and heathenish, with their enlightened doctrines. Therefore, if we are willing to be saved, why are we not saved? If a thirsty man refuses to drink pure cold water,—and if a hungry man refuses to eat delicate victuals,—and a naked man refuses to put on clean and valuable apparel,—is it not his own fault? The chief means of being saved from death, is by faith towards God; consequently, the man who has a complete faith, ought to keep God's commandments, according as they appear in the Holy Scriptures, and leave off all evil works, and do all good works. There are three things in the heart of man which lead to all manner of evil, viz. covetousness, envy, and ignorance: and thus men, in consequence of these chief evils, or on account of covetousness, envy, and the ignorance of the true religion, do sin, by word, deed, and thought; they commit murders, thefts, and adulteries: by their words, they lie, backbite, talk roughly, so as to hurt a man's feelings; take the name of God in vain, and say other bad things; and in their thoughts covet the things and property of others. They are envious of the prosperity of others, and think that there is no God; all these things happen on account of the above said covetousness, envy, and ignorance: all these evils are against his salvation. These things he ought to forsake; and ought to give alms according to his circumstances. He ought to speak courteously to others, and to conduct himself, in all his actions, so as not to be prejudicial to others, but beneficial; to consider the lives of all others as his own; these are the good works. Therefore, my brethren, let us endeavour to forsake all the aforesaid evil things, be confirmed in good works, and not to err from the right paths; but to lead those into the right paths, and to participate of the redemption of Christ, and the love of Almighty God; SO SHALL WE SAVE THEIR SOULS FROM DEATH, AND HIDE A MULTITUDE OE SINS.

The third Report of the Colombo Bible Society contains the following notice of our friend PETRUS: —

" Another example of conversion in the person of Sree Dharma Panditta Tirrunancy, chief priest of a temple in the neighbourhood of Galle, is perhaps still more remarkable; for his natural abilities and acquired learning had given him a weight and authority among his brethren that could not fail to attach him to his heathen profession. But there was nothing in the vague principles and idolatrous worship of the Budhist religion that could satisfy his acute and reflecting mind. Doubt, and distrust, and perplexity harassed his thoughts, and he began to long for some more rational system of rewards and punishments, than a succession of unconscious transmigrations: some more consolatory prospect of futurity, than a cheerless *Newana*, or the perpetual tranquillity of everlasting annihilation.

"While he was labouring under this mental anxiety, the Rev. Mr. Clough, one of the Wesleyan Missionaries, arrived, and settled in his neighbourhood. To him the wavering Budhist earnestly applied for a solution of his difficulties; and a few conversations with such an earnest advocate of Christianity, convinced him that his peace of mind would not be restored by an adherence to the superstitions of his unenlightened forefathers.

"When Mr. Clough observed his pressing inquiries upon the subject of the Christian religion were continually increasing, he presented him with one of the copies of the Cingalese Gospels, which he had received from this Society; and after a few more interviews, in which objections were started, doubtful points discussed, and difficulties explained, the priest of Budhu resolved at once to abjure the erroneous system in which he had been educated, and to profess the religion of Christ.

"One very remarkable circumstance that took place during the interval between his forming this resolution and his baptism, well deserves to be brought forward to your notice. Upon the celebration of some Budhist festival, a Bana Mandooa had been erected, and many priests were assembled from different temples to distribute alms, and preach to the people. It is customary, on such occasions, for the minister of highest rank, or greatest learning, to exhort and instruct his brethren of the priesthood in a discoure upon the virtues of Budhu, and the excellence of his religion: Sree Dharma Panditta was called upon to perform this office; but instead of choosing for his theme any of the legends of Budhist tradition, the subject that he selected was the Gospel of St. Matthew.

"To the astonishment of his yellow-robed hearers, he opened that sacred volume, and read and expounded for their edification, during the whole of the night, the authentic history of our Blessed Saviour. No tumult or disturbance arose: the priests listened with mute and respectful attention to the earnest address of one of their brotherhood, who, convinced of his own error, sought only to remove their delusion."

No. XIII.—*Inscription referred to* p. 261.

TO
CAPTAIN GUALTERUS SCHNEIDER,
Of the Royal Engineers,
𝔗𝔥𝔦𝔰 𝔆𝔲𝔭
Is presented, as a small Token of grateful Esteem,
For his kind and *gratuitous* Services, in
Superintending the Erection of the
WESLEYAN MISSION ESTATE
IN COLOMBO:
By his Faithful and Obliged Friends, and Servants,
THE WESLEYAN MISSIONARIES.

Colombo, August, 1817.

No. XIV.—p. 263.

PUBLICATIONS. The following works were issued from the Mission Press from August 1816 to December 1818:—

English.

1, A Sermon in the Kandyan Provinces, delivered in the Governor's Tent, by Mr. Bisset.—2, Sunday School Union Spelling Book, Part I. *four editions*, 4000 copies.—3, 4, Second and Third Part ditto, *two editions*, 2500.—5, Fletcher's Address.—6, Hopkin's Ten Commandments.—7, Baldæus's Jaffnapatam.—8, Abridged Hymn Book.—9, Wood's Catechism; each 500.—10, Gospel Warning, a Sermon on the Death of John Jenny, *two editions*, 2500.—11, Fox's Geography and Solar System, 600.—12, Callaway's Abridgment of Sutcliffe's Grammar, 500.—13, Ditto Extracts from Dyche's Guide, 1000.—14, Hymn Book for Baptist Mission.—15, Milk for Babes, for ditto, 500 each.—16, Alphabets, Class Papers, &c. for Native Schools, 30,000.—17, Annual Reports, and Anniversary Sermons of Colombo Auxiliary Bible Society.—18, Assembly's Catechism for the Dutch Consistory, 500.

Dutch and Portuguese.

19, Catechism for the Dutch Consistory, 500.—20, Wood's Catechism.—21, Wesley's Instructions, 500 each.

—22, Fox's Short Catechism.—23, Ditto First Lessons *two editions each*, 3700.—24, Ditto Portuguese Hymns.— 25, Portuguese Liturgy, each 250.—26, Newstead's Portuguese Hymn Book.—27, Ditto Sermon on the Mount, 800.—28, A Religious Book for the Roman Catholic Mission, 500—29, Portuguese Common Prayer Book for Archdeacon Twisleton, 500.

Singhalese.

30, The New Testament, *demy quarto, for the Bible Society*, 1000.—31, Part of an Edition of ditto, *demy octavo*, 3500, *ditto.*—32, Our Lord's Parables.—33, Ditto Miracles, 1000 each, *ditto.*—34, Green's Principles, *for the Colombo Treatise* Society, 1000.—35, Dialogue on the Bible Society, between a Mohandiram and his Friend, by Sir Hardinge Gifford, *for ditto.*—36, Folly of Idolatry, *for ditto*, 1000.—37, Wesley's Instructions.—38, Wood's Catechism, each 500.—39, Clough's Translation of the Liturgy, *two editions*, 3000.—40, Ditto with the Offices, or occasional Services, 500.—41, Callaway's Vocabulary, English, Singhalese, and Portuguese, 500.—42, Ditto Spelling Book, *two editions*, 2500.—43, Ditto Two Word Books, 3400.—44, Fox's Dictionary, Portuguese, Singhalese, and English, 400.—45, Prayers for Catechumens, 1000.—46, The Lord's Prayer, Te-Deum, Ten Commandments, &c. 2000.—47, Hymn Book, 1000.—48, Dialogue between a Budhist Priest and a Christian Missionary, 3000. [This tract is annexed.]—49, The old Catechism, for the Government Schools, 1500.

Tamul.

50, Our Lord's Parables.—51, Ditto Miracles, *for the Bible Society*, 1000, each.—52, Folly of Idolatry, *for the Treatise Society*, 1000.—53, Wesley's Instructions.—54, Wood's Catechism, 1000 each.—55, Prayers, &c. (No. 45) 1000.—56, Part of Mr. Squance's Tamul Grammar, &c. &c.

A CONVERSATION

BETWEEN A

BUDHIST PRIEST AND A CHRISTIAN MISSIONARY,

AT BELLIGAMME.

Missionary.—Good morning my friend.—Will you give me leave to ask you a few questions about your religion?

Priest.—Very willingly, Sir, if they are not too difficult; for I am not very learned in the religion.

M.—Pray how long have you been in the situation of a Budhist Priest?

P.—Only about twenty years.

M.—Then I suppose you are able to answer any question about the Budhist religion, as you have studied it for so many years.

P.—Sir, there are so many books of our religion, that it would take a man's whole life to understand them all; and hence it is that I cannot engage to answer any difficult questions relative to it.

M.—That is very candid: tho' I fear such a hard religion cannot be good for poor ignorant people.

P.—Yes.

M—But I will promise not to ask any questions of a learned nature.—Will you be so good as inform me to whom it is you pray, and make your offerings in your temple, from time to time.

P.—To Budhu and to his Sermons.

M.—But why do you pray to Budhu?

P.—Because he was a god.

M.—I rather think, my friend, that you are mistaken there.—Did you never hear of two Budhist books, called Raja-ratnaw-Cary, and Raja-Vally?

P.—I have heard of them, but never read them.

M.—Well, I have got them translated into the English language: and those books say that Budhu was the son of a king, in Dambadiva, or the main land of India; and that he came over to Ceylon, and established here.

P.—It may be so. Our religion teaches that Budhu was a good man, who, by his holy life and excellent Sermons, became afterwards a god.

M.—My friend, you must be aware that there is a great difference between a man and a god.

P.—Certainly there is.

M.—How then can you think that Budhu, who was but a man like yourself, should become a god? And how can you honour him as a god, by building temples to him, and bowing before his image, when your own religion tells you he was once but the son of a king, and hence only a man like yourself?

P.—But he was a good man.

M.—Allowing that he was a good man, still that does not constitute him a god.

P.—But Budhu preached excellent doctrines, and we worship him on account of his doctrines.

M.—I doubt the goodness of some of his doctrines; tho' others of them may be good.

P.—They are all good and true.

M.—Do you not believe that a good man may sometimes say false things through ignorance?

P.—Certainly.

M.—But we ought not to follow his ignorance, even supposing him to be a good man, if we can get, at the same time, better instruction.

P.—We are very well satisfied with our religion, and do not want to be taught any new religion. You are a gentleman from Europe, where there are a number of learned people. Your religion is good for you European gentlemen; and our religion is good for us Singhalese people.

M.—But have not Singhalese people souls, as well as Europeans?

P.—I suppose they have; but we cannot tell much about those high things.

M.—My friend! believe it:—Singhalese people have souls as well as others; and it as much concerns them to know the true doctrine as it does Europeans!

P.—The doctrines of Budhu are all true; and we have lived in this faith for many generations.

M.—Budhu may perhaps have been a good man; but I think all he said was not true.—Did not Budhu teach that there is no Supreme Creator and God? and that all things in the world made themselves?

P.—The learned priests of our religion say that the world made itself.

M.—That is a doctrine which I cannot believe, because it cannot be true. Every thing must have had a beginning; and hence must have had a Maker. All things were made by the great God, who himself never had any beginning, and will never have any end.

P.—We have not learned that in this country.

M.—What would you think if the Aratchy of this place were to publish it abroad that there was no Modeliar in this district; and that therefore the people must pay all their respect and obedience to him the Aratchy?

P.—I should think he was mad.

M.—But what would the Modeliar do, if all the poor people were to pay him no kind of respect, but were to take their presents and make all their obedience to the Aratchy?

P.—Of course he would be very angry.

M.—Ah! my friend! Budhu is the Aratchy: God Almighty is the Modeliar. The people of this country pay no respect to God Almighty. They are worshippers of Budhu, but none worshippers of the true God! Surely God must be angry with such a people! Let me advise you to think seriously of this! To the good and true doctrines of Budhu, I would recommend you to pay the strictest attention. But remember the Modeliar is greater than the Aratchy; and there is a God in Heaven who is greater than Budhu, and the Maker and Preserver of us all. Think of that God! Pray to that God! Strive to please that God! Be sorry that you have lived so many years without knowing him! And begin to pay him the worship which is due! If you confess your sins he will pardon you, for the sake of our Lord Jesus Christ: and will give you his Holy Spirit to make you good; that you may go to Heaven when you die, and live with him for ever. "This is a faithful saying, and worthy of all men to be received; that Jesus Christ came into the world to save sinners."—" God so loved the world, that he gave his only begotten Son, that whosoever believeth in him should not perish, but have everlasting life."—" Ho! every one that thirsteth! Come ye to the waters: and ye that have no money, Come ye: Come, buy wine and milk, without money and without price."—" The spirit and the bride say Come, and let him that heareth say Come, and whoever will, let him come, and take of the water of life freely."—" Blessed are the people which are in such a case : yea, blessed are the people whose God is Jehovah."—" If thou seek him, he will be found of thee ; but if thou forsake him, he will cast thee off for ever."

THE LORD'S PRAYER.

Our Father which art in heaven. Hallowed be thy Name ; Thy kingdom come; Thy will be done in earth, as it is in heaven : Give us this day our daily bread ; and forgive us our trespasses, as we forgive them that trespass against us : And lead us not into temptation : But deliver us from evil : For thine is the kingdom, and the power, and the glory, For ever and ever. *Amen.*

THE GRACE.

The Grace of our Lord Jesus Christ, and the love of God, and the fellowship of the Holy Ghost, be with us all evermore. *Amen.*

Having been especially favoured by the insertion of our notifications in the Government Gazette, it has been suggested as desirable to preserve the following extracts in this Appendix.

I. *Advertisement and Contributions in favour of the Missionary Place of Worship in Colombo, designated the Wesleyan Mission House.*

To the Editor of the Ceylon Government Gazette.

SIR,

Having been solicited, by some of your constant and respectable readers, to publish the subjoined Advertisement and List of Subscriptions, I have taken the liberty to forward them to you, and to request the favour (should they not encroach too much on your columns,) that you will be so good as to insert them in your weekly paper.

I have the honour to be, Sir,
Your obedient, humble Servant,
W. M. HARVARD.

Main Street, Pettah, June 11, 1815.

AN ADDRESS TO THE INHABITANTS OF COLOMBO, &c.

The Wesleyan Missionaries beg leave respectfully to lay before the kind friends of Christianity in this Province, that they have for some time deeply lamented the situation of the Pettah and its suburbs, with respect to Christian knowledge—many of its inhabitants are without any opportunity of Religious Instruction; and many, especially of the poorer class, are seriously sunk in their moral condition.

The Missionaries take the liberty to say, that, in their opinion, the state of this people is in a great measure owing to the want of interest in their religious concerns; and that, if some additional attention were devoted to them, they humbly hope their increased improvement would more than repay it.

In this they are confirmed by the fact, that the few meetings they have already established for religious purposes, have been considerably encouraged by the inhabitants of the Pettah and its suburbs; and, they are happy to add, that a reformation is already perceivable in some, and that several others appear very desirous of religious instruction.

These appearances, together with the pressing solicitations of several who have offered to assist so far as their circumstances will enable them, have encouraged the Missionaries to attempt the erection of a Place of Worship in the suburbs of the Pettah, for their accommodation.

For this purpose they have made the purchase of an estate, chiefly occupied by old buildings, and situate in Cayman's Street, nearly opposite Mr. Cadell's residence. And, though their plan is as plain and economical as possible, yet the expence will be rather considerable, added to the original purchase-money of the estate.

On this account the Missionaries humbly and earnestly request the kind assistance of those who wish well to the Christian cause, and who may consider their plan as likely to prove useful. They beg the liberty to say, they will be thankful for the smallest Donations, and assure their kind friends, that their benevolence shall be most carefully disposed of, and, they trust, will not " lose its reward."

Main Street, Pettah, June 11, 1815.

APPENDIX. 367

[LIST, No. 1.]

SUBSCRIPTIONS ALREADY RECEIVED.

	Rix Dol.		Rix Dol.
His Excellency Lieut-Gen. Sir R. Brownrigg, K.G.C. Governor, &c. &c.	500	James Gay, Esq.	50
		J. Badger, Esq.	100
		W. Tolfrey, Esq.	50
The Honourable Sir Alex. Johnston, Knt. Chief Justice	500	C. Layard, Esq.	50
		E. Bletterman, Esq.	20
		S. D. Wilson, Esq.	50
The Honourable John Rodney	100	R. M. Sneyd, Esq.	20
		John Hart, Esq. Bombay	175
The Honourable R. Boyd, Esq.	250	Mrs. Hart.	87 6 Frs.
		Lieutenant-Col. O'Connell.	50
The Honourable J. W. Carrington, Esq.	100	Lieutenant Col. Gordon.	50
		Captain Bates.	20
The Hon. and Rev. T. J. Twisleton	100	Captain Prager.	20
The Rev. G. Bisset	200		
Colonel Kerr, Commandant.	100	P.S. As several Gentlemen, desirous of promoting this undertaking, have not yet favoured us with the amount of their intended Subscription, we hope, on a future day, to insert the list of Subscribers complete.	
Colonel Young.	100		
Dr. High.	100		
James Sutherland, Esq.	50		
A. Cadell, Esq. Pay-Master General	100		
E. Tolfrey, Esq.	50	W. M. H.	

[LIST, No. 2.]

To the Editor of the Ceylon Government Gazette.

SIR,

I beg the favour of you to insert in your next paper the following list of Subscriptions towards our intended Place of Worship, which we have received in the course of the last few days; and have the honour to remain,

Your obliged and obedient Servant,

W. M. HARVARD.

Main Street, Pettah, June 26, 1816.

	Rix Dol.		Rix. Dol.
H. R. Sneyd, Esq. Provincial Judge of Galle	100	C. A. E. Raymond, Esq.	50
		Anonymous	35
L. Sansoni, Esq.	50	J. F. Lorensz, Esq. Fiscal	25
J. Campbell, Esq. Quarter-Master of His Majesty's 73d Regiment	50	Mrs. and Misses Lorensz	25
		C. C. Unlenbeck, Esq.	25
		J. Gambs, Sen. and Jun.	35
The Clerks of the Colombo Commissariat, viz. The Messrs. Lansberg, 25 r. ds. Conderlag, 20. Treck, 15. Murtier Jonklans, Schrooter, Vandendriesen, Jantz, Mattice, and Kelart, 5 r. ds. each	100	Mrs. Fretz, Sen	40
		Mrs. Potken	30
		D. C. Fretz, Esq.	50
		J. Burnand, Esq.	30
		The Clerks of the Columbo Cutchery. The Messrs. Frisken, 10. Blacker, 10. De Vos, De Run, and Dias, 5 each	35
Mr. C. Carr, Fort Constable	30		
Barend De Waas	100	Mr. C. W. Hoffman	25

APPENDIX.

	Rix Dol.
The Messrs. J. Holst and B. Brohier	20
Mr. J. W. De Waas	16
Messrs. R. Morgan, P. Jonklaas, B. Alviz, J. P. Siebel, C. A. Spaas, C. G. Kalenberg, F. Smith, H. J. Doebratz, W. Kelart, Jongbloed Schokman, 10 each	110
The English Lodge of Ancient and United Free Masons, No. 419	20
Anonymous	50
Messrs. Storke, Vandendriesen, and Micholle	30
Messrs. P. Jantz, G. Dupuy, P. Ebert, H. T. Labrony, J. Heyse, Dr. Lorentz, J. Coopman, J. Labrooy, J. Ebert, P. Gratian, H. De Run, C. Pfieffer, N. Bergman, A. Martensteyn, A. C. Jantz, A. De Vos, H. P. Claassen, Potger, P. Kalenberg, T. Loos, 5 r. ds. each	100
Sundry small sums	31
Mrs. Wouter's Children	3
Mr. Lorenson	6
Mr. R. and M. Williams	10
The Messrs. H. W. Calenberg, P. T. Nonis, J. B. Ludekens, J. H. Maas, F. C. Vaneyck, W. T. and J. A. Shomagher, Mathyaz, Pfieffer, J. Brohier, N. C. Ernest, 5 r. ds. each	65
Mr. Andrew Bratt	15

P.S. The Missionaries request the indulgence of their kind Friends, if, through inadvertence, any of them should find their names to have been omitted. This they will endeavour to remedy in a future list.

[LIST, No. 3.]

To the Editor of the Ceylon Government Gazette.

SIR,

I have taken the liberty to transmit you the names of a few more kind Subscribers towards our intended Place of Worship in the suburbs of the Pettah, and which I beg the favour of you to insert in your next paper; and trust our generous friends will favour us with the same candid indulgence which they have hitherto kindly exercised towards us, should any of them discover their names to have been inadvertently omitted.

I have the honour to be, Sir,
Your obliged and obedient Servant,
W. M. HARVARD.

Main Street, Pettah, July 10, 1815.

	Rix Dol.
H. Giffard, Esq. Advocate Fiscal	200
E. W. Mead, Esq. Provincial Judge of Calpentyn	100
W. Granville, Esq. Collector of Galle	45
T. Eden, Esq. Provincial Judge of Colombo	50
A few Friends at Jaffna	100
The Clerks, &c. of the sitting Magistrate at Colombo, Mr. J. Krikenbeck, Sec. 15, E. W. Staats, 5, J. J. Ondatjie, 5, G. Kriekenbeck, 6, Bon J. F. Dias, 10, Gregory De Zoyzas, 10	51
W. A. Kriekenbeck, Esq. Notary Public	15
Mr. D. Gratian	15
Mr. J. G. Hillabrand	15
Messrs. J. G. Andriess, L. W. Lourenz, J. H. Demmer, 10 r. ds. each	30

	Rix Dol.
Messrs. A. N. Martensa, P. M. Ondatjie, Waanderwall, S. Calpooram, J. W. De Neys, H. De Haan, Dr. Touissaint, G. T. Ebert, W. Ferwerde, G. Siergertz, J. Isaackz, J. C. Barber, M. F. Dickman, W. T. Ledulx, 5 r. ds. each	65
Sundry small sums	12
John Gerard Kriekenbeck, Esq. Advocate	10
A Corporal	10
The Rev. Mr. Armour, Cingalese and Portugese Preacher	50
The Rev. Mr. J. J. Perara, Cingalese Preacher	25
The Rev. Christian David, and a few of the Malabar Congregation at Columbo	75
The Rev. Mr. Oudatjie, Malabar Preacher	25
The Rev. Mr. Franciscus, do.	25
Mrs. Sutherland	10
M. Dias, *Lama Etena*	10
Louisa Jeronymus, *Lama Etena*	15

NATIVE CINGALESE HEADMAN.

	Rix Dol.
Don David Hangakoon, Maha Modeliar	50
Louis De Saram, late 2nd Maha Modeliar	25
Abraham De Saram, 2nd Maha Modeliar	30
Johan Godfried Philipas, 3rd Maha Modeliar	20
Christofel De Saram, 4th Maha Modeliar	25
A. De Rajapaxse, Maha Modeliar	40
Don Philiph Samerkoon, Don Jacobus Dias, J. Jacobus De Saram, Don Simon De Melho, Johannes Louis Pereira, Don Adrian De Alvis, Don H. Dasnaike, Don S. P. Samerkoon, A. De Alvis, H. De Saram, G. De Saram, Geradus Mendis, Don C. Welliwatee, 10 r. ds. each	130
Martinus De Saram	25
Barend De Silva	20
Don Carolus De Livera	30
J. Paulus Perera	26
John Louis Perera	20
Don David De Alvis	25
J. De Silva Thombo Holder	25
Simon Cornelius De Abreu	25
Jacob A. Pierris, Don A. De Thomas, J. W. Dias, J. G. Perera, 8 r. ds. each	32
Don C. Dias, Don S. De Livera, A. Dias, Don Louis De Livera, Don D. Goonatilaka, 5 r. ds. each	25
Sundry smaller Sums	15

[LIST, No. 4.]

To the Editor of the Ceylon Government Gazette.

SIR,

Thanking you for the obliging notice which you took, in a former number, of the Opening of our Place of Worship in this place, myself and Colleague beg the favour of you, if not inconvenient, to insert the following short List of Subscriptions, which yet remains to be published—Some of the generous Donations therein have been received since the Opening; and with the others we have been favoured at various times, since our last List appeared in your Paper.

At the end of the Two Opening-Sermons, which are preparing for the Press, will be printed a complete and correct List of all our kind Subscriber's names.—Gratefully acknowledging your past favours, I have the honour to remain,

SIR,

Your much obliged and very obedient Servant,
W. M. HARVARD.

Wesleyan Mission House,
Colombo, March 20th, 1817.

	Rds.	F.
Amount already Advertised......	5,553,	6

	Rds.
His Excellency Lieut. Gen. Sir Rob. Brownrigg, Bart. K.G.C. *Governor*, &c &c. a Second Donation	300
The Hon. Sir W. Coke, Knt. *Puisne Justice*	300
Lieut. Col. Hardy, *Deputy Quarter Master General*	30
N. Mooyart, Esq. *Sitting Magistrate of Jaffna*	100
Enclosed in an *envellope* with the following sentence written in Dutch—*This comes from a Christian by name*	50
The late Jacob Burnand, Esq.	30
The late Mr. D'Esdenden of Galle	20

	Rix Dol.
Mrs. Reynolds of do.	50
Mrs. Conradi of do.	50
Mrs. Halwachs of do.	100
Mrs. Rabinall of do.	150
The late *Capt.* Fred. Keller of Colombo	35
Mr. P.	10
Anonymous	25
Mr. Ferdinand, *Wolfendal-Street*	15
Serjeant S.	5
Corporal S.	5
The amount of a Bass Viol sold at Batticaloa with the late Rev. W. Ault's estate (a Donation)	70

II. *Address relative to the Sunday School.*

TO THE INHABITANTS OF THE PETTAH AND ITS NEIGHBOURHOOD.

A becoming observance of the Sabbath-day is what every good Christian will strive to promote.

We cannot expect that persons will perform their duties as Christians, unless they are, in the first place, instructed what duties they ought to perform.

Persons who are grown up, and engaged in worldly business, have little or no time to devote to the purpose of learning.

Youth is the season to cultivate the mind with useful knowledge;—youth is the seed-time of life; and those who do not neglect the seed-time, may, with good reason, expect a gratifying harvest.

There are many who would be glad to have their children taught to read; but they are so poor, that they cannot pay money for their instruction.

No undertaking can be more suitable to the sacred duties of the Sabbath-day, than to take such poor children by the hand, and teach them to read the Bible, without receiving any other reward than the satisfaction of promoting the great cause of Christianity, and the pleasure of showing our gratitude for the advantages which we ourselves have enjoyed.

The Wesleyan Missionaries have the pleasure to inform the inhabitants of the Pettah, and its neighbourhood, that they intend to open a Sunday School, for the instruction of poor children in the English language, and in the Principles of Christianity, on Sunday next, the 4th of June. And, as they will gladly teach all who come, without any kind of payment, they hope and beg that the inhabitants will send their children or servants, that they may learn to read the Holy Scriptures.

The Missionaries are peculiarly happy to begin the establishment of Sunday Schools in India,* on the birthday of our beloved Sovereign, King George the Third; because, before his lamented affliction, our good King expressed the Christian hope, that the time might soon come, when every child in his dominions would be able to read the Word of God.

The School will begin at 12 o'clock, and be concluded by 3 o'clock, that it may not interfere with any of the other duties of the Sabbath-day.

Mrs. Harvard will take the charge of the girls, and one of the Missionaries will endeavour always to be present and superintend the instruction of the boys.

The Missionaries are glad to say, that two or three young persons have kindly promised to assist in this Christian work; and, they will thank any persons of good moral reputation, if they will likewise come forward and assist in teaching the Poor to read.

N.B. Persons desirous of having their children or servants instructed in this Sunday School, are requested to attend themselves, or to send some one with the children, in order that their names may be properly entered on the School book.

The School will be opened at the Mission House in Cayman's Street, opposite Mr. Cadell's garden.

See page 263, Note.

III. *Encouraging Letters in favour of the Design.*

[No. 1.]

From His Excellency Lieutenant General Sir Robert Brownrigg, G. C. B. Governor, &c. of Ceylon.

"*King's House, May* 20, 1815.

" Gentlemen,

" I have not read your letter of this morning without receiving sincere satisfaction, both from the nature of the object which you propose to accomplish, and from the manner in which your intentions are expressed. It has long given me serious concern to observe the low state of morals among that class of inhabitants to which you allude; and I should highly value any judicious attempt to raise and improve their condition. Your laudable and industrious exertions have convinced me that you are in earnest in your Missionary pursuit. I believe that your labours will be producttve of great good; and your zeal appears to be so tempered with discretion, that I am satisfied that nothing but what is good will be the result.

" In regard to the immediate subject of your letter, it gives me pleasure to hear that some of the inhabitants have come forward to solicit your instructions, and to offer their own contributions towards the expence of a place of worship. Their desire to learn strongly marks their capability of improvement; and I cheerfully shew my approbation of their voluntary proposal of assistance, by giving some aid towards carrying their plan into execution. I beg you will accept for that purpose the enclosed draft for five hundred rix-dollars; and be persuaded, that I shall always listen with a lively interest to such propositions as may be rationally expected to produce an amendment in the religion and morals of every class of people under this government.

" With my anxious wishes for the health and success of yourselves, and the other gentlemen associated with you,

" I am, Gentlemen,

" Your faithful humble servant,

" ROBERT BROWNRIGG."

" *To the Rev. Messrs. Harvard and Clough.*"

APPENDIX.

[No. 2.]

From the Honorable Sir Alexander Johnstone, Knight, Chief Justice of Ceylon.

"Col-petty, May 25, 1815.

"GENTLEMEN,

"I have had the pleasure to receive your letter of the 22nd instant. A very long residence on this island, and a very attentive consideration of the different prejudices which prevail among the people, convinced me many years ago, that the surest method which his Majesty's government could adopt for improving the moral character of the inhabitants, would be to encourage a sufficient number of zealous Missionaries to establish themselves in different parts of the Island, whose sole object it should be to instruct the natives in the *real* principles of Christianity, and to superintend their religious conduct.

"When I was last in England I communicated my sentiments upon the subject to Mr. Wilberforce, and to many of his friends; and I was extremely happy to learn, by letters which you were so good as to bring me from those gentlemen, that they concurred with me in opinion, that it was in some measure owing to what I had said to them, that the late Rev. Dr. Coke had determined to establish a Mission in this Island.

"The conversion of the Budhuist priest at Galle, and the interest in favour of Christianity which you have already excited among the natives in this province, as well as among those in the provinces of Galle, Jaffna, and Batticalao, most clearly prove the salutary effects which have been produced by your exertions. The respect and the influence which the propriety of your mode of life has obtained for you among the several classes of people, and the unremitting attentions which you pay to the sacred duties of your office, will, I have no doubt, secure your complete success in the great work which you have undertaken.

"Allow me to enclose you a draft for five hundred rix-dollars; and to add, that whenever it may be in my power, I shall always be happy to afford you any assistance that you may require. I have the honor to be, with great esteem,

"Gentlemen,
"Your very faithful and obedient servant,
"ALEXANDER JOHNSTONE."

"*To the Rev. Messrs. Harvard and Clough.*"

[No. 3.]

From the Honorable Sir William Coke, Knight, Puisne Justice of Ceylon.

"*Colombo, January 4th,* 1817.

" Gentlemen,

" I am infinitely obliged to you for the opportunity you have afforded me of contributing to the accomplishment of your very praise-worthy efforts in favor of religion and morality in this Island. I shall be most happy to add my name to the support you have received from others, and I will give directions to forward my subscription to you in the course of a few days. Believe me,

" Gentlemen,
" Very faithfully and truly yours,
" W. COKE."

" To the Rev. Messrs. Harvard and Clough."

[No. 4.]

From a Provincial Judge in a distant Province.

In reply to a letter of thanks which we had sent him for a generous donation, which, unasked, he had transmitted to us, on seeing our Subscription List in the Government Gazette.

" Gentlemen,

" The mite I subscribed is by no means worthy of the grateful return you have made. I assure you, it gives me great satisfaction in being able to assist so pious an undertaking, which effectually lays the foundation of an institution so glorious to the British character, and the success of which every Englishman ought to have at heart; an institution, whose only aim is that of spreading the light of the Gospel over the heathen world, without the least wish or hope of pecuniary remuneration. This is a disinterestedness which worldly-minded men justly admire, but have not resolution to imitate. I am, Gentlemen, a sincere well-wisher to your Society, and trust you will receive sufficient inducement to persevere in your undertaking.

" Most faithfully yours,"
&c. &c. &c.

" To the Rev. Messrs. Harvard and Clough."

No. XV.—p. 272.

ROMAN CATHOLIC MISSIONARIES. The following copy of a letter from the Rev. *P. S. Pereira*, one of the most respectable members of this Mission, may be interesting, as an evidence of the friendly understanding which subsisted between us.

"*Church of St. Luisia, Colombo,*
22d *Nov.* 1818."
" REV. SIR,
" It is with much concern I have to inform you of the lamented demise of the Superior and Vicar-General *Padre Joaquin Monroy*, which took place last night; after he had laboured for our Lord Jesus Christ in this Island for upwards of twenty-nine years. The funeral will take place at five o'clock this evening. Please to communicate the same to your brother Missionaries.

" Leaving you and your family to the protection of the Supreme Disposer of all things, I remain, with due respect,
" Reverend Sir,
" Your most obedient, humble Servant,
" P. S. PEREIRA."
"*The Rev.* W. M. HARVARD,
Wesleyan Mission-House."

No. XVI.—p. 279.

VILLAGE PREACHING. Extracts of letters from Mr. Clough.

[No. 1.]

"*Colombo, August* 30, 1815.

" We spend our Sabbaths in visiting the villages from five to ten miles round Colombo, preaching to the people, and catechising the children by interpreters. At present, there are two native preachers (together with Mr. Armour, who preaches in Singhalese) who act in concert with us. We hold a preachers' meeting at our house every Friday, to report the labours of the past Sunday, and fix our stations for the following one. By this means, we generally supply 13 or 14 villages with preaching on the Sabbath-day. Our congregations begin to increase, and we have, in some places, four or five hundred of the poor natives regularly attending preaching, consisting chiefly of persons who have been baptized, but most of them are ignorant, even of the plainest doctrines of Christianity. And, in general, we find it difficult to give them clearly to understand, that the religion of Christ is designed to change the heart; and that our Saviour saves men from hell, by saving them from the practice, the guilt, the power, and the love of sin. New as these doctrines may appear to most of them, we constantly enforce them wherever we go. We have no doubt, but in a little time, God will begin to work, by the saving energies of his Spirit, and experimental godliness will spread like *fire among stubble.* For this we labour and pray unceasingly, and encourage ourselves with the idea, that our dear fathers and brethren, as well as thousands of our Christian friends, in our native land, are uniting their ardent supplications with ours at the throne of grace, that God will hasten this most desirable period. Even so, Lord grant it! Amen! Amen!

"In some villages, a general reformation has taken place. The people that disregarded the Sabbath, and considered it only as a common day, have now the greatest reverence for, and attachment to it. Instead of buying and selling, labouring, or going about taking pleasure, they crowd to hear the word of God preached. And several of the villages are as free from labour, trade or traffic, and noise, as most of the towns and villages in England. These appearances may well, and indeed do encourage us.

"There is a place called Callaany, ten miles from Colombo, in the interior, which, according to the history of Budhu, he visited in the course of his travels, and left the print of his foot in the bottom of a large river, which runs close past it, (a circumstance which is also said to have happened upon Adam's Peak, in the centre of the island.) Here they have built a large pyramid, of immense height, and a temple close to it. Here also, they hold an annual festival in the month of May: and such is the veneration of the Singhalese for that particular spot, that, on these occasions, they come from every part of the island, considering it highly meritorious to bring their presents, and pay their vows to their favourite god. In the month of May last I visited it twice. In my first visit, I went in company with Mr. Armour, the two converted priests, and several of the native catechist masters. On our arrival at the place, a native Christian, a man of some note, offered us the use of a garden, which was close to the temple, to preach in while we stayed there. But, while they were erecting a shade to screen us from the heat of the sun, a poor man who had gone up into a very high cocoa-nut tree to extract toddy, (a liquid from which they distil arrack,) fell down close to the shade, and was killed. The noise and confusion of the idolatrous multitude, at this time, exceeding every thing I ever witnessed before; indeed, I began to think that my situation, and that of my companions, was rather a dangerous one. For, if they had begun to imagine, that the god was angry with the person who had granted us this favour, and suffered this punishment to happen as a judgment for his kindness to us, who had come there to recommend another religion, it is impossible to say what they might have done, while irritated by such reflections. We were in the middle of this distracted crowd, who filled the air with the cry, Hi ho, Hi ho, i. e. Alas! Alas! a term used by the natives expressive of deep lamentation. But just as if Providence had determined that nothing should harm us, a magistrate, who was a particular friend of ours, and who had been sent by the governor to keep order during the festival, came up, took us to his lodgings, and sent round to inform the people, that I should preach there immediately. We soon had a large congregration; I stood in the front of his Bungaloe, upon a rising ground, and preached to them from John iii. 16, *God so loved the world,* &c. and Mr. Armour was my interpreter. Towards the close, I improved the awful misfortune of the poor man, by endeavouring to refute one of their favourite principles—the doctrine of Transmigration. Mr. Armour concluded with prayer. And it was a most pleasing scene, to see so large a company, who had assembled from different parts of the island, to worship a large image, fall down, some upon their knees, and some upon their faces, in the open air, and, for once, offer up their worship to Jesus, *who is over all, God blessed for evermore!* The next morning, when they buried the poor man, a great company assembled to attend him to his grave. The magistrate also went, and as he came pretty near, he heard a noise as though the people were quarrelling; but, when he got close to them, understanding their language very well, he heard they were debating upon the subject of Transmigration. One man was endeavouring to make it out, that according to the life which the deceased had lived, he had now entered into such a beast. Another, who had kept in mind the observations which I had made the day before, observed, " What fools we are to believe such things; only think what the minister said about it yesterday." Then he began to reason with the people, which produced the noise and confusion: but as soon as they saw the magistrate, they were silent. However, they made inquiries when the minister would visit them again; and requested the magistrate to invite me. When I received this intelligence, I promised to visit them again before the feast closed. But when the priests heard of this, their chief sent to the magistrate to say, that on my second visit, he would hold a public dispute with me in the open air, in the presence of the people, to prove that the religion of Budhu was superior to every other religion in the world.

" On a day appointed, we set out early in the morning, with a larger party than we had before; and brother Harvard made arrangements to accompany us. For several miles before we came to the place, the road was covered with people going and returning. I stopped several large companies of them, and spake to them upon the impropriety of spending their time, their strength, and their property, upon such unprofitable journies. The chief arguments they used in favour of their conduct was, that their forefathers had done the same, and they only followed that religion because they had been taught it from their youth. However I spoke of the superiority of the Christian religion, which instructs us in the knowledge of that God who made the world, whose goodness and mercy are equal to his power, and tells us that He is present alike in all places, can bless us with all that we need to make us happy both in this life and in the world to come, and has promised to do so, if we apply to Him in a proper manner. I said, you have been travelling several days, with your presents to offer to your god, and now you are returning, what benefit have you received? Did your god ever speak to you? No. Did he smile on you? No. Did he look at you, or give you to understand, in any way, that he was much pleased with you? No. What assurances have you then that Budhu is more your friend now than before you left your home? None. Now, said I, if you had stayed at home, and prayed to that God who made the world, he would have heard your prayer; and he, being a Spirit, can speak to our spirits, and assure us, that he approves of us, and will bless us: we need not go long journies, and take large presents; he can do it in our own houses. Many of them seeming much pleased and surprised, promised to take my advice, begin to pray to that God who could hear them, and never more attend the temple-worship.

" On our arrival we went to the temple, and, oh! my dear Sir, what you would have felt to see the ceremonies of that day! My paper will not allow me to enter into a description of them, but should you desire it, I will send you an account of the temple, and the manner in which they go through their whole ceremonies. We considered, however, that we had no right to interrupt them on their own ground: so we went to the magistrate's house, who received us very kindly. But, at this time, all the priests (I suppose forty in number,) had left the temple, and retired to a private house very near; as we supposed, to be out of the way. Consequently, I went to find the man who had sent me the challenge to a public dispute; and when I had got out, I saw a great multitude collected together in the front of the house. But when I came thither, to my surprise, he had made his escape; and none of the other priests would enter into the subject. This had a singular effect upon the surrounding multitudes, many of whom began to think that he had run away, because he was not able to defend the religion of Budhu, in opposition to the Christian religion. I preached to them, and then went to join my companions at the magistrate's house. When I got thither, I found another large company assembled, and one of the converted priests making a speech to them in his yellow robes, (the Budhuist's priest's uniform,) and so admirable it was, that it electrified the whole multitude; when he concluded, a shout of approbation immediately resounded from them. Brother Harvard then preached a most appropriate sermon to them, from Rom. i. 16, and the magistrate was his interpreter. These things occasioned, as may be supposed, considerable noise. And the inhabitants, both of Calaany, and other places have sent us petitions to go and preach to them. There is at Calaany, at this time, a subscription begun, to build a new church for us to preach in; and the poor creatures have petitioned the government to assist them. I have also the pleasure to inform you, that subscriptions have been begun with the most flattering success, at four other villages, for the erection of new churches. These are circumstances which, I believe, were not frequent in this island before. It is to us a source of great joy, but we feel our minds in one respect a little pained. The people are excessively poor, as there is no kind of trade, and we cannot afford them any relief, as we have no licence from our Connexion at home to do it; so we are forced to lay the matter before government, and they have kindly undertaken to assist them.

"Some of the happiest moments that I ever spent in my life, are those employed in preaching to the poor neglected Singhalese. I was preaching the other Sunday, at a village, to a large company; and after sermon, the head man, with some others, brought forward a man who had been caught breaking the Sabbath, in a very public manner. They placed him in the front of the pulpit, in the presence of all the people, and the headman charged him with selling arrack. Other witnesses were produced to prove he had often been guilty of it, "after the Missionaries had said so much upon the subject." At first, he seemed much displeased at being exposed before so many people by the headman. I spoke to him in a very close manner, told him how sinful it was for a Christian to violate the express command of God; that one sin would be punished by the Lord as well as another; and that the same authority that forbade murder, forbade sabbath-breaking: consequently, any thing he might say upon that head, would not clear him of being guilty in the sight of God. He soon publicly confessed his crime, became a true penitent, and begged my pardon; then he begged the headman's pardon, and hoped God would pardon him, promising that he would never do the like again. Now, said I, you must not think hard thoughts of the headman, for bringing you up here; for, I am sure that he wishes to have you all good Christians, that you may be happy both in this and the future world. He replied, "I am sure of that; for the conduct of the headman towards the whole village, of late, makes me think, that he wishes to do us good, and to have all the people in his district happy, or he would not labour so much as he does." Upon hearing this several burst into tears; and, as soon as loud weeping would permit, they began to bless God, for sending the Missionaries, and working such a change in the headman; adding, "they could never thank God enough for these wonderful things: for, a little time back, they were all living like beasts, without any kind of instructions or thought of God. But now God had sent the Missionaries, and they hoped that he would reward them for their trouble; they could only pray for us, which they did both night and day." I could not but mingle my tears with theirs; and surely, thought I, God has put honour upon me, in permitting me to be a witness of such things in an heathen land. Oh! how I wished that all infidels, and enemies to Missionary exertions, had only been present to witness this affecting scene. I regret that I have not an opportunity to multiply facts of this kind."

[No. 2.]

Colombo, February, 1816.

"All classes of Europeans appear actuated, in one way or another, to be of some use to the inhabitants of this place; and I believe our Mission has the approbation of the whole settlement: the conduct of His Excellency the Governor towards us having had a considerable influence on the public mind in our favour. He is ever kind, ever attentive, and ready to enter into any thing we lay before him. Sir Alexander Johnstone, the Chief Justice, is also extremely kind to us, and gives us many pleasing proofs that we have in him a warm friend. But we owe a great deal to the Hon. and Rev. T. Twisleton, the senior chaplain and principal of the schools. His public situation gives him almost an unbounded degree of influence among the natives, and that affords him a fair opportunity of doing much good among them. Though he has been our constant friend since our first arrival in Ceylon, yet of late he has been more remarkably kind, and endeavoured, all in his power, to forward the grand design of our Mission. To this end, he has laboured to give us as much influence among them as he could; and to convince them (as he expresses it,) *that we are all one.* He has repeatedly taken Mr. Harvard and myself in his own carriage, out upon little journeys, for twenty or thirty miles distant from Colombo, where we spend our time in preaching in the native churches, to large congregations, assembled by orders that are previously sent out by him. At the same time he makes provision for others to accompany us; so that our parties are in general pretty large; and we spend a few days and then return; and all the expenses he bears himself. I have no doubt but it would be interesting to you to have the particulars of all our visits, as they are so closely connected with our Missionary work. To give you an idea how we spend our time on these occasions, I will give you a hasty sketch of one of our last. On this excursion, we were accompanied by three Church Missionaries, who had just come to the island. About seven o'clock, on the Tuesday morning, we left Colombo, and went to Galkeese, about seven miles distance, and one mile from the Governor's country-house. At half-past eight, Mr. Harvard preached to the natives from Rom. xv. 4. His Excellency the Governor and Lady Brownrigg, and two of the Aides-de-camp, were present. From thence we went to Morotto, six miles farther, and here we had a very large congregation. Mr. Norton, one of the church Missionaries, preached after Mr. Armour had opened the service, by singing and prayer. Mr. N. was followed by our converted priest, who gave them a warm exhortation of about twenty minutes, and then I concluded with a short exhortation and prayer. Here we dined, and then went to Caltura, about sixteen miles farther, and here we met with Mr. Squance, from Galle, who preached to the people a sermon in Portuguese. At this place we stayed all night. Next morning, a very numerous congregation came together from many miles round the country.

At ten o'clock in the forenoon the service began, and I preached to them from James iv. 7. Then the converted priest got up, and spoke for some time. Then Mr. Chater, the Baptist Missionary, preached from Luke ii. 10, 11. Mr. Armour concluded by singing and prayer. In the afternoon the people assembled again. Mr. Greenwood preached from *Now is the accepted time, &c.* The converted priest got up again, and then Mr. Armour spoke to them for some time, and dismissed the congregation. At seven in the evening, another congregation assembled. Mr. Schroeter, a German, another of the Church Missionaries, preached, and Mr. Armour interpreted it into Portuguese. He was followed by Mr. Squance and Mr. Chater, who gave exhortations in Portuguese, and concluded with prayer. Thus ended the services of such a day as the inhabitants of that place never before witnessed. In the evening we received a letter of thanks, drawn up and signed in behalf of all the inhabitants of Caltura, by several of the principal men of the place. Here we stayed all night; next morning we set out for Pantura, ten miles, where we found another very large congregation waiting. We began the service by singing and prayer. Mr. Norton then preached. After him, Mr. Schroeter gave them an exhortation. Then the converted priest stood up again. This was the first place where he met with any opposition. In the middle of his discourse, a shrewd man, supposed to be a Kappooa, stopped him, and began to reason with him in the public congregation. At first it caused some disturbance among the people, but when the priest began to reply to the Kappooa's objections, all was silent, and he soon silenced the man. When he had done, Mr. Harvard concluded by an exhortation and prayer. At this place we took a little refreshment, and then proceeded to the Governor's house at Mount Lauvinia, about ten miles, all the party having had a previous invitation to dine with his Excellency. Here we spent the day, and in the evening reached home."

[No. 3.]

"*Colombo, December* 15, 1817.

" I had a very interesting Missionary journey last week. On Saturday the 13th inst. I went to a village in the jungle called ———; it is about 20 miles from Colombo. This whole country is awfully devoted to the worship of devils, and this village especially, which contains 2000 inhabitants. I expected before I went that I should not meet with the most pleasant treatment, knowing as I did the character of the people. The works of the devil make his servants very obvious in all countries; but when people are publicly, and by profession, devoted to the devil, it generally gives them an appearance of savage ferocity. However, I determined to make the attempt; and in a cross journey, which I was making about four days before, I called upon the native head-man of that country, who lived about six miles from the village, and told him of my intention to go to the place which was under his command, and attempt to establish a Christian school for the instruction of their children. The head-man smiled when he heard what I had to say; and with a degree of astonishment that we should think of looking upon such a barbarous people, exclaimed, " O Sir! that people are no better than (or are living like,) beasts!" Well, said I, my friend, *if their state be bad, there is the greater need that we should go to them;* and I appointed a day, and begged he would accompany me, to which he very cheerfully consented. On the day appointed I set out with brother Fox, being then at his station at Caltura; and when we got there, we found the head-man had sent to apprise them of our coming, and the natives had constructed a most beautiful little shed, which we found a most welcome retreat, after having travelled ten miles under a *vertical sun*. A number of the inhabitants had assembled, and all the *inferior* head-men of the place. I soon found some had come to argue the matter with us; however, after about an hour's conversation, which had been carried on by both sides, I began, and told them plainly and pointedly of their situation, and of our wishes respecting them; upon which they seemed much pleased and satisfied, and the inferior head-men gave me all their names, and said they would rejoice to have such a school; and though they had kept back their children, so that we did not see one, except by accident, they promised to build a school, and would send 100 children to be taught. They assured me they would forward the list of names in the course of the week: thus I left them."

APPENDIX.

Extracts of letters from Mr. Lynch.

[No. 1.]

Madras, February 27, 1817.

From Tranquebar to this place, my journey was tolerably pleasant. I was met near this by three brethren, and stopped with Mr. Durnford. Here are twelve persons in a class; I have met them, and think some of them are converted. On my arrival I waited upon the Governor, who expressed great satisfaction as to the character given me by Sir Robert Brownrigg, but said, as I was not the person authorized from England, he would lay my case before the Council, and allowed me to call again in a few days. This was on Friday the 14th instant. He seemed a little surprized to find that there are no Wesleyan Methodist Missionaries at Madras; as he thought Mr. Lovelass was one of them.

Yesterday I had a second interview with his Excellency, who informed me, I might remain till the will of the Court of Directors was known; and when I stated that I only intended to remain till Mr. Harvard could take his appointment at Madras, he said, in that case, there was no objection.

I intend to open my mission on next Sunday morning. Already several have proposed subscribing for the building of a chapel; one has proposed 100 pagodas. I spent a truly profitable evening with Mr. Thompson; he is all life and zeal. I met there a young chaplain, who is stationed near Madras, who has every appearance of deep piety. I had to promise to visit him and his pious lady on next Thursday, the 27th instant. Every Thursday he has a meeting at his own house for the soldiers and others. A Mr. Knill has lately come out to Mr. Lovelass. He scatters life wherever he goes.

[No. 2.]

Madras, May 12, 1817.

Though I have but very little of any importance to write to you, yet, as a ship is to sail in a few days, I consider it my duty to give you what little information I can. By the letters which I wrote to Mr. Buckley, you are informed of my arrival and reception here, and the number and state of the little society. And, thank God, we are still going on pretty well. I believe six of our society are happy in God, and several more are pressing into the kingdom. I am under the necessity of preaching from three to five times a week; and feel that three times fatigues me more than fourteen times used to do in Ireland. Our present place, though large enough, is exceedingly unfavourable, as it has no circulation of air through it; and is so hot, that women are often obliged to keep fanning themselves all the time: and I never preach, but I am thrown into the highest state of perspiration. And yet we cannot get a better place unless we were to go to the expence of eight or ten pounds a quarter. At present our congregations are tolerably good; but would be much better if we had a chapel; and, as yet, I have no prospect of a suitable place.

No. XVII.—p. 280.

Copy of a Letter from the Honorable the Chief Justice, acknowledging the receipt of the Committee's Present of Mr. Wesley's Works.

"Colombo, 24th August, 1816.

" SIR,

" I beg leave to return, through you, to the Committee of the Wesleyan Methodist Missionary Society in London, my warmest thanks for the very valuable set of Mr. Wesley's Life and Sermons which they have done me the honor to send me. The pious and benevolent character of that great man, and the extensive influence which his doctrines have acquired in Europe and in America, will make me read his works with interest and with pleasure.

" I am, I assure you, most highly flattered by the terms in which you are so obliging as to express yourself with respect to any little attention which I may have had it in my power to shew the different members of your Society who are on this Island. The line of conduct which they have uniformly observed, renders it the duty of every Christian to co-operate with them in the cause in which they are so zealously engaged; and I shall always feel happy in having an opportunity of publicly evincing the sentiments of respect which I entertain for their proceedings.

" I request that you will do me the favor to present my kind compliments to all your Missionary brethren; and that you will believe me to be, with great esteem,

" Sir,
" Your very obliged and faithful servant,
" ALEXANDER JOHNSTONE."

" *To the Rev. W. M. Harvard,*
  Secretary to the Conference."

No. XVIII.—p. 289.

Copy of Resolutions passed at a meeting of the Committee of the Colombo Auxiliary Bible Society, held at the King's-House the 7th of July, 1816.

Present.

Hon. Sir ALEXANDER JOHNSTONE, Vice President,
Hon. Rev. T. J. TWISLETON,
Dr. HIGH,
C. E. LAYARD, Esq.
W. TOLFREY, Esq.
Rev. G. BISSET, Secretary.

Resolved, that Mr. Harvard's superintendence of the Press of this Society is of essential consequence, and that his removal from Colombo would be greatly detrimental to the success of their grand object, an early completion of Mr. Tolfrey's Singhalese translation of the New Testament.

Resolved, that the Secretary do write to the Wesleyan Missionaries, enclosing a copy of the above Resolution.

Signed by order of the Committee,
G. BISSET, *Secretary.*

Extract from the proceedings of the Colombo Auxiliary Bible Society, at their Fourth Annual Meeting, held on the 4th of August, 1816.

Resolved, that the thanks of this meeting be given to the Conference of the Wesleyan Missionaries, for their obliging readiness to comply with the wishes of the Committee, by changing the destination of the Rev. Mr. Harvard, and permitting him to reside at Colombo, for the purpose of superintending the Press of this Society.

Signed by order of the Meeting,
G. BISSET, *Secretary.*

No. XIX.—p. 293.
TABLETS
To the Memory of Dr. Coke and Mr. Ault.

Sacred
To the Memory of
THE LATE REVEREND THOMAS COKE, L.L.D.
Of the University of Oxford,
GENERAL SUPERINTENDENT OF THE WESLEYAN METHODIST MISSIONS;
Who was an ardent lover of immortal souls, and
A zealous and persevering Friend and Advocate of Christian Missions
Among the Heathen!—
By his Instrumentality, Liberality, and Personal Exertion,
The Wesleyan Methodist Missions
Were introduced & established in all the Four Quarters of the Globe!
Their Success in the Conversion of Sinners lay nearest his heart,
And was one of the chief sources of his joy
While on earth.—
THOUSANDS OF REAL CONVERTS WILL HAIL HIM BLESSED
IN THE GREAT DAY.
His last principal Undertaking was
The Introduction of this Mission to ASIA:
For this purpose, like that primitive and eminent Missionary, St. PAUL,
He withstood the earnest entreaties of his numerous Friends!
And, at the advanced age of 67 years,
He left his native and much-beloved Country,
Under the express sanction of the BRITISH GOVERNMENT,
And bearing Letters testimonial
From several of the principal Characters IN THE STATE!
Being accompanied by Six other Missionaries,
The Rev. Messrs. Lynch, Ault, Erskine, Harvard, Squance, & Clough,
And burning with fervent zeal
For the Conversion of the Inhabitants of India,
He was followed by the tears and prayers of anxious multitudes.—
His Constitution, however, sunk under the Change of Climate,
And from intense Application to preparatory Studies.
He died on the Voyage, May the 3d, 1814,
Happy in that Saviour whom he had so successfully preached to others;
And his mortal Remains were committed to the Deep,
In Lat. 2° 29′ S. & Lon. 59° 29′ E.
This Tablet, inscribed by his surviving Missionary Companions
And Sons in the Ministry,
Is designed as a public and constant Memorial
Of their unceasing respect, affection, and reverence for his
Person and Character.
August, 1816.

Sacred

To the Memory
OF THE LATE REVEREND WILLIAM AULT,
Wesleyan Methodist Missionary,
Who, having laboured with great Acceptance, in England,
As a Minister of the Gospel,
For many years,
Voluntarily Sacrificed the scenes of Popularity and Friendship,
With which he was surrounded,
For the arduous and less flattering Occupation
Of a Christian Missionary.—
On his Arrival in Ceylon,
His sphere of Labour was Batticaloa, and its Environs,
(On the Eastward of the Island.)
His anxious Exertions for the Spiritual Good of the Natives
Of that Place,
Evidenced the Purity of the Motive
Which introduced him into the Missionary Work.
Every Cottage in his District had received his Pastoral Visits,
And had Echoed with his affectionate, familiar, and efficacious Advice!
Even the Heathen beheld him—revered him—loved him,
And committed their Children to his Care,
Consenting to their Use of the Bible, as their principal School-Book!
His Missionary race was short:
He died among the People of His Charge,
"In sure and certain Hope,"
April the 1st, 1815,
After labouring among them only Eight Months!
Over his Grave,
The Inhabitants of Batticaloa erected, at their own Expense,
A Monument of his Worth,
And of the Admiration, with which it had inspired them.
He was beloved and respected
By all Descriptions of Men;
From the most inferior Member of His Flock, at Batticaloa,
To the highest existing Authorities in the Island;—
They all paid a Tribute to his Memory!
This Stone was erected
By his affectionate surviving Fellow-Labourers,
The Wesleyan-Methodist Missionaries in Ceylon,
As a lasting Token of their warmest regard.
August, 1816.

On the completion of our premises, we addressed two Circulars to our obliging Subscribers; No. 1, *to our own countrymen; No.* 2, *to our friends among the native and country-born Inhabitants, announcing to them our opening services.*

[No. I.]

Wesleyan Mission House, Pettah;
December 16*th*, 1816.

WE beg respectfully to inform you that our Place of Worship, towards which you were so kind as to favour us with a subscription, in the last year, is now completed; and and that we intend to open it for Divine Service on Sunday next, the 22nd. Instant.—From a variety of circumstances, no less painful to our own feelings, than tending considerably to encrease the expences of our concern, we are sorry it has been so long in hand. We however beg to assure you the cause of delay has not rested with either of us; as we have spared neither expence nor personal exertion, to bring it to an earlier completion.

Since beginning to build, we have been obliged to enlarge our original plan.—Our various and multiplying concerns requiring more room, we have been under the necessity of purchasing three adjoining small estates.—These purchases, and the Expences of the various buildings, have altogether risen to upwards of 30,000 Rix Dollars.*—By this amount, however, we are provided with a commodious place of worship—an excellent double dwelling-house—a large room for our Sunday and Day-Schools — buildings for our printing, book binding—and letter-foundry departments;—likewise for warehouses, and other useful purposes.—The whole forms a complete Missionary Establishment, though on an extremely limited Scale; and we hope will produce advantages which will not be confined to one generation.

In our place of worship, which, for the sake of distinction, we have called " The Wesleyan Mission-House," we intend to carry on regular English preaching, on the Sunday Evenings, at Seven o' Clock—and in Portuguese,

---

* The total Amount of Subscriptions is about 7,000 Rix-Dollars.—For the Surplus we have been under the Necessity of drawing upon our Funds at home: in the Hope, however, of being able in the course of Time to liquidate, by various Means, the whole Expence.

on the Tuesday Evenings, at the same hour: and as our Missionaries acquire the Languages, we hope other Evenings will be similarly occupied in preaching in others of the native tongues.

Some few of our respected friends having suggested, that if we were to have an early Sunday Morning Service, with the use of our venerable and excellent Liturgy, they might sometimes make it convenient to attend, we have had no hesitation in adopting the hint; and though we do not expect large congregations at that time, we hope we shall find no difficulty in raising a small one.——We have, in consequence, fixed on seven o'Clock, as the usual hour, on a Sunday Morning; and intend to conclude, at all events, by a quarter past eight.—This will prevent any interference with the services, either of the English, Dutch, or Portuguese Churches; and we hope will be the means of benefitting some, without either opposing or inconveniencing any.——From these arrangements, we shall have a kind of double opening-service, on Sunday next. —One of us will preach in the morning, and the other in the evening.

In case any of our generous friends, the subscribers, and others, should find it convenient to honour our Mission House with their presence, on either of these occasions, we shall be most happy to accommodate them with convenient seats.——We are thankful to say that his Excellency the Governor and Lady Brownrigg, have kindly intimated their obliging intention of being present.

We should not have taken the Liberty to trouble you at so great a length; but we feel it a grateful duty to state to you every particular relative to our intended proceedings; especially when we are about to occupy a place of public Worship, which we assuredly should not have erected, but for the generous sanction and assistance, which we have received from yourself, and others of our benevolent countrymen and friends on this island.

We have the pleasure to remain with sentiments of the sincerest gratitude and respect

Your much obliged, and
Very obedient servants,
W. M. HARVARD,
B. CLOUGH.

To———

[No. 2.]

Wesleyan Mission House, Pettah;
December 17th, 1816.

We have the pleasure to inform you that our new place of worship, towards the erection of which you so kindly subscribed last year, is now completed; and that we intend opening it for divine service on Sunday next, the 22nd. instant.—One of us will preach in the morning, and the other in the evening: and, we are thankful to say, that his Excellency the Governor and Lady Brownrigg, have kindly intimated their obliging intention of being present.

We shall be extremely happy to see you on the occasion, and hope you will always consider yourself, together with any of your Family or Friends, as extremely welcome to a seat in the Mission House, at any of the Public Meetings for Religious Worship.

The times of our usual Services will be——for preaching in English, on Sunday Mornings, at Seven o'Clock; to conclude by a Quarter past Eight, at farthest; and on Sunday Evenings, at the same Hour.—On Tuesday Evenings, at Seven o'clock one of us intend to preach in the Portuguese language.——And on Saturday Evenings, at the same hour, we shall have our usual Prayer Meeting: the Services to be conducted in the English, Dutch, and Portuguese languages.

Our Sunday School will in future be kept in a long School-Room, adjoining to the Mission House; and, as it will be continued on a new plan, we hope our Friends will be inclined to send their Children or Servants, for the purpose of being instructed in the English language and in the principles of Christianity.

As it respects our various Religious Services, we shall always endeavour to fix them at such hours, as will not clash with those of any other church in this place.—It is far from our wish to interfere with the exercises or usefulness of any other body of Christians whatsoever.—Our only aim and desire is to be as instrumental as we can of spreading abroad the knowledge of the Saviour, whom "to know, is life eternal."

Praying that God may abundantly bless our Mission-house, and every other place of worship in this populous town, to that desirable and important end, we remain,

Yours very sincerely,
W. M. HARVARD,
B. CLOUGH.

To———

The following account of the opening is extracted from the Ceylon Government Gazette of Saturday, January 4th, 1817.

" In some of our former papers we inserted the names of the Subscribers towards the erection of the New Wesleyan Mission House in the Pettah. We have now the satisfaction to announce the opening of it and the first performance of divine worship which took place on Sunday the 22nd ultimo.

"The morning service began at 7 o'clock when the prayers according to the Liturgy of the Church of England were read by the Rev. W. M. Harvard and an appropriate sermon was paeached by the Rev. B. Clough, on Psalm cxxii. verses 6, 7. — *Pray for the peace of Jerusalem, they shall prosper that love thee — Peace be within thy walls and plenteousness within thy palaces.* From which the preacher enlarged on the prosperity of the Christian Church, and pressed the work of promoting it as a common duty binding upon all Christians to the utmost of their power.

"The morning service was well attended and some of the principal gentlemen of the Settlement were present.

" In the evening Mr. Harvard preached from Luke ii. verse 14.—*Glory to God in the highest, and on earth peace, good-will towards men,* and noticed the Christian Revelation as a means of effectively displaying the Glory of God, as providing abundantly for the happiness of man, and as powerfully exciting religious devotion.

" The evening was remarkably fine, and the place was so crowded that at an early hour every seat was occupied. The Hymns were judiciously selected, and the voices aided by a small but well toned organ produced an excellent effect. So large and attentive a congregation engaged in the solemnities of Religious Worship in this remote part of Christendom presented a most pleasing sight, and must have been highly gratifying to the Subscribers in general as well as to those active individuals under whose superintendence the building has been completed.

" His Excellency the Governor who with his accustomed benevolence and zeal to promote Christianity sanctioned and generously assisted the Missionaries at the commencement of their undertaking, attended their place of worship on this interesting occasion and was accompanied by Lady Brownrigg.

" There were also present the Hon. and Rev. T. J. Twisleton and his family, the Hon. J. Rodney and family, Lady Johnstone, Col. Kerr, Col. Young, Lieut. Col. O'Connel, Lieut. Col. Hardy, A. Cadell, Esq. W. H. Kerr, Esq. C. E. Layard, Esq. J. Badger, Esq. the Rev. G. Bisset, and several other of the principal gentlemen of the Civil and Military Establishment.— Many of the respectable Dutch and native Inhabitants attended; and persons of almost every class crowded round the doors unable to gain admittance.

" The building is about one mile from the Fort. It is substantial and well adapted to the purpose of hearing. The form is almost an amphitheatre with three rows of elevated seats nearly all round. It is finished in that style of neatness and simplicity which is most suitable to a Missionary place of Worship. We consider it to be a valuable addition to the number of buildings already dedicated to the service of the Christian Religion in this populous neighbourhood: and we sincerely hope it will prove in every respect answerable to the laudable and zealous intentions of those who planned the design, and of those generous Subscribers who promoted their undertaking."

No. XX.—p. 304.

THE SECOND MAHA MOODELIAR. The copy of a letter from this excellent man will be interesting. The youth to which it contains a reference was the son of the *Maha Moodeliar;* whose kindnesses to Mr. Erskine have been recorded in page 164; and for whom the author is happy to have this opportunity of expressing his sincere regard.

" *Kandy,* 20*th March,* 1818.

" MY DEAR SIR,

" I have received your very kind letter of the 25th ultimo. I am sorry I did not acknowledge it sooner, and am more so to hear that you had so much affliction lately in your Family.

The present circumstances at this place I fear will detain us long in Kandy, and the anxiety I have to return to my Family, though great, does not make me at all uneasy, when I reflect that I am serving a person to whom I am much indebted.

I had great pleasure in reading that your School at Pantura is so much to your satisfaction; and any thing that lies in my power, so feeble as it is, I am ready to do at all times for the good of our countrymen and the success of your beneficent endeavours. For I know you are not like a gardener who strives to bring all the trees of the garden to one height and bulk; to do which one cannot without cutting and reducing large trees to level with small ones: and consequently injure those which are larger and valuable.

I am very much obliged to you for the account you gave me of young Ilangakkoon, I have no doubt that you and Mr. Clough will do every thing for him, to deserve the grateful thanks of myself and his Father, who, I am confident will not forget the least attention shown to his family: and returning my best thanks for your kind wishes.

"I remain, Dear Sir,
"Your sincere friend and servant,
"A. D. SARAM."
"The Rev. Mr. Harvard, Mission House, Colombo."

No. XXI.—p. 306.

ADDRESS AND REPLY OF THE CHIEF JUSTICE.

"*Wesleyan Mission House, Colombo,*
August 23, 1817.

"HON. SIR,

"From the favorable manner in which you have been accustomed to look upon our character and pursuits in this Island, the lively interest in our success and prosperity which you have always manifested, and the essential counsel and aid which you have never ceased to offer us in our Missionary Work, we are urged by a grateful and unanimous impulse to address you on your approaching departure from this country; and are persuaded that you will at once excuse the intrusion, and accept of this sincere expression of our sentiments and feelings.

"Led to this scene of Missionary labour instrumentally by the representations of it which you gave to some of the leading characters of our Connexion in England, we have been taught by our Society to look up to you as an honorable friend and well-wisher of our undertaking. And we have not been disappointed. You have generously entered into our views, you have in many instances most disinterestedly marked out for us stations of usefulness and plans of exertion; and your well-timed cautions, advice and support, have oftentimes been of the most essential service to us in circumstances of difficulty and discouragement, as well as in those of a less difficult and more gratifying complexion.

"It would, therefore, be an omission which would be unbecoming our station, and the kind attention with which you have honored us, were we not to repeat to you on this interesting occasion our grateful acknowledgments of all the various public favors, as well as unseen and effectual assistances, which we have from time to time received from you in the furtherance of our common object. And in this we shall be united by the thousands of our friends in the United Kingdom in particular, as well as by all who wish well to the cause of the Gospel in general.

"Permit us then, Honorable Sir, to offer you our warmest and most respectful thanks; and to assure you, that while we shall never forget the Honorable name which has so invariably stood among the foremost of our friends in this distant land, so we shall not cease to pray, that you, with every branch of your family, may be ever remembered for good by our *Divine Master*, even by that *Jesus* whose name you have earnestly desired that we publish with success among the *benighted* inhabitants of this country; and who hath said, those who honor him he will honor—and, that a cup of cold water disinterestedly given in his name shall not lose its reward.

"Having been instrumental in introducing us to our present sphere of action, you have beheld us in a humble measure entering upon our work. As yet, but little saving effect has been produced. We are, however, we trust, laying the foundation for future usefulness; and we intend patiently and perseveringly to proceed in imparting the knowledge of the Gospel, until it shall please God to render the communication thereof signally effectual to the salvation of the Heathen. We are in no doubt as to the final result; we are persuaded it will be glorious.—The day may be distant, but we are sure it will come, and know it is approaching, (may we be permitted to see it,) when the degrading worship of unholy demons shall universally give place to the pure and peaceful service of Jesus our Immanuel, and when the populous jungles of Ceylon shall resound with the high praises of Him who came to seek and to save that which was lost.

"Though at a distance from you, we trust we shall still be allowed a place in your solicitude; and as you have obligingly made yourself acquainted with our whole economy and situation, we beg to request your services with our Committee and friends in England, that we may continue to be supported and reinforced in such a way as to render our endeavours increasingly efficient. They will thankfully receive your various communications, and we shall no less thankfully enjoy the beneficial consequences of them in our work from time to time. This consideration tends to lessen the regret that we feel at losing your personal residence among us in this country, and we entertain the hope that it may yet be the will of Providence to return you again personally to assist His work in the Eastern world.

"We cannot, Honorable Sir, but refer with feelings of respectful sympathy to the immediate cause of your present removal to Europe. The kindred and Christian solicitude of your esteemed and respected Lady, especially for the improvement of the female part of the rising generation, renders our loss two-fold. May the wishes of her Ladyship be fully carried into effect; and especially may the rising Institution near your late residence, which was the object of her daily attention and superintendence, continue to flourish, and ever be a source of pleasing satisfaction to its benevolent Foundress, whose name the children of that place will always be taught by us to revere and esteem.

"We ardently hope that the voyage and change may be the effectual means of restoring her Ladyship's health, and that you may very shortly find yourself in your native land, surrounded by your numerous and cheerful family under the most pleasing possible circumstances.

"With no common sentiments and emotion do we draw to the conclusion of a letter already too long—were it not that gratitude is sometimes allowed to exceed limits prescribed by ordinary rules—and commending you and amiable partner and family, to the grace and keeping of our Lord Jesus Christ, we remain,

" Honorable Sir,
" Your much obliged, and
" Thankful, humble servants,
" Signed by order, and in behalf of the Conference of the Wesleyan Methodist Missionaries in Ceylon,

" W. M. HARVARD,
Secretary."

" *The Hon.* SIR ALEXANDER JOHNSTONE, *Knight, Chief Justice of the Island of Ceylon.*"

"To the Conference of the Wesleyan Methodist Missionaries on Ceylon.

"*Galle*, 30th *August*, 1817.

"GENTLEMEN,

"I beg that you will accept of my sincere and grateful thanks for the very kind and the very flattering manner in which you have been so obliging as to communicate to me your resolution of the 22nd ult. The respect which I entertain for your Society at large, as well as for those members of it in particular with whom I have the honor to be personally acquainted, make me fully aware of the weight which is due to your opinions; and nothing, I assure you, could be more gratifying to my feelings, than to receive so unanimous a mark of your approbation.

"It is with infinite satisfaction I learn from you, that your Society in England do me the honor to consider me in some measure as the original cause of the establishment of your Mission on this Island. The benefit which the country has derived from your unremitted exertions, notwithstanding the innumerable and unforeseen difficulties which you have had to encounter, is acknowledged by every unprejudiced person who is acquainted with the real nature of your proceedings; and the extensive effect which has already been produced by your pious exertions, will enable your friends to look forward with confidence to what may hereafter be expected from your zeal and from your perseverance.

"The progress which the members of your Society have made in acquiring a knowledge of the different languages that prevail in this country; the extent of the information which you have collected, relative to the religion, sciences, customs, manners, and local prejudices of the people; the the care with which you have educated natives to officiate as preachers; the assiduity with which you have yourselves instructed the inhabitants on religious and moral subjects; the number and the variety of the English books which you have translated; the ready assistance which you have afforded to the Bible Society, in completing and printing the new translation of the Testament; the great improvement which you have introduced into the method of printing at Colombo; and the moderate prices at which you have circulated the most useful works—are unequivocal proofs of the pains which you have taken to disseminate, by every means in your power, a knowledge of Christianity, and a bias in favour of its doctrines.

T

"The admirable plan upon which you have established your Schools in the vicinity of Colombo, Negombo, Pantura, Galle, Matura, Batticalao, and Jaffnapatnam, has excited an universal anxiety amongst all classes, and amongst all descriptions of the natives, to have similar schools opened in every part of these settlements. The rule which you have so wisely adopted, of selecting such persons only for Masters, as may be deemed fit for the situation by the heads of the different families whose children they are to instruct, has warmly interested those who are parents in the success of your undertaking; and the voluntary manner in which they have offered you their assistance, is a decided indication of the popularity of your system. An attentive observation of the character of the people of this Island for a period of fifteen years, enables me to form some conjecture as to the probable effect of this system; and I have no hesitation whatever in stating it to you as my decided opinion, that should you meet with the support which you deserve in England and this country, you will realize, ere long, the hopes of those who are the most sanguine in their expectations of the ultimate success of the cause of Christianity in Asia.

"The kindness with which you express your wishes for the recovery of Lady Johnstone, and the terms in which you are pleased to mention her earnest, though feeble endeavours, to promote the establishment of the School at Colpetty, are most flattering to her. She begs me to return you her sincere thanks, and to assure you how much she regrets that the distressing, very melancholy state of her health, has prevented her of late from attending so regularly as she wished, to an institution, the success of which has never failed, under all her sufferings, to be a source of real consolation to her mind. It was her intention, had her health permitted of her remaining in this climate, to have promoted many other institutions of a similar nature; and under the urgent necessity which she now feels of her immediate return to Europe, she reflects with the greatest pleasure upon all those benevolent measures which your Society, from motives of the purest philanthropy, has adopted for the education and religious instruction of the native inhabitants of both sexes in every part of this Island. I have the honor to be, with great respect and esteem,

"Gentlemen,

"Your most obliged and faithful servant,

"ALEXANDER JOHNSTONE."

No. XXII.—p. 308.

NATIVE SCHOOL PRICES.
1818.

	Rds.	Fans.	Pice.
Making Gentlemen's Fine Shirts, with Frills	1	0	0
Do. do. do. without do	0	9	0
Do. Coarse or Night do	0	6	0
Do. Pocket Handkerchiefs	0	0	3
Do. Neck-Cloths	0	1	0
Do. Gentlemen's Drawers	0	4	0
Do. Children's Pantaloons, with Frills	0	6	0
Do. do. do. without do	0	4	0
Do. Ladies' Petticoats, with Bodies	0	8	0
Do. do. do. without do	0	4	0
Do. do. Shifts, with Frills	0	9	0
Do. do. without do	0	6	0
Do. Baby Shirts, with Sleeves	0	1	2
Do. do. without do	0	1	0
Do. do. Night Gowns, with Frills	0	6	0
Do. do. Frocks, tucked	0	8	0
Do. do. Night Caps	0	4	0
Do. do. Pillow Slips, with Frills all round	0	3	2
Do. do. Long Pillow Slips, with Frills	0	2	0
Do. Goodree Slips, with Frills	0	6	0
Do. Sheets, per pair	0	6	0
Marking, per Letter	0	0	1
Do. 2 Numbers	0	0	1

N.B. *The Profits of all Work done in the Wesleyan Mission Native Free-Schools, are equally divided as follows:—One Third to the Worker—One Third to the Mistress—and One Third to the General Reward-Box of the School.*

No. XXIII.—p. 311.

Mr. JAMES SUTHERLAND, JUN.—Under date of Jan. 3. 1820, Mr. Newstead writes as follows:—

" Both the Governor and Lady Brownrigg took a very kind leave also of our dear young friend who was with me, and adverted to the services of Mr. Sutherland, his late father, with the highest respect. I should also mention, that on the same day I waited on the Hon. Robert Boyd; who has hitherto been the guardian of our young friend, in connexion with the Mission; and who committed him fully into our entire care; as his own decided wish and intention is to spend his future life among us, devoted to the service of God as a Missionary to the heathen. Mr. Boyd entirely approves of his choice, after having so long and so maturely deliberated on the important point: and assured our young friend, as his father had done before, that he accounted him happy to have become associated with those whom he was perfectly convinced would be his kind and permanent protectors; and was pleased that he had directed his views to a profession at once so honourable and so useful. Our dear young friend, therefore, will be proposed to travel among us at our approaching meeting; and I am very thankful to add, that I believe him, from two years' experience, to be every way worthy of our kindest regards. May Jehovah be his guide!"

No. XXIV.—p. 319.

MRS. FOX. The following respectful notice of our excellent Sister Fox appeared in the Government Gazette, Saturday, December 5, 1818:—

" DEATH.] Early in the morning of the 3d instant, at the Mission House, Galle, whither she had been removed for the change of air, the wife of the Rev. W. B. Fox, Wesleyan Missionary, of Caltura, leaving two infant children to learn the greatness of their loss, and an affectionate husband, and many friends, to cherish the remembrance of her Christian virtues and excellencies.

" This much respected lady having abandoned the comforts of her own domestic circle, in order to accompany her husband, in his Missionary line of duty, unhappily brought with her to this Island, a constitution which had been seriously undermined by the effects of a violent cold caught in England, which finally terminated in consumption.

" For many months her numerous and affectionate friends have been buoyed up with those hopes of her recovery, which that uncertain, but fatal complaint frequently excites. She had appeared to have derived effectual relief from the removal from Caltura to Galle. But an unerring Providence has disappointed their fond expectations: yet while they bow with submission to the stroke, they will continue to lament her loss."

The Author adds a tribute of affection and respect from the pen of the Rev. R. Newstead, dated Colombo, December 21, 1818.

ON THE DEATH OF MRS. FOX.

Beloved Sister, O farewell!
(A word, how painful, who can tell
    Where kindred hearts unite?)
We dwell upon the mournful theme,
Thy flight from earth, in our esteem
So like a short, uneasy dream,—
    The phantom of a night!

But 'tis a real, heart-felt woe,
That wrings the heart with mis'ry's throe,
    The heart of those bereft;
Thy stricken spouse, thy infants dear,
Thy friends, who bathe with many a tear
Thy memory, with a love sincere,
    The circle thou hast left.

From our endear'd, our native land,
We came together hand in hand
    To serve our Jesus here;
And Jesus first hath call'd thee home,—
Thy spirit beckons us to come,—
And we shall follow to the tomb,
    When Jesu's voice we hear.

We bid thee tenderly farewell,
Thy virtues we forbear to tell,
    They're written in the skies:
Awhile we trace thy upward flight,
And follow on in Jesu's might;
To yonder blissful world of light;—
    To meet in paradise.

No. XXV.—p. 323.

Extract of a letter from the Rev. G. BISSET, dated Colombo, May 27, 1817.

" Attached as I am to the Established Church, I must regard the Wesleyan Missionaries as by far the most efficient instruments in propagating the Gospel in Ceylon. As such I cannot but rate them highly in point of utility; and in regard to their individual conduct, it has been always marked with a propriety and discretion, that entitle them to the personal esteem of the Clergy, as well as to the protection and favour of the Government of the Island."

The excellent spirit which breathes throughout the following letter, from the Rev. MARMADUKE THOMPSON, of Madras, renders it a truly valuable Missionary document. It is addressed to one of the Wesleyan Missionaries in Ceylon.

Madras, May 7, 1816.

Dear Sir,

"I am much concerned to see, how many days I have suffered to elapse without acknowledging, as I should have done, the receipt of your draft for 25 pagodas, which has been duly accepted. You will, however, kindly excuse me, I am sure, when you hear that it has been occasioned chiefly by illness. I have been laid by for more than two months, under a low, tedious illness, which greatly incapacitates me for any business, Could I indeed have followed my own inclination, I should certainly have written to you immediately on the receipt of your letter—it afforded me so much pleasure, from the delightful strain of a true Missionary spirit and lively faith, and piety which pervaded it. You have already been long enough in this part of the world, I dare say, to know the importance of Christian communion, and how refreshing such things are. Accept my best thanks for the kind manner in which you and Mr. ―― have received my little endeavour to assist you in the matter of books, and for the freedom and information of your letter. Believe, I shall ever be happy to undertake any thing for you in Madras, if only you will inform me with any order you wish executed, how I may forward it with the greatest readiness, and the least expence to yourself. It has ever been a pleasant thing to me, one of the advantages of my situation, for which I am very thankful, to be occasionally the friend and agent of Missionaries, to help them onward in the good way they have chosen; and if you can employ me with any advantage to your Mission, believe me you will highly gratify me. Only let me, at the very outset, warn you, that you are dealing with an invalid, who cannot always be as alert as he would wish.

"I have heard, from time to time, of your Missionary labours, and of all the Methodist Missionary labours, with great delight, and bless the Lord for all his goodness to you, and the prosperity he has shewn you. Go on, dear brethren, be strong in the Lord, and in the power of his might. See whom you serve—think what is his service—and the end thereof; and may it be a perpetual joy to you, that he hath called you to be Missionaries. It is a good part which you have chosen, and I will venture to assure you, that none better know how to appreciate it than the heathen natives themselves.

" And here I must beg to protest strongly against an opinion entertained by some persons, that Missionaries need larger salaries, and more means of outward shew than they possess, to gain upon the natives. I will confidently say, and appeal to the history of every esteemed Missionary in India from Ziegenbalg through Swartz downwards to the present day, that it is quite a mistake. A Missionary's *character*, if indeed he be a truly consistent Christian, is more than a thousand pagodas a month in their account; and of that character they consider exercises of self-denial, mortification of appetites, a cheerful poverty, to be essential parts. And who indeed does not? Of the whole world, a Missionary no doubt should most know how to want—to endure hardships: and in general, it is the striking contrast between the piety, abstinence, and cheerful lowliness of the Missionary, and the excesses of other Europeans, that so exalt Missionaries, as we really find them to be, in the eyes of the natives.

"The late General Gowdie, of this Establishment, when in command of the Northern Division of the Madras Army, having his head-quarters at Vizagapatam, took the late Missionary from the London Society, Mr. Cran, with him in one of his military tours, as a diversion to Mr. C. for the benefit of his health. Mr. Cran, ill as he was, contrived to preach as he went to the natives; and such was the impression of Mr. Cran's character on the natives, that General Gowdie declared to me, he really appeared to be regarded by them as the greatest, at least the most important man in the whole party.

" Encourage, strengthen each other with these things: and may the Lord make one and another of you a light to lighten the heathen, to the glory of his own adorable name; as was Cran and his companion De Grange, who soon followed him to his reward; Swartz, Gericke, and many others; who had neither large incomes, nor made any greater outward display than you yourselves may be able to do. It will be a pleasure to me to hear from you occasionally, as you may find opportunity, and especially if you can turn my acquaintance to any good account to your Mission.

"And now, dear Sir, heartily commending you, Mr. ——, and all your brethren to the grace of God our Saviour, whom we serve, desiring to be much remembered by you and them, I remain,

"Yours most sincerely,
"M. THOMPSON."

FINIS.

Printed by J. Haddon, Tabernacle Walk.

www.ingramcontent.com/pod-product-compliance
Lightning Source LLC
Chambersburg PA
CBHW022111080426
42734CB00006B/89